Lean Six Sigma
for the Office

Series on Resource Management

The Intimate Supply Chain: Leveraging the Supply Chain to Manage the Customer Experience
David Frederick Ross
ISBN: 1-4200-6497-5

A Supply Chain Logistics Program for Warehouse Management
David E. Mulcahy and Joachim Sydow
ISBN: 0-8493-0575-6

Hands-On Inventory Management
Ed C. Mercado
ISBN: 0-8493-8326-9

Retail Supply Chain Management
James B. Ayers and Mary Ann Odegaard
ISBN: 0-8493-9052-4

Sustaining the Military Enterprise: An Architecture for a Lean Transformation
Dennis F.X. Mathaisel
ISBN:1-4200-6224-7

Operational Excellence: Using Lean Six Sigma to Translate Customer Value through Global Supply Chains
James William Martin
ISBN: 1-4200-6250-6

New Methods of Competing in the Global Marketplace: Critical Success Factors from Service and Manufacturing
by William R. Crandall and Richard E. Crandall
ISBN: 1-4200-5126-1

Supply Chain Risk Management: Minimizing Disruptions in Global Sourcing
by Robert Handfield and Kevin P. McCormack
ISBN: 0-8493-6642-9

Rightsizing Inventory
by Joseph L. Aiello
ISBN: 0-8493-8515-6

Integral Logistics Management: Operations and Supply Chain Management in Comprehensive Value-Added Networks, Third Edition
by Paul Schönsleben
ISBN: 1-4200-5194-6

Supply Chain Cost Control Using Activity-Based Management
Sameer Kumar and Matthew Zander
ISBN: 0-8493-8215-7

Financial Models and Tools for Managing Lean Manufacturing
Sameer Kumar and David Meade
ISBN: 0-8493-9185-7

RFID in the Supply Chain
Judith M. Myerson
ISBN: 0-8493-3018-1

Handbook of Supply Chain Management, Second Edition
by James B. Ayers
ISBN: 0-8493-3160-9

The Portal to Lean Production: Principles & Practices for Doing More With Less
by John Nicholas and Avi Soni
ISBN: 0-8493-5031-X

Supply Market Intelligence: A Managerial Handbook for Building Sourcing Strategies
by Robert B. Handfield
ISBN: 0-8493-2789-X

The Small Manufacturer's Toolkit: A Guide to Selecting the Techniques and Systems to Help You Win
by Steve Novak
ISBN: 0-8493-2883-7

Velocity Management in Logistics and Distribution: Lessons from the Military to Secure the Speed of Business
by Joseph L. Walden
ISBN: 0-8493-2859-4

Supply Chain for Liquids: Out of the Box Approaches to Liquid Logistics
by Wally Klatch
ISBN: 0-8493-2853-5

Supply Chain Architecture: A Blueprint for Networking the Flow of Material, Information, and Cash
by William T. Walker
ISBN: 1-57444-357-7

Introduction to e-Supply Chain Management: Engaging Technology to Build Market-Winning Business Partnerships
by David Frederick Ross
ISBN: 1-57444-324-0

Supply Chain Networks and Business Process Orientation
by Kevin P. McCormack and William C. Johnson with William T. Walker
ISBN: 1-57444-327-5

The Supply Chain Manager's Problem-Solver: Maximizing the Value of Collaboration and Technology
by Charles C. Poirier
ISBN: 1-57444-335-6

Lean Performance ERP Project Management: Implementing the Virtual Lean Enterprise, Second Edition
by Brian J. Carroll
ISBN: 0-8493-0532-2

Basics of Supply Chain Management
by Lawrence D. Fredendall and Ed Hill
ISBN: 1-57444-120-5

Lean Six Sigma
for the Office

James William Martin

CRC Press
Taylor & Francis Group
Boca Raton   London   New York

CRC Press is an imprint of the
Taylor & Francis Group, an **informa** business

Crystal Ball® is a registered trademark of Oracle® Software Corporation.

Minitab® software is a registered trademark of Minitab, Inc.

MATLAB® is a trademark of The MathWorks, Inc. and is used with permission. The MathWorks does not warrant the accuracy of the text or exercises in this book. This book's use or discussion of MATLAB® software or related products does not constitute endorsement or sponsorship by The MathWorks of a particular pedagogical approach or particular use of the MATLAB® software.

CRC Press
Taylor & Francis Group
6000 Broken Sound Parkway NW, Suite 300
Boca Raton, FL 33487-2742

© 2009 by Taylor & Francis Group, LLC
CRC Press is an imprint of Taylor & Francis Group, an Informa business

No claim to original U.S. Government works
Printed in the United States of America on acid-free paper
10 9 8 7 6 5 4 3 2 1

International Standard Book Number-13: 978-1-4200-6879-5 (Hardcover)

Library of Congress Cataloging-in-Publication Data

Martin, James W. (James William), 1952-
    Lean six sigma for the office / James William Martin.
        p. cm.
    Includes bibliographical references and index.
    ISBN 978-1-4200-6879-5 (alk. paper)
    1. Total quality management. 2. Six sigma (Quality control standard) 3. Office management. 4. Service industries--Quality control. I. Title.

HD62.15.M3744 2008
658.4'013--dc22   2008011862

Visit the Taylor & Francis Web site at
http://www.taylorandfrancis.com

and the CRC Press Web site at
http://www.crcpress.com

Contents

Foreword xi

About the Author xv

Introduction...xvii

STEP 1: ALIGN IMPROVEMENT OPPORTUNITIES

1   Strategy Alignment 3
    Overview 3
    What Is Kaizen?..4
    Strategic Alignment 8
    General Deployment Strategies...10
    Reducing System Complexity 17
    Outsourcing Processes 18
    How to Deploy Lean in Three Steps 22
        Step 1: Align Improvement Opportunities 23
        Step 2: Plan and Conduct the Kaizen Event 24
        Step 3: Implement Solutions and Change Behaviors.............25
    Important Elements of a Lean System..26
        Understand the VOC 26
        Reduce Product and Process Complexity.................................28
        Deploy Lean Six Sigma Teams...29
        Implement Performance Measurements 29
        Create Value Stream Maps...29
        Eliminate Unnecessary Operations..30
        Implement Just-in-Time (JIT) 30
        Develop Supplier Networks 31
        Implement Visual Controls and Pull Systems 32
        Continuously Update Process Technologies.............................32
    Summary..32
    Suggested Reading..33

2 Project Identification...35
  Overview 35
  Lean Supply Chain 36
  Conducting a Lean Assessment...39
  Breaking Down High-Level Goals and Objectives 41
  Project Identification—Process Analysis...43
  Typical Project Examples 45
  Key Metric Definitions 46
  Project Charter Example..50
  Prioritizing Projects 51
  Summary..55
  Suggested Reading..56

3 Lean Six Sigma Basics 57
  Overview 57
  Understand the Voice of the Customer (VOC)...61
  Create Robust Product and Process Designs to Reduce Complexity 64
  Deploy Lean Six Sigma Teams...67
  Performance Measurements 69
  Create Value Stream Maps (VSMs)...70
  Eliminate Unnecessary Operations...74
  Implement Just-in-Time (JIT) Systems 76
      Reorganize Physical Configurations 78
      5S and Standardized Work 80
      Link Operations 82
      Balance Material Flow 84
          Bottleneck Management 85
          Transfer Batches..87
      Mistake Proofing 87
      High Quality..89
      Reduce Setup Time (SMED) 90
      Total Preventive Maintenance...92
      Level Demand 94
      Reduce Lot Sizes...96
          Mixed-Model Scheduling...98
  Supplier Networks and Support..98
  Implement Visual Control and Pull Systems—Kanban 100
  Continually Update Process Technologies 102
  Summary..105
  Suggested Reading...106

STEP 2: PLAN AND CONDUCT THE KAIZEN EVENT

4 Kaizen Event Planning..**111**
Overview 111
Prepare for the Kaizen Event..113
Select a Project Charter...116
Assign a Project Leader and Team Members.......................116
Reserve a Conference Room 117
Obtain Supplies and Equipment...118
Ensure Facilities Are Available, Including Breakout Rooms...........118
Ensure Support Personnel Are Available to Assist the Team 118
Collect Process Information of Floor Layouts, Workflows, and
Procedures..119
Collect Information on Operational Cycle Times................120
Taking Pictures of the Area to Be Improved 121
Obtaining Examples of Process Breakdowns 122
Obtaining Examples of Best-in-Class Process Conditions 122
Developing a Schedule for the Kaizen Event.......................123
Communicating the Event..124
Marking Areas for the Event..124
Setting Up Flip Charts and Organizing Other Materials.............124
Kaizen Event Communication Letter 125
Kaizen Event Kickoff Agenda 126
Conducting the Event...127
Bring Team Together to Discuss Roles and Responsibilities 127
Discuss Operational and Financial Objectives of the
Kaizen Event..128
Conduct Team Training as Required....................................128
Create Detailed Value Stream Maps and Layouts of the
Process Workflow...129
Facilitate to Ensure Full Participation of Team...................129
Collect Data at Every Operation...131
Analyze Data and Develop Prioritized Improvements...........136
Change the Process..137
Apply 5S and Mistake-Proofing Methods...........................137
Evaluate the Kaizen Event..138
Summary..139
Suggested Reading...140

5 Data Collection and Analysis...**141**
Overview 141
Value Stream Mapping 143

Brown-Paper Exercise 149
Process Characterization.. 151
Simple Analysis of Process Data... 160
Process Mapping—SIPOC... 163
Cause-and-Effect (C&E) Diagrams 164
Five-Why Analysis 165
Histogram... 167
Pareto Chart 168
Box Plot.. 169
Scatter Plot 170
Time Series Graph 170
Control Charts 172
Example: Analyzing Job Shadowing Data.. 175
Example: Inventory Analysis and Reduction.. 177
Summary... 182
Suggested Reading... 184

6   **Process Improvement** **185**
Overview 185
Common Process Changes 185
Control Tool Effectiveness and Sustainability...................................... 194
Root Cause Analysis and Improvement Strategies................................ 196
Examples Using Common Process Workflows....................................... 199
        Example 1: Financial Forecasting.. 200
        Example 2: Accounts Receivable... 202
        Example 3: New Product Market Research 204
        Example 4: New Product Development.. 205
        Example 5: Hiring Employees 208
        Example 6: Supplier Performance Management 210
Identifying and Prioritizing Improvement Opportunities 212
Summary... 213
Suggested Reading... 215

STEP 3: IMPLEMENTING SOLUTIONS

7   **Building a Business Case for Change**... **219**
Overview 219
Change Readiness.. 223
Project Transition 225
Building a Business Case for Change.. 226
Cost–Benefit Analysis 227
Key Stakeholder Analysis... 229
Infrastructure Analysis.. 233

Scheduling Process Change Activities 234
Communication 235
Summary..236
Suggested Reading..237

8   Implementing Solutions **239**
Overview 239
Key Questions 240
Control Plan Requirements..241
Important Control Tools 242
Statistical Process Controls 244
Measurement System Improvements..254
Failure Mode and Effects Analysis (FMEA)..255
Other Control Tools 258
Quality Control Plan 259
Communicating the Proposed Changes to Management.......................259
Follow-Up Activities 261
Creating Metric Dashboards..263
Summary..263
Suggested Reading..265

9   Reinforcing New Behaviors and Organizational Change **267**
Overview 267
Process Change across Global Supply Chains 269
Summary..274
Suggested Reading..275

Conclusion **277**

Appendix 1: Crystal Ball® Software **285**

**Appendix 2: Minitab® Statistical Software and Quality Companion
            by Minitab**..**295**

Appendix 3: Figures and Tables...**299**

Glossary **305**

Index **321**

Foreword

My goal in writing this book is to provide a simple reference to plan and conduct Kaizen or rapid improvement events in service systems and office environments in particular. Although no one book could possibly contain every tool, method, and concept currently used to improve operational performance and productivity, I have brought together in *Lean Six Sigma for the Office* a practical reference of tools, methods, and concepts that have been developed specifically for service environments to enable a reader to quickly understand Lean Six Sigma concepts to rapidly improve his or her process using Kaizen events. Kaizen means to "to take apart" and "to make good." In our discussion we will use the terms *Kaizen* and *rapid improvement* synonymously because rapid improvement is our focus. These rapid improvement events usually span just several days but have as their objective immediate process improvement by local work teams.

The key tools, methods, and concepts that are contained in this book have been condensed from my Lean Six Sigma consulting and graduate teaching assignments over the past 30 years. These assignments were in diverse service industries across the world, such as banking, insurance, procurement, research and development, accounting, sales and marketing, finance, food and retail distribution, and logistics. Extensive research was also conducted to develop new ways to collect and analyze information from dynamic process workflows that are virtual and widely geographically dispersed across the world. This new and expanded process improvement information will help your team identify and execute Kaizen projects to increase your organization's operational efficiency and customer satisfaction.

Service systems have unique operational characteristics that are different from those found in manufacturing. As an example, in service industries, the flow of information in various formats, as opposed to materials or physical objects, is measured and analyzed by a Kaizen team. This does not imply that the flow of information and materials is not measured within both types of systems, but only that the flow of information, in the form of transactions, predominates within service systems. As an example, in service industries, most of the work is virtually contained within information technology (IT) systems. Or if it is in physical form, then it appears in the form of data collection forms, exception lists, requests for information, orders, invoices, and other summarized informational formats processed or transformed by a system. As a result, data collection and analysis methods must be highly modified in some systems to capture essential operational information when it occurs.

In summary, a major focus of this book is a discussion of methods to efficiently collect and analyze operational data to improve service system operations. However, the activities required to do this work are usually very difficult because a process workflow may span several locations across the world. This greatly complicates a team's improvement efforts in globally dispersed work environments. As an example, operational information may be gathered across several globally dispersed organizational functions using disparate IT systems and platforms. Common examples of these IT systems include business process management (BPM), business modeling and analyses (BMAs), business intelligence (BI), business activity monitoring (BAM), enterprise application integration (EAI), and workflow management (WM) systems. Each of these systems varies in its ability to measure, monitor, and control process workflows. As an example, there is a hierarchal relationship between these systems because business process management (BPM) systems integrate several IT platforms or systems, as opposed to business activity (BAM) monitoring, which monitors the flow of transactions across several workflows, but not normally between different IT platforms. As an example, BPM systems manage business modeling specifications such as business design goals and objectives, middleware specifications such as hardware components, software, telecommunications, and the structuring mechanisms for data collection management and object location. Also, BMA platforms are lower-level systems that specify rules to model a process workflow. The other IT systems discussed above are useful in analyzing, monitoring, and controlling specific process workflows and functions. A major goal of this book will be to show how data can be collected across disparate IT platforms and similar hierarchal systems.

A common approach taken by some manufacturing consultants, when deployed within a service system, is to integrate manufacturing methodologies with a few modifications relevant for system analysis and improvement. As part of these operational assessments, modified tools and methods are used to collect and analyze process data to identify improvement opportunities. However, the resultant system improvements may be unwieldy, and in some situations somewhat embarrassing. As an example, I have seen process improvements degenerate into a set of inconsequential controls. Examples include applying a pull system to drinks in a refrigerator or marking off where flip charts should be positioned and similar minor and even annoying activities. The same situation can occur in manufacturing where improvements require a high level of manual intervention for their maintenance. In these types of situations, the resultant impression made on professional service workers is that organizational effort and resources have been applied to a process without significant business benefits. These actions tend to detract from the usefulness of Lean Six Sigma when it is applied within an office environment. Also, office cultures are different than those found in manufacturing because process workflows may be globally dispersed and rely heavily on IT. As a result, more elegant and practical methods are required to improve and sustain the productivity of service systems. In other words, the work done by service professionals must be measured differently than that in manufacturing environments.

As a result of these observations and opinions, a major goal of writing this book is to document the lessons I have learned deploying Lean Six Sigma in industries such as banking, insurance, mutual funds, manufacturing, and retail operations, as well as many other service systems to create a practical and hands-on reference written for people who need a concise and practical source of information to rapidly improve their service operations anywhere in the world. The nine chapters comprising this book contain more than 150 figures, tables, and road maps covering a range of practical topics, such as project identification and alignment, cultural transformation and team building, data collection activities, and the application of simple tools and methods to analyze the data collected from dynamic and virtual systems that may contain numerous integrated process workflows. Understanding these topics will help ensure that your organization's operational systems meet customer needs and expectations. Each of the nine chapters also contains checklists and evaluation tools. These are provided in the form of Excel templates to help your organization identify areas for operational improvement. In this context, the book also emphasizes the importance of strategic alignment of Kaizen events and improvement projects as well as considering the impact of organizational culture on process improvement activities. In later chapters of the book, key elements of a change model are also discussed in the context of transitional improvements to the process owner and local work team. In summary, this book has been written from a viewpoint that people and the cultural aspects of process improvement are as important as the Lean and Six Sigma tools and methods that are used to identify and execute process improvements. It is my opinion that effective and sustainable organizational change can be accomplished by applying the proven principles found in this book.

I must thank Raymond O'Connell, my Auerbach senior editor, for encouraging me to write this book. Also, I thank Jeff Ozarski of Minitab® Statistical Software and Quality Companion by Minitab™ as well as Lawrence Goldman, senior manager of product marketing of Oracle's Crystal Ball® software for complimentary copies of their software. Finally, I thank my family, my clients and Providence College graduate students who have provided the inspiration for this book as well as Elaine Kowansky, president of Gelrad Consulting, and her husband, Ram Josyula, for their support this past year.

About the Author

James W. Martin is president of Six Sigma Integration, Inc., a Lean Six Sigma consulting firm located south of Boston, and the author of the books *Operational Excellence: Using Lean Six Sigma to Translate Customer Value through Global Supply Chains* and *Lean Six Sigma for Supply Chain Management: The 10-Step Solution Process*. As a Lean Six Sigma consultant and master black belt for more than ten years, Mr. Martin has trained and mentored more than 1,500 black belts, executives, deployment champions, and green belts in Lean Six Sigma methods, including supply chain applications, and has led successful Lean Six Sigma assessments across Japan, China, Korea, Singapore, Malaysia, Thailand, Australia, North America, and Europe. This work included organizations in retail sales, residential and commercial service, banking, insurance, financial services, measurement systems, aerospace component manufacturing, electronic manufacturing, controls, building products, industrial equipment, and consumer products. He has also served as an instructor at the Providence College Graduate School of Business since 1988. He teaches courses in operations research, operations management, and economic forecasting as well as related quantitative subjects, and counsels MBA candidates from government organizations and leading corporations. He holds an MS in mechanical engineering, Northeastern University; an MBA, Providence College; and a BS in industrial engineering, University of Rhode Island. He also holds several patents and has written numerous articles on quality and process improvement. He is a member of APICS and has certifications in production and inventory management (CPIM) and integrated resource management (CIRM). He is a member of the American Society for Quality (ASQ) and is a certified quality engineer (CQE).

Introduction

Over the past several years, the tools, methods, and concepts of Lean manufacturing have been increasingly applied to the characterization and improvement of service process workflows. Although this information is generally useful, it is usually a fact that data collection and analysis activities are more difficult in service applications. Also, it is generally found that process improvements in service systems rely to a great extent on implementation of information technology (IT) countermeasures to eliminate the root causes related to high cycle time, low yields, and high transaction cost. As an example, in a manufacturing system, a Lean assessment team will work in a coordinated manner to obtain quantifiable information relative to operational metrics such as cycle time, uptime, yield, inventory, setup time, and similar metrics. In this assessment work, teams are deployed across several manufacturing process workflows to physically count materials and collect operational information from the workflows. In these applications, data collection is challenging but straightforward. This is because machine operations are very repeatable hour to hour and day to day, which enables operational data to be gathered over several machine cycles to improve its accuracy. Also, auditors can usually return to a manufacturing process to obtain confirmatory data to support their analysis and recommendations.

In contrast, service systems are heavily dependent on a combination of manual and computerized work tasks. This makes it difficult to directly observe process transactions within these systems without using modified data collection strategies. However, an advantage in service environments is that data is easily stored in these IT systems. As a result, large amounts of data can be collected and analyzed. Admittedly, in contrast to manufacturing, in service workflows having a low manual work content it may be relatively easy to map and track work transactions. This is especially true in more advanced IT systems having business modeling and analyses (BMAs), business intelligence (BI), business activity monitoring (BAM), and workflow management (WM) systems. These systems actively track information at key points in a process. In fact, process workflow models can be built and analyzed to estimate the impact of various operational changes and their combined impact on operational cycle times, cost, and process yields. As an example, in modern call centers, numerous statistics are collected to monitor how many customers enter the system, how long they wait to have their calls answered, if their calls must be escalated to supervisors, how many customers must call back into the call center, and any other complaints they may have expressed to the call center agents. Offline, this information can be used to create network simulation models that enable an organization to adjust its systemwide capacity by location and shift within a call center to meet expected demand on the network or system and to evaluate the impact of making various process improvements. These types of service industries are actually ahead of many manufacturing systems in operational analysis. However, complicating the system dynamics in service systems may be the numerous manual operations and their associated work tasks, which are integrated with advanced IT systems. Highly complicated work tasks may inhibit the efficient collection of data in a system. As an example, a call center system is usually a highly standardized back-office system consisting of numerous manual work tasks. This creates a situation in which data collection using methods similar to those found in manufacturing may be difficult. This is especially true if service systems consist of professionals such as attorneys, accountants, financial analysts, engineers, procurement and human resources personnel, and similar professionals whose work activities are characterized by integrated and complicated work tasks.

In the chapters of this book, we will be discussing several assessment methods that can be used to successfully collect operational information from highly automated process workflows within service systems. Some of these methods include the automatic capture of transaction events by an IT system, the "shadowing" of office workers to observe them in relation to their work behavior, an analysis of interfacing systems, reports, and other methods such as conducting audits of e-mail systems. We will discuss these data collection activities in much detail in the upcoming chapters of this book, with a heavy emphasis on using IT systems to automatically capture information for an operational assessment team. In these assessment activities, improvement teams are brought together on either a long-term basis as Lean Six Sigma teams or shorter term as Kaizen or rapid improvement teams.

An operational assessment begins with the creation of a specialized map that is called a value stream map (VSM). VSMs are important tools that are useful in collecting and analyzing operational data related to how customers value work. In this context, value is defined as product or service features that a customer needs and values. This type of customer perspective encourages a team to eliminate internal work tasks that are not valued by customers, that is, non-value-adding (NVA) activities, and improving those activities that customers value, that is, value-adding (VA) activities. This has proven to be a very useful concept. As an example, it has been found that many work tasks that organizations do every day have little relationship to those that are considered important to an organization's customers. Common examples include the inspection or testing of work, reworking activities, and similar internally facing activities.

In a hands-on operational assessment using a VSM, a team is brought together to create a VSM using sticky notes on a wall. These notes describe the performance of financial and operational metrics as well as the relationships between various operations. Assessment teams also "walk the process" to verify that the VSM is correct in both its structure or layout and the metric quantification described by the sticky notes. In service workflows, the quantification of a VSM can be done, in part, using system time stamps to capture the status of all transactions within a process workflow. In parallel, physical audits can be conducted to verify the accuracy of the process information. Gathering the information necessary to build a VSM also requires capturing the information of numerous related activities at manual and technology interfaces. As an example, audits of operations containing high manual work content can be conducted to count and classify e-mails by their type and frequency. Also, employees' time budgets can be analyzed by auditing personal calendars to identify NVA work such as poorly organized meetings. People can also be shadowed for several days to determine the percentage of time spent on various work tasks. In regard to an operational assessment of equipment, the quantity and timing of materials converted or produced by equipment can be measured to calculate production rates. Financial and operational reports that record NVA expenses such as material, direct labor, premium freight, overtime, and similar expenditures can also be analyzed during an operational assessment. Finally, interviews and similar data gathering methods can be used to analyze a process workflow. In summary, a major goal of this book is to use data collection methods that are useful in the analysis of service workflows to demonstrate, using practical examples, the methodologies necessary to organize and deploy Kaizen events for rapid process improvement.

A second major purpose of this book is to demonstrate the key tools, methods, and concepts of Lean Six Sigma using several common examples of office processes. These common examples will be used to show how to create operational performance baselines, identify improvement opportunities, and execute projects to "Lean out" a process workflow. These examples have been taken from finance, accounting, marketing, design engineering, human resources, and procurement. The focus of the nine chapters comprising this book is the deployment of Kaizen events from a global supply chain perspective. This is because globalization has had a dramatic impact on the design of process workflows over the past several decades. The global impact has been particularly dramatic where work tasks have been outsourced to increase their value content. However, our discussion will also apply to geographically localized or smaller organizations.

A third major objective of this book is to provide readers with an easy-to-follow road map using Excel templates to successfully plan and execute Kaizen events in service systems. This is because over the past several years, I found it was difficult to find in one place a clear road map, checklists, or other templates showing how to plan and conduct Kaizen events in office environments. Data collection and analysis templates are particularly needed for office applications to provide a turnkey approach. This book contains these types of tools and templates. I have also brought together the latest Lean Six Sigma tools, methods, and concepts to enable your team to quickly analyze and improve its process workflows. Many of these tools and methods are currently used in manufacturing systems, but they have been modified to apply to the process workflows that characterize service system operations.

A fourth major goal of this book is to show how to strategically align a Lean Six Sigma operational assessment and develop projects that can be executed using the approach that a Kaizen event provides to reduce cycle time and transaction cost and increase process yields. A major problem with many Lean Six Sigma activities and Kaizen events in particular is that strategic alignment is often missing. As a result, their business benefits are difficult to quantify because process improvements tend to be disconnected from organizational goals and objectives. In Chapter 1, we will begin our discussion of Lean Six Sigma for the office by showing how to reduce a system's complexity and also to strategically align projects prior to their deployment as Kaizen events. However, this discussion will also be useful, at a higher level, to drive full-scale Lean Six Sigma deployments across global supply chains as well as to analyze a single-process workflow. To reiterate, the focus of this book is to show how to execute Kaizen events for rapid process improvement in a global supply chain.

As a result of these objectives, this book has been written in a modular manner to enable a Kaizen team to plan and conduct a Kaizen event in a systematic manner with alignment to an organization's strategic goals and objectives. This book is organized in three major sections. These include the alignment of process improvement opportunities, the planning and execution of a Kaizen event, and implementation of solutions identified during a Kaizen event. The alignment of improvement opportunities includes several key topics. These topics are necessary to ensure that an event is strategically aligned with an organization's goals and objectives. Alignment is an important concept because Kaizen events require the use of organizational resources. Also, their resultant solutions must be sustained over time by local work teams. It is thus important that Kaizen events are effectively coordinated to achieve their intended business benefits.

The first section of this book is divided into three chapters. These include strategy alignment, project identification, and a discussion of several important operational elements that are characteristic of a Lean system. Strategy alignment implies that Kaizen events will be linked to higher-level organizational goals and objectives. This reinforces the concept that the deployment of projects should be to improve high-priority work areas. Prioritizing implies that business benefits have been quantified and meet minimum financial or other requirements. Also, it forces an evaluation of the correct tools and methods to identify and eliminate the underlying root causes of a process problem as it was identified by a team's project charter. It provides a high-level discussion of several related topics. As an example, the first chapter discusses strategy alignment, a review of Lean Six Sigma deployment mechanics, project identification at a strategic level, deployment communications, and the alignment of Kaizen projects with an organization's goals and objectives. Chapter 1 concludes with a high-level discussion of major Lean tools and methods. Chapter 2 discusses how to deploy higher-level organizational goals and objectives via actionable project charters. Project charters should be highly quantified from an operational perspective and financially justified prior to their deployment. They should also be aligned and deployed in an integrated rather than an ad hoc manner. Chapter 3 provides an in-depth analysis of Lean tools and methods. It begins with a discussion of the voice of the customer (VOC) and shows why reducing complexity at all levels throughout an organization is important to increasing productivity. The chapter then continues the discussion of major Lean tools, methods, and concepts from Chapter 1, but on a more detailed level. Specific topics include:

Deploying Lean Six Sigma team's performance measurements
Creating value stream maps (VSMs) of major process workflows
Eliminating unnecessary operations within these workflows
Implementing just-in-time (JIT) systems to eliminate process waste
Reorganizing workflow configurations
Implementing 5S and standardized work
The linkage and spatial relationships between operations
Balancing material flows
Bottleneck management
Using transfer batches
Mistake proofing
Improving quality
Reducing setup time
Deploying total preventive maintenance (TPM)
Leveling demand
Reducing lot sizes
Deploying mixed-model scheduling systems
Creating supplier networks
Implementing visual controls and pull systems using Kanban
The importance of continually updating process technologies

The second section of this book includes Chapters 4 through 6. These three chapters provide a logical road map of the sequential activities that are necessary to plan and conduct Kaizen events. Chapter 4 discusses several important Kaizen event planning activities. These include:

Key roles and responsibilities
Selecting project charters
Identifying team members, including the leader and facilitators
The logistics of meeting rooms and similar supporting resources
The collection of key operational data such as floor layouts, existing maps of process workflows, work and inspection procedures, and operational metrics

These operational metrics include operational cycle times related to job setups, processing, inspection, transport, and waiting. Other important topics discussed in Chapter 4 include the importance of documenting a current process by taking pictures and obtaining real examples from the area serving as the focus of a Kaizen event. This documentation is shown to be useful in revealing process issues. In this context, it is helpful to compare worst versus best performance to identify opportunities for improvement. In addition, Chapter 4 discusses the activities that are necessary to develop a schedule for a Kaizen event and communicate an event. Our discussion of VA operations from Chapter 3 is continued in Chapter 4. This discussion includes estimating production rates, scrap and rework percentages, downtime percentages, capacity levels, setup times, and similar metrics operation by operation. Chapter 5 discusses how to collect and analyze data using Lean and Six Sigma tools and methods. Important Lean tools and methods include VSM, spaghetti diagrams, developing time standards, auditing processes, and job shadowing. Six Sigma tools include cause-and-effect (C&E) diagrams, X to Y matrices, five-why analysis, checklists, histograms, Pareto charts, box plots, scatter plots, time series graphs, and control charts. Chapter 6 concludes the second section of this book. Major topics of Chapter 6 include management presentations of the Kaizen team's findings to secure management support for the project's improvement recommendations. Key elements of these presentations include an analysis of financial and operational data, implementation activities, lessons learned (what did and did not work), the presentation of findings to management, root cause analysis, and countermeasures (mistake proofing, standardized work, training, etc.) to eliminate each root cause. Chapter 6 ends with a discussion of how the project's lessons learned can be translated to other work areas. The discussion in Chapter 6 is focused on office workflows. These include new product forecasting, accounts receivable, new product marketing research, new product development, new employee hiring, and supplier performance management (SPM).

The third section of this book discusses the implementation of a Kaizen or rapid improvement team's solutions. These implementation topics include how to build a business case to management for the new process changes, implementing the actual solutions, and reinforcing new organizational behaviors. Related topics include tying project improvements to a team's root cause analysis, developing effective process controls and systems, training people to use new process controls, estimating a project's business benefits, conducting a risk analysis of the improvements, and transitioning a project to a process owner and local work team. In these discussions, our goal will be to develop long-term and sustainable process improvements that are aligned with an organization's strategic goals and objectives.

ALIGN IMPROVEMENT OPPORTUNITIES

1

Chapter 1

Strategy Alignment

Overview

Today's office environments are a complex mixture of employees, consultants, and technologies that are integral parts of global supply chains. As an example, an accounts receivable department may reside in one country, but several of its core functions are performed across the world. In this context, sales and marketing functions may be geographically dispersed, with customers located in different countries. The invoicing process itself may be modularly designed to service customers based on their cultural, language, or other demographical considerations. Also, an invoicing process's employees and suppliers may be geographically dispersed across the world. In global supply chains, simple and standardized operational systems will tend to have lower cycle times and cost as well as higher quality levels than more complex systems. Simplifying and standardizing processes is a major focus of the Lean tools and methods that are the subject of this book. These tools and methods have been shown to be the most direct way to simplify, standardize, and mistake proof process workflows to translate the needs and requirements of customers through operational systems. This is called translating the voice of the customer (VOC). It will be shown that the application of Lean tools and methods is straightforward, but the process of deploying Lean across an organization is difficult. Organizations always find that Lean deployments require hard work, patience, effective resource allocation, and significant personal involvement of their employees and management.

Unfortunately, many organizations have difficulty applying Lean methods consistently over time due to myriad reasons. These include a genuine failure to properly instruct people on Lean concepts, organizational apathy, a general lack of management support, and a failure to continuously measure and improve operational performance. Employee training is also important in a Lean culture because employees must use the proper tools and methods to analyze and improve their operational work tasks. Also, there are many subspecialties or disciplines within a Lean culture that need extensive on-the-job training from experienced facilitators. As an example, maintenance, job setups, and conducting Kaizen or rapid improvement events require knowledge and practical experience. A major difficulty as well as strength of Lean deployments is that they are a hands-on and practical set of tools and methods that must be learned sequentially in a consistent manner over time.

Organizational apathy is another reason for the failure or suboptimization of many Lean deployments. These dysfunctional situations occur for many reasons, including a lack of prioritization by management, a lack of resources, and a lack of employee accountability. Prioritization issues occur when projects are not selected or strategically aligned by deployment managers. In contrast, if projects are selected and properly aligned, then an organization will be able to incorporate them into its operational planning process. This would force key stakeholders to complete the projects to meet an organization's annual operating plan. Resource issues normally follow from the fact that projects must compete with other important projects within an organization. Projects that are not strategically aligned by management will have a low priority and lack sufficient resources for their execution. The third major reason for organizational apathy is that employees do not have the proper incentives to focus on Lean projects. Properly setting incentives to support a Lean deployment requires that an employee's annual performance contract has specific tasks that support a Lean initiative. Employees will only work on tasks that they know will be measured and rewarded by management. If an organization does not require its employee to support a Lean initiative, then it will fail in practice. In summary, Lean initiatives, and Kaizen events in particular, should not be deployed in isolation with an expectation that they may be expanded in the future or that their improvements will be sustained over time.

What Is Kaizen?

The planning and execution of Kaizen events is the focus if this book. Figure 1.1 defines *kai* + *zen* as "to take apart" and "to make good." The power of this methodology is that continuous-improvement teams can use Kaizen, or more specifically Lean tools and methods, to analyze or take apart their process workflows and their associated operational work tasks using simple analytical tools such as process mapping. Then they can improve or make good their process. An advantage of deploying Kaizen events is that process improvements are usually achieved over several days through an intensive workshop. In this workshop a process workflow or area is analyzed and process changes are made based on the analysis. However, "kai" + "zen" = "to take apart" and "to make good."

Continuous improvement teams analyze process
workflows using simple analytical tools and make
immediate improvements.

Figure 1.1   What is Kaizen?

although Kaizen events are very powerful rapid improvement tools, they are used much too infrequently in many service organizations. This is due to a variety of reasons. One reason is that attention may be diverted by other initiatives such as Six Sigma. Six Sigma initiatives require extensive training in statistical analysis tools and a subsequent phased project execution methodology. The phases are define, measure, analyze, improve, and control (DMAIC). We will discuss these five phases in Chapters 5 and 6, when simple data analysis tools are described in the context of several office processes. A problem with the DMAIC approach is that a project's completion time may take several months. This is because it is difficult to bring everyone together at once to analyze and eliminate process problems. Also, depending on the specific project application, the use of complicated statistical rather than Lean tools and methods contributes to a long project execution cycle time. This does not mean that DMAIC does not have its place or cannot be accelerated, but only that it is often misapplied in practice. These situations tend to create employee frustration at the slow pace of the project activities, which is due to the overly complicated analyses. In other words, in my consulting work, I have found that many Six Sigma projects that have been deployed in office environments would have been best executed using Lean or Kaizen methods. Many people have recognized this fact, and in recent years the term *Lean Six Sigma* has been created to emphasize using the correct process improvement tools and methods in an integrated approach to process improvement. As mentioned above, some data-intensive and complicated root cause investigations may require a Six Sigma–style project execution using its highly structured problem-solving methodology. However, for an organization to obtain timely business benefits from its process improvement activities, it is important that its improvement projects are properly selected, prioritized, and executed using the correct tools and methods. In my opinion, the greatest process improvement potential within office environments is by strategically aligning and executing projects using Kaizen methods, but in an integrated Lean Six Sigma environment.

Table 1.1 compares the major characteristics of Lean, Six Sigma, and Kaizen methodologies. It is obvious that there are many similarities between the three methodologies relative to their project identification, improvement objectives, and the tools utilized for process improvement. As an example, all three methodologies begin with an identification of operational performance gaps through an analysis of financial and operational metrics or through an intensive analysis of process workflows. Performance gaps that are identified by such analyses represent opportunities

Table 1.1 How Do Lean, Six Sigma, and Kaizen Compare?

Lean	Six Sigma	Kaizen
Identify performance gaps and create project charters to close the gaps.	Identify performance gaps and create project charters to close the gaps.	Identify performance gaps and create project charters to close the gaps.
Projects requiring process analysis tools and several weeks or months for execution are selected for a full Lean evaluation.	Projects requiring statistical analysis tools and several weeks or months for execution are selected for a full Six Sigma evaluation.	Projects requiring process analysis tools and only several days for execution are selected as Kaizen projects.
Train and deploy improvement teams around project charters.	Train and deploy improvement teams around project charters.	Train and deploy improvement team around a single project charter.
Align process analysis and improvement with the voice of the customer (VOC) using a value stream map (VSM).	Align process analysis and improvement with the voice of the customer (VOC) using a value stream map (VSM) or quantitative customer information related to complaints, warranty, lost sales, and similar information.	Align process analysis and improvement with the voice-of-the-customer (VOC) using a value stream map (VSM) of the process workflow or a floor layout of the work area associated with the project charter.
Use VOC and simple process analysis tools to eliminate non-value-adding operations and the root causes for poor performance from a process	Use VOC and simple or complex data analysis tools to eliminate the root causes for poor process performance.	Use VOC and simple process analysis tools to eliminate non-value-adding operations and the root causes for poor performance from a process.
Standardize and mistake proof remaining operations using several Lean tools including 5S, SMED, TPM to increase value adding content.	Build models relating the poor performance represented by an output metric (Y) to the root causes or key inputs (Xs).	Standardize and mistake proof remaining operations using several Lean tools including 5S, SMED, TPM to increase value-adding content.
Optimize a process workflow to ensure its operations meet the takt time with a high adding-value content.	Optimize the process relative to Y by changing the levels of the Xs.	Optimize the process workflow to ensure it operations meet its takt time with a high adding-value content.

for teams to improve process workflows. In this identification work, a first step is to create actionable project charters that are aligned with an organization's business goals and objectives. These project charters are carefully defined and structured to close one or more gaps in operational performance. However, different performance gaps may require different toolsets to identify, analyze, and eliminate the root causes for poor operational performance. As an example, those projects requiring simple process analysis tools and several weeks or months for execution may be selected as candidates for a Lean deployment. However, projects requiring advanced statistical analysis tools and several weeks or months for execution may be selected for a Six Sigma deployment. In contrast, projects requiring simple process analysis tools in a localized work area and only several days for their execution may be selected as Kaizen or rapid improvement projects. The employee training activities are then aligned with the required tools and methods necessary to identify and eliminate the root causes for the process problems. In other words, training activities should be specific to business opportunities as well as the anticipated root cause analysis. It should also be noted that Kaizen projects will most likely use a subset of Lean and perhaps some of the less complex Six Sigma tools and methods. We will discuss this approach in the upcoming chapters of this book.

All three improvement methodologies use similar analytical tools, although Six Sigma goes a few steps further with regard to statistically based methods. Common tools and methods include identifying the VOC, building value stream maps (VSMs), analyzing floor layouts of the local work area, and applying simple quality tools for data analysis. This data analysis often includes an analysis of quantitative information. Specific examples include customer complaints, warranty expenses, failure incidents, lost sales, and similar information. These types of project opportunities as well as others are incorporated into a project charter's problem statement and objectives. It should be noted that a project charter should already have been aligned with the VOC prior to selection of any of the three methodologies or assignment to an improvement team. Kaizen projects or events, in particular, will often require the use of simple tools such as process mapping, work standardization, mistake proofing, and similar methods to identify and eliminate non-value-adding (NVA) operations from process workflows, as well as other causes of poor process performance. NVA operations can be immediately eliminated from a process because they are not valued by external customers. In contrast, value-adding (VA) operations are integral to a process because they are necessary to satisfy external customers. VA operations cannot be eliminated from a process workflow without customer permission or a redesign of one or more operational work tasks. A third classification of operational work tasks is defined as business value-adding (BVA) operations. BVA operations are not valued by an external customer, but must remain part of a process workflow due to technology or regulatory constraints that are independent of a customer's requirements. Kaizen events use the VOC and simple process analysis tools to identify and eliminate non-value-adding operations as well as the causes for poor process performance. Kaizen events are a major Lean improvement methodology and heavily use Lean tools and methods. These tools and methods include work standardization, mistake-proofing operations, single minute exchange of dies (SMED), and total preventive maintenance (TPM). In addition, 5S methods are applied to process standardization and improvement. 5S is defined as the following activities: sorting, setting in order, shining, standardizing, and sustaining. In combination, these tools and methods are used to increase the value-adding content of simplified, standardized, and mistake-proofed process workflows. Another major improvement objective of Lean and Kaizen projects is to simplify, standardize, and mistake proof a process workflow to ensure it will meet its takt time with a high value-adding content. Takt time is the work time available to produce one unit from a process. As an example, if there are 100 available minutes per day in a process and 10 units must be produced per day, then the takt time will be calculated as 100 minutes/10 units = 10 minutes per unit. We will discuss these and other Lean tools and methods in Chapter 3, as well as subsequent chapters.

It has been mentioned that Six Sigma projects may require complex data analysis tools to eliminate the root causes for poor process performance. A principal goal of the Six Sigma initiative is to build quantitative statistical models that show relationships between poor performance represented by output metrics (Ys) relative to their identified root causes or key process inputs (Xs). Common Lean tools and methods used in Six Sigma projects include work standardization, mistake proofing, 5S, SMED, and TPM to increase the value-adding content of an improved process. Six Sigma projects optimize the process outputs, or Ys, by changing the levels of the process inputs, Xs, in a predetermined pattern based on a project's analytical work. Our discussion of Six Sigma tools and methods will be at an elementary level. But this discussion will be sufficient because the simpler Lean tools and methods will be required in data collection and analysis as well as the implementation of countermeasures or process controls.

Strategic Alignment

Strategic alignment is critical to ensure resources are efficiently utilized to achieve business goals and objectives. Consistently achieving business goals and objectives, if they are the right ones in the first place, will increase organizational productivity, enable an organization to meet its commitments to key stakeholders, and increase shareholder value. This concept is qualitatively shown in Figure 1.2, and it is equally applicable for not-for-profit as well as commercial organizations because all organizations need to reduce process waste to increase quality and lower cost for their constituents. In this context, the operational effectiveness and efficiency of an organization can be measured by the alignment and value content of its products and services when measured against customer requirements. Measures of organizational effectiveness and efficiency can be integrated using productivity metrics regard-

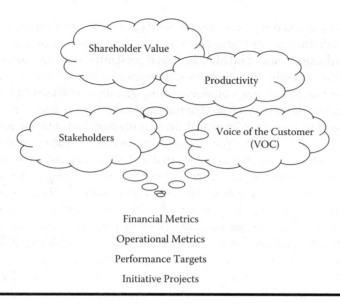

Financial Metrics

Operational Metrics

Performance Targets

Initiative Projects

Figure 1.2 Strategic alignment.

less of the organizational structure. Productivity metrics are ratios of outputs and inputs. Outputs are revenues or other sources of income that may be adjusted based on exchange rates. Inputs are labor, material, and similar expenses or resources that are used to support sales activities. Organizations having strategically aligned and well-managed operations, including all supporting activities, should have higher productivity ratios than nonaligned or poorly managed organizations.

Organizational productivity has a direct impact on an organization's key stakeholders, including its shareholders if it is a commercial enterprise. Some executives dismiss stakeholder interest as irrelevant to running a business, but this is a mistake because these stakeholders include shareholders, employees, governmental regulatory agencies, suppliers, and other constituents associated with an organization's supply chain. These stakeholders can positively or negatively impact an organization's productivity and long-term success. Once an organization sorts out its strategic goals and objectives, relative to its productivity and shareholder economic value-added (EVA) targets, these high-level financial targets are translated into lower-level financial and operational metrics and improvement targets. It should be noted that EVA is defined as the income shareholders receive for their investment in an organization. Although there are several complementary versions of the EVA calculation, one of the easiest to understand is that EVA is an organization's operating profit adjusted for the cost of capital. These lower-level metrics are then successively communicated down through an organization along with improvement targets. The linkage between strategy and its operational execution is made through initiatives of one type or another. These initiatives are aligned to financial and operational metrics based on the anticipated root cause analysis, which is necessary to close performance gaps.

Every initiative has its unique tools and methods that are used to identify, analyze, and eliminate specific types of root causes. As an example, if a process workflow's lead time is too long, then Lean methods can be used to analyze the VOC and use this information to simplify, standardize, and mistake-proof the remaining value-adding (VA) operations with the workflow. On the other hand, if an organization has a problem with low process yields, then a model may be required relating several process input variables (Xs) to their output variables (Ys). In these situations, complex statistical analyses, based on Six Sigma methods, may be required to analyze the root causes for a process problem. There are also many other initiatives or toolsets that can be used to increase organizational productivity. As an example, if an organization needs to improve its equipment uptime or availability, then perhaps the tools and methods associated with total preventive maintenance (TPM) may be useful in these improvement activities.

General Deployment Strategies

The specific strategies that organizations use to deploy initiatives vary depending on their strategic goals and objectives. However, successful deployments have similar success characteristics. These include an alignment with organizational strategy, project charters, resource commitments from senior management, and the training of people in the use of an initiative's tools, methods, and related concepts. Relative to strategic alignment, it is important that an initiative produce tangible business benefits for an organization. These usually take the form of well-defined projects systematically executed to improve process workflows. Other success characteristics may include clear and consistent communications at several levels within an organization, using appropriate communication channels, to show the benefits of a deployment as well as the impact on key stakeholders. These are the success characteristics that help ensure the long-term effectiveness of an initiative.

The specific form or structure of an initiative relative to its deployment may vary across industries and even in organizations within the same industry. As an example, some organizations deploy an initiative using people on a part-time basis. These part-time process improvement experts will usually have other job responsibilities. On the other hand, some organizations may take people out of their functional roles and integrate them on a full-time basis within an initiative to accelerate the creation of its business benefits. Although both strategies may be successful, a part-time strategy will result in a significantly longer cycle time to implement improvement projects. However, an advantage of a part-time approach is that a stand-alone function is not created within an organization. This deployment model avoids the situation in which employees who have been assigned full-time to an initiative must eventually be assimilated back into the organization at a future date.

Also, the deciding factor between full- versus part-time roles and responsibilities to a great extent depends on available projects as well as business benefits. The net business benefit of projects per person must be in multiples of that person's annual salary to assign them to an initiative on a full-time basis. Another differentiating characteristic between initiatives relates to an organization's initial level of expertise. As an example, some organizations hire external consultants to plan and execute their initiative. Others deploy an initiative using internal resources that have been trained on basic principles of an initiative. In this latter situation, a deployment's success will depend on the internal capability of an organization. Another differentiating characteristic of successful initiative deployments is a requirement that they have financial as well as operational benefits. In contrast, poorly deployed initiatives do not have this requirement, or poorly execute it in practice. If the business benefits of projects are not rigorously justified prior to their deployment, then the resources that are necessary to execute them will be hard to justify. In this context, some organizations focus only on cost savings, while others have a more balanced project deployment strategy. It has been found that a balanced project selection process works best. In a balanced selection process, projects may be created to improve customer and stakeholder satisfaction as well as increase sales revenue or reduce operational expense. In the discussions that follow, we will continue this deployment discussion by showing common and differentiating deployment characteristics of the Lean and Six Sigma initiatives.

There are several proven methods to select projects to ensure deployment objectives will be met in practice. The first is a financial analysis of an organization's operations to identify performance gaps. As an example, if expenses are too high or have been increasing over time, then it may make sense to deploy projects to reduce these expenditures. A second method requires an operational analysis using performance reports to analyze poor metric performance of the various process workflows. As an example, if there are issues relative to long cycle times or high error rates, then projects can be created to eliminate these problems. A third method in project identification is to actually study a process using a value stream map (VSM), and then to "walk the process." This method is very useful because it identifies actual work activities being done within a process workflow day in and day out. In fact, many work activities never appear on management reports and may not be known by process owners. The objective of walking a process is to identify non-value-adding (NVA) operational work tasks from a customer perspective. Some common NVA work tasks may include operations that are part of rework loops and those having quality or other problems.

Project benefits are cross-referenced to the resources that are required to meet the organization's deployment schedule once a Lean Six Sigma deployment team identifies a group of projects that will improve its organization's productivity. This approach will preclude the deployment of projects having known solutions or which can be executed through capital expenditures. Important characteristics of these types of projects are that their solution is not known, they align with organizational goals, resources are available to complete them, and they do not depend on other projects that have high implementation risks. A successful deployment is highly dependent on successfully managing organizational communication at all levels. The creation of effective communications depends on engaging communication and human resource professionals with an organization to help with deployment activities. Effective communications must be simple, consistent, and promoted frequently across an organization. In Chapter 8 we will discuss several strategies that a Kaizen team can use to increase the effectiveness of their communications.

The organizational structure of an initiative's deployment is important because it determines how an initiative is positioned within an organization relative to project prioritization and resource allocation. This concept is shown in Table 1.2. Top-down initiatives have a hierarchal structure that facilitates resource allocation to projects based on their business benefits and priority. A top-down and aligned deployment is the most effective way to ensure that projects will be assigned resources and there will be employee accountability for project identification and execution. In contrast, bottom-up deployments will usually have an informal structure that allocates resources to projects based on local priorities. A problem with this approach is that projects may not be aligned with an organization's goals and objectives, making their project prioritization difficult. This situation will tend to result in poor project prioritization and a nonoptimum allocation of organizational resources. Informal or isolated deployments are not efficiently aligned or resourced, and as a result, their project benefits are difficult to sustain over time.

Roles and responsibilities also depend on a deployment's structure. As an example, hierarchal deployments have well-defined and formal roles and responsibilities for all participants. In contrast, bottom-up deployments will usually have informal roles and responsibilities based on the functional areas that are impacted by a project. Informal or isolated deployments will usually have no formally identified roles and responsibilities. This makes their execution difficult. Also, their business benefits are usually minor because process improvements cannot be sustained over time. Roles and responsibilities are important because they facilitate a clear understanding of who is leading and supporting a Lean Six Sigma deployment and its projects. Clearly defined roles and responsibilities show people where to look for resources, technical and financial advice, as well as the necessary approvals to move a project forward. Although initiatives may have differing names for their major roles and responsibilities, their basic roles and responsibilities are usually very similar in form. As an example, every initiative needs leaders, support people, and people to directly improve its process workflows.

Table 1.3 lists several commonly defined roles and responsibilities that are commonly found in Lean Six Sigma deployments. A deployment leader develops strategically aligned plans that integrate projects and their required resources, including project teams. Aligning business benefits with available resources helps in their prioritization and team selection. Deployment leaders also coordinate operational assessments to identify project charters. Project charters form the basis

Table 1.2 Comparing Deployment Strategies

1. Deployment Strategies	Driven Top Down	Driven Bottom Up	Isolated
2. Organizational Structure	Hierarchal and formal allocating resources based on business priorities.	Informal and allocating resources based on local priorities.	No organizational structure and personality dependent.
3. Roles and Responsibilities	Formalized based on benchmarked deployments.	Informal and based on project types.	No identified roles or responsibilities.
4. Benefit Identification	Formalized through operational and financial assessments and integrated into annual strategic plans.	Benefits are realized informally and seldom exceed planned goals and objectives.	Benefits are isolated and may actually be negative if capital is required or root cause analyses are incorrect.
5. Resource Prioritization and Allocation	Resources can be optimally prioritized and allocated by on identified projects relative to other productivity drivers.	Resources are prioritized at a local level or not at all. Projects are usually incremental to current goals and objectives.	No resource prioritization and allocation may be nonexistent, resulting in project execution if there are nonutilized resources.
6. Communication	Formalized communication at all levels throughout an organization using multiple channels.	Informal communication at local levels.	No communication at all unless there is a major breakthrough.
7. Execution	Project execution is time phased and based on resource availability and business benefits to achieve productivity gala and objectives.	Project execution is dependent on other business priorities and typically lags schedules.	Project execution is dependent on available time of the people participating in the initiative.
8. Organizational Integration	Complete and sustainable long-term goals.	At a local level, but not sustainable over time.	None.
9. Continuous Improvement	Visibility enables continuous improvement over time to achieve strategic goals and objectives.	Depending on business priorities continuous improvement is sustainable only short-term for a few years.	Not sustainable.

Table 1.3 Deployment Roles and Responsibilities

Role	Responsibility
Deployment Leader	A person who develops strategic plans to ensure improvement opportunities and business benefits are aligned with resources.
Process Owner	A person responsible for the process in which improvements are made as well as the team members.
Kaizen Event Sponsor	A person who provides resources for the Kaizen event.
Kaizen Event Facilitator	A person who coordinates the planning, execution, and follow-up activities related to an event.
Team Members	The people who analyze and improve a process.
Green Belts/ Black Belts/ Lean Masters	Experts in Six Sigma or Lean tools, respectively.
Support Personnel	People who support the team in its Kaizen activities. These include maintenance, finance, and information technology, as well as other professionals.

on which a deployment's schedule and business benefits are analyzed, and serve as a basis for subsequent project prioritization activities. Lean Six Sigma teams are subsequently deployed based on the prioritization of project charters. These are very important responsibilities that, if well executed, will ensure a successful Lean Six Sigma deployment. In contrast, if project charters are not based on a firm analysis of financial and operational data, only minor business benefits will be realized by an organization. This situation creates a drag on a deployment because resources are required to support projects, but their return on investment (ROI) is low. It should be noted that a common definition of ROI is net income divided by total investment. In these situations an organization may redirect a Lean Six Sigma deployment's resources to other business priorities. In summary, a deployment leader's role is extremely important to Lean Six Sigma deployments and requires that he or she be at a director or vice presidential level within an organization. Lean Six Sigma deployments also have other important roles and responsibilities. As an example, the role of project champions is critical. Champions help coordinate operational assessment, obtain resources for project teams, provide advice, and work with key stakeholders to keep projects on schedule. A third important champion role relates to supporting data collection and analysis activities, as well as the implementation of process improvements. In summary, process owners are responsible for the day-to-day work activities within a process, including its local work team and other resources.

Table 1.3 lists several additional roles and responsibilities that are associated with a Lean Six Sigma deployment. These roles include team members, green and black belts, Lean masters, and various support personnel such as maintenance, finance, information technology, and other professionals. Roles and responsibilities may also be modified by deployment leaders because the degree of technical expertise required for a particular project will vary. As an example, if a project is expected to be heavily Lean-based and deployed across several organizational functions, then a Lean expert should join the team. On the other hand, if a project's root cause analysis is expected to be heavily data-based, then a black belt expert may be a better choice to join a team. The roles and responsibilities of support personnel may also vary. As an example, a project's root cause analysis and improvements may require the expertise of maintenance, logistics, or accounting experts to assist a team with its work.

Kaizen events will also have several specialized roles and responsibilities to get a team up and running very quickly, that is, in a matter of hours, because these events only last several days. As an example, Kaizen events rely to a great extent on their event sponsor and facilitator. A sponsor may be a process owner, executive, or other key stakeholder. One major role of a sponsor is to provide the necessary resources, including facilities, for an event. Resources may include training rooms, materials, trainers, access to phones and e-mail, and equipment. An event facilitator will be a person who coordinates the planning, running, and follow-up activities associated with an event. There will be a great deal of interaction and coordination between an event sponsor and its facilitator. Team members are people who analyze and improve a process workflow. They are selected based on the project charter's problem statement and objective. Support personnel include maintenance, finance, information technology, and other professionals who are required to support an event by quickly providing information, equipment, and other resources. The types of support people may change depending on the type of project.

The business benefits created by a top-down deployment are usually significantly higher and accrue at a faster rate than those from bottom-up or isolated deployments. The reason is that business benefit identification and project execution in top-down deployments are formalized through operational and financial assessments and integrated into an organization's annual strategic plan. In contrast, the business benefits associated with bottom-up or isolated deployments seldom exceed an organization's planned goals and objectives. In fact, they may actually be negative if capital is required to execute the project's solutions without sufficient payback or ROI. Top-down driven deployments also efficiently prioritize and allocate resources to a project's work activities because projects are normally selected based on their productivity impact. On the other hand, in bottom-up or isolated deployments, resources are prioritized at a local level or not at all. This latter situation may result in a conflict with other competing priorities. Also, bottom-up and isolated projects are not usually incremental to current goals and objectives, which may result in double counting of business benefits against other projects. Another problem associated with bottom-up or isolated deployments is that their projects either have a long completion cycle time or are seldom completed on schedule.

Communication is another important characteristic of a successful Lean Six Sigma deployment. In this context, it is important that deployment leaders effectively communicate at all levels of their organization using multiple communication channels. The communication should be modified to match its intended audience. Properly communicated information helps secure resources for a Lean Six Sigma deployment and its projects. It should be noted that even in a hierarchically structured, top-down deployment, initial process improvements will usually be targeted to just a few areas within an organization. It is also very important in this early deployment strategy that a Lean Six Sigma deployment's benefits be communicated with the larger organization. This is because an expansion of a Lean Six Sigma deployment will be dependent on buy-in from the rest of the organization. Negative information regarding a deployment, including a lack of quantified business benefits, will result in little buy-in from the larger organization. In contrast, positive information will increase buy-in from key stakeholders. Communication should also be done at several organizational levels using a multitude of communication channels. This is not usually possible in bottom-up deployments because other initiatives having higher prioritization will be competing for the same communication channels. Finally, it is very important that an organization send simple and consistent messages across its organization to reinforce its Lean Six Sigma deployment objectives. However, in bottom-up or isolated deployments, effective communication is usually prevented from reaching a large audience because it is not aligned with organizational priorities.

These successful deployment characteristics directly impact the ability of an organization to execute its Lean Six Sigma improvement projects. My experience has been that top-down and aligned projects will be executed several times faster than nonaligned projects. Also, their resultant business benefits will be several times higher. This is why an organization should insist that every project, regardless of the initiative, be formally evaluated and approved using standardized procedures prior to its deployment. It has been shown that the long-term sustainability of process improvements is only possible in a well-structured and top-down driven deployment. In summary, it is difficult to sustain process improvements in bottom-up or isolated Lean Six Sigma deployments.

To place this discussion in a specific context, over the past 15 years, I have been involved with perhaps 20 or more Lean Six Sigma deployments using a variety of deployment models in small and large organizations. In the smaller organizations the annual revenue was as low as $20 million per year, and in the largest organization it was more than $100 billion. I recall that one large organization did a great job training its deployment leaders and champions. Also, its financial and operational assessment activities were particularly well done in advance of project assignment. As a result, several well-defined project charters were created for black belts prior to their arrival to training activities. Projects also closed ahead of schedule and with an average savings of several hundred thousand dollars. In contrast, another financial services organization deployed projects poorly and, after training more than 100 black belts, had saved an average of less than $10,000 per project. These were very large organizations. The disparity of business benefits between similar organizations was startling. In my opinion, the difference between these similar organizations was in the up-front deployment planning and project selection activities. Assigning improvement roles on a full-time basis will also increase and accelerate a deployment's cost savings.

Most recently, I have been consulting with a major corporation that created a new department. In this organization, the process improvement strategy was to create and modify processes to align them with customer requirements. In other words, the intent was not to focus on cost savings, but rather on process improvements. This organization has been very successful in improving its operations. However, cost savings and revenue benefits have also been created by these projects. The message I want to convey is that an organization needs to select projects based on strategic considerations. These considerations may include cost savings, cycle time reductions, quality improvements, increases in customer satisfaction, or other relevant business benefits, as well as a combination of one or more of these benefits. This is where some people have become confused: the tools and methods of Lean Six Sigma should be used to help execute strategy, not be stand-alone programs divorced from an organization's goals and objectives.

Reducing System Complexity

The tools, methods, and concepts of Lean Six Sigma can be effectively utilized to reduce system complexity at all levels within an organization. In fact, the greatest productivity gains from a Lean Six Sigma deployment may be attained by their application at an organizational level to reduce overall system complexity prior to actual project selection activities. As an example, an operational assessment may identify redundant facilities or other excess system capacity that should be eliminated from an organization's processes. In other words, it would make no sense to deploy improvement projects unless their benefits would exist for a considerable period of time. Table 1.4 shows several basic concepts that have been useful in reducing a system's complexity. One of the most important is to first ensure that all

Table 1.4 Reducing System Complexity

Voice of the Customer (VOC)	Understand customer value and ensure products and processes have a high value content.
Product and Service Rationalization	Analysis of profitability, volume, and strategic impacts to products or services, which determine if they be should done internally or externally.
Product or Service Design	The elimination of components or optimization of the relationships between remaining components of a system.

organizational activities are aligned with the voice of the customer (VOC). This is because any process workflows or operational work tasks that are not aligned with the VOC may be immediate candidates for elimination. In other words, a very effective way to reduce system complexity is to identify and eliminate products, services, process workflows, operations, and work tasks that have no value content. Eliminating organizational complexity up front, prior to initiating improvement activities, will prevent false starts and resource waste.

Another way to simplify a system is to analyze the profitability of its product or services as well as their volume and strategic impact. Also, the cost of major process workflows and their associated operations can be analyzed prior to project deployment. These types of analytical activities may lead to a discontinuance, outsourcing, or modifications to the design of the low-profit products, services, and their process workflows. In addition, products, services, and process workflows can be redesigned using Lean and Design for Six Sigma (DFSS) concepts to simplify, standardize, and optimize relationships between remaining components of a system. Effective product rationalization can have a major impact on an organization in that it eliminates products having low profitability or other negative attributes. The underlying concept is: Why should we improve a process workflow for a product that is not profitable? Rationalizing profits can also be done from several perspectives. One perspective is, of course, profitability. In this scenario, products, services, or processes with low profitability are eliminated from an organization. Another approach is to eliminate or consolidate similar products, services, and processes to increase their volumes for economy-of-scale advantages. A third approach is to outsource the production of low-volume products, services, and processes. There may also be additional rationalization strategies that may depend on a specific industry or organization. Service rationalization is analogous to product rationalization. In this context various service packages are evaluated for their customer impact and profitability relative to an organization's starting goals and objectives, as well as its core competencies. The rationalization of process workflows requires a careful review of where products or services should be performed as well as the design of their associated work processes. In summary, reducing system complexity through rationalization is an important activity prior to deploying improvement activities, because it would make no sense to allocate resources to improve process workflows that add no real value to an organization or will be eliminated at a future date. In other words, it is more efficient to work within a process workflow that will continue to exist in the future.

Outsourcing Processes

Many organizations have come to rely heavily on their outsourced teams to work on many back-office operations and associated work tasks, but also increasingly on processes that directly touch both internal and external customers. In these environments, there are many examples of successful and not-so-successful outsourced work activities. In my previous book, entitled *Operational Excellence— Translating Customer Value through Global Supply Chains*, I discussed several major considerations when outsourcing work to other countries having diverse cultures, languages, or other barriers to the transfer of work. In this current discussion, I will review a few of the major considerations of outsourcing work as it impacts a global team's process improvements when they plan and execute Kaizen events.

Over the past several years, I have observed the work activities of several international subsidiaries of major corporations in environments having cultural and language barriers between various organizational entities across the world. In these situations, I noted that several key success factors enabled global teams to mature into high-performance work teams. As an example, several years ago, several colleagues and I formed several international teams at one major corporation. These teams spoke Japanese, Korean, English, Hindi, and Mandarin. We met our goals and objectives ahead of schedule relative to other teams because we organized at a local level respecting cultural values, but coordinated our Lean Six Sigma improvement activities at a global level from Singapore. At the end of eight months, the deployment work was completely outsourced to these teams and the deployment was expanded throughout Southeastern Asia.

It is not uncommon for managers of a parent organization to not fully realize the impact of language and cultural differences when they outsource work to another country. Of course, it is obvious that the local people do not speak the language, but managers of the parent organization believe that properly translating current work and inspection procedures into a local language is all that is necessary to transfer the outsourced process workflow. To some extent this is because the key managers of a local subsidiary with which they interact often do speak the language of the parent organization. The assumption is that information will be correctly translated by local managers to their workforce. However, this translation step often goes missing or is not properly done. Exacerbating this problem are situations in which major breakdowns occur because work standards, inspection procedures, equipment setup and maintenance information, and similar information are not provided in the local language or are simply summarized at a higher level. Key facilitators and engineers may also be relocated within a subsidiary for a long period of time, but this may not always be effective. A serious complicating factor may be that the people sent over to facilitate the transfer of work and technology may be arrogant or ignorant of the local customs of the employees with whom they work. These situations occur despite the fact that these people are well educated. In fact, I recall listening to an executive from a major U.S. corporation who had little respect for his local workforce even though he majored in anthropology in college. Also, I have seen many employees who would be considered to be sub par except for the fact that they speak a local language. I have also seen the same situation in reverse, when local managers who speak a parent organization's language and are familiar with its customs have an attitude that the parent organization's influences stop at their door and they run their subsidiary according to their own standards, but with enforced financial accountability by their parent organization. These situations occur when the hiring managers of a parent organization have not fully investigated the backgrounds of their local managers. I am not going to discuss the cultural issues further because there are more complete sources of such information for this subject. However, I will continue this discussion from an operational perspective relative to important activities organizations should consider when they outsource portions of their work activities or deploy Kaizen events across outsourced process workflows to increase productivity.

Organizations outsource process workflows to other locations and organizations for a variety of reasons, including expanding operational capacity without high risk or cost. As an example, a call center, which has a high direct labor cost, could create a subsidiary in a low-wage location. Organizations may also need to be near new customers or critical suppliers. Another reason to outsource work is technology constraints. In these situations, an outsourcing partner may have unique patent positions or specialized knowledge that would be costly or impossible to independently develop. A process workflow may also be under severe environmental controls, but if there are few environmental controls at a subsidiary's location, it may make sense to outsource the work. It may also be necessary to move sources of supply and production closer to new international markets. As an example, McDonald's would obviously want to locate new stores closer to its international customers as well as modify its style and appearance. Menus may also be changed to match local customer's preferences. Along this line of thought, there may be local country or regional rules that mandate that a parent organization locate its subsidiaries or develop local partnerships within a country. Developing partnerships may enable an organization to quickly obtain cultural expertise at a local level. Consultants could also be retained by an organization. Another reason for outsourcing work is that an organization may want to focus on its core process workflows without the distractions from peripheral processes.

There are a variety of factors that relocation or outsourcing teams should consider to minimize the risk to their organizations when an organization thinks about outsourcing its work to international locations. First, cultural factors must be considered by a relocation team. These include cultural norms and values as well as the political and religious tolerance levels of the local government. It was discussed above that an organization usually retains consultants or develops partnerships to ensure that it understands and respects the cultural values and norms of its subsidiary's employees. Demographic factors such as population size and density, the age distribution of a population, its education levels and skills, and language proficiencies are other important relocation considerations. From an economic risk perspective, the major considerations include a country's economic stability, its available infrastructure and capital, as well as the types and availability of equipment, labor, suppliers, and customers. Finally, legal and regulatory factors such as a local government's taxation policies, and internal political stability, as well as the geopolitical stability of the region are major considerations in a relocation decision.

Once all the major factors have been fully considered by a relocation or outsourcing team, then the specific activities necessary for an efficient transfer of process workflows are an important consideration. In this context, from an operational perspective, organizations outsource their work for several reasons. These include higher productivity and customer service as well as more efficient supplier relationships. Organizations will also seek to increase the degree of information sharing throughout their global supply chain as well as the percentage of intangible to real assets and service augmentation. A critical enabler of outsourcing work is to increase the value content of a process through its simplification and standardization. Lean Six Sigma methods are especially useful in these activities because they directly increase the value content of a process. The deployment of Lean Six Sigma methods with other initiatives will create global process workflows that can dynamically respond to changes in customer demand across the world. In summary, a major goal of a Lean Six Sigma deployment is a desire to migrate work to where it will have the highest value content anywhere in the world.

Because outsourcing work is important, it is important that it be executed well at an operational level. It has been my experience that many people do not understand the level of detail that is required to properly transfer or build a new process workflow within a country having different languages or customs. What may, at first, appear as extremely well-documented work and inspection instructions in one work environment may be totally confusing at a second location in another part of the world. This is because a language conveys a great deal of context and implied meanings. Admittedly, many engineers who design products have understood these concepts. Also, to the extent that they do understand, their product transfers to other locations may be better executed than the transfer of service designs and processes. This is because a transfer of service processes creates new challenges because local customs, values, and preferences often have a direct impact on the final form of a service. This form will usually be radically different from that which is offered within a parent organization's country. McDonald's is a good example of an efficient transfer of service processes because its facility designs and menus are customized to local consumer preferences, laws, and regulations. Accounting processes are another example in which the process workflows, tools, and templates must be modified to meet local accounting standards, as well as those of a parent organization. In these situations, using Lean tools and methods, but with a Six Sigma voice of the VOC translation process, is often the best overall approach. Effectively translating the VOC from an external to an internal perspective will ensure a project's specifications are communicated prior to developing a schedule for outsourcing work activities. Once the VOC has been effectively translated, then simple and standardized process workflows can be developed to meet an outsourcing project's goals and objectives. Process workflows should also be mistake proofed and documented to a very detailed level. Also, to the greatest extent possible, process documentation should not rely on a particular language format, but rather use visualization examples. In other words, the most efficient way to communicate process instructions across diverse cultures and countries is through 5S visualization methods. Once a process has been fully documented so that its work procedures can be unambiguously understood, then the next step is to select facilitators and transfer agents who respect and speak the local language. Ideally, these will be local people who have been well trained by the parent organization. Finally, local employees must be well trained to use the new work methods. A rigorous set of follow-up activities, including audits, must also be designed into a process workflow to prevent future process breakdowns.

How to Deploy Lean in Three Steps

A goal of this book is to provide an easy-to-understand and self-contained reference for office professionals to enable the deployment of Lean Six Sigma methods, and in particular Kaizen or rapid improvement events, to increase and accelerate your operational performance. The nine chapters comprising this book follow the high-level road map shown in Table 1.5. The road map is divided into three sections, or steps. These steps include an alignment of improvement opportunities, the planning and execution of Kaizen events, and changing behaviors. The nine chapters discuss strategy alignment, project identification and deployment, Lean Six Sigma basics, Kaizen event planning, data collection and analysis, process improvement, building a business case for process changes, implementing solutions, and reinforcing new organizational behaviors. We will briefly discuss the major topics of these nine chapters and move into increasing detail in subsequent chapters.

Table 1.5　How to Deploy Kaizen Events in Three Steps

Step 1—Align Improvement Opportunities	1. Strategy Alignment
	2. Project Identification
	3. Lean Six Sigma Basics
Step 2—Plan and Conduct the Kaizen Event	4. Kaizen Event Planning
	5. Data Collection and Analysis
	6. Process Improvement
Step 3—Implement Solutions and Change Behaviors	7. Building a Business Case for Change
	8. Implementing Solutions
	9. Reinforcing New Behaviors
	10. Organizational Change

Step 1: Align Improvement Opportunities

Although this book will describe the specific activities that are necessary to successfully deploy Lean Six Sigma in an office environment, we will begin our discussion of Lean Six Sigma at an organizational rather than a process workflow level. The first important concept in this discussion is that all planned Lean Six Sigma activities should be aligned with senior management's goals and objectives. Alignment is achieved by identifying operational performance gaps related to an organization's required goals and objectives. A second major concept is that a well-balanced business case for a Lean Six Sigma deployment must be made to senior management to secure the necessary resources to carry out improvement activities. Development of a business case will also facilitate Lean Six Sigma deployment activities by requiring a prioritization of projects, including the Kaizen events. As an example, higher priority will be given to projects that provide the greatest business benefits to an organization. In this context, Table 1.6 lists three key considerations that are necessary when developing a business case. First, the business benefits discussed in a business case should be directly related to performance gaps. These gaps will be evident as non-value-adding (NVA) work tasks. Improvement opportunities occur by eliminating the performance gaps to increase production rates and capacity and reduce scrap and rework percentages, downtime, setup time, inventory, and similar metrics.

What are business benefits? People may disagree on how to properly characterize a project's benefits. However, at a basic level, every project should produce benefits at least as great as the resources it consumes. A financial analysis is the most useful way to evaluate and prioritize a project's business benefit relative to other projects. In a financial analysis, expenses, sales allowances, and revenue

Table 1.6 Building a Business Case for Improvement

What Needs to Be Done	How It Gets Done
1. Identify performance gaps and productivity opportunities.	Analyze cost and revenue drivers, customer issues, supplier interfaces, core processes that are broken, regulatory issues that pose risk relative to strategic goals and objectives.
2. Identify opportunities in new products and services to improve performance, move technology, lower risks, and increase market share.	Apply Lean Six Sigma and Design for Six Sigma methodologies to reduce and manage technical, supplier, customer, scheduling, cost, and other project risks.
3. Break the opportunities into linked and actionable project charters.	Develop baselines and improvement targets for business and financial metrics aligned with business opportunity.

increases can be used to show the financial impact of a project. This information can be found within an organization's profit-and-loss (P/L) statement, which is shown by way of example in Figure 2.5. As a second option, an analysis of an organization's balance sheet will show the amount of money an organization has invested in various assets. These assets include accounts receivable, inventory, plant and equipment, and others. The conversion of an asset increases the cash available to an organization. It also reduces interest expenses if money has been borrowed to purchase or finance an asset. This extra money gained through an asset conversion can be invested in operations that have a high rate of return. A third category is cost avoidance projects. These projects prevent higher expenses or increase revenue in future time periods. There may also be other projects that may directly increase revenue or reduce cost. These usually focus on improvements in service or product design. There are many other types of projects that may have a significant business impact, but no direct financial benefit. These may be designed to improve key stakeholder satisfaction. Once performance gaps have been identified through financial and operational assessments, project charters are created to enable process improvement teams to improve their processes. These topics will be expanded in Chapter 2 when we discuss the creation of project charters for Lean Six Sigma deployments. It should be noted that not all projects will require the use of Lean or Six Sigma tools and methods. As an example, some projects may be better executed through a capital expenditure, or if a solution is known, they should be executed using standard work methods. Also, there will be a subset of Lean projects that can be identified for execution over only several days using a Kaizen event or workshop. In Kaizen events, the required activities include the up-front selection of a cross-functional team to execute a project charter, allocating other resources, planning, and conducting the Kaizen event. Final activities include integrating process improvements into the daily work activities of the local work team. As part of a Kaizen event, an improvement team also makes management presentations and develops plans to ensure all unfinished tasks are completed according to a schedule. In summary, a Kaizen event is a set of activities that analyze and improve a process workflow using Lean and simple data analysis tools to identify and eliminate the root causes of poor process performance.

Step 2: Plan and Conduct the Kaizen Event

Once Lean Six Sigma projects have been identified and scheduled for deployment, they are categorized by the toolsets required to execute them. As an example, those requiring extensive data analysis will be classified as Six Sigma projects, while those requiring major changes in process workflows will require an integrated Lean approach. However, projects having a limited scope and which can be executed in a very short time horizon, such as three to five days, can be deployed as Kaizen events. These events have proven very useful in service organizations to quickly improve operations by simplifying, standardizing, and mistake proofing operations. In later chapters of this book we will discuss Kaizen events in more detail and provide templates to enable an improvement team to plan and conduct Kaizen events within their process workflows. It will be shown that planning a Kaizen event is a structured process consisting of numerous sequential activities that are designed to focus a team on a valid business problem and obtain the necessary resources to schedule and execute all the work activities associated with an event.

In a Kaizen event, people can come together and complete their work activities in a matter of days, but subsequent follow-up activities may be required to complete any unfinished work tasks. At the beginning of an event, an improvement team is trained on how to complete the various Kaizen activities, which include collecting and analyzing data from the process workflow being improved, as well as developing countermeasures to eliminate the root causes of process problems. In Chapters 4 and 5 we will provide several Excel templates to help a Kaizen team collect and analyze process data. Several simple and easy-to-use Six Sigma tools are also discussed in Chapter 5. Once data has been collected and analyzed from a process workflow, a Kaizen team develops a list of countermeasures that can be immediately implemented within a process. This information is directly communicated to the process owner and local work team.

Step 3: Implement Solutions and Change Behaviors

Organizational change is a complex process that requires convincing a majority of an organization that the new behaviors that are required to sustain process improvements produce advantages for their organization. There are proven success characteristics that will support the activities necessary to implement a Kaizen team's recommended process changes. In Chapters 7 to 9, we will show how to build a business case for process improvements based on a Kaizen team's root cause analysis and its recommended countermeasures or solutions, and then manage the change aspects of their project. This discussion will focus on the importance of acting on fact by linking project improvements to their root cause analysis and developing effective process controls that are linked to root causes. Other important change activities will be shown, to include training employees to use new work procedures, effectively transitioning a project to the process owner, applying tools and methods to sustain process improvements, integrating the process improvements with other organizational initiatives, and reinforcing new behaviors through a modification of an organization's rewards and recognition systems.

The basis for effective organizational change requires that solutions to process problems are sustainable. But in order for solutions to be sustainable, they must directly eliminate the root causes for poor process performance and be easy to maintain by local work teams. In other words, irrelevant and complicated solutions will fall into disuse over time. Also, solutions must create real value for an organization, and in particular for a process owner and local work team. If a Kaizen project has these characteristics, then its improvements will have a high probability of long-term success. Over an extended period of time, organizational behaviors can be positively influenced by a Lean Six Sigma deployment. However, an organization must create and execute a large number of projects to change organizational behavior. It has been shown by John P. Kotter that, in some corporate cultures, organizational change may take between 15 and 20 years. But this is true only if it is also a high organizational priority with the proper rewards and recognitions. In other words, employees must use, on a daily basis, the new tools and methods that have been identified as the countermeasures necessary to eliminate the root causes for poor process performance. In summary, a critical mass of employees must willingly practice new behaviors for an extended period of time, and the new behaviors must be positively reinforced by an organization through its reward, recognition, and incentive systems as well as its ongoing communications.

Important Elements of a Lean System

Figure 1.3 shows ten key elements of a Lean system. These elements will be briefly discussed to provide some context around our discussion in Chapters 2 and 3. Then we will expand our Lean discussion in later chapters relative to these ten elements and introduce additional Lean and Six Sigma concepts. Because of the high information technology (IT) content of service workflows, we will discuss how Lean and Six Sigma tools and methods can be applied in these highly automated service processes. Our focus will be the rapid process improvement of office processes using Kaizen events.

Understand the VOC

Understanding the voice of the customer (VOC) is a powerful way to immediately identify and eliminate process waste. However, the VOC may be completely misunderstood or unknown when an organization substitutes its voice for that of its external customers. The process of identifying and analyzing the VOC is based on a rigorous set of activities that are firmly based on modern market research methodologies. In our present discussion, it is assumed a Kaizen team has a quantifiable listing of current customer requirements that have been correctly translated through sales, marketing, and design engineering. This implies that an organization has gathered information describing customer needs and value expectations by market segment, and then correctly translated this information into internal requirements and specifications. This VOC translation process is important because a Kaizen team will need to compare quantifiable customer specifications

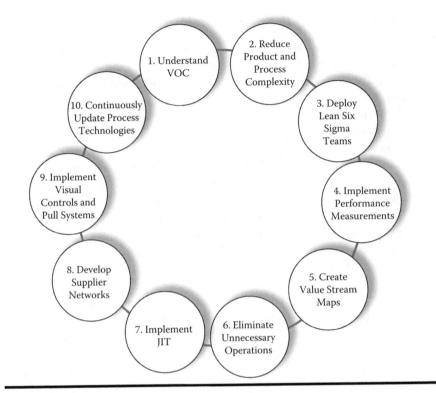

Figure 1.3   Ten important elements of a Lean system.

Table 1.7   Translating the Voice of the Customer (VOC)

1. Market segmentation.
2. Customer demographics and distribution channel.
3. Market research.
4. Customer themes or critical-to-quality (CTQs) characteristics.
5. Translation of CTQs into specifications (Ys).
6. Comparison to process performance.
7. Identification of performance gaps.
8. Development of projects to close performance gaps.

with current process performance. These comparisons will be made using value stream maps (VSMs), operational reports, and data collected directly from the process workflow being analyzed by the Kaizen team. Table 1.7 shows how customer needs and value expectations are successively translated into major themes or critical-to-quality (CTQ) characteristics related to quality, time, cost, or similar characteristics, then quantified into internal specifications, or Ys.

Reduce Product and Process Complexity

The importance of reducing process complexity at every level of an organization by eliminating unprofitable or noncore products, services, and processes has been discussed earlier in this chapter. In this context, it is also important that a Kaizen team look for ways to reduce process complexity at a project level by identifying and eliminating the causes of non-value-adding work from a process workflow. As an example, suppose a Kaizen team were assigned a project to reduce travel expenses. There may be several reasons for higher-than-expected expenses. First, high travel expenses may be caused by general business conditions, which may include higher fuel costs or competitive pressures. Second, people may also be making unnecessary trips, or they may be incorrectly arranging their travel by not following policies regarding travel partners or routing. In these latter situations, projects can be created to analyze and lower travel expenses. As an example, because reducing the frequency of business trips will directly lower travel expenses, it may make sense to investigate this key factor and simplify the system prior to deploying Kaizen teams to reduce expenses. As another example, when incoming customer calls are not answered by call center agents within an expected time period, due to any one of several reasons, customers will usually call back into a call center; this increases the incoming call volume. In some call centers this increase may exceed 25 to 50 percent of the initial incoming call volume, effectively decreasing available system capacity. An increase in call volume creates many other process breakdowns. These include longer customer waiting time and mistakes. These conditions increase the overall complexity of a system. However, the mechanics of how a call center operates are well known. For this reason, it would make sense to attack the reasons for the incremental call volume, then work on the remaining process issues. As an example, suppose the incoming call volume were related to a process issue connected to rebates for software products. In this hypothetical process, a customer tears off a UPC code and completes a questionnaire or form and sends it to a rebate collection center. These reverse logistics systems are very complicated processes and require significant organizational resources for their management. Although a Kaizen team could map the process operation by operation to improve its workflow, if the rebate process could be automated or eliminated to reduce the system's complexity, this work would not be necessary. Reducing a system's complexity would also eliminate myriad related problems, such as returned mail, customer complaints, receiving rebate documentation from customers, and mailing rebates. How could this be accomplished? When I make purchases at Best Buy and similar stores, some manufactures allow me to go online and enter a rebate code. No other information needs to be sent to obtain a rebate. In contrast, other manufacturers maintain complicated and manually intensive rebate processes as described above. In summary, Kaizen teams are more effectively utilized once a process has been simplified at a higher level using the VOC as a guideline and best-available operational practices.

Deploy Lean Six Sigma Teams

Problem-solving teams are an integral part of a Lean system. However, prior to assigning resources such as a Kaizen team to a project, it is important to understand how projects support business goals and objectives. For this reason, organizations should create executive steering committees to develop their Lean Six Sigma deployment plan and schedule based on an alignment with organizational goals and objectives. In addition, it is important that an organization develop reward and recognition systems to reinforce its deployment level by level throughout the organization. Communication is very important in these efforts. This is especially true prior to and during team engagement because people need to understand why they have been asked to be part of a Lean Six Sigma deployment as well as a particular improvement team. In this regard, a consistent organizational message facilitates team formation and related work activities within an organization. After the deployment's infrastructure has been created by an executive steering committee, project charters are created using operational assessments of major process workflows. Once selected, team members are trained to use tools, methods, and concepts that are directly related to the process analysis and improvements required by their project charter. We will discuss these important topics in later chapters of this book.

Implement Performance Measurements

Unless a system has been properly designed up front, a successful deployment of a Lean Six Sigma initiative takes several years of continuous improvement. Integral to a successful Lean Six Sigma deployment is the measurement of key system attributes in the form of financial and operational metrics related to cycle time, cost, and quality. Financial and operational metrics will show a Kaizen team how process performance improves from an initial baseline. In this context, there are several key Lean Six Sigma metrics that enable teams to identify areas where process improvements should be made to increase productivity. In fact, many organizations create metric dashboards to track their higher-level metrics. This provides visibility to the lower-level metrics that drive their performance. We will discuss these concepts in more detail in subsequent chapters.

Create Value Stream Maps

One of the key strengths of Lean Six Sigma is the simplification of a process workflow and its operational work tasks. However, process simplification does not imply that operations or work tasks can be arbitrarily eliminated from a process. On the contrary, operations must be shown to be unnecessary or non-value-adding (NVA) in satisfying customer requirements prior to their elimination. A key analytical tool to document and analyze non-value-adding operational work tasks is a value stream map (VSM). A VSM is a quantified description of a process workflow. It shows operational relationships and helps differentiate value-adding (VA) from NVA operational work tasks. There is also a third value category called business value adding (BVA). This category consists of NVA operational work tasks that cannot be eliminated from a process due to technology or regulatory constraints and requirements. However, over time, an organization's improvement goal should be to also eliminate BVA operations for its process workflows. In these environments, process simplifications can be implemented at several levels within an organization. As an example, it was mentioned earlier that facilities, products, services, and processes can be eliminated from an organization if they are considered to be noncore to its strategic goals and objectives. But at a lower organizational level, NVA operational work tasks within a facility's workflows can also be eliminated using Lean, Six Sigma, or other important improvement methodologies, such as Kaizen teams, to lower cycle times and cost as well as increase process yields.

Eliminate Unnecessary Operations

It may make sense to either eliminate non-essential markets or reorganize the ways in which operations are spatially oriented to each other once a process has been simplified. As an example, some process layouts have been shown to be more efficient than others because of their design. For example, discrete part manufacturing operations that are laid out as U-shaped work cells are usually more efficient than other process layouts. This is because a U-shaped work cell integrates all operations within it. This type of work cell design enables easy staffing of a work area because employees can switch from one work station to another within the work cell. In contrast, a linear flow of materials for low-volume operations may make it difficult to assign workers to different operations when demand on the work cell fluctuates over time. Once a process workflow has been simplified and its operations organized efficiently, its work operations must be standardized to minimize their variation. Standardization ensures work is performed the same way every time by any worker. As a result, work standardization reduces cycle time and costs and improves the overall yield of a process. The specific methods used to lay out work operations and standardize process workflows will be discussed in later chapters.

Implement Just-in-Time (JIT)

A full implementation of a Lean system (excluding Six Sigma activities) requires a level demand pattern with minimum variation. Estimates of maximum allowable month-to-month maximum demand in medium-volume systems are approximately

±10 percent of average monthly demand. However, it is obvious that few systems have demand variation this low. This is why it is difficult to apply such important Lean methods such as pull scheduling systems to completely integrate process workflows as a Lean enterprise. However, there are several actions an organization can take to minimize the impact of the variation in external demand on its system. First, it could minimize its sales promotional activities. As an example, many retailers offer their customers special incentives to purchase their products and services. In contrast, several major retailers such as Wal-Mart have everyday low pricing of their products. Everyday low pricing tends to minimize demand variations on a system. This has an effect of increasing the probability that capacity can be matched to demand time period to time period. In other words, products and services will more likely be available when customers want to purchase them. This eliminates the myriad rework processes that must be deployed to manage customer complaints.

Level loading of demand, in the context of a pull system, will be discussed in later chapters of this book. In a pull system, operational capacity is aligned and linked to external customer demand. This is the reason that level-loaded demand is so important. In pull systems, operations are linked through either manual or electronic systems that order products or services from upstream operations only when they are needed by downstream operations. In a manual system, Kanban cards are used to authorize the movement of materials through a system. A detailed description of these systems will be provided and discussed in later chapters, but at this time it should be noted that pull systems help to minimize work-in-process (WIP) inventory and ensure capacity is efficiently utilized to meet actual rather than forecasted demand.

Develop Supplier Networks

Lean systems depend on the complex interaction of several organizations across a supply chain. In service organizations, these supply chains are often global and consist of several information technology (IT) platforms as well as their supporting systems. In these complex systems suppliers and customers must work together to standardize operations and efficiently match operational capacity across the supply chain to external and internal demand. In complicated global supply chains, it is important that partnerships be created between all participants to ensure complementary workflow systems. This is especially important with respect to the strategic as well as tactical goals and objectives of the supply chain. As an example, we want to avoid situations in which participants suboptimize a supply chain's financial and operational performance. To simplify, standardize, and mistake proof the numerous operations that are characteristic of global supply chains, it is important that suppliers understand basic Lean Six Sigma concepts.

Implement Visual Controls and Pull Systems

Controlling the flow of information and materials through a global service system can be complicated and prone to error. An important concept in Lean systems is that information and materials should flow uninterrupted between the operations of a process. This requires that the status of all workflow objects within a system be known and that simple rules are used to move objects from one operation to another based on external demand, or a pull signal. Pull systems may be visual using physical signal cards, that is, Kanban cards, or electronic and reside within the IT systems making up a process. The exact procedures or mechanics of how these types of scheduling systems are created will be discussed in Chapters 3 to 5. At this point in our discussion, it is important to simply understand that the many improvement activities of a Lean Six Sigma process are designed to move information and materials, without interruption between process workflows, through the system or supply chain.

Continuously Update Process Technologies

Information technology drives the efficiency of service operations as manual operations are eliminated from process workflows and mistake-proofing systems are deployed within remaining workflow operations. Later in this book we will discuss some of the major IT platforms in more detail. This discussion will describe how to collect information from highly automated systems and use it to implement process improvements. It will be shown that it is important that the people imbedded within a highly automated process are trained to perform the newly integrated work tasks as they are updated and improved over time. In these situations, process technologies and their associated manual work tasks should be developed in unison to maximize their combined efficiency.

Summary

Today's office environments are a complex mixture of employees, consultants, and technologies that are integral parts of global supply chains. This complexity often results in process breakdowns that increase cycle time and cost and lower quality. The balance of this book will focus on the application of Lean Six Sigma tools and methods in office environments within global supply chains. Another important focus of this book is rapid process improvement using Kaizen events. The deployment of Kaizen events requires Lean tools and methods, but also several simpler Six Sigma tools. A comparison of the similarities and differences between these three related improvement methodologies was shown in Table 1.1. It was shown that the three methodologies use similar analytical tools. Regardless of the specific methodology or combination of methodologies employed by an organization, deployment strategies must be aligned with an organization's strategic goals and objectives to increase productivity and shareholder value. As an example, an important part of process improvement is the selection of projects to improve workflows. In this improvement work, the tools, methods, and concepts of Lean Six Sigma can be used to reduce system complexity at all levels within an organization. In addition, product or services can be rationalized from a profitability, volume, or strategic impact viewpoint. It was also mentioned that problem-solving teams are an integral part of a Lean Six Sigma deployment. In summary, a successful deployment of a Lean Six Sigma initiative takes several years of continuous-improvement work in which tools and methods are used in a logical sequence.

Suggested Reading

Larry Bossidy and Ram Charan with Charles Burck. 2002. *Execution—The discipline of getting things done*. Crown Business, New York, NY.

Stan Davis and Christopher Meyer. 1998. *Blur—The speed of change in the connected economy*. Reading, MA: Addison-Wesley.

John Donovan, Richard Tully, and Brent Wortman. 1997. *The value enterprise—Strategies for building a value based organization*. New York: McGraw-Hill.

Thomas L. Friedman. 2006. *The world is flat*. New York: Farrar, Straus and Giroux.

Robert S. Kaplan, ed. 1990. *Measures of manufacturing excellence*. Boston: Harvard Business School Press.

John P. Kotter. 1996. *Leading change*. Boston: Harvard Business School Press.

James W. Martin. 2007. *Lean Six Sigma for supply chain management*. New York: McGraw-Hill.

———. 2008. *Operational excellence—Using Lean Six Sigma to translate customer value through global supply chains*. New York: Auerbach.

James M. McTaggart, Peter W. Kontes, and Michael C. Mankins. 1994. *The value imperative—Managing superior shareholder returns*. Free Press, New York, NY.

Michael E. Porter. 1990. *The competitive advantage of nations*. Free Press, New York, NY.

Jae K. Shim and Joel G. Siegel. 2001. *Handbook of financial analysis, forecasting and modeling*. 2nd ed. Englewood Cliffs, NJ: Prentice Hall.

G. Bennett Stewart III. 1990. *The quest for value*. Boston: Harper Business.

John Tschohl. 1996. *Achieving excellence through customer service*. Best Sellers Publishing, Minneapolis, MN.

Thomas E. Volkmann. 1996. *The transformation imperative*. Boston: Harvard Business School Press.

Chapter 2

Project Identification

Overview

In business, improving financial and operational metrics requires bringing people and resources together to identify and execute projects. These projects should have clear objectives of the types of work that needs to be done and how work activities should be organized and assigned to team members. In this context, work activities are identified as sequenced activities that are used to build a project plan. A project plan describes work activities in terms of their resource requirements and schedule. It should also be noted that work activities have time durations, resource requirements, and an objective or expected outcome when an activity has been completed. Work activities can also be broken down into lower-level work tasks. In other words, work activities are operations within process workflows, and work tasks reside within operations. Alternatively, work activities can be aggregated into milestones that are major components of several work activities. A project consists of several milestones that in turn consist of several completed work activities. Work activities can be broken down into operations, and finally into work tasks.

Projects also exist in several forms. These can be classified according to their intended objectives as well as the types of resources required to execute them. In this book we will focus our discussion primarily on the application of Lean tools and methods to rapidly improve a process. However, some of the simpler and more useful Six Sigma tools will also be discussed relative to data collection and analysis. Along this line of thought, it should be noted that some improvement projects, which require in-depth statistical analysis, may be more effectively deployed and executed using Six Sigma tools. These types of projects may also require experimentation or testing of potential solutions. This testing methodology is called a pilot study. In addition, other types of improvement projects may require a purchase of capital equipment or other toolsets to eliminate the root causes for poor process performance. However, all improvement projects and their associated work activities, resource requirements, and schedules must be described using a formal project charter. Using formal project charters to create Kaizen projects is an important topic of this book.

The objective of a Kaizen event or project is the improvement of financial and operational metrics over a very short time frame, which is usually measured in days. The term *financial* implies that improvements focus on expense reductions, increases in cash flow through asset conversions, or revenue increases. *Operational* implies that a linkage has been made between the operational metrics that will be improved and their associated financial metrics. In this context, Lean methods will be used to improve operational metrics that have been correlated with a project's financial metrics and targets. Typical high-level operational metrics in service processes include process yield and cycle time. At a lower level, operational metrics may include scrap and rework percentages, capacity utilization, inventory investment, job setup time, maintenance effectiveness, equipment uptime, as well as many other types of metrics. As an example, an operational assessment may show that high inventory levels are caused by long lead times. In these types of analysis, it should be possible to create a simple model that relates a lead-time reduction in days to the reductions in inventory investment required to maintain customer service levels. As a second example, if warranty expense is very high, then it should be possible to investigate one or more of its root causes and eliminate them from a process to reduce warranty expense.

Projects should also be formally documented using project charters. Project charters describe where a project will be deployed, its objectives, and the resources required for its execution. Integral to a well-written project charter are well-defined financial and operational benefits. In addition to this basic information, a project charter should document the extent of a process problem, the project's objectives, and its team and key stakeholders. Project benefits should also be time phased and evaluated against their implementation costs to calculate the net business benefits of a project. Later in this chapter we will discuss the major characteristics of project charters, how to create them, and provide an example using an Excel template.

Lean Supply Chain

Lean systems are characterized by having a high value-adding (VA) content across their operations and work tasks. This implies their work operations are organized in a way in which a process workflow is aligned with customer value expectations. A high value-adding content also implies that work is done efficiently and without waste to meet external customer demand. In addition, Lean supply chains are characterized by having high asset utilization efficiencies. In other words, they do more work with fewer resources and are thus "Lean." It will be shown in later chapters of this book that in a Lean system, work should be "pulled" through a process using a time-based external customer demand signal called the drumbeat or takt time of a process. In this context, external demand is pulled though a process operation by operation starting with those operations that are closest to the final customer. In an advanced Lean system, materials and information flow from one operation to another in single-unit quantities using visual control systems. In Chapter 3, it will be shown that an effective deployment of a Lean system requires that its participants sequentially deploy several key operational elements. These operational elements consist of several Lean tools, methods, and concepts that evolve over time and build on each other. This evolution of sequenced process improvements increases an organization's operational capability by eliminating non-value-adding (NVA) work tasks from a process workflow. Some of the more important operational elements include a pull-based demand scheduling system having a predetermined production rate called a takt time, operational stability through work standardization and mistake proofing, as well as the deployment of continuous deployment teams within an integrated supply chain. A takt time is the time required to create one unit of production. It is calculated as available production time divided by required production quantity. We will discuss these tools and methods as well as others in subsequent chapters.

A system's leanness can be measured from several perspectives using benchmark statistics. As an example, a quantified value stream map (VSM) can be used to calculate the time duration of value-adding (VA) operations relative to the total cycle time required to produce a product or service, to calculate a percentage of value-adding time. A second method is to measure asset utilization efficiencies across an organization's process workflows. A truly Lean supply chain should have higher asset utilization efficiencies than its competitors. As an example, inventory turns is one measure of asset utilization. Inventory turns is calculated in a manufacturing process by dividing the total cost of goods sold (COGS) by the average monthly inventory investment necessary to maintain the COGS level. As an example, if COGS is $1,200 and the average monthly inventory investment is $100, then the inventory turns ratio is calculated as 12. In a service system, one measure of asset utilization efficiency can be calculated as the total cost center budget divided by the average investment necessary to maintain the system's available capacity. As an example, if a call center has a total budget of $12 million per year and an asset base of $1 million, then its asset utilization efficiency would be 12. The asset base may include building, equipment, and similar capitalized costs. In either scenario, it makes sense to continuously drive down the invested resources and capital in the denominator of the ratio.

Improving the value-adding content of a system is also very important to an organization for several reasons. The first is to increase its productivity and competitive position. This is because more than 50 to 80 percent of all organizational costs are associated with the materials, people, and equipment within a system.

The second reason is to create operational systems that cannot be easily emulated by competitors. A Lean competency will enable an organization to gain a productive advantage over its competitors. This higher productivity can be used to invest in more-efficient processes and equipment or to increase market share. In this context, depending on the industry and functions within an industry, superior operational performance may be critical to an organization's strategic goals and objectives. Examples include airline operations, the back-office systems of financial institutions, procurement systems, and others in which profit margins are very low. In other organizations, the development of unique products or services may be very important in executing strategic goals and objectives. Examples include the entertainment and other service industries having a very high degree of customer-facing operations as opposed to back-office operations. However, an organization that creates simpler and more repeatable processes will also have higher customer satisfaction levels because its operational performance will be more consistent and standardized. But it should be noted that a high degree of operational standardization does not imply a lack of operational flexibility. On the contrary, simple and standardized systems can often be designed to quickly satisfy changing customer requirements. An example is United Parcel Service, which is characterized by highly standardized work procedures, but which can easily adapt its systems to accommodate major demand variations due to seasonality. These variations in demand may require a 100 percent increase in operational capacity.

Key benefits of an effective Lean system are low operational cost, low cycle time, and high process yields. The superior performance of a Lean system is due to its operational simplification obtained by eliminating NVA work as well as the standardization and mistake proofing of the remaining VA work tasks. A key characteristic of an effective Lean system is also its low variation of internal demand. Internal demand in a Lean system is maintained at a constant level with minimum variation to enable an organization to more effectively plan and execute its work schedules. But stability is directly proportional to the degree to which the design of products or services and their process workflows can be standardized and use common components or work elements. In service industries a process design is also heavily influenced by the available information technology (IT) platforms. These IT platforms or systems are used to increase capacity across a system to enable more effective operational planning and flexibility in meeting external customer demand wherever and whenever it may occur. As an example, international call center networks manage demand on their system by transferring waiting calls anywhere in the world depending on available local capacity and demand. In contrast, dysfunctional supply chains exhibit friction at their organizational or functional interfaces. This friction is caused by conflicting priorities in the form of divergent goals and objectives that are often seen as competing financial and operational metrics. As a result, the ability of a dysfunctional system to meet external customer demand is often poor due to a misalignment of capacity at various operations within its process workflows. These interfunctional conflicts may be caused by myriad reasons. A common example in some organizations is the friction that may occur between sales and marketing versus operations. In these situations, sales would like to sell more products and services, but operations would like to provide the products or services as efficiently as possible. In dysfunctional organizations, sales may be tempted to sell products or services based on incentives regardless of available operational capacity or the most efficient production sequence. This tends to lower overall profitability of a product or service. In this context, available capacity includes materials, people, and equipment that are used to produce products and services as well as their efficient usage. To avoid these types of problems in complex service systems, conflicting goals and objectives are managed using various communication vehicles, such as meetings, conference calls, and e-mails, with varying degrees of success.

In contrast, in a Lean system, all operational capacity is aligned using specialized scheduling systems called pull production to produce products and services to meet daily customer demand. In these systems, customer demand has been stabilized, at least initially, to produce a minimum amount of internal variation between operations. Also, the entire system, including customers, suppliers, and production operations, is synchronized using common financial and operational metrics. In well-designed Lean systems, all participants have these aligned financial and operational incentives specified by written contracts. These system attributes contribute to production operations that efficiently utilize a system's available capacity to satisfy external customer demand for products and services. In these systems, alignment is accomplished by an elimination of "functional silos" in favor of highly connected operations that "pull" materials and information through a system's process workflows to produce products and services for customers.

Conducting a Lean Assessment

Conducting an operational assessment will ensure that a Lean Six Sigma deployment will be aligned with an organization's goals and objectives. In other words, the Lean Six Sigma improvement projects identified through an assessment will be focused on those operational areas that will provide the greatest business benefits to an organization. Assessment activities require an analysis of financial and operational reports, interviews of key stakeholders, analysis of customer and supplier complaints, and the value stream mapping (VSM) of major process workflows. In this context, an assessment is a structured investigation of productivity opportunities within an organization's process workflows. Some examples include finance, accounting, sales and marketing, procurement, and other major functions. It should be noted that assessment activities should be deployed from higher to lower operational levels of an organization. Periodic operational assessments are important to an organization. This is because they identify projects that can be prioritized based a minimum return on investment (ROI) or other prioritization criteria that meet strategic goals and objectives. Assessments also help create a deployment infrastructure from which Kaizen events can be deployed at lower levels of an organization. Finally, an operational assessment also enables local management and team members to assist in developing projects to directly improve their operations. But these projects are also integrated at higher levels of an organization.

The basis of an operational assessment includes analysis of financial and operational reports to identify performance gaps. In addition, interviews are conducted in which key stakeholders identify additional project opportunities. These additional project opportunities may include process workflows having long cycle times, low yields, or high cost. However, it is important that potential operational improvements be thoroughly tied to financial metrics to directly increase organizational productivity. Integral to all the assessment activities is VSM of major process workflows by local work teams. The operations within a process are mapped and quantified to create the VSM. After a preliminary VSM has been created by an assessment team, the process owner, and the local work team, the accuracy of the VSM is verified by actually "walking the process" operation by operation. When a VSM has been verified and analyzed, it is also important to capture, through written or electronic methods, the financial and operational information necessary to create project charters. In this creation process, project charters should have a fully developed problem statement and quantified objectives that are tied to a financial analysis. This information is used to develop a business case for a single project or several. In addition, a project charter should identify the resources necessary to execute the project. A major issue with operational assessments is that teams may identify improvement opportunities in a subjective and anecdotal manner without a rigorous quantification methodology using project charters. In fact, a good test of the success of an operational assessment should be a stack of project charters that are immediately actionable by an organization. An assessment is not complete if project charters have not been well defined from both a financial and an operational perspective. Do not let an assessment team leave your facility without completing its project charters to your satisfaction. A failure to create project charters implies an assessment team was not able to effectively quantify operational performance gaps or financial and operational metric linkages. This situation will eventually result in local improvement teams having to create their own project charters. This will lengthen their project's deployment schedule.

In any initiative, it is important to identify a deployment leader and create an executive steering committee to ensure a deployment's strategic and tactical alignment. A top-down deployment is the foundation on which a successful change initiative is created and deployed across an organization. A failure to gain senior management's commitment through these enabling organizational structures or to develop clearly defined roles and responsibilities results in an isolated and ineffectual deployment. In these situations, project teams cannot obtain required resources and project benefits are poor. These types of deployment problems are exacerbated by poor project selection and conflicts with other organizational priorities. In chapter 1 we discussed the major roles and responsibilities of a Lean Six Sigma deployment using Table 1.3. In this discussion it was shown that roles and responsibilities should be integrated into a Lean Six Sigma deployment using leadership and middle management workshops. These are also called executive and project champion training, respectively. Workshops are used to provide training on the tools and methods of Lean and Six Sigma as well as a hands-on demonstration of how assessments are deployed, their tools and responsibilities, as well as key deployment success characteristics. An executive workshop is designed to show key decision makers and stakeholders how a deployment works and the types of improvement opportunities that are possible in their organization. Case studies are also used to show the typical business benefits, required resources, and types of the organizational changes that can be expected for the deployment. These leadership discussions also include a description of the deployment's schedule and required resources. In contrast, project champion training is focused at lower levels of an organization and is aligned with one or more major workflows associated with each champion. Project champions help an assessment team identify and fully scope projects and guide improvement teams through training and project execution. An important output of these executive and project champion workshops is a deployment model that is customized to the organization.

Breaking Down High-Level Goals and Objectives

Figure 2.1 shows how an organization's high-level goals and objectives can be broken down into actionable Lean Six Sigma projects. In some organizations this project identification method is called a critical-to-quality (CTQ) flow down. This tool enables a team to work from the higher-level strategic goals and objectives of their executive team down to lower levels of their organization to identify projects at an operational level. Once identified using this method, projects will be properly aligned throughout an organization. As an example, Figure 2.1 shows how facility XYZ would use this method to reduce its operating expenses. The total operating expense is shown to be $1 million dollars (100 percent). Using the CTQ flow-down method, the $1 million dollar operating expense of this facility is successively broken down to identify actionable projects. At the first level of the analysis, operating expenses are broken down by work area within the facility. In this analysis, work area A is shown to represent 50 percent of the total operating expense, or $500,000. Drilling down to a next lower level shows that overtime expenses of work area A represent 30 percent of the total operating expense of facility A, or $300,000. Continuing this analysis to lower levels of the facility within work area A, it can be seen that machine uptime represents approximately 67 percent of the overtime expense within work area A, or 20 percent of the total facility expense. Finally, the setup expense due to overtime in work area A is shown to represent 10 percent of the total expense of facility XYZ and is identified as a project opportunity. At

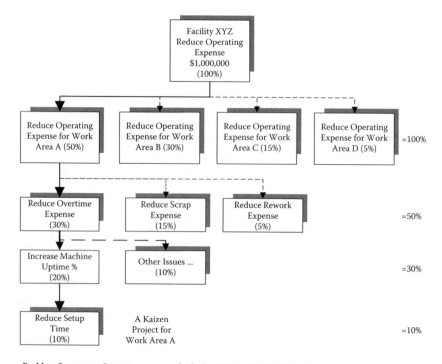

Problem Statement: Operating expenses for facility XYZ are $1,000,000 for fiscal year ending December 31. Facility overtime expense for work area A represented 50% of the total facility operating expense across all four work areas ($500,000). Problems with machine available in work area A represented 20% of the total XYZ facility expense or $200,000. Setup time issues represented 50% of the machine availability incidents or 10% of the total XYZ facility operating expense.

Project Objective: Reduce setup time by 50% within one week using a Kaizen event focused within work area A.

Figure 2.1   Project identification—breaking down high-level goals.

this point in an analysis, this project opportunity may represent a smaller Kaizen project that can be executed over several days, or a Lean or Six Sigma project. Lean and Six Sigma projects are typically executed over a longer period of time.

A problem statement for this project's charter might be written as:

> Operating expenses for facility XYZ are $1,000,000 for the fiscal year ending December 31. Facility overtime expense for work area A represents 50 percent of the total facility operating expense across all four work areas ($500,000). Problems with machine availability in work area A represented 20 percent of the total annualized facility XYZ operating expense, or $200,000. Setup time issues represented 50 percent of the machine availability incidents, or 10 percent of the total facility XYZ operating expense. The project's objective is to reduce setup time by 50 percent within one week using a Kaizen event focused within work area A to save $50,000.

The CTQ flow-down methodology is a good way not only to ensure that projects are aligned with senior management's goals and objectives, but also to actually identify potential project areas by analyzing financial and operational metrics. However, there is one word of caution. A large operating expense does not imply it is all waste. In other words, areas having a smaller total expense may have a higher percentage of actual process waste and, as a result, may be a better candidate for project selection. A financial analysis may point us toward high areas of expenditure, but additional analyses are required to show performance gaps that can form a basis for improvement projects.

Project Identification—Process Analysis

In addition to using a CTQ flow down to identify projects, a direct operational analysis of process workflows can be conducted at several hierarchal levels within an organization. These levels are shown in Table 2.1 and include a system, a process workflow, an operation, a work task, and a work element level. An analysis of a system includes mapping interrelationships between several process workflows. This is usually at a supply chain or organizational level because it describes several different organizations or organizational functions. There are many process workflows at a system level, including customers, suppliers, other external stakeholders, as well as the organization itself. Common internal workflows include functional entities such as sales, marketing, finance, design engineering, procurement, operations, logistics, suppliers, and customers. In Chapter 3, we will discuss the application of VSM to several common process workflows. Also, individual process workflows and their operations can be value stream mapped and analyzed by an improvement team. At a lower level, a process workflow consists of a discrete set of operations and their work tasks, which provide specific families of products or services. These workflows can be mapped and analyzed by an improvement team to create actionable project charters. Within process workflows there are various operations. An operation is a set of integrated work tasks that produce a portion of a product or service. Operations are also interconnected in serial or parallel workflows that create a subsystem network at a process workflow level.

Organizations are systems composed of major process workflows such as accounting, human resources, and similar functions. As an example, an accounts payable process workflow can be broken into several major operations, some of which include setting up invoices to be paid, paying invoices, and conducting audits of paid invoices. In human resources (HR), major operations necessary to hire people might include gathering job requisitions and comparing them to available applicants, setting up interviews between job applicants and hiring managers, and making job offers to new hires. Each of these operations contains lower-level work tasks that have well-defined functions. Examples of lower-level HR work tasks related to hiring an employee include the various activities necessary to set

Table 2.1 Analytical Levels of Process Analysis

Analytical Level	Definition	Examples
I. System	Several process workflows making up an organization or a larger supply chain.	Sales & Marketing, Finance, Design Engineering, Procurement, Production, Logistics, Supplier, and Customers.
II. Process Workflow	A discrete set of operations designed to provide a product or service.	Accounting workflow provides invoicing, tracking, and management.
III. Operation	A set of work tasks within a process workflow that is used to execute a well defined function.	A single accounts payable clerk checking a few major customers.
IV. Work Task	A combination of work elements used to execute a single work task.	An accounts payable clerk completing one of several forms.
V. Work Element	The most basic motion associated with a work task including manual and equipment operations used in combination to execute a single work task.	The motions required to execute a work task such as completing an accounts payable form.

up an interview for a job applicant, the related activities necessary to compare job requisitions to available applicants, and similar types of operations. Finally, a single work task can be broken into work elements. Work elements are the smallest breakdown of work. These are the most basic motions associated with completion of a work task, including motions related to manual operations used in combination with equipment and tools to execute a single work task. An example would be the various motions necessary to complete an accounts payable form.

A quantification of key metrics is also important to fully analyze a system's operational performance. As an example, Figure 2.2 shows the higher-level concept behind process mapping at several analytical levels with respect to important Lean metrics used in Lean deployments. As an example, the percentage of value-adding to non-value-adding time across all operations is a critical measure of a system's leanness. The goal of a Lean deployment is to become lean by eliminating work activities that do not add value. The second metric shown in Figure 2.2 measures a system's production rate. A production rate, at an operational level, would be measured as the operational output per unit time. However, if a production rate is used to measure a larger system, then it will be balanced relative to a system's bottleneck resource that controls the throughput rate of the system. In addition

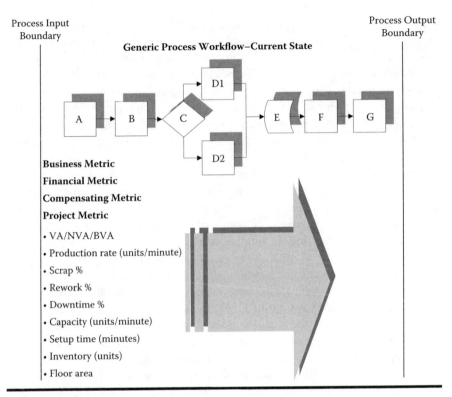

Process Input Boundary

Process Output Boundary

Generic Process Workflow–Current State

A → B → C → D1

C → D2

D1 → E → F → G

Business Metric

Financial Metric

Compensating Metric

Project Metric

- VA/NVA/BVA
- Production rate (units/minute)
- Scrap %
- Rework %
- Downtime %
- Capacity (units/minute)
- Setup time (minutes)
- Inventory (units)
- Floor area

Figure 2.2   Project identification—process analysis.

to the metrics shown in Figure 2.2, there are several others that vary by industry, organizations within an industry, as well as functions within an organization. The specific Lean metrics shown in Figure 2.2 will be discussed in detail in Chapter 3. Subsequent chapters will provide examples of how to calculate and analyze these types of Lean metrics.

Typical Project Examples

The specific types of Lean improvement projects vary by industry as well as organizational function within an industry. These organizations include manufacturing, financial institutions, retail organizations, governments, hospitals, and even educational institutions. In these diverse organizations, projects are routinely created to improve process efficiencies, effectiveness, and compliance to regularity rules, or to provide other business benefits. Table 2.2 shows project examples for several major service functions. These functions include finance, marketing, sales, product design, procurement, human resources, and operations. Projects within these disparate functions may also have common themes. These are usually associated with rework, inspection, audits, and other non-value-adding (NVA) work. On the other hand, some projects may be unique to a particular function. This latter category of projects may include improvements to cash flow, financial ratios, and other cash management systems within a finance function. Financial projects can also be created to improve an organization's asset utilization ratios, such as reducing inventory investment at constant sales or reducing investments in plant and equipment. Projects specific to marketing include increasing market penetration, improving brand awareness, improving customer satisfaction, optimizing pricing levels, and improving channel gross margin. Specific projects within a sales function may include increasing the number of new customers or their profitability, increasing sales into new markets, improving sales force effectiveness, improving sales force productivity, increasing the sales success rate per sales person, or improving the gross margin of a product or service. Specific improvement projects within product design include reducing design cycle time, increasing the number of new products, reducing design errors, and reducing the standard costs controlled by design engineering. Typical projects created to improve procurement operations include increasing forecasting accuracy, reducing data error rates of procurement systems, improving supplier on-time delivery, and increasing inventory turns. Projects found within human resources (HR) include increasing employee retention rates, simplifying the new-employee hiring process, improving employee satisfaction, reducing lost-time accident rates, and improving the effectiveness and efficiency of employee training. Operational projects may include increasing process yields, reducing lead time, reducing standard costs associated with operations, reducing warranty expense, reducing the incident rate of returned goods, reducing scrap and rework, improving schedule attainment, reducing job setup times, improving on-time delivery, increasing system availability, and reducing the floor area required by operations. This list shows that the numbers of potential process improvement projects available to increase an organization's productivity are numerous.

Key Metric Definitions

A metric, as we define it in this book, exists at several organizational levels and can be defined from several perspectives, but at a basic level, a metric is a quantified measure of performance. In Lean Six Sigma deployments there are four high-level metrics from which we define lower-level operational metrics such as lead time, yield, and others. These higher-level metrics are shown in Table 2.3 and include business, financial, project, and compensating metrics. Business metrics can be aggregated across an organization and are usually described in percentages. An example would be comparing warranty costs as a percentage of revenue across several facilities. This enables an organization to compare, on a volume-adjusted basis, the relative financial and operational performance of the facilities. Another common method used to create a business metric is adjustment by production

Table 2.2 Typical Project Examples

Finance	Marketing	Sales	Product Design	Procurement	Human Resources	Operations
■ Eliminate NVA operations within finance i.e., rework, inspection, audits, and unnecessary reviews.	■ Eliminate NVA operations within marketing.	■ Eliminate NVA operations within sales.	■ Eliminate NVA operations within product design.	■ Eliminate NVA operations within procurement.	■ Eliminate NVA operations within human resources.	■ Eliminate NVA operations within operations.
■ Improve cash flow.	■ Increase market penetration.	■ Increase the number of new customers.	■ Reduce design cycle time.	■ Improve forecasting accuracy.	■ Increase employee retention.	■ Increase yield.
■ Improve productivity.	■ Improve brand awareness.	■ Increase customer profitability.	■ Increase the number of new products.	■ Reduce the incident rate of data errors.	■ Simplify the new employee hiring process.	■ Reduce operation lead-time.
■ Reduce inventory investment.	■ Improve customer satisfaction.	■ Increase sales in new markets.	■ Reduce design errors.	■ Improve supply on-time delivery.	■ Improve employee satisfaction.	■ Reduce standard costs associated with operations.
	■ Optimize pricing.	■ Improve sales force effectiveness.	■ Reduce standard costs controlled by design.	■ Increase inventory turns.	■ Reduce lost time accident rates.	■ Reduce warranty expense.
	■ Improve channel gross margin.	■ Improve sales force productivity.		■ Reduce standard cost controlled by procurement.	■ Improve the efficiency of employee training.	■ Reduce returned goods.
	■ Improve net promoter score (NPS).	■ Increase sales success rate.		■ Reduce floor area required by inventory.		■ Reduce scrap and rework.
		■ Improve gross margin per customer.				■ Improve schedule attainment.
						■ Reduce job setup time.
						■ Improve on-time delivery.
						■ Increase system availability.
						■ Reduce floor area required by operations.

volume. Additional examples of commonly used business metrics are asset utilization efficiencies, inventory turns, and percentage of lost time. A second metric category includes financial metrics. However, absolute numbers may also be important. As an example, if a facility has a high percentage of warranty cost relative to its revenue, but a very small absolute warranty expense, then improvement projects may better prioritized using both warranty percentages of total revenue and total warranty expense. This may force prioritization of improvement projects for a different facility. Business and financial metrics in the form of percentages, monetary units, and production volumes can be linearly allocated down through an organization and also aggregated upward. This is why they are useful in measuring overall organizational performance.

Financial metrics include revenues, expenses, and cash flows. These metrics have a monetary basis and can be described in monetary units or their ratios. Project examples include expense reductions relative to warranty cost, the cost of goods sold (COGS), interest expense, customer allowances, and revenue adjustments and reductions in general administrative expenses. Revenue projects are often deployed to increase product and service gross margin and to reduce adjustments to sales or other discounted expenses. Cash flow projects are often used to increase asset utilization rates. A common example is improvement of an inventory turns ratio in which less inventory investment is required to support a constant production level as measured by GOGS. Another example is improvements in equipment utilization efficiency.

Project metrics are usually focused at an operational level. When a project metric has been improved, there should also be a direct improvement in a project's business and financial metrics. This is why it is important that project metrics be clearly linked to higher-level business and financial metrics. In this way, as the root causes for poor operational performance are eliminated from a process workflow, business benefits can be easily calculated to provide a financial justification for the resources that are required to improve the process workflow. As an example, recall that an inventory turns ratio is a business metric calculated as a ratio of COGS divided by average inventory investment. Also, inventory investment in monetary units, such as U.S. dollars, is its correlated financial metric. It is known that a product's inventory turns ratio is impacted by its lead time, demand variation, and required unit service level. In this example, lead time is the initial project metric. In this context, it is both an operational and a project metric. However, lead time is also impacted by a product or item's lot sizes, quality problems, or supplier delivery issues. These lower-level root causes may change the project metric to a lower-level metric such as reducing lot size or improving process yield percentages to reduce lead time. However, a clear line of sight or linkage must always be maintained across all metrics to ensure process improvements are translated throughout an organization at their appropriate levels. In this example, higher-level metrics may include increasing a product's inventory turns ratio, that is, a business metric to reduce its inventory investment, that is, a financial metric by decreasing its lot size, that is, the project metric. A fourth metric category contains compensating metrics. Compensating

Table 2.3   Key Metric Definitions

Metric Type	Definition	Example
Business	Metrics that can be linearly applied throughout an organization.	Percentages, dollars, and similar common units of measurement that can be linearly allocated and aggregated throughout an organization such as asset utilization efficiencies, inventory turns, percentage lost time, etc.
Financial	Metrics that have a monetary basis and are represented in monetary units or ratios.	Dollars, cash flow, expenses, revenues.
Project	Metrics that are used at a lower operational level to tie the business and financial metrics to root causes.	If the business metric is increasing inventory turns that are found to be impacted by lead-time. The project becomes reducing lead-time to improve inventory turns while maintaining customer line fill rates. Inventory investment in dollars is also reduced as turns increase. Lead-time could also be found to be impacted by large lot sizes, quality or supplier issues that would change the project metric to one of these lower-level operational metrics.
Compensating	Metrics that are used to provide insight into the impact of a project on the total system and typically show the impact on internal and external customers.	Customer satisfaction and retention, employee satisfaction and retention.

metrics are used to ensure a project's improvements are balanced relative to each other as well as with the goals and objectives of various organizational stakeholders, including external customers. As an example, we would not want to increase revenue but lose profit margin on the increased sales. Also, we would not want to increase sales for one customer but lose other customers due to conflicting production schedules. Additional examples of compensating metrics include maintaining customer satisfaction and retention levels, maintaining employee satisfaction and retention levels, and not increasing expenses in another area of an organization due to a cost reduction project in a second operational area.

Project Charter Example

Project charters exist in several formats. Some are relatively simple in that they do not provide financial or operational information, while others provide very detailed information. The most useful versions of project charters are Excel-based and contain a rigorous financial analysis, including ROI and payback calculations for a project. This financial information is also linked with a detailed operational analysis. In other words, the project charter contains all the information necessary to prioritize and deploy a project within an organization. The information supporting the operational analysis must be verified and analyzed to a level of detail that will enable a team to be formed and a process owner identified to obtain local organizational support for the project. It should be noted that several projects may be necessary to fully eliminate an operational problem from a process workflow. Project charters are very important to place a Lean Six Sigma deployment on firm footing, and organizations will make a serious mistake if they do not insist that their consultants and managers rigorously define project charters in advance of their deployment. This is because significant reductions in a team's project execution cycle time will be possible if it is provided with a well-supported and well-written project charter. In this context, it is especially important that Kaizen projects also have well-written and well-quantified project charters because they must be executed in a matter of just days, and a false start will delay a team's scheduled activities.

A project charter is also a communication vehicle that shows an organization and its key stakeholders the business benefits expected from execution of a project. It is a communication vehicle because it describes the extent and frequency of a process problem as well as its historical impact on an organization, from both financial and operational viewpoints. In summary, a project charter describes the resources necessary to execute a project, as well as a financial analysis of its expected benefits versus implementation costs. This enables a calculation of a project's net benefits by time period. Figure 2.3 shows that a project charter also contains administrative information that describes where a project will be deployed and its team members. The specific information used to construct Figure 2.3 contains an example of an accounts receivable project. When the average collection time of accounts receivable is reduced, then the interest expense required to borrow against the receivable is saved in proportion to its rate, the amount of the receivable, and the reduction in the number of days. In this example, an improvement team would be organized to reduce the number of accounts receivable write-offs that occur between 31 and 60 days. The interest rate is assumed to be 10 percent. The project charter, shown in Figure 2.3, also shows that the expected savings must be adjusted by subtracting the project costs from the projected savings amount, to calculate a net benefit from the project.

Administrative Information

Project Name	Reduce Cycle Time in Accounts Receivable (A/R) Process

Chartering Organization	Accounting	Project Complexity	Medium
Champion	Joe	Resources	Attached
Project Start	July	Est. Project Duration	5 Days	Probability of Success	High

Problem Statement: The average cycle time between provision of services and receipt of payment averages 60 days with a range between 30 and 90 days (30 our payment terms). The result is lost interest expense from money that should be collected no later than 30 days from invoicing. The average A/R balance is $15 million between 31 and 60 days; $10 million between 61 and 90 days and $5 Million over 90 days.

Project Objective: To reduce the accounts receivable cycle time by 50% in the 31– 60 (15 days) to save $61.6 K ($15 MM) *(15 Days/365 Days)*10% = $61.6 K

Business Metric	% Invoice Amount per Category	Financial Metric	Lost Interest Expense
Project Metric	Days Late (>30 Days)	Other Metrics	TBD

Financial Summary – Initial Projected Savings

	P & L						Comments
	Cost Sales	SG & A	Operation Expense	Depreciation	Interest Expense @ 10%	Total P & L	
One-time cost savings					$ 61,643	$ 61,643	
Project Costs					$ 5,000	$ 5,000	
Net Benefit	$ –	$ –	$ –	$ –	$ 56,643	$ 56,643	

Soft Savings

Estimated Capital

Team Information

Team Leader:

Team Members:

Name	Role	Expertise	% Time

Figure 2.3   Project charter example.

Prioritizing Projects

Prioritization of projects is also important to ensure that productivity improvements are obtained with minimum resource expenditure. There are several strategies that can be used to prioritize projects prior to their deployment. Some of the most common are shown in Figure 2.4. These include identifying strategic performance gaps through an analysis of an organization's strategic goals and objectives over and above projects that have already been identified to close performance gaps.

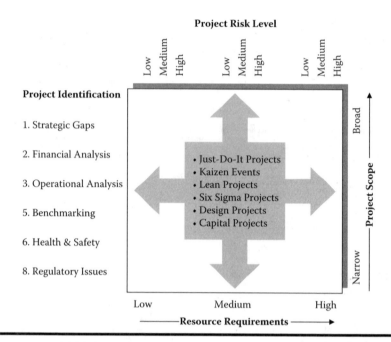

Figure 2.4 Prioritizing projects.

Project identification activities usually include a series of executive interviews and workshops. In these activities, executives and their teams discuss their strategic goals and objectives. Any performance gaps not already identified may be a useful source of project ideas to meet goals and objectives. A second common project identification method includes a financial analysis of an organization's profit-and-loss (P/L) statements and balance sheet. Examples are shown in Figures 2.5 and 2.6. P/L statements describe the relationships between revenues and expenses. An analysis of P/L and balance sheets can also be conducted at several levels, including at a facility and product line. In these analyses, either large revenue or expenditure differences between similar groups may help identify projects. Financial information is always useful in creating project charters because it is directly aligned with an organization's financial goals and objectives. A financial analysis should also include a review of an organization's balance sheet. A balance sheet is a snapshot of an organization's assets, liabilities, and shareholder's equity. Shorter-term assets include cash on hand as well as accounts receivable. Longer-term or fixed assets include land, facilities, and equipment. In this context, projects can be identified by analyzing asset utilization ratios and comparing them to benchmark targets. As an example, typical projects that will improve asset utilization ratios may include reductions in accounts receivable cycle time and other asset levels to free up invested capital. The liability category on a balance sheet includes accounts payable, loans payable, and similar accounts that an organization is obligated to pay in the future.

Profit and Loss (P/L)

(Millions)	Current Year	Previous Year
Revenues		
Net Sales	$100	$90
Other Income (Net)	$20	$10
Total Revenues	**$120**	**$100**
Expenses		
Cost of Sales	$5	$5
Selling, General and Administrative	$20	$18
Operating Expenses	$70	$60
Depreciation	$10	$8
Interest	$5	$4
Total Expenses	**$110**	**$95**
Income Before Taxes (30%)	$10	$5
Taxes (30%)	$3	1.5%
Net Income	**$7**	3.5%
Shareholder Return on Equity	**8%**	4.4%

Figure 2.5 Generic financial statements—profit-and-loss statement.

The information contained in financial statements will always be a good source of project ideas for improvement teams. Continuing our discussion of Figure 2.4, an operational analysis includes a review of operational metrics, including their trends over time against performance to target. Comparisons between similar operations that exhibit variation in performance are always useful in identifying improvement projects. However, projects identified using an operational analysis must also be financially evaluated to show how they will benefit an organization. Another useful method that is commonly used to identify projects is process mapping. In this regard, value stream mapping (VSM) is particularly useful in project identification. VSM is a major focus of this book, and it will be discussed in Chapters 3 to 5. An advantage of constructing a VSM is that it provides information not found in either financial or operational reports. This is especially true when it is verified using process walk-throughs to verify a team's initial VSM and performance estimates. Benchmarking is another useful method that can be used to identify projects. Benchmarking activities compare current performance of an organization's systems and process workflows against those of similar organizations. Finally, any issues related to health and safety or poor adherence to regulatory standards may also serve as a good source of improvement projects.

In the center of Figure 2.4 is a listing of major toolsets or initiatives. The execution of a project may require different types of tools and methods. As an example, process simplification and standardization projects would greatly benefit from using Lean tools and methods. On the other hand, projects requiring complicated

Balance Sheet

(Millions)	Current Year	Previous Year
Current Assets		
Cash	$20	$15
Temporary Cash Investment	$10	$6
Notes and Accounts Receive	$50	$40
Inventories at Average Cost	$60	$70
Total Current Assets	**$140**	**$131**
Fixed Assets		
Buildings	$10	$12
Land	$15	$14
Vehicles	$5	$6
Equipment	$25	$30
Total Fixed Assets	**$55**	**$62**
Total Assets	**$195**	**$193**
Liabilities and Shareholders' Equity		
Current Liabilities		
Notes payable	$10	$12
Accounts payable	$20	$22
Total Current Liabilities	**$30**	**$34**
Long-term Liabilities		
Long-term debt	$80	$80
Total Long-term Debt	**$80**	**$80**
Total Liabilities	**$110**	**$114**
Shareholder's Equity	**$85**	**$79**

Figure 2.6   Generic financial statements—balance sheet.

data collection and analysis activities would most likely benefit from the use of Six Sigma tools and methods. In this context, a project charter is also a useful vehicle in assigning the correct toolset and improvement team to specific projects. As an example, if the root causes of a process problem could be easily identified and also have a known solution, then an improvement team could immediately implement the known solutions. In other situations, perhaps simple root cause analysis is required to identify and eliminate a process problem over several days. These projects could be assigned to Kaizen teams for solution. Other projects may require an extended set of analyses and improvements before a process problem can be completely eliminated. Finally, more extensive process problems may require product or service redesign or capital expenditures.

Figure 2.4 also shows that projects should be prioritized according to their scope, resource requirements, and risk levels. In this context, projects that touch several process workflows or organizational functions may have either a higher or lower prioritization than other projects, depending on their benefits and risks as well as their anticipated resource requirements. As a result of these considerations, projects may be deployed at different times. The prioritization strategy shown in Figure 2.4 is a useful way to visualize the many factors that may impact the deployment of projects.

Summary

Improving the performance of financial and operational metrics requires bringing people and resources together to identify and execute projects. Lean and rapid improvement using Kaizen events will be the focus of our discussion in the next several chapters. Lean systems are characterized by having high value content because of the continuous elimination of process waste. A Lean system and its process workflows can also be characterized by low operational cost and cycle time as well as higher quality. This is in contrast to competitive systems that have not been "leaned out." In this context, an operational assessment is important to ensure that a Lean Six Sigma deployment and its projects will be aligned with an organization's goals and objectives.

Project alignment is accomplished through an analysis of financial and operational reports. In this analysis, performance gaps are identified and converted into projects of various types. Figure 2.1 showed how an organization's high-level goals and objectives can be broken down into actionable Lean Six Sigma projects using a critical-to-quality (CTQ) flow down of key organizational goals. In addition, an operational analysis of process workflows can be conducted at several organizational levels to identify additional projects by continuing the CTQ flow down into lower levels of an organization. Figure 2.4 showed there are several other methods that can be used to identify and prioritize Lean Six Sigma projects. It was also mentioned that the specific forms of Lean Six Sigma improvement projects vary by industry as well as function within an organization. Roles and responsibilities are also an important element of Lean Six Sigma deployments.

An important aspect of project selection was an analysis of key financial and operational performance metrics. A metric, as we define it in this book, is a quantified measure of process performance. Metrics and related information used to describe a project are incorporated into a project's charter. A project charter is a communication vehicle that shows an organization and its stakeholders the business benefits expected from execution of a project. Assessments can be used to create actionable project charters. These project charters can then be prioritized for assignment to improvement teams. Prioritization of project charters is also important to ensure that resources are available to the improvement teams and the correct toolsets are used to identify and eliminate the root causes of a process problem.

Suggested Reading

J. Kent Crawford. 2006. *Project management maturity model.* 2nd ed. Center for Business Practices Series. Vol. 8. New York: Auerbach.

Harold Kerzner. 2005. *Project management: A systems approach to planning, scheduling, and controlling.* 9th ed. New York: Wiley.

Hans J. Lang and Donald N. Merino. 1993. *The selection process for capital projects.* Wiley Series in Engineering and Technology Management. New York: Wiley.

James W. Martin. 2007. *Lean Six Sigma for supply chain management.* New York: McGraw-Hill.

James W. Martin. 2008. *Operational excellence—Using Lean Six Sigma to translate customer value through global supply chains.* New York: Auerbach.

Joseph P. Martino. 1995. *Research and development project selection.* Wiley Series in Engineering and Technology Management. New York: Wiley.

Parviz F. Rad and Ginger Levin. 2007. *Project portfolio management tools and techniques.* New York: IIL Publishing.

Chapter 3

Lean Six Sigma Basics

Overview

In this chapter we will discuss the basic tools, methods, and concepts of Lean in the context of six common process workflows found in most organizations. These common workflows include financial forecasting, accounts receivable, new product marketing research, new product development, and supplier performance management. Our goal is to use these workflows to demonstrate how to implement Lean Six Sigma within service and office operations. In this discussion we will take Lean concepts that have been successfully applied to manufacturing operations and develop analogues to service and office operations. The discussion will follow the sequence shown in Table 3.1. But prior to beginning our discussion, we will introduce and discuss the seven classic forms of process waste, shown in Figure 3.1, from a Lean perspective. Other factors exacerbate the occurrence of process breakdowns. These include a lack of procedures, poor training methods, a lack of process standardization, poor process design, as well as variable demand, which strains a system's available capacity. Available capacity is calculated as design capacity minus normal allowances for things such as employee breaks and other expected losses in system capacity. Actual capacity is calculated as available capacity minus unexpected losses due to process breakdowns.

Figure 3.1 shows the seven classic forms of waste. The first process waste is overproduction. Overproduction results when an operation is utilized at a production rate that is higher level than the demand rate. As an example, if the actual demand on a procurement process is 100 purchase orders per day, but it produces an additional 100 purchase orders per day, then we have overproduced purchase orders.

Table 3.1 Ten Key Steps to Implementing a Lean System

1. Understand the voice of the customer (VOC)
2. Create robust product and process designs—reduce complexity
3. Deploy Lean Six Sigma teams
4. Performance measurements
5. Create value stream maps (VSMs) of major workflows
6. Eliminate unnecessary operations within workflows
7. Implement just-in-time (JIT) systems—eliminate waste
7.a. Reorganize physical configurations
7.b. 5S and standardized work
7.c. Link operations
7.d. Balance material flow
7.d.1. Bottleneck management
7.d.2. Transfer batches
7.e. Mistake proofing
7.f. High quality
7.g. Reduce setup time
7.h. Total preventive maintenance
7.i. Level demand
7.j. Reduce lot sizes
7.j.1. Mixed-model scheduling
8. Supplier networks and support
9. Implement visual control and pull systems—Kanban
10. Continually update process technologies

To a casual observer, this does not seem like a bad idea, especially if people are idle, but if external demand changes, we may find that the purchase orders created in advance may require rework, and in the end, the labor costs may actually be higher. Also, if a process is operated at or near its available capacity level, then mistakes may be made that require rework. Overproduction occurring in complicated systems will degrade available capacity as the number of job setups increases. We will show that an effective way to prevent overproduction is by linking production operations with a system's bottleneck resource. In turn, the bottleneck is linked to external customer demand using a rate-based takt time. This is called a pull scheduling system. In summary, a bottleneck resource controls the flow of material or information through a system. These concepts will be discussed in this chapter.

A second form of process waste is waiting. This is because waiting for an operation to be performed reduces its available capacity because people, equipment, and

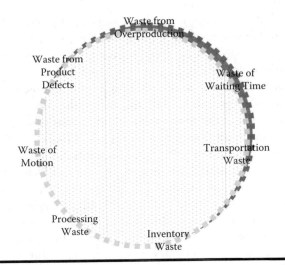

Figure 3.1   JIT philosophy—the seven major types of process waste.

work are idle for a period of time. This lost time cannot be recovered once it is lost. If a bottleneck resource is left waiting or starved for work, then a system loses its capacity. In other words, a system's throughput is proportional to its bottleneck's production rate. As an example, if a production rate at a bottleneck operation is 100 units per hour and this resource is idle for two hours, then the system has permanently lost 200 units of production unless overtime can be used to make up for the lost production. Another problem with materials or information waiting at any operation on a system's critical path, where it is not continuously moving through a process, is that the overall lead time of a system is increased in proportion to the waiting time. Because time that is lost at a bottleneck is directly dependent on conversions of invested material and labor into sales dollars, there is a monetary loss when lead time is increased within a system. This is because inventory levels increase and revenues either decrease or are lost. Inventory in this context can be thought of as stored materials, information, or other forms of work. In summary, excessive waiting has a direct negative impact on a system's productivity.

The unnecessary transport of materials and information is a third form of process waste. This is because unnecessary movements of materials and information require time and resources. In an office environment, the unnecessary transport of materials of information can be seen when people must search for each other or meeting rooms, people who interact to a high degree are not located next to each other, or people must search sharepoints and other information depositories for information over and over from one folder to another. In manufacturing, unnecessary movements are usually associated with the transport of materials. This is problematic because materials are costly to move from one location to another. Also, they may become damaged or lost in the transportation process. In this and later chapters we will show how to map the movements of people, information, and materials to identify non-value-adding transportation activities.

A fourth type of process waste is excess inventory. Inventory waste is created when an operation overproduces relative to external customer demand or downstream operations break down, resulting in high levels of upstream work-in-process (WIP) inventory. These process breakdowns disrupt the flow of work, effectively increasing the variation of the flow of materials and information within a system. Inventory waste can also occur due to arbitrary policies that set inventory levels too high relative to lead time and service targets. The major problem with excess inventory is that it requires materials and labor to build it in advance, but if demand patterns should change, there is either too little or too much available material. In these situations, excess or obsolete inventory will build up within a process. Also, process breakdowns are exacerbated because excess inventory hides production problems. In other words, production problems are discovered only when the inventory is eventually shipped to external customers. This discovery may be months or years after it was produced. In an office environment, examples of excess inventory can usually be found in the form of promotional and marketing literature that is printed months and years in advance of when it is needed. Another example is when people are hired in advance of expected work, but when the work does not materialize, they are redundant. Obsolete inventory is excess inventory that cannot be used due to several reasons. These include design changes to products or services that cause previous versions of the product or service to not be suitable for sale to customers. Obsolescence is also caused by poor demand management, technology improvements, and changes in customer preferences. Operational problems caused by obsolete inventory occur when it takes up space or must be inventoried, protected, or transported from one location to another.

The fifth process waste is the unnecessary processing by an operation that consists of people, machines, or a combination of both. Processing waste occurs when an operation produces a product or service independent of its external demand. This occurs when an operational resource such as a machine or person is utilized at a rate that exceeds its system's demand rate. In fact, a resource should only be activated based on pull demand signals linked to external customer demand. These pull signals are translated by a system's takt time. Processing waste decreases available capacity because products or services are produced without having a customer. This results in higher operational cost due to increases in inventory for the products or services that have no demand and expediting of products that were displaced from their production schedule.

Waste of motion, the sixth process waste, occurs when work is not performed using a standard method, including its procedures, materials, and tools. A standard method is created using time and motion studies and similar analytical studies. It is the one best way to perform the work using current technology, procedures, materials, and tools. Any deviation from a standard work method will result in motion waste. As an example, an employee not using a standardized work method may have to position work components several times or rework them if mistakes occur. An employee may also have to search for work components, tools, and other equipment. These non-value-adding (NVA) activities extend a system's lead time, waste its available capacity, and fatigue employees. Mistakes are also easily made in these types of situations. Unnecessary motion also occurs in office environments. Examples include looking for information or people online or within an office environment. In fact, I recall an example of a call center process flow in which the average time to answer a customer's incoming call and provide the required information to the customer was twice the targeted span of time. After a root cause analysis it was found that call center agents did not have standardized scripts or the information necessary to answer customer questions. In fact, in some situations, more than 20 computer screens had to be accessed to obtain the information required to answer a customer's questions. In this and later chapters we will discuss several methods that will help to minimize the unnecessary movement of materials and information in office environments.

The seventh form of process waste is caused by defects. The occurrence of either product or service defects necessitates that the defective work product be thrown away, i.e., scrapped or reworked to bring it up to a required standard. Defective products or services must be redone without cost to satisfy customers. There are myriad possible defects in office environments. Some of the most common include mathematical mistakes, sending incorrect information, or having to do any work task more than once for the same job. Defects exist when common office terminology includes terms and phrases like *rework, reanalyze, resend, reship, call again, set up a meeting twice, not everyone responded to the e-mail,* and similar situations in which the work must be done one or more times.

Lean and Six Sigma are the two major process improvement initiatives used to reduce and eliminate one or more types of these seven types of process waste. Lean uses the voice of the customer (VOC) to evaluate a process from a customer's perspective to identify and eliminate non-value-adding (NVA) operations and work tasks from a process. Value-adding (VA) operations, which remain within a process workflow after a process improvement, are then standardized and mistake proofed to ensure a production system remains stable over time. Six Sigma also uses several Lean tools and methods throughout its five phases, but it is more focused on the analysis of process data using statistical methods. These Six Sigma phases are called define, measure, analyze, improve, and control. They will be discussed in Chapters 5 and 6 in the context of simple data analysis. Process improvement programs rely on combinations of both initiatives as well as others.

Understand the Voice of the Customer (VOC)

Process improvement activities should be aligned with organizational goals and objectives as well as VOC. The basis of Lean methods requires understanding

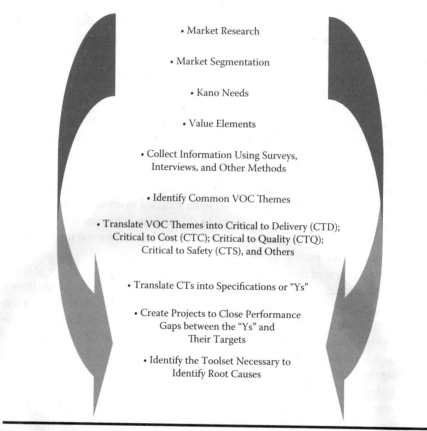

- Market Research

- Market Segmentation

- Kano Needs

- Value Elements

- Collect Information Using Surveys,
  Interviews, and Other Methods

- Identify Common VOC Themes

- Translate VOC Themes into Critical to Delivery (CTD);
  Critical to Cost (CTC); Critical to Quality (CTQ);
  Critical to Safety (CTS), and Others

- Translate CTs into Specifications or "Ys"

- Create Projects to Close Performance
  Gaps between the "Ys" and
  Their Targets

- Identify the Toolset Necessary to
  Identify Root Causes

Figure 3.2   1. Voice of the customer (VOC).

which attributes of a product or service are really important to customers to design products and services that meet their needs and value expectations. Figure 3.2 shows a structured set of activities that will enable an organization to methodically identify, analyze, and incorporate the VOC into their products and services. As a brief summarization of Figure 3.2, the process begins when external customers are categorized by their market segment and interviewed to identify needs and values. Needs are identified through an interview process developed by Dr. Kano and include basic, performance, and excitement needs. Basic needs are product or service attributes expected by a customer as a basis for their use. As an example, if a person goes to a market to purchase food, his or her expectation is that common foods will be available in good condition. He or she does not get excited if milk and bread are available at an average cost. This makes this product attribute a basic need. On the other hand, performance needs differentiate one competitor from another along dimensions of cost, time, or quality. Referring again to the market example, some markets may offer special foods or beverages or perhaps lower cost.

Customers who value these products or service attributes will differentiate one competitor from another. Excitement needs are product or service characteristics that customers do not expect but which meet a need that a customer did not realize he or she had before encountering the new product or service characteristic. An example would be the home delivery of a market's products or customized services during the market experience, such as free merchandise or a completely new type of food.

In addition to Kano needs, customers can be interviewed to identify their value expectations. Value expectations are analyzed by using five dimensions: time, price, utility, functionality, and relative importance. Different customers will have different expectations of how long they should wait for a product or service, what a fair price should be to purchase it, and how it should function. In addition, its usefulness will vary by customer market segment, as well as its relative importance to customers. Classifying customer value expectations using the three Kano needs and five value elements by market segment will provide a very good starting point from which to identify and analyze the VOC. VOC information, when it is properly gathered, will enable an improvement team to analyze a process workflow and determine how its products and services, as well as their internal production processes, are aligned with customer value requirements. Internal customers also have a voice. But it is more aligned with the voice of the business (VOB). VOB considerations include increases in profit margins and sales, reductions in expenses, increases in cash flow, improvements in employee safety, and similar internal goals and objectives. An improvement team must take a holistic approach to process improvement by considering both the VOC and VOB in balance.

Once customers have been segmented, their VOC information is collected using informational surveys, interviews, and related methods. Surveys can take many forms, including personal interviews, focus groups of several people, online survey questions, mailings, and visiting a location to observe how a product or service is used in practice by customers. Survey design and management is a complicated set of activities that require consultation with experts to maximize their informational content at minimum survey cost. In addition to actively soliciting customer information, organizations can analyze customer complaints and returned goods and warranty histories as well as industry and trade association databases.

Common VOC themes are identified after the VOC information has been collected from customers using one or more collection methods. These themes are translated into critical-to-delivery (CTD), critical-to-cost (CTC), critical-to-quality (CTQ), and critical-to-safety (CTS) performance metrics. These performance metrics are subsequently quantified by translation into internal specifications, or Ys. Projects can be created to close performance gaps between the Ys and their performance targets. Initiative toolsets are aligned with each project, based on its anticipated root cause analysis. Lean and Six Sigma are the toolsets we will be discussing in this book in the context of Kaizen events.

Create Robust Product and Process Designs to Reduce Complexity

It is very important that an organization "Lean" itself out at a higher organizational level prior to the deployment of Lean Six Sigma teams at a local level. This is because a system's complexity impacts its cycle time, cost, and quality. As an example, it would make no sense to improve a process workflow if it was going to be eliminated in the future. Also, it may not make sense to improve process workflows having very low or negative profit margins if they are noncore to an organization and should be outsourced to another organization. In this context, the implication is that even after process improvements, the profitability will not be sufficient to justify continued production of a product or service. A common solution to these situations often requires outsourcing products or services to other organizations that can also produce them at a lower cost and higher quality levels. Service process workflows can be simplified by adapting generally accepted tools and methods that have been in use in manufacturing organizations for decades. As an example, operations, work tasks, physical parts, and other design components may be eliminated from a product or service if they do not increase its value. In these situations, incremental features may have been added over time to a product or service without verifying that they increase customer value or meet customer Kano needs. Misunderstandings may also have occurred that resulted in an addition of wrong features. In addition to an elimination of nonessential service offerings, those that remain part of a product or service design may be combined or presented to customers in unique ways. An example could be the use of self-service facilities that eliminate manual work tasks from a process workflow. In summary, simpler product and service designs as well as their processes will fail at a lower rate. Also, their cost and assembly time will be reduced if design features can be configured to aid easy assembly and use.

Table 3.2 lists seven key concepts to reduce product or service complexity. The first key concept recommends that an organization only design and produce products or services that add value from its customer's perspective and are profitable. As an example, at any given time an organization produces many product or services that, for various reasons, may not be in demand by customers or whose profitability may be low or negative. This situation may be caused by operational inefficiencies or sales and marketing problems. In these situations, a good way to understand how products and services impact an organization is to prioritize them by profitability and gross margin. It is surprising how many products and services are negative contributors to an organization. Elimination of these nonprofitable products and services will reduce an organization's complexity and improve its profitability. A major goal of this book is to encourage the removal of products and services that are not part of an organization's core product and service portfolio.

A second key concept shown in Table 3.2 is that product and service simplification strategies should be applied to create designs having a minimum number of

Table 3.2   2. Create Robust Product and Process Designs to Reduce Complexity

Concept	Classic Manufacturing	Service Analogy
1. Ensure it is the right thing to do. Be effective. Don't do things that will not add value or be profitable.	Produce profitable products that customers need using the correct technology.	Produce the correct services and information customers need using the correct technology.
2. Simplify what is left by using fewer components, standardized components, and merging components into composite units.	Use design for manufacturing (DFM) methods simplify products and their processes.	Use design for Six Sigma (DFSS) and Lean methods to simplify systems and their process workflows.
3. Design so the product can only be assembled one way to avoid errors.	Use asymmetrical design features to ensure components can be assembled in just one way. Example: Only allow certain product configurations.	Use self-checking logic to prevent service errors or detect them as soon as their occur.
4. Design so the product does not require tools or, if necessary, only simple tools.	Use features that enable snap-fit of components.	Create procedures using visual systems so anyone can do the work. Example: Self-service systems such as airport check-in.
5. Methodically evaluate the product using design for Six Sigma (DFSS), prototypes, pilots, models, simulations and other methods to understand its performance prior to commercialization.	Fully test new product designs prior to releasing them to manufacturing.	Test new service systems under controlled market research conditions. Use proven tools and methods, such as failure mode and effects analysis (FMEA) and simulations.

continued

Table 3.2 (continued)   2. Create Robust Product and Process Designs to Reduce Complexity

Concept	Classic Manufacturing	Service Analogy
6. Mistake proof the product's production process	Use mistake-proofing strategies including eliminating "red flag" conditions, prevention of error conditions, and immediate defect detection.	Using information obtained from market research studies, the FMEA, simulations, and other evaluation tools and methods, develop mistake-proofing strategies. Example: If customers order a product pr service, enable the system to verify data accuracy such as credit card information.
7. Continually evaluate production performance and the VOC.	Develop product and process control plans to ensure the new design meets the VOC.	Develop product and process control plans to ensure the new service meets the VOC.

standardized, consolidated, and modular components. In this context, Design for Manufacturing (DFM) and Design for Six Sigma (DFSS) methods can be used to simplify products or services by eliminating and aggregating their components. In this book, Lean methods will be used to simplify the process workflows used to produce products and services in office environments.

A third key concept is to apply mistake-proofing methods to a simplified product or service so it can be constructed or assembled in just one way. This will avoid assembly and related types of errors. In other words, it is important to ensure that the production of products and services are mistake proofed once they have been released to production. Mistake proofing product and service designs is facilitated by simplification, standardization, and functional testing. However, once released within a production process, additional mistake-proofing strategies can be employed to prevent errors within a production process. These can be categorized as the elimination of "red flag" conditions, the prevention of error conditions, and immediate defect detection. These concepts will be discussed later in this chapter. In the design of service systems, mistake-proofing strategies are developed using information obtained from market research studies, the design failure mode and effects analysis (FMEA), simulations, and on-site customer testing. In manufacturing, a common design strategy is to use asymmetrical design features to ensure components can be assembled in just one way. As a second example, when purchasing a computer from Dell through the Internet, customers are only allowed to configure their product or service in certain ways to avoid component incompatibilities of the product. Mistake proofing is also very widespread in service processes to prevent or detect errors as they occur. As another example, a zip code can be used to cross-verify an address to verify its accuracy.

A fourth key concept in the design of products or services is to ensure a product or service can be assembled or configured very easily without the use of complex tools or procedures. A common example is designing a product in a way in which its components are snap-fit together. In service workflows, an analogous application is to use easy-to-understand visual systems that enable anyone to do work tasks. An example would be designing a self-service system at an airport check-in in such a way that anyone can easily check himself or herself in for his or her flight by selecting seat assignments and using baggage check-in options. In this process, all the information that a customer needs to complete a transaction resides within a kiosk.

A fifth key concept advocates fully testing new products or services, under actual conditions of customer usage. This evaluation process will help to identify their failure points to optimize performance. Methodically testing a new product or service is done using key DFSS tools and methods. These include building prototypes, running pilot evaluations, building and analyzing models, conducting simulations, and using similar methods to analyze product or system performance prior to commercialization. In summary, it is important to fully test new products and service designs prior to their release to production operations and the external market.

The sixth and final key concept in creating robust product and service designs is continually improving them over time. In these improvement activities, it is important that their performance is aligned with the VOC. Continual process improvement is only possible through the deployment and use of relevant performance measurements to monitor, manage, and improve process performance. In this context, an important focus of this book will be a discussion of commonly used Lean and Six Sigma performance metrics in office environments.

Deploy Lean Six Sigma Teams

In the following chapters we will show how Lean Six Sigma teams are deployed in support of improvement projects. In our current discussion, it is important to state that improvement teams should not be deployed in a nonaligned manner across an organization. This concept has been discussed several times in previous chapters. Unfortunately, many Lean Six Sigma deployments have not been properly aligned, and as a result, they have failed to deliver the anticipated business benefits to their sponsoring organization. One reason may be some are deployed bottom up through an organization or at a tactical level and sponsored by just a few people. However, this not does imply that process improvements should not be made at a local level by teams, but only that more significant improvements can often be made if projects are prioritized and strategically aligned up front, prior to their deployment.

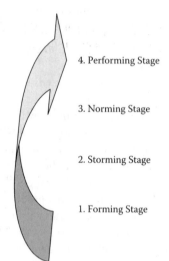

4. Performing Stage

3. Norming Stage

2. Storming Stage

1. Forming Stage

1. Select the team based on the project charter

2. Manage the four stages of team growth

3. Train the team in the proper tools and methods of problem identification, data collection, analysis, and process change

4. Identify root causes of the problem

5. Continuously improve team performance

6. Celebrate success!

Figure 3.3   3. Deploy Lean Six Sigma teams.

Process improvements will also be easier to sustain when an initiative is properly aligned with an organization's goals and objectives. An organization's leadership should also provide the necessary resources to support Lean Six Sigma activities to the extent that they are aligned with organizational goals and objectives. An important element of leadership support is actively communicating deployment information in a simple and consistent manner. This is especially important as higher-level deployment goals and objectives are translated down to successively lower levels of an organization. Another important leadership responsibility is to realign or create incentive systems to remove barriers to change.

Case studies have consistently shown that developing high-performance work teams depends on several common success factors related to a team's maturation process. A team maturation process consists of the four stages shown in Figure 3.3: forming, storming, norming, and performing. The interval of time a team spends within a given stage varies by the team and organization, but it has been shown that some teams move through the four stages very quickly, while others do not. In the latter situations, these teams usually lack effective facilitation and are dysfunctional in one or more ways. In contrast, several common key success factors that help create a high-performance work team are the diversity, both culturally and psychologically, and the reinforcing skill sets of its members. Another success factor is the creation of effective facilitation roles and responsibilities to ensure that differences of perspective are respected within a team. Diversity is particularly important in creating a high-performance work team because different perspectives help a team focus on data collection, analysis, and improvement activities. However, different perspectives require patience and respect between a team's members. It has been found that an efficient way to improve team performance is through active facilitation by impartial observers of team meetings. In addition to cultural and other diversity factors, team members should also have supporting skills that will enable their team to move through its root cause analysis and implement solutions to eliminate the process problem. The roles and responsibilities shown in Table 1.3 would be a good starting point in Lean Six Sigma team selection.

Figure 3.3 also shows six key steps that will help to ensure a team's success relative to its maturation process. First, a team should be selected to support a project charter that formalizes a project's objectives, business benefits, available resources, and other expected deliverables. A project charter also enables a team's project leader to select team members based on the process workflow that is the focus of the charter. This selection process should include team members upstream, downstream, and internal to the process workflow described by the project charter. In the second step, the team leader adds facilitators to the team to enable it to quickly move through its maturation cycle. Team facilitators may be either internal or external resources. It should also be noted that although team members may have unique skill sets, additional team training may be necessary depending on a project's anticipated root cause analysis. In these situations, team training will usually focus on various types of problem-solving methods, including Lean and Six Sigma. After training, a team will be fully prepared to conduct its root cause analysis. Finally, if a team is a natural work group that has been organized around a process workflow rather than just one project, continuous-improvement methods should be applied to measure and improve team performance over time. Continuous improvement occurs when team members provide suggestions for how to improve their team's performance. Finally, as a team succeeds, it should periodically celebrate its success as an incentive to continue its work.

Performance Measurements

Performance measurements are necessary to monitor, manage, and improve process performance over time. In this context, they are useful in identifying performance issues within a process workflow to create project charters. Although there are hundreds of different performance measurements across diverse industries and functions, an organization will usually use just a handful of critical operational, financial, and customer satisfaction metrics to manage its operations. Common performance measurements used in Lean Six Sigma deployments, at an operational level, include:

1. Percentage of value-adding (VA) content or time
2. A system's production or throughput rate (units per minute)
3. Scrap percentages
4. Rework percentages
5. Downtime percentages of equipment and people
6. Available production capacities of operations in units per time
7. Setup time and the cost of jobs at various operations within a process workflow

Operational Performance Measurements

Work Area: Accounting	Average Job Cost:	$22.75	Date: July
Operation: Accounts Payable	Units Per Shift:	50	Auditor: Joe
Process Owner: Mary	Shift Cost:	#######	Takt Time: 8.4 Minutes/Unit (50 units in 420 Minutes)
Operation Number: 4TD	Available Time (Minutes):	420	

Operation "Accounts Payable"

Key Metrics	Baseline	Week 1	Week 2	Week 3	Week 4	Week 5	Week 6	Week 7	Week 8	Week 9	Week 10	Week 11	Week 12	Week 13	Week 14	Week 15	Week 16	Average	Improvement %
1. Value Adding %																			
2. Production Rate (Units/Shift)																			
3. Scrap%																			
4. Rework %																			
5. Downtime %																			
6. Capacity (Units/Shift)																			
7. Setup Time (Minutes)																			
8. Inventory (Units in Queue)																			
9. Floor Area																			
Additional Metrics (Depending on Industry or Function)																			
A. Total Process Workflow Cycle Time																			
B. Number of Problem Solving Teams																			
C. Number of Customer Complaints																			
D. Number Employee Suggestions																			
E. Warranty Expense/Incidents																			
F. Returned Goods Expense/Incidents																			
G. Annualized Savings																			
H. Percentage Scheduled Jobs Missed																			
Additional Metrics (Depending on Industry or Function)																			
1. First Pass Yield (Rolled Throughput Yield-RTY)																			
2. Profit/Loss																			
3. Inventory Efficiency (Turns)																			
4. On-Time Supplier Delivery																			
5. Forecast Accuracy																			
6. Lead Time																			
7. Unplanned Orders																			
8. Schedule Changes																			
9. Overdue Backlogs																			
10. Data Accuracy																			
11. Material Availability																			
12. Excess & Inventory																			

Figure 3.4   4. Create performance measurements.

8. Inventory investment operation by operation
9. Allocated floor space required for production of products and services

Organizations also track financial measurements related to revenue, expenses, and cash flow; customer metrics related to market share and repurchase intent; as well as a multitude of similar metrics. The reason we will focus our discussions on these nine operational metrics is that they are applicable to any operation in both manufacturing and service industries. In a Lean Six Sigma initiative it is important we identify and define the correct metrics, measure their performance over time, and close performance gaps through the deployment of projects as shown in Figure 3.4.

Create Value Stream Maps (VSMs)

A Lean Six Sigma team creates a VSM to describe, analyze, and improve a process workflow. Creating a VSM requires that people be brought together to create a graphical representation of their process. It is important that these people have an understanding of how their process actually operates day in and day out. After an initial VSM is created, operations are quantified using at least the nine metrics mentioned above in Step 4, as well as other relevant operational metrics, such as those shown in Figure 3.4. The sequence of activities necessary to bring a team together to create a VSM will be discussed in Chapter 4, but at a high level, they include

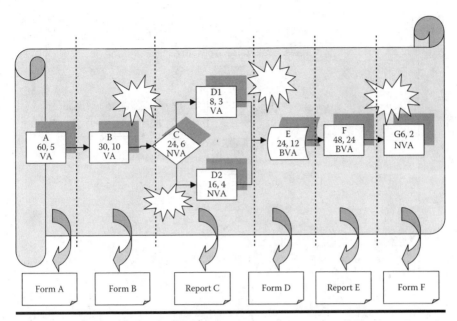

| A 60, 5 VA | B 30, 10 VA | C 24, 6 NVA | D1 8, 3 VA | D2 16, 4 NVA | E 24, 12 BVA | F 48, 24 BVA | G6, 2 NVA |

| Form A | Form B | Report C | Form D | Report E | Form F |

Figure 3.5   5. Create value stream maps (VSMs) of major workflows.

bringing together a diverse, high-performance work team to map and quantify the various operations of a major process workflow.

Figure 3.5 shows a generic version of a VSM. Recall that a VSM identifies VA, NVA, and BVA operations within a process workflow. VA operations are required to meet customer needs and value expectations. NVA operations are not needed in a process and can be eliminated. BVA operations are not required to meet customer expectations, but must remain part of a process due to technological or other system constraints. The VSM shown in Figure 3.5 describes the spatial relationships between operations as well as the average and standard deviations of operational cycle times. If reducing cycle time is a team's goal, this type of VSM will help identify the critical path though a process workflow. A critical path controls a system's throughput as measured at its longest cycle time. In Figure 3.5, the first number represents the mean cycle time of an operation, and the second number represents the standard deviation of cycle time for the same operation. As an example, the mean cycle time of operation A is 60 seconds, with a standard deviation of 5 seconds. In the example contained in this book, all operations are assumed to have normally distributed (symmetrical) cycle times. In addition, each operation has been labeled as VA, NVA, or BVA to help analyze the process and identify simplification opportunities. The team's immediate process improvement goal will be to eliminate all operations that are identified as NVA. A second improvement goal is to standardize and mistake proof the remaining operations. These and other Lean and Six Sigma improvements will help reduce the cycle time of the process. As part of its VSM building activities, an improvement team brings together examples of management

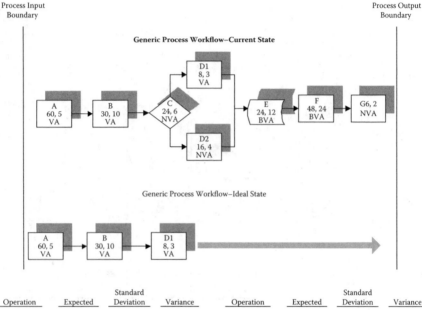

Process Input
Boundary

Process Output
Boundary

Generic Process Workflow–Current State

Operation	Expected	Standard Deviation	Variance
A	60	5	25
B	30	10	100
C	24	6	36
D2	16	4	16
E	24	12	144
F	48	24	576
G	6	2	4
Total:	208		901
95% CI of Cycle Time:			266.83

Operation	Expected	Standard Deviation	Variance
A	60	5	25
B	30	10	100
D1	8	3	9
Total:	98		134
95% CI of Cycle Time:			120.69
Average % Improvement:			–53%

Figure 3.6   Takt time calculation.

reports, data entry forms, and other information that is used to record, analyze, and report process information. These various forms, reports, and data entry forms are shown in Figure 3.5 with several starbursts. An advantage of creating a VSM and similar process maps is that they clearly show the complexity of a process workflow as well as its financial and operational performance as a visual representation of a process. In addition to the VSM, quantified metrics, and operational reports, related information describing the contributing factors to process breakdowns, including their occurrence frequency, is also shown on a VSM. These process breakdowns are also highlighted using starbursts. In this context, the starburst represents potential Lean Six Sigma improvement projects.

As part of VSM quantification, a system's takt time should also be estimated in the manner shown in Figures 3.6 to 3.8. Figure 3.6 summarizes the cycle time information of the VSM shown in Figure 3.5. It can be seen that in the current process workflow, the total average time to produce one unit of material or information

All analyses are in seconds:

		Initial Process		
	Operation	Expected Time	Standard Deviation	Variance
A		60	5	25.0
B		30	10	100.0
C		24	6	36.0
D2		16	4	16.0
E		24	12	144.0
F		48	24	576.0
G		6	2	4.0
Total		**208.0**		**901.0**

Demand per shift:	800.0
Allowed time (breaks):	3,600.0
Available time:	25,200.0
Takt time =	**31.5**
(seconds per unit)	

Theoretical minimum operations or stations:

Time to produce one unit:	208.0
Takt time	31.5
Number of people:	**6.6**

Figure 3.7   Takt time calculation—original process.

is 208 seconds. However, if only VA operations and work tasks remained within the process workflow, then the average cycle time would be reduced to 98 seconds. This is a 53 percent reduction in cycle time over the current process. Figure 3.7 also shows that the demand per work shift is 800 units, and the available time for each work shift is calculated as 25,200 seconds. The takt time can be calculated as 31.5 seconds to produce each unit. In other words, no production unit should take more than 31.5 seconds to assemble. The assumption is that there were eight hours per work shift and only one hour was lost due to lunch and resting breaks. This means one unit must leave this system every 31.5 seconds. Referring again to the current process map, the total operational time required to produce one unit is 208 seconds, which is calculated by summing the average cycle times for all operations. Dividing the total time to produce one unit by the system's takt time shows that the required number of people or work stations to produce 800 units per work shift is 6.6, or rounded to 7.0. The next step in this analysis is to allocate

All analyses are in seconds:

Final Process

Operation	Expected Time	Standard Deviation	Variance
A	60	5	25.0
B	30	10	100.0
D1	8	3	9.0
			0.0
Total	**98.0**		**134.0**

Demand per shift:	800.0
Allowed time (breaks):	3,600.0
Available time:	25,200.0
Takt time =	**31.5**
(seconds per unit)	

Theoretical minimum operations or stations:

Time to produce one unit:	98.0
Takt time	31.5
Number of people:	**3.1**

Figure 3.8   Takt time calculation—future state.

the operational work tasks to work stations in such a way that the total cycle time at any work station remains below the system's takt time. It should be noted that if the NVA operations of the process workflow could be eliminated, then the required number of work stations would be reduced to 3.1 because the required production time would be reduced to 98 seconds per unit, but the takt time would remain at 31.5 seconds per unit. However, the resources necessary to produce a unit would have been reduced as a result of the process improvements.

Eliminate Unnecessary Operations

Once a VSM has been created, it can be analyzed to differentiate between NVA, VA, and BVA operations and work tasks. This will enable a Lean Six Sigma team to immediately simplify its process workflow to concentrate on improving the value-adding components. Recall that non-value-adding operations are those not

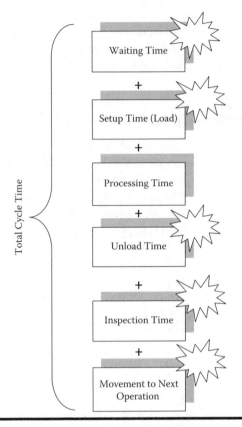

Figure 3.9   6. Eliminate unnecessary operations within workflows.

required by an external customer, and by team agreement they can be immediately eliminated from a process workflow without adverse consequences. Typical non-value-adding operations include rework stations, inspection activities, inefficient work methods, and similar activities, such as those discussed relative to Figure 3.1. Another good way to characterize NVA operations is to consider them to be any operation or work task that adds unnecessary cost, extends cycle time, or adversely impacts product or service quality. Also recall that BVA operations have no inherent value to a customer, but are required to be performed, at least on a short-term basis, due to technological, operational, or regulatory constraints. VA operations are required by external customers. However, unnecessary work tasks may remain within value-adding operations. In summary, the immediate improvement strategy should be to quickly eliminate NVA operations and optimize the remaining work tasks contained within BVA and VA operations. On a longer-term basis, BVA operations can also be eliminated through technological and operational improvements. Figure 3.9 shows another viewpoint of how to identify unnecessary operations within a process workflow. Many processes contain time components, which include waiting, setup, unloading, inspection, and unnecessary movement. If every operation on a VSM can be broken down further into the categories shown in Figure 3.9, then additional improvement projects can be created by identifying non-value-added time components or work tasks within value-adding operations.

Implement Just-in-Time (JIT) Systems

Many people think that a just-in-time (JIT) system can be implemented by increasing the throughput of material and information through a system or by reducing work-in-process (WIP) inventory levels. This ad hoc approach to a JIT implementation will most likely shut down portions of a process when its operations are starved for materials or information by upstream operations. This situation may also be caused by fluctuations of demand or lead time. Lead time is extended by a large number of process breakdowns, including late deliveries, rework and scrap, and similar operational issues. In contrast, a successful JIT implementation depends on stable external demand, which is reflected in a takt time, operational stability, and continuous operational improvement activities. These concepts are shown in Figure 3.10.

The first key building block of a JIT system is stable demand. Stable demand implies that operations and work tasks within a process can be synchronized to external demand using a takt time. But this presupposes a predictable external demand pattern. This original JIT concept was created as part of the Toyota Production System (TPS). However, the TPS is characterized by a relatively constant external demand whose level has been estimated as ±10 percent deviation from the average monthly unit demand. In contrast, variation of external customer demand often exceeds ±10 percent for most industries. This situation makes it difficult to establish a stable takt time. As a result, organizations have been forced to modify the original

Stable Demand		Operational Stability		Continuous Improvement	
1.	Continuous Flow	1.	Robust Designs and Processes	1.	High Performance Work Teams
2.	Pull System/ Kanbans	2.	Standardized Work	2.	Basic Problem Solving Tools
		3.	Mistake Proofing		
		4.	Single Minute Exchange of Die (SMED)	3.	Advanced Problem Solving Tools (Six Sigma)
		5.	Total Productive Maintenance		
		6.	Supplier Support		

Figure 3.10   7. Implement just-in-time (JIT) systems—eliminate waste.

TPS to suit their specific operational requirements. However, to the extent that a system's demand variation can be reduced, operational stability will be increased, and the deployment of pull production scheduling systems will be easier.

As a result, operational stability is a second key building block of an effective JIT system. It is achieved by creating robust product and service designs up front, prior to release to production. Production work tasks must be standardized and mistake proofed to prevent the occurrence of processing errors. Errors increase the operational variation of a process and hence its cycle time. There are, of course, many other tools and methods that are necessary to stabilize production operations. A few of the more important ones include single minute exchange of dies (SMED), or techniques to quickly set up jobs, total productive maintenance (TPM) to ensure equipment availability, quality improvements, and development of supplier support systems. It should also be noted that TPM is a key initiative used to increase system availability through an effective design of maintenance systems. In this context, TPM activities include ensuring the availability of equipment, people, and procedures when they are needed by production. Supplier support systems are also important because they directly impact internal operational takt times through on-time deliveries as well as material availability and quality. Supplier support systems are created using a variety of methods, including formalized written contracts and the application of Lean, Six Sigma, and other initiatives within supplier facilities. A supply chain should also optimize its asset investment by positioning assets at optimum locations within a supply chain. In fact, a "Lean" supply chain should have higher-asset utilization efficiencies than its competitors.

The third building block of an effective JIT system is the continuous improvement of operational work tasks over time. These improvements can be broadly categorized into time, quality, and cost. Common continuous-improvement activities include the deployment of high-performance work teams as well as the training and use of basic and advanced Lean and Six Sigma problem-solving tools. Chapter 5 discusses many of these problem-solving tools and methods and applies them to the analysis and improvement of service systems and office processes. Chapter 6 also discusses many Lean and Six Sigma tools and methods, but with application to six common process workflows found in office environments. There is significant synergy among the three JIT building blocks. As a result, high-performance work teams and the application of basic problem-solving tools facilitate the creation of systems having a high degree of operational stability. This facilitates the continuous flow of materials and information.

A complicating factor in the deployment and application of JIT methods is that they were developed by Toyota for a manufacturing environment. These manufacturing environments have unique characteristics, such as stable external customer demand. However, over time, Toyota has modified many of its Lean methods for use in its service workflows, such as procurement, design engineering, and logistics. Other industries and organizations have also made modifications to the original Toyota Production System (TPS), which range from minor to major.

As a result, Lean systems have been implemented with varying degrees of success across very diverse industries. However, the results have often fallen short of expectations because building a "Lean" organization is hard work and must be done in a phased and sequential manner. Some organizations just do not have the patience for a continuous-improvement approach. It has been repeatedly shown that a successful deployment of a Lean system takes years of continuous effort using performance metrics to monitor organizational performance against targets. In this book I will discuss the most common financial and operational metrics, but leading organizations use a more extensive approach to the measurement and improvement of their processes. As an example, Kobayashi developed 20 key performance measurements that enable an organization to establish an initial performance baseline and then measure process improvements against these baselines over time. These 20 keys include the following metrics:

1. Clean and tidy
2. Participative management style
3. Teamwork on improvement
4. Reduced inventory and lead time
5. Changeover reduction
6. Continuous improvement in the workplace
7. Zero monitoring
8. Cellular manufacturing
9. Maintenance
10. Disciplined, synchronized, rhythmic working
11. Management of defects
12. Supplier partnerships
13. Constant identification and elimination of waste
14. Worker empowerment and training
15. Cross-functional working
16. Scheduling
17. Efficiency
18. Technology
19. Conserving energy and materials
20. Using the most efficient design methods

We will discuss some of these metrics in subsequent chapters using data collection and analysis templates and examples of common process workflows found in offices.

Reorganize Physical Configurations

It is difficult to understand the real impact that the physical configuration of a process workflow can have on its efficiency. As an example in a continuous process,

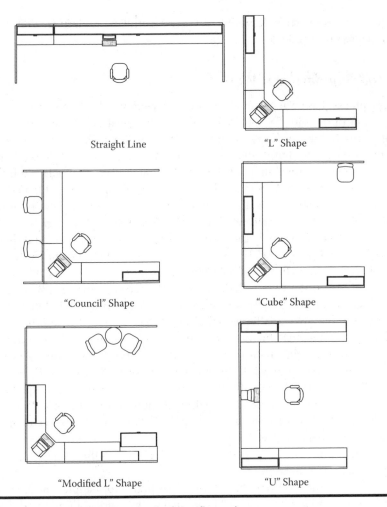

Figure 3.11   7.a. Reorganize physical configurations.

a straight line will often be the most efficient physical configuration. However, in many situations, such as a discrete parts manufacturing environment, it has been found that U-shaped work cells are more efficient than straight-line work-flow designs. This is because cross-trained workers can move more easily between equipment as local demand on equipment and people changes. Also, U-shaped work cells enable employees to work more than one work station if demand on the work cell decreases. In this context, a U-shaped work cell facilitates balancing of materials and information to the work cell's takt time. Figure 3.11 shows, by way of example, several different physical configurations of an office. These physical configurations are available within Visio® software and include straight lines, L shapes, council shapes, cube shapes, modified L shapes, and U shapes. There may also be variations of these common designs, depending on the work environment.

We will discuss the reconfiguration of process workflows to decrease cycle time in later chapters of this book.

5S and Standardized Work

Once a process has been optimally physically reconfigured, 5S methods are applied to its work operations. 5S applications may be designed either into a new process or after the fact using Kaizen events. 5S is an acronym that stands for sorting, setting in order, shining, standardizing work tasks, and sustaining the improvements. These are defined in Table 3.3. The sorting of work materials and information requires that a work area be well organized based on the flow of materials and information through its operations, and that nonessential materials and information be removed from the same work area. In other words, only materials and equipment that are necessary to do the required work tasks for the job at hand should be located within a work area. The 5S sorting process is analogous to cleaning your desk of all nonessential items. In an office process, sorting work enables a person to concentrate on the work at hand rather than become distracted by extraneous materials. A clean and orderly workspace also makes it easier to find materials and information that are actually needed to do current work tasks. Another example is cleaning up a sharepoint work area that contains numerous extraneous work files. Disorganized sharepoints can waste a lot of time when employees cannot find electronic folders and the information needed to do their work. A process that is clean and orderly will also have a lower cycle time and higher quality. Red tagging is the most useful method to eliminate nonessential materials from a work area. In a red-tagging exercise, materials and equipment that have been red tagged should be removed from a work area after a short review period. This review period enables the people who are part of the work area to verify the red-tagged items are not required for production.

Setting in order requires that all materials and information that remain in a work area after 5S has been applied be located in their proper location. This makes it easier to find them when needed for production. In fact, in some work areas, the location of all materials and equipment is labeled or marked off so there are just one or a few places to locate them for production. Setting in order also facilitates inventory and material control because materials can be easily seen to be in their assigned storage or staging areas. Operational efficiency will be increased directly in proportion to the ease in which workers can find their work materials and tools. Referring again to the sharepoint example, when a sharepoint's information storage and retrieval rules are standardized, relative to how information is placed and accessed, the efficiency of information storage and retrieval will be higher. As one last example, imagine creating a predefined location for every tool used in your home. The tool is always placed there and it is always easy to locate for use.

Shining requires that everything within a work area be maintained clean. This is important to help identify abnormal conditions within a work area and equipment

Table 3.3 7.b. 5S and Standardized Work

5S Category	Classic Manufacturing Application	Service Application
1. Sorting	Separate materials and tools that are needed in a work area from those that are not needed using a red tag. This minimizes the time it takes to look for things.	Maintain clean work areas and eliminate materials or information that is not needed to do the work. Example: Dump old files.
2. Set in order	Ensure there is one location to place those items remaining in the work area.	Ensure computer files are properly documented for easy access; place all tools, equipment, and information within easy access of the worker.
3. Shine	Ensure all tools, equipment, and the work area are clean. Abnormal conditions such as oil leaks and rework are easier to see under these circumstances.	Maintain work areas that are clean so abnormal conditions can be easily seen.
4. Standardize	Ensure products are designed using standardized components and manufacturing processes, and that the work is performed the same way every time.	Ensure work tasks are performed in a standardized manner using checklists, procedures, and instructions. If the work is complicated, then separate operations that can be standardized (back office) and ensure the customized operations are tightly controlled.
5. Sustain	Use control plans and deploy continuous improvement teams.	Use control plans and deploy continuous improvement teams.

maintenance issues. A classic example is placing white floor mats under equipment to identify if oil is leaking. This visual check facilitates equipment maintenance, which contributes to higher equipment availability. In an office environment, similar examples include keeping an office clean and well organized so work can be completed without any distractions. Distractions waste time and may cause work mistakes. As an example, in some organizations a once-per-month cleanup activity is used to encourage employees to discard materials such as obsolete reports and other miscellaneous items that are no longer necessary to complete current work tasks.

Standardization is the fourth S in a 5S system. Standardization implies that the work will be done the same way every time. Consistency reduces process variation, which contributes to a stable takt time. As an example, it has been repeatedly shown that if work tasks are done differently from one employee to another, or one job to another, then cycle time and cost will increase and quality levels decrease. However, work tasks should be standardized only after a careful study has been made under typical production conditions. Time and motion studies or process audits are used to help determine how operational work tasks should best be done. In time and motion studies, process analysts, who are often industrial engineers, break process operations down into their elemental work tasks for a detailed analysis. There are several ways to determine how a work task should be optimally done. One includes breaking an operational work task down into its elemental motions and then consulting standardized time and motion tables. Another method uses a micro motion camera to record how people do a work task, then optimizing its motions using standard work and ergonomic methods. In summary, these analytical studies can be used to determine the best way to do work tasks. The result will be tools, methods, instructions, and other necessary work materials and information that are easily accessible to the people doing the work.

The fifth S is maintaining the self-discipline to sustain the improvements. Sustaining improvements is facilitated by deployment of high-performance work teams using problem-solving tools and methods. An integral part of sustaining process improvements is measuring performance using well-defined financial and operational metrics. Metrics are an important discussion throughout this book. However, sustaining process improvements also requires management commitment and resources. This is the reason that all Lean Six Sigma activities must be aligned up front with organizational goals and objectives.

Link Operations

It was mentioned earlier in this chapter that the physical configuration of the operations within a process workflow has an important impact on its operational efficiency. This is because physical configurations may either enhance or inhibit the flow of materials and information between operations. As an obvious example, the materials must travel the longer the cycle time to complete a work task unless inventory or other forms of capacity have been made available for production. In contrast, the shorter the distance, the lower the cycle time. But this discussion becomes more interesting when operations are linked together in various ways either physically or virtually across the world. As an example, several years ago, I worked with a manager to make process improvements across several packaging lines. Each production line packaged different products. As a result, the people who worked on each packaging line were either busy or idle, depending on the available work. It was also difficult to bring materials to the various packaging lines. It was found

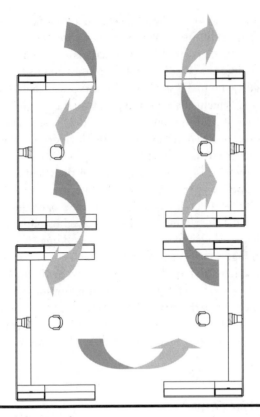

Figure 3.12 7.c. Link operations.

that the reason the lines were isolated was that people had to walk around conveyors to adjust or load machines. A solution was found in locating the packaging machines inside two adjacent packaging lines so one person could adjust and load both machines. As a result, employees could work either or both packaging lines by simply turning around to face the other line. The flexibility to assign employees to adjacent packaging lines contributed to the smooth flow of material through the process. Figure 3.12 shows how these operational concepts can be applied within an office environment using a U-shaped physical configuration. In this example, work in the form of materials or information enters the work cell or office area, moves around the work cell, and exits at the same point that it initially entered the work cell. The advantage of using a U-shaped work cell is that workers can be assigned one or more operations within the cell and work flows through it as a single unit traversing each operation. In other words, the lot size is effectively one unit of work. A U-shaped physical configuration and its unique operational linkage prevents inventory buildup within a work cell. It also enables direct labor to be increased or decreased in a manner similar to that in the packaging line example discussed above.

As a first step in an analysis of an office area, a floor layout or similar process map is created to identify operational work tasks that comprise a process. This layout is then analyzed relative to the flow of materials and information. The goal of this analysis is to reduce the complexity of the process and increase its value-adding (VA) content. Figures 3.6 to 3.8 show how these types of analysis are completed in practice. After improvements have been made, work tasks can be completed using a minimum number of work stations or people. The physical layout of people and machines varies in an office environment due to a high degree of automation. As an example, in global and virtual office environments, information is moved through information technology (IT) systems anywhere in the world almost immediately. In linking these types of operations, the key concept is to keep the materials or information flowing without interruption from one operation to another. This implies that functional interfaces should be removed by eliminating unnecessary setups, inspections, waiting, and similar non-value-adding (NVA) work tasks such as those shown in Figure 3.9. Also, the key principles of operations research (OR) are directly applicable to global IT subsystems. OR methods, including queuing theory in particular, are very helpful in designing, analyzing, and improving global IT systems. As an example, these types of IT systems must have adequate capacity to provide products and services in an environment in which demand dynamically impacts a system, but at a reasonable cost. OR methods are useful in these types of analyses.

Balance Material Flow

Once a process workflow has been standardized and its operations linked, the flow of material or information can be balanced across its work stations. Balanced implies that there is no significant over- or underloading of a system's capacity. In other words, no work station or group of related work operations has a cycle time that exceeds the system's takt time. But external demand requirements are still met in practice. As discussed earlier in this chapter, the takt time is calculated as the available time per-unit time divided by the required production rate per-unit time. Every operation is balanced to the system's takt time and not allowed to exceed it even if additional capacity such as workers or equipment must be added at an operation. As an example, if the available time per day is eight hours and eight units are required, the system takt time is calculated at one unit per hour. As a second example, if available production time per day is 480 minutes (8 hours multiplied by 60 minutes per hour) and the demand is 80 units per day, then the system's takt time will be calculated as 6 minutes per unit. This means that every six minutes one unit of production must be completed by every operation or work station within the process workflow. On the other hand, it is a common situation in which one or more work stations are underloaded relative to their takt time and have excess capacity. However, when a work station is overloaded, a second work

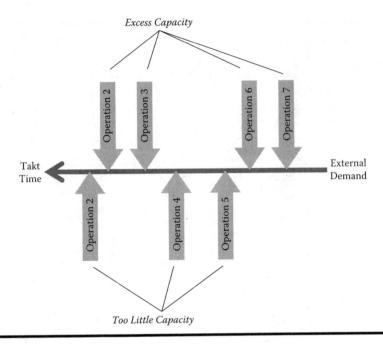

Figure 3.13   7.d. Balance material flow.

station may be added in parallel to ensure that the flow of work is balanced relative to the system's takt time. This concept is shown in Figure 3.13. Figure 3.13 implies that operations having cycle times exceeding a system's takt time should be provided with additional capacity, but those having cycle times lower than the system takt time may be combined with other operations within or across work stations to eliminate excess capacity. Alternatively, one or more process improvements may be made to reduce operational cycle times through an elimination of non-value-adding (NVA) work tasks. As we continue our discussion of Lean tools and methods, it will become obvious that it is important to balance the flow of work through a system at operational, process workflow, office, facility, and supply chain levels.

Bottleneck Management

In any system, a certain sequence of operations will constrain the flow of work. This sequence of operations is called a system's critical path. A critical path is a sequence of operations having the longest total cycle time compared to any other parallel path through the system. It has also been known that only one operation, at a single point in time, on the critical path will control workflow through a system. This single operation is a called a system's bottleneck resource. A bottleneck operation must be able to meet its system's takt time because it controls the flow of materials and information through a system. This means that nonbottleneck operations will

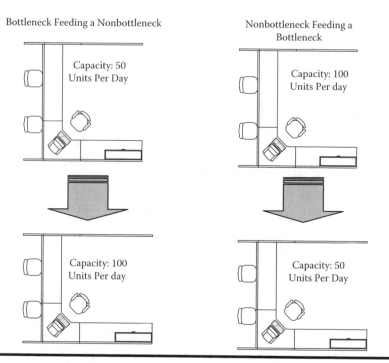

Figure 3.14 7.d.1 Bottleneck management.

be periodically idle or not utilized if production rates exceed the bottleneck's rate. In other words, operations should only be activated when they are needed to support a system's bottleneck to meet its required takt time. Put another way, they are utilized to meet their required activation level as determined by demand on the bottleneck operation. As a result, organizations have developed several strategies to maintain an uninterrupted flow of work through their bottleneck operation.

Figure 3.14 shows how the concept of a bottleneck operation applies within an office environment. In the first scenario, a bottleneck operation feeds a nonbottleneck operation. In the second scenario, the sequence is reversed. In either scenario, the production rate of all resources or operations must be subordinated to a system bottleneck's demand. Another important concept is that a bottleneck must be activated and utilized to meet the system's takt time. In situations where a bottleneck cannot meet its demand, process improvements should first focus on increasing the bottleneck's capacity, because increasing capacity elsewhere does not increase the overall throughput rate of a system. However, if process improvements cannot provide sufficient capacity to enable a bottleneck to meet its required takt time, then other strategies can be used to increase its capacity. As an example, a bottleneck operation could be utilized over multiple shifts or additional workers, and equipment could be added to the system to support the bottleneck. As a final comment, other operations, called capacity constrained resources, may at times become a bottleneck under certain conditions. Value stream mapping (VSM) techniques are very useful to fully understand operational capacity at every operation within a process, including its bottleneck.

Transfer Batches

Using transfer rather than production batches is another key concept in maintaining the flow of work through a system. Transfer batches move material or information from one operation to another as soon as the preceeding operation has completed its work. In contrast, a production batch sends completed units to a downstream operation only after all units in the production batch have been produced and can travel together as a batched lot. It has been shown that using transfer batches can significantly reduce a system's total cycle time or lead time. As an example, Figure 3.15 compares the lead time through a process workflow having three operations, A, B, and C, using either a transfer or production batch system. Ten units are moved through the system. The total cycle time to produce the ten units is 60 minutes when using a process batch system versus just 24 minutes using a transfer batch system. This cycle time reduction, of approximately 60 percent, was obtained by simply changing the rule used to release production from one operation to the next in sequence. The concept of transfer batching is directly applicable to office operations. As an example, the turnaround time will be faster when expense reports are immediately reviewed by a supervisor and sent to an accounting department rather than batched with those of several other employees.

Mistake Proofing

Mistake proofing operations and work tasks also helps balance the flow of work through a system, because unexpected interruptions to the flow of work are prevented from occurring, or their frequency is reduced. As a result, mistake proofing helps a system maintain its takt time because defects are prevented or are quickly detected when they occur. Figure 3.16 shows several common strategies used to mistake proof operations. The most effective mistake-proofing strategy is to design a product or service so it cannot fail when used by customers. Mistake-proofing strategies may also include several levels of protection. At a first level, red-flag conditions can be identified and eliminated from a process. Red-flag conditions include a lack of training or procedures, a lack of effective measurement systems, frequent changes to jobs, long cycle times to complete a job, jobs that are produced infrequently, and poor environmental conditions, such as noisy, dirty, and poorly lit work areas. It has been well documented that red-flag conditions contribute to the creation of error conditions within a process. In turn, error conditions contribute to the creation of errors and defects. Because red-flag conditions are easy to see and eliminate, it is usually a good idea for process improvement teams to immediately

Process Batch

		Unit									
Time	Operation	1	2	3	4	5	6	7	8	9	10
2	A	2									
2	B	2									
2	C	2									
2	A		2								
2	B		2								
2	C		2								
2	A			2							
2	B			2							
2	C			2							
2	A				2						
2	B				2						
2	C				2						
2	A					2					
2	B					2					
2	C					2					
2	A						2				
2	B						2				
2	C						2				
2	A							2			
2	B							2			
2	C							2			
2	A								2		
2	B								2		
2	C								2		
2	A									2	
2	B									2	
2	C									2	
2	A										2
2	B										2
2	C										2

(60)

Transfer Batch

		Unit									
Time	Operation	1	2	3	4	5	6	7	8	9	10
2	A	2									
2	B	2	2								
2	C	2	2	2							
2	A		2	2	2						
2	B			2	2	2					
2	C				2	2	2				
2	A					2	2	2			
2	B						2	2	2		
2	C							2	2	2	
2	A								2	2	2
2	B									2	2
2	C										2

(24)

Figure 3.15 7.d.2 Transfer batches.

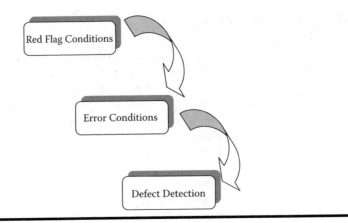

Figure 3.16   7.e. Mistake proofing.

eliminate them prior to process improvement work. A next lower level of mistake proofing, assuming products and services were effectively designed and red-flag conditions have been eliminated from a process, is to detect error conditions known to cause defects. An example would be monitoring the status of various components of copying equipment to prevent paper jams by shutting the machine down and requesting maintenance prior to additional copying. The lowest level of a mistake-proofing strategy is to detect the occurrence of a defect as soon as it occurs, to prevent the creation of additional defects. This is typically done by activating an alarm to warn operators, or automatically shutting down equipment.

High Quality

Table 3.4 lists several process improvement activities that contribute to higher quality levels within an organization. These activities have a cumulative impact on an organization because they prevent or correct process breakdowns. The list of activities includes the proper design of products and services using Design for Six Sigma (DFSS), the correct design of the resultant process workflows, the reduction of complexity using Design for Manufacturing (DFM), and other cutting-edge tools and methods that reduce system complexity through product and service standardization. Standardization can be achieved through the use of common materials, generous design tolerances, and off-the-shelf rather than customized components. It is also important to ensure that work and inspection procedures are easy to follow and people have been trained in their usage. Mistake proofing and effective root cause analysis contribute to higher quality levels, as the causes of failure are systematically identified and eliminated from a process.

DFSS activities are a structured set of tools and methods that systematically identify, prioritize, and translate the voice of the customer (VOC) through an organization into the design of its products and services. Effectively translating the VOC

Table 3.4   7.f. High Quality
"Zero Defects"

Product design	Design products using the voice of the customer (VOC), Design for Six Sigma (DFSS), Design for Manufacturing (DFM), and other cutting-edge tools and methods.
Reduce complexity	Simplify and standardize product and service designs and their production processes to eliminate non-value-adding work tasks that only contributes defects to the ultimate product or service.
Standardize	Use common materials, generous design tolerances, and off-the-shelf rather than customized components. Ensure work and inspection procedures are easy to follow and people have been trained in their usage.
Mistake proofing	Analyze the final product or service design to make it impossible to fail during assembly or customer usage. Eliminate red-flag conditions, detect error conditions, and prevent defects from occurring.
Effective root cause analysis	It is important to use problem-solving tools and methods to identify the reasons or root causes for higher-level problems or process breakdowns.

ensures that customer requirements are integrated into operational work tasks. Another added advantage of effective VOC translation is that products and service will contain a higher value-adding content than otherwise. DFM can be considered a subset of DFSS because its tools and methods are heavily utilized by DFSS programs. However, DFM was originally developed as a stand-alone methodology that enabled manufacturing and now service industries to simplify, standardize, and make other important improvements to the design of their products and services, which simplify their production. In many ways, Lean methods reflect the basic concepts of the original DFM methods, but to the design or modification of process workflows. Standardization is an example of a set of tools and methods that are integral to DFSS methods but were originally developed as stand-alone improvement activities. Also, they are the basis of the Lean 5S philosophy. Root cause analysis will be discussed in Chapters 5 and 6 in the context of Lean and Six Sigma tools and methods. The major tools and methods described in Table 3.4 have been successfully applied to improve process workflows in office environments. We will continue our discussion of Lean Six Sigma for the office by application of these concepts in subsequent chapters.

Reduce Setup Time (SMED)

SMED is an acronym for the single minute exchange of dies. It is a set of tools, methods, and concepts designed to reduce the time required to set up a job. Although

Table 3.5 7.g. Reduce Setup Time (SMED) "Single Minute Exchange of Die"

Improvement Opportunity	Key Improvement Tasks	Service Operation Applications
1. Identify setup elements	Map out in sequence all the elements, i.e., work tasks required to set up a job. Characterize them as VA, NVA, and BVA. Eliminate NVA work tasks from the setup process.	Break the setup of a job down into its smallest work tasks. Example: Use process maps and develop a sequential list of work tasks.
2. Separate internal from external setup	Identity those work tasks that can be done offline and do not directly impact production.	Identify work tasks that can be completed prior to the job setup. Example: Information could be collected prior to a meeting as opposed to during a meeting.
3. Move elements to external setup	Offline work tasks can be scheduled independent of the job setup. But these tasks should also be studied using SMED methods and simplified offline, but with lower priority than online tasks.	Study internal setup work tasks and make design modifications to the process to convert them to external work tasks.
4. Simply, standardize, and mistake proof remaining elements	Study the internal or in-line setup work tasks and eliminate or standardize them. Design mating dies so they fit together only one way and can be mated and adjusted without tools.	Study those work tasks that remain part of the internal or online setup of a job. Simplify and standardize these work tasks using Lean and information technology (IT) methods.

its origin was in manufacturing, the tools and methods of SMED are analogous to office processes. There are several key activities integral to an effective SMED program. These are described in Table 3.5. The first key SMED activity is the identification of individual work tasks associated with setting up a job. The analysis requires mapping and creating sequential lists of the work tasks required to set up a job, and then classifying them as value-adding (VA), non-value-adding (NVA), or business value-adding (BVA) work tasks. The goal of a SMED analysis, which is similar to other Lean activities, is to eliminate NVA work tasks immediately from the setup of jobs. As an example, in office operations, SMED activities would consist of creating a process map of the work tasks required to set up a typical job, such as invoicing a customer. In this type of analysis the work tasks would be analyzed for their value content, efficiency, and relative relationships to each other to look for ways to reduce invoicing cycle time, improve quality, and reduce the cost of the invoicing transaction. Integral to this type of analysis is identifying ways to automate portions of a process. A second key SMED activity is the identification and separation of internal from external work tasks that are associated with setups. External setup work tasks can be done offline, at convenient times, and do not directly impact the overall cycle time for setting up a job or production schedules. In other words, these work tasks can be completed prior to the online setup of a job to save production time. In an office environment, an example of this concept is collecting information prior to meetings to reduce the time necessary to bring a team up to speed relative to the discussion at hand. Another example would be prescreening job candidates using the Internet by asking them job-specific questions. If an answer is not a yes, then they would be excluded from further consideration to reduce the cycle time of the candidate evaluation process. A third key SMED activity is the conversion of internal to external work tasks through design modifications. In a manufacturing environment, this usually requires a modification to manufacturing tooling or product designs. In an office environment examples would be reducing the number of required sign-offs of a job or enabling an information technology (IT) system to extract information from disparate databases and insert this information into an invoice. The extracted information would include names, addresses, amounts to be paid, or at a more complicated level, the customer's credit history. A fourth key SMED activity is the simplification, standardization, and mistake proofing of the remaining internal and external work tasks. These important activities will reduce job setup mistakes and avoid increases in the cycle time. As an example in manufacturing environments, tooling is designed asymmetrically, so mating dies fit together only one way to avoid mistakes. Also, in other situations dies and tooling may have design features that enable them to be assembled and adjusted without using special tools. This reduces overall cycle time to set up a job. A fourth key SMED activity requires a continuous analysis of the remaining internal work tasks using Lean tools and methods.

Total Preventive Maintenance

Total preventive maintenance, which is also called total productive maintenance (TPM), is a set of tools, methods, and philosophies that are developed to ensure that equipment and people are available for use when needed at a predetermined probability or reliability level. Table 3.6 lists three key strategies that will help to ensure a system's availability. The first TPM strategy begins with an analysis of operational equipment relative to its classification into major equipment categories. In manufacturing environments, common examples may include categories related to

Table 3.6   7.h. Total Preventive Maintenance (TPM) "Preventive...Autonomous...Predictive"

Improvement Opportunity	Key Improvement Tasks	Service Operation Applications
1. Eliminate breakdowns	Analyze operational equipment by major category, i.e., pumps, vehicles, compressors, etc., for their required maintenance frequencies, and integrate their required maintenance into a TPM program. Analyze maintenance failures and develop strategies to eliminate their root causes.	Analyze equipment and people to determine their availability. Develop strategies to increase and sustain system availability.
2. Maintain standard production rate	Do not run equipment at rates exceeding their design. Analyze equipment production rates below standard and eliminate their root causes.	Do not run equipment or work people at their capacity for extended periods of time. Identify the root causes of worker sickness, lateness, terminations, and resignations. Ensure work conditions are ergonomically designed and maintained for workers.
3. Reduce yield loss at start-up	Analyze the types of start-up scrap related to maintenance issues. Identify and eliminate their root causes.	Identify, analyze, and eliminate worker and equipment errors due to fatigue or ergonomic issues.

pumps, vehicles, compressors, and others. The reason for the classification of equipment into categories is that common maintenance policies can be applied to equipment having a common design because they may use similar replacement parts and service technologies. As part of the classification of equipment, an ongoing analysis of maintenance failures is also used to identify projects to eliminate their failures. The overall production capacity will be increased to the extent that the incident rates of process breakdowns are reduced. In an office environment, system availability depends on several interacting components. These include information technology (IT) databases, analytical algorithms, input/output devices and their associated systems and platforms, the professionals doing the work of moving materials and information through process workflows as well as other peripheral equipment, and information that is necessary to ensure service systems are available for use.

A second key strategy is to use equipment only at its standard production rate. In other words, equipment should not be operated at rates exceeding its design specifications. If additional capacity is needed to maintain a system's takt time, then additional pieces of equipment should be employed to meet production requirements, or equivalently, could be operated for longer periods of time. This means additional work shifts should be used to meet production requirements. In other words, equipment should not be operated or people worked at or beyond their available capacity for extended periods of time. Available capacity is defined, for our purposes, as a system's design capacity minus adjustments due to expected losses of capacity. On the other hand, if equipment performs below its rated standard production rate, then an analysis is required to identify and eliminate the root causes for these lower-than-anticipated production rates. In this context, it is important to measure the actual capacity that is available to do work. It is less than a system's available capacity due to unexpected process problems. These problems include rework, scrap, and schedule disruptions that degrade a system's available capacity. To avoid degradation of actual capacity or even to expand it back to the expected level of availability, an organization should identify the root causes of its process breakdowns. In office environments, these may include worker sickness, employee lateness, terminations, and resignations. Ergonomic considerations are also important to ensure people remain healthy and their working activities are efficient.

A third key strategy is to reduce yield loss at job start-up to increase actual capacity. This requires an operational analysis of process breakdowns using Lean and Six Sigma methods. Many systems have issues associated with wasted time and resources, i.e., the seven basic process wastes shown in Figure 3.1. These seven wastes directly impact a system's maintenance efforts as they relate to the maintenance of equipment, IT system, and employee capacities. In summary, in office environments, it is important to use Lean Six Sigma methods to identify, analyze, and eliminate process wastes that contribute to longer cycle times, lower quality, and higher transaction costs.

Level Demand

In addition to basic process improvements that increase system performance, the more advanced JIT systems also require level external demand to establish and maintain a stable takt time. Figure 3.17 shows five common demand patterns: level, normal, erratic, seasonal, and demand impacted by sales promotions. There are many other types of demand patterns, but these five common patterns will illustrate the relevant concepts. In our discussion, *level* implies unit demand variations in the range of ±10 percent, *normal* implies that unit demand fluctuations

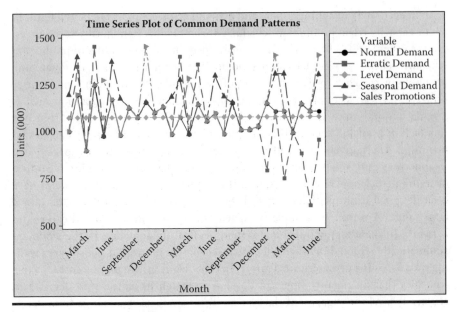

Figure 3.17   7.i. Level Demand.

are ±25 percent, and *erratic* could imply fluctuations of more than ±100 percent of average unit demand. In addition, demand patterns could exhibit seasonal fluctuations, promotional spikes, and other patterns specific to certain industries. However, level does not imply that there is no variation in external demand, but only that variation of demand should not exceed a system's available capacity and disrupt its takt time.

The ability of a supply chain to stabilize the external demand that is placed on its participants varies by industry as well as by the organizations within a given industry. However, some supply chains may have options that will help reduce their variation of demand. The most important option is not to engage in marketing and sales promotional activities or otherwise manipulate their external demand patterns. This is because these types of activities tend to increase demand variation and are often major contributors to the deterioration of a supply chain's ability to match its capacity to fluctuating demand. These conditions will lower a supply chain's productivity. A simple example of this concept is the demand that is placed on Wal-Mart's numerous retail stores versus that which is placed on some of its direct competitors. Wal-Mart's products exhibit relatively stable demand patterns precisely because Wal-Mart does not overpromote its products. In contrast, many of its competitors routinely promote their products. The result is higher inventory investment. In summary, product or service promotions have the effect of artificially manipulating external demand patterns throughout a supply chain's participating organizations. These situations may adversely impact a system's asset utilization efficiency and capacity.

Not accurately matching supply and demand across a supply chain will result in excess capacity when production schedules are empty due to nonutilized resources. On the other hand, when capacity is constrained due to overloading of production schedules, customer service levels deteriorate. Unfortunately, an efficient matching of supply or capacity to demand may not be possible, due to inefficient resource utilization. As an example, it is very common to enter a service operation such as a bank, hospital, store, or restaurant and wait for an inordinate period of time due to a lack of available agents. This situation is usually caused by poor operational planning. Alternatively, demand on a system may be higher than expected due to abnormal causes, which may preclude efficient operational planning regardless of staffing efficiency. However, even in these situations some service systems have been designed to immediately expand their capacity as demand fluctuates over a large range. A common example is capacity planning within a global call center network. In these highly integrated systems, calls from anywhere in the world are automatically rerouted to other call centers within the network if a customer's waiting time exceeds a predetermined target. In other words, there may be cost-effective strategies that an organization can develop to match its capacity to demand to effectively level the capacity of the system. These strategies may range from developing common product or service designs, to increasing operational flexibility, to forming partnerships with other organizations, including the outsourcing of work to reliably increase available capacity at low cost.

Reduce Lot Sizes

The concept of lot size is common in manufacturing systems. But it is also analogous to service system operations. As an example, the larger a lot or batch or work, the longer the lead time before the next operation will receive the batch of work. A lot or batch of work could include several invoices, expense reports, résumés, or similar types of work that require analysis by an office worker. The concept of a lot or batch is also similar to our previous discussion of transfer versus process batching, which was described in Figure 3.15. Recall in transfer batching that units of work are immediately transferred to the next operation rather than batched together. However, a reduction in the size of a production lot implies that it has fewer units or work to begin with. This difference is apparent in situations in which lot sizes are larger than required because of contractual or technology constraints. In other words, our goal should be to create small lot sizes to enable a flexible capacity response to external demand, and to produce them using a transfer batch methodology to further reduce their production lead time. In this context, minimizing the size of a production lot is a concept that is slightly different than transfer batching. It should also be noted that many of the Lean concepts we have discussed in this chapter will also help reduce lot size. As an example, the application of SMED principles will enable more frequent job setups, which can be subsequently

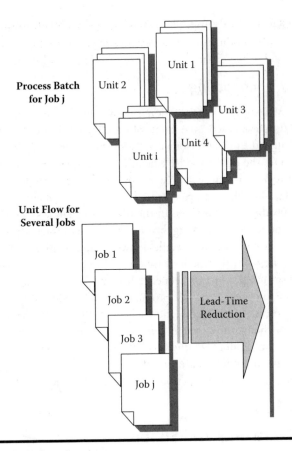

Figure 3.18   7.j. Reduce lot sizes.

translated into reductions in lot size, and yield improvements will not require that extra work be performed to make up for lost production.

The ultimate goal of JIT and Lean system deployments is to continuously move the production of work from larger lots or batches toward a single unit flow production system in which the size of a lot is one unit of work. The advantage of single unit flow systems is that they enable the dynamic matching of supply or capacity to external demand. In these systems, a product or service's lead time will be reduced to that required to produce a single unit of different production sequences of products and services. The result will be lower inventory or other resource investment and higher customer service levels. Figure 3.18 shows a unit flow concept from a slightly different perspective using invoices. This concept can be seen when a person goes to an airport kiosk and obtains a boarding ticket or requests upgrades, earlier flights, or other services; this is single unit flow production because different jobs or requests for boarding assignments are processed in unit flow quantities person by person if kiosks are available. An alternative system is to require people to queue up behind an agent for various types of services, some of which require waiting in different lines.

Mixed-Model Scheduling

As lot sizes are reduced, a production system will be able to move toward a mixed-model production schedule. Some of the characteristics of such a scheduling system were implied in the previous discussion of lot size. Our purpose here will be to demonstrate the mixed-model scheduling concept using the simple example shown in Figure 3.19. In this example, it can be seen that five products or services labeled A, B, C, D, and E are produced over five working days using batched and mixed-model production schedules. In the batched schedule system, the lead time to produce a product is five working days because each of the five products requires one day to meet its production schedule. However, in the mixed-model production schedule it can be seen that the lead time is reduced to just one working day, or by 80 percent, as the production sequence becomes hourly rather than daily. This implies that the lot sizes of the five products are also reduced by 80 percent. The advantage of a mixed-model production scheduling system is that it can dynamically respond to changes in external demand. As an example, if the demand for a product A temporarily doubles, then its production amount can be immediately increased if its subcomponents are available. Alternatively, if demand temporarily decreases, then product A's production amount can be immediately decreased.

Supplier Networks and Support

A supply chain should be integrated through operational competencies and contractual obligations. In other words, the creation of high-performance supply chains requires that all their participants work together to enhance their productivity and shareholder economic value added (EVA). In addition, Lean, Six Sigma, and similar operational initiatives should be effectively deployed by the participants of the supplier chain. Supply chains should promote mutually beneficial activities between participants, rather than being dominated by the interests of a few large organizations. A supply chain becomes noncompetitive as external competition increases when dominant organizations pass on their operational inefficiencies to other participants. In these situations, a dominant organization has no incentive to improve its operational efficiency when it passes on higher production costs to its suppliers through price and other concessions. In some industries, this practice results in deterioration of a supply chain's ability to invest in infrastructure, people, and equipment. In the final phases of this deterioration, the profit margins of all supply chain participants eventually become threatened, and more efficient competitive

Day	Hour	Production Sequence	Mixed-Model Sequence
1	1	A	A
1	2	A	B
1	3	A	C
1	4	A	D
1	5	A	E
1	6	A	A
1	7	A	B
1	8	A	C
2	1	B	D
2	2	B	E
2	3	B	A
2	4	B	B
2	5	B	C
2	6	B	D
2	7	B	E
2	8	B	A
3	1	C	B
3	2	C	C
3	3	C	D
3	4	C	E
3	5	C	A
3	6	C	B
3	7	C	A
3	8	C	B
4	1	D	C
4	2	D	D
4	3	D	E
4	4	D	A
4	5	D	B
4	6	D	C
4	7	D	D
4	8	D	E
5	1	E	A
5	2	E	B
5	3	E	A
5	4	E	B
5	5	E	C
5	6	E	D
5	7	E	E
5	8	E	A

Figure 3.19 7.j.1. Mixed-model scheduling.

supply chains may become dominant. Many industries within the United States have been good examples of supply chain deterioration and extinction. These industries include consumer electronics, automobiles, and, more recently, services of all types, to name just a few examples. At an operational level, the best way to maintain supply chain competitiveness or dominance is to deploy initiatives to increase organizational productivity.

A key performance measure of a successful supply chain is its asset utilization efficiency. High asset utilization efficiencies require that a supply chain's assets be positioned at points where capacity is needed to satisfy demand. As an example, in a manufacturing supply chain, inventory investment, at various points in the system, is used to minimize the overall investment within the system that is required to satisfy external demand. An optimum allocation of inventory investment, using proven analytical methods, also ensures that minimum quantities of subcomponents are positioned across a supply chain. Other supply chain assets, including people, plants, and equipment, can be similarly allocated. This is especially true if suppliers and customers are dispersed nationally or internationally. Key Lean tasks and methods can also be applied to increase supply chain production. Figure 3.20 shows a mixed-model scheduling example. In summary, a supplier network or supply chain should be designed to increase its asset utilization efficiencies and position capacity so it has the highest value-adding content.

Implement Visual Control and Pull Systems—Kanban

A key component of a Lean system is deployment of a pull scheduling system to move work through the system in pace with external customer demand. This is in contrast to systems where work is scheduled in anticipation of future customer demand using statistically based forecasts. In push scheduling systems, capacity is out of synchronization with actual customer demand due to demand or capacity fluctuations. This situation results in wasted capacity because actual demand is higher or lower than that which was originally forecast. In manufacturing organizations using a pull scheduling system, visual or electronic signals called Kanbans or cards are used to notify upstream work stations when work is needed by downstream operations.

Pull systems have been deployed with varying degrees of success depending on the industry and organization. As an example, the pull scheduling system was originally popularized by Toyota manufacturing. In Toyota's manufacturing system it has been estimated that external customer demand varies by approximately ±10 percent. Also, Toyota's manufacturing systems are highly simplified, standardized, and mistake proofed through more than 50 years of cumulative improvements. In these environments, visual and manual control systems have been shown to be highly efficient in scheduling the work at upstream manufacturing operations. However, the efficiency of a pull system varies by industry and the organizations

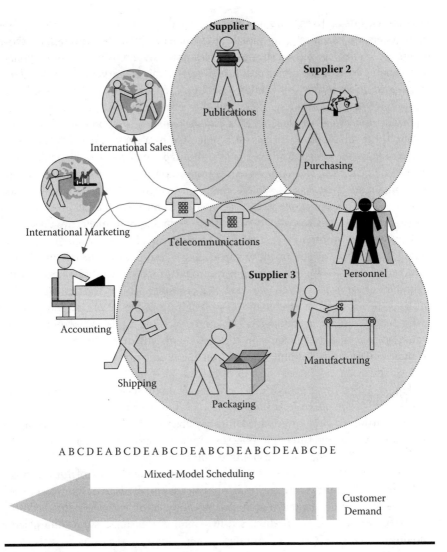

Figure 3.20   8. Supplier networks and support.

within an industry. As an example, in some industries external demand is highly seasonal and fluctuates by more than ±100 percent of its average monthly demand. Pull systems may also be difficult to implement in these types of environments, in which external demand is highly variable.

However, the question is often asked: How does the concept of pulling demand through a system apply to service and office environments in particular? Whereas in manufacturing it makes sense to move baskets or containers of materials from one machining center to another using Kanban cards, modified methods are necessary to deploy pull systems in office environments. As an example, in McDonald's restaurants, buffer inventories are utilized to reduce customer waiting time, but most orders are made to order based on customer request. In other words, these orders are "pulled" or moved though the restaurant system using electronic signals or Kanbans. In fact, customer orders in Burger King and several other fast food services are more highly differentiated because they are made to order based on a high degree of customization. There are other systems in which customers initiate a job or order. An example is when a patient requests an appointment to visit a doctor. Once an appointment has been requested by a patient, paperwork is completed to move the patient (the work object) through the medical evaluation process. However, in contrast, this same system becomes a push system when appointments are made in advance. As an example, many medical and dental appointments are made by office assistants one year in advance. This push scheduling process forces follow-up phone calls to patients when their annual appointments are due. Also, appointments must often be rescheduled, resulting in a loss of capacity in the time period in which an appointment was made and a heavy work schedule in a future time period. In the case of an accounts receivable process, the process begins when a product or service has been provided to a customer. This is the pull signal that initiates the accounts receivable process to begin its sequence of operational work tasks. In contrast, an accounts receivable process using a push scheduling system would prepare customer invoices in anticipation of providing a product or service. In these situations, if customer demand for the product or service is not realized, then the invoice must be reworked or discarded.

Figure 3.21 shows a generic office example of a pull scheduling system. We can consider this example to be a site visit at a job fair. In this example, 100 visitors arrive each hour. They are divided into groups of 20 people. Each person has 36 seconds to answer three questions by employers at each station. This system will schedule 800 people over 8 hours at 100 people per hour. The assumption in this simple example is that customers arrive for service at the rate of 100 per hour. It should be noted that there are more sophisticated methods to design and operate this type of system using queuing models in combination with the pull scheduling system. Queuing models are discussed in several of the suggested readings at the end of this chapter.

Continually Update Process Technologies

In a Lean system technology is important to ensure higher process yields and move materials and information through process workflows with more efficiency. However, the emphasis of a Lean system is not on technology itself, but rather on the use of technology to support employees in their work. In this context, technology should be flexible to meet changing technological needs. This concept is shown in Figure 3.22. In manufacturing systems, the goal is to use simple and flexible equipment. Redundant equipment can also be utilized or left idle

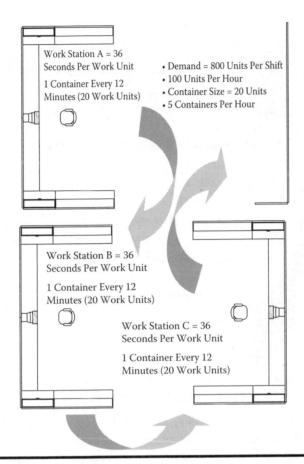

Work Station A = 36
Seconds Per Work Unit

1 Container Every 12
Minutes (20 Work Units)

• Demand = 800 Units Per Shift
• 100 Units Per Hour
• Container Size = 20 Units
• 5 Containers Per Hour

Work Station B = 36
Seconds Per Work Unit

1 Container Every 12
Minutes (20 Work Units)

Work Station C = 36
Seconds Per Work Unit

1 Container Every 12
Minutes (20 Work Units)

Figure 3.21   9. Implement pull systems in offices using visual controls and Kanban.

to meet a system's takt time. This is because the machines are simple and less costly than more complex machines. Simpler machines are also more reliable and easier to maintain. In contrast, many less efficient organizations utilize very complex machines. Although these replace several manual work tasks, they are often expensive to maintain and may become bottlenecks if their throughput rates are lower than other productive resources.

In office environments, information technology systems exist at several levels of sophistication. Also, the degree of work task automation may vary from none to extensive. In the balance of this chapter we will discuss the evolution of the major information technology (IT) systems that have transformed office environments into global systems moving materials and information continuously around our world. Although IT systems have been around for more than 50 years, we will begin the discussion around mid-1990, when the use of e-mail became common. It may be difficult for people not familiar with work practices prior to the widespread use

• Business Process Management Suite (BPMS)

• Business Process Management (BPM)

• Business Process Modeling and Analysis (BMA)

• Business Intelligence (BI)

• Business Activity Monitoring (BAM)

• Enterprise Application Integration (EAI)

• Workflow Management (WM)

• E-Mail

Figure 3.22   10. Continually update process technologies.

of e-mail to understand that the business world was characterized, at that time, with written documents and extensive bureaucracies that slowed down the review and approval of office work to a trickle. The development of e-mail enabled large segments of the global workforce to exchange information very rapidly, as was shown by the dramatic reductions in lead time using transfer rather than process batching. This is because e-mails are usually sent without formal approvals. Also, there has been an acceleration in the development of software and hardware technologies that has resulted in increasingly sophisticated systems to create, manage, and improve process workflows. These advances have pushed organizational productivity to higher and higher levels.

Workflow management (WM) systems evolved from simple electronic versions of manual work tasks to advanced adaptive systems that can be dynamically reconfigured to match capacity to demand. In other words, the systems rule sets and work sequences of process workflows can also be modified using these systems. Earlier versions included Excel spreadsheets and customized software written for specialized applications. More recent versions include Internet-based WM systems that can be reconfigured in minutes, to match changes in workflow structure. A next step in the evolution of IT systems began when users wanted to integrate diverse IT platforms, including software and hardware systems, to reflect geographically dispersed workflow configurations. Initially, these activities were at a local level, but they have now been integrated into Internet-based applications. These integration activities are called enterprise application integration (EAI). Business activity monitoring (BAM) systems were being developed in parallel to WM and EAI systems. BAM systems are based on extensive rule sets that enable routing of information across systems and provide status information, including drill-down capability, to lower-level metrics and work tasks. A common example is modern call center software that monitors incoming and outgoing call volumes and similar transactions and reports their status dynamically. These systems both control and monitor the transaction volumes across a call center's network. A natural extension of BAM is business modeling and analysis (BMA). BMA enabled users to simulate changes in system inputs to evaluate their combined impact on the system. In the call center example, depending on the sophistication of the software, users can conduct offline simulations of changes in employee staffing and other variables. This information is used to determine optimum capacity levels, by location, across the system to maintain target customer service levels. These customer service levels are measured by the waiting time and the quality of information provided to customers. A business process management suite (BPMS) is used to integrate the diverse software and hardware platforms to manage the capacity necessary to maintain the flow of materials and information across global supply chains.

Process technologies such as these are important to the deployment of Lean Six Sigma systems in office environments. At a first level, IT systems enable the automation of work tasks. Automation simplifies, standardizes, and mistake proofs a process workflow in proportion to the reduction in its manual work tasks. In addition to automation benefits, intermediaries are also eliminated from process workflows, which increases the flow of work through a system. At a next higher level, IT systems bring together diverse information from across a global supply chain and analyze it using predetermined rule sets to provide information that is useful in making decisions. At still higher system levels, modern IT systems enable a system to be reconfigured based on changing process workflows. These topics are relevant to a Kaizen or rapid improvement team that must collect and analyze data from IT systems to modify or create models of its process workflows. In this context, various types of IT subject matter experts are essential to execute most Lean Six Sigma projects that are deployed in offices and to support Kaizen events.

Summary

In this chapter, we discussed the basic tools, methods, and concepts of Lean production. This discussion began with a review of the seven basic forms of process waste that Lean is designed to identify and eliminate from a process. It was also shown that all process improvement activities should be aligned with organizational goals and objectives as well as the voice of the customer (VOC). VOC information is analyzed and translated into an organization's internal workflows to identify work tasks that are value adding (VA), business value adding (BVA) and non-value-adding (NVA). Operational information is also used to provide a focus for process improvement projects. A system's complexity should be reduced to decrease its cycle time and cost and improve its quality. In this context, it was recommended that a system's complexity be reduced and obvious process break-downs be eliminated, if possible, prior to deploying improvement projects so as to not waste resources improving processes that will be eliminated in the future.

The chapter then continued to discuss the major Lean tools and methods. The first step in process improvement activities should be an operational assessment and the creation of a value stream map (VSM). A VSM describes major process workflows and their key financial and operational metrics, including the system's takt time. It was also shown that once a VSM has been created, it can be analyzed to identify non-value-adding NVA work tasks. In this discussion, NVA work tasks were eliminated and Lean methods were applied to simplify, standardize, and mistake proof the remaining work tasks. These process improvements were made to stabilize the system's takt time to pull work through a process. It was also mentioned that in any system, a certain sequence of operations will constrain the flow of work through a process workflow. This is its critical path. A bottleneck resource will be on a system's critical path. Several useful methods were also presented to accelerate the flow of work through a system. The numerous Lean concepts presented in this chapter can be utilized by an organization to create high-performance supplier networks in which all parties work together to enhance their productivity and shareholder economic value added (EVA).

Suggested Reading

Sanjiv Augustine. 2005. *Managing agile projects*. Upper Saddle River, NJ: Prentice Hall.

Thomas Fabrizio and Don Tapping. 2006. *5S for the office: Organizing the workplace to eliminate waste*. New York: Productivity Press.

Eliyahu M. Goldratt and Jeff Cox. 1986. *The goal*. 2nd ed. Great Barrington, MA: North River Press.

Paul Harmon. 2003. *Business process change—A manager's guide to improving, redesigning, and automating processes*. San Francisco: Morgan Kaufman Publishers.

Peter Hines, Richard Lamming, Dan Jones, Paul Cousins, and Nick Rich. 2000. *Value stream management*. New York: Prentice Hall.

Kobayashi Iwao. 1995. *20 keys to workplace improvement*. New York: Productivity Press.

James W. Martin. 2007. *Lean Six Sigma for supply chain management*. New York: McGraw-Hill.

James W. Martin. 2008. *Operational excellence—Using Lean Six Sigma to translate customer value through global supply chains*. New York: Auerbach.

James M. Morgan and Jeffrey K. Liker. 2006. *The Toyota Product Development System*. New York: Productivity Press.

Ken Schwaber. 2003. *Agile project management with scrum.* Redmond, WA: Microsoft Professional.

Rajan Suri. 1998. *Quick response manufacturing—A companywide approach to reducing lead times.* New York: Productivity Press.

James P. Womack and Daniel T. Jones. 1996. *Lean thinking—Banish waste and create wealth in your organization.* New York: Simon & Schuster.

PLAN AND CONDUCT THE KAIZEN EVENT

2

Chapter 4

Kaizen Event Planning

Overview

Kaizen events are workshops in which processes are analyzed and improved in a matter of days. This process improvement approach is very applicable to office environments in which many of the root causes for process breakdowns are due to communication issues within and across departments. Bringing people who interact across the many process boundaries that are characteristic of global supply chains is always a useful way to understand a process problem from different organizational and cultural perspectives. It should be noted that not every process problem can be analyzed and eliminated within a few days. However, larger-scale projects should only be created to understand the causes of more complicated problems. Understanding how to identify and deploy rapid improvement projects is important because too many Lean Six Sigma projects are focused on a three- to five-month Six Sigma problem-solving methodology. In my experience with thousands of projects, I have found that perhaps up to 80 percent or more require basic Lean tools and methods for their solution. In fact, in many situations, Kaizen events would have been the most useful process improvement approach. However, Lean and statistical problem-solving tools are important and will be discussed in Chapter 5. In summary, an overly complicated improvement methodology is usually not necessary to improve office processes. Why complicate an improvement project and waste valuable resources and time?

In this chapter we will discuss the activities required to plan and execute a Kaizen event in an office environment. In this discussion, we will show the step-by-step activities that are necessary to successfully prepare and conduct Kaizen events. Our

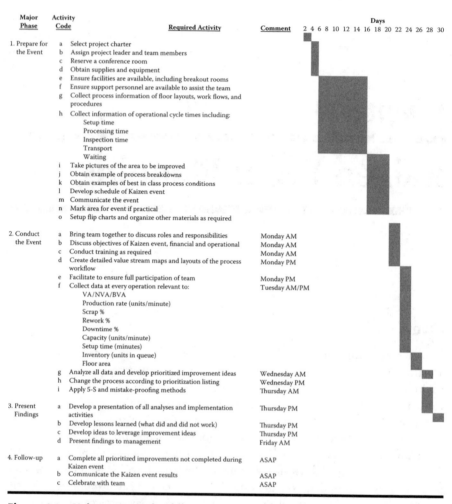

Major Phase	Activity Code	Required Activity	Comment	Days
1. Prepare for the Event	a	Select project charter		
	b	Assign project leader and team members		
	c	Reserve a conference room		
	d	Obtain supplies and equipment		
	e	Ensure facilities are available, including breakout rooms		
	f	Ensure support personnel are available to assist the team		
	g	Collect process information of floor layouts, work flows, and procedures		
	h	Collect information of operational cycle times including: Setup time / Processing time / Inspection time / Transport / Waiting		
	i	Take pictures of the area to be improved		
	j	Obtain example of process breakdowns		
	k	Obtain examples of best in class process conditions		
	l	Develop schedule of Kaizen event		
	m	Communicate the event		
	n	Mark area for event if practical		
	o	Setup flip charts and organize other materials as required		
2. Conduct the Event	a	Bring team together to discuss roles and responsibilities	Monday AM	
	b	Discuss objectives of Kaizen event, financial and operational	Monday AM	
	c	Conduct training as required	Monday AM	
	d	Create detailed value stream maps and layouts of the process workflow	Monday PM	
	e	Facilitate to ensure full participation of team	Monday PM	
	f	Collect data at every operation relevant to: VA/NVA/BVA / Production rate (units/minute) / Scrap % / Rework % / Downtime % / Capacity (units/minute) / Setup time (minutes) / Inventory (units in queue) / Floor area	Tuesday AM/PM	
	g	Analyze all data and develop prioritized improvement ideas	Wednesday AM	
	h	Change the process according to prioritization listing	Wednesday PM	
	i	Apply 5-S and mistake-proofing methods	Thursday AM	
3. Present Findings	a	Develop a presentation of all analyses and implementation activities	Thursday PM	
	b	Develop lessons learned (what did and did not work)	Thursday PM	
	c	Develop ideas to leverage improvement ideas	Thursday PM	
	d	Present findings to management	Friday AM	
4. Follow-up	a	Complete all prioritized improvements not completed during Kaizen event	ASAP	
	b	Communicate the Kaizen event results	ASAP	
	c	Celebrate with team	ASAP	

Figure 4.1 Kaizen event checklist.

goal will be to build on the Lean concepts presented in Chapters 1 to 3. Chapter 4 will form a basis for continuing our discussion of Lean Six Sigma in subsequent chapters, with an emphasis on the rapid deployment of Kaizen teams. It will be shown that Kaizen events require the involvement of team members and supporting people for several days. For this reason, it is important to plan these events very carefully. Also, Kaizen events are very fast paced. As a result, their schedules may be adversely impacted if event planning is poorly coordinated.

Our discussion of Kaizen event planning and execution will follow the sequential list of activities shown in Figure 4.1. These activities are divided into four major sections with each containing sets of activities structured to be completed within several days. These major sections include "preparing for the event," "conducting the event," "presenting the findings," and "follow-up." The first two sections will be discussed in this chapter, except that data collection and analysis will be discussed in Chapter 5. The reason data collection and analysis is discussed separately is due to the many tools and methods that are required to support these activities. The sections entitled "presenting the findings" and "follow-up" will be discussed in Chapters 6 to 8, along with several examples of common office workflows. These workflows include finance, accounting, sales and marketing, product design, human resources, and procurement.

Prepare for the Kaizen Event

We have already discussed the importance of ensuring that improvement activities are aligned with an organization's strategic goals and objectives, and that these should be reflected in a project's charter. In this context, deployment leaders have a major responsibility to identify where Kaizen events should be deployed and the business problems they will focus on. Also, deployment leaders have a responsibility for ensuring the Kaizen teams have the resources required to execute their project. The purpose of these deployment activities is to help provide the anticipated business benefits, as described by the project charter, for their organization.

The activities required to prepare for a Kaizen event are listed in Table 4.1. Event preparation is the first major section of activities. The preparation of an event begins several weeks prior to bringing a team together. These preparation activities include developing an actionable project charter, assigning team members, securing facilities and other resources, and communicating the event to the people who are involved with the improvement activities. Important information describing a project should also be incorporated into its charter. Recall that chapter 2 discussed several important concepts related to project identification as well as the creation and prioritization of project charters. Once a project charter is developed, a team leader, team members, and a facilitator are assigned as members of the core Kaizen team. Their selection is based on the project's problem statement and objectives. The project charter also describes the area in which the team will focus their improvement efforts as well as the process owner and local work team. Additional information includes the required supporting personnel and the project's anticipated business benefits. It should also be noted that an important factor in the success of these events is the availability of historical data describing the process as well as financial and operational metrics. This information should be gathered by an organization's deployment leader and the Kaizen team's leader several weeks prior to a rapid improvement event. This will accelerate a team's root cause analysis and improvement activities. Identifying a team's members, in advance, also enables an organization to begin communicating an event's goals and objectives. This will help a team obtain organizational support for their activities. In an office environment these activities are particularly important because team members tend to be very busy professionals working across several organizational functions. In many

Table 4.1   1. Prepare for the Kaizen Event

a. Select project charter.
b. Assign project leader and team members.
c. Reserve a conference room.
d. Obtain supplies and equipment.
e. Ensure facilities are available including breakout rooms.
f. Ensure support personnel are available to assist the team.
g. Collect process information of floor layouts, work flows, and procedures.
h. Collect information of operational cycle times including:
Setup time
Processing time
Inspection time
Transport
Waiting
i. Take pictures of the area to be improved.
j. Obtain example of process breakdowns.
k. Obtain examples of best in class process conditions.
l. Develop schedule of Kaizen event.
m. Communicate the event.
n. Mark area for event, if practical.
o. Set up flip charts and organize other materials as required.

situations, they may be located across the world. In these organizations, communication is one of the most important planning activities of a deployment leader.

Other important preparatory activities include reserving meeting rooms and conferencing facilities that include video and audio capability, providing catering services, and purchasing the necessary supplies and materials for group activities. Video and audio conferencing facilities are critically important if a team is geographically dispersed across the world. In these situations, a core team may be working at one location but need to confirm its root cause analyses and improvement recommendations with other teams in other locations. An example would be when one part of a process workflow resides in, say, the United States, but the balance of the workflow resides in India or China. In these situations, the client-facing portion of the workflow may need to be modified to make the operational-facing activities more efficient. Modifications include adding or eliminating operations, or changing their operational sequences, and adding or deleting approval authorizations, or creating entirely new workflows to replace those that currently exist. Relative to other supporting materials and information, every situation is different, but the concept is to have everything a team may need to complete its work activities in one place so time is not lost looking for them. It is also very important that a Kaizen event be held within or near the work area being analyzed so a team can see firsthand the layout of operations, equipment, materials, procedures, and other materials and information comprising a process. This will also enable a team to make their improvements without traveling back to a work location. In addition, a conference or breakout room (also called a war room) should be made available to a Kaizen team both during and for a period of time after an improvement event. The reason for reserving conference rooms for an extended period of time is that not all the improvement activities may be completed during a Kaizen event. This may occur for various reasons, so a team may need to access the information gathered during an event over time. Also, a team's value stream map (VSM) and other relevant information should remain visible and available for an extended period of time to enable the process owner and local work team to use the information to make additional process improvements. It is interesting that in manufacturing organizations, these reserved rooms are a common practice because process improvement activities are ongoing. It is also interesting to note that, in my experience, war rooms seldom exist in office environments. The absence of war rooms in office environments sends a message that process improvement activities are isolated events. In many organizations, a lack of continuous-improvement activities reflects a general apathy toward the need for process improvement by office professionals and their management. The result has been a continued focus on improvement activities in an organization's back-office operations rather than the client- and supplier-facing operations, which are dominated by finance, accounting, sales and marketing, product design, human resources, and procurement. It has been my experience that sustained process improvement in these functions is seldom encouraged by an organization's senior management, despite the many articles and research we may read to the contrary. Noncompliance and a lack of engagement in service organizations are, in my opinion, rampant. In fact, if it were not for increased automation, productivity in many of these organizations would most likely be much lower or negative.

In addition to reserving conferencing rooms and materials necessary to support team activities, various support personnel will usually be necessary to help collect and analyze process information and then help make the required process changes. These changes often include moving equipment and office partitions, obtaining information from computerized systems, or making minor changes to computer coding. In manufacturing applications, these support people may include plumbers, electricians, and similar people if equipment must be moved or upgraded to support improvement activities. In service operations, support people may include financial analysts, software programmers, and facility management people. In the balance of this chapter we will discuss the activities necessary to select a team's project charter, prepare for a Kaizen event, communicate an event, develop an event kickoff agenda, and conduct the Kaizen event.

Select a Project Charter

An organization should be continuously identifying ways to increase its productivity and shareholder economic value added (EVA). Recall that the financial components of productivity and shareholder economic value added (EVA) were discussed in Chapter 1 relative to project selection. Identifying productivity opportunities is a formal process that results in the creation of project charters. These project charters are then deployed across an organization to help achieve its goals and objectives. The activities necessary to create and prioritize project charters were discussed in Chapter 2. In our current discussion, we will assume that a project charter has been created and forms the basis for deployment of a Kaizen team. In this context, the project charter directs a team to a specific process workflow or a portion of a workflow that requires improvement. In its root cause analysis, a team uses a project charter's objectives to clearly align its goals and objectives. In summary, the objective of a Kaizen event is to execute the team's project charter objectives.

Event leaders or coordinators use the checklist shown in Figure 4.1 to plan and schedule an event's activities. The goal is to ensure that all major activities are executed on schedule, leaving only miscellaneous activities to be completed after an event. It should also be noted that complicated projects may require extensive process and data analysis or capital expenditure to attack the root causes of their process breakdowns. However, complicated projects may not be good candidates for a Kaizen event, which last only three to five days, if their root cause analysis and improvements are expected to take weeks or months to execute.

Assign a Project Leader and Team Members

A Kaizen event leader is assigned to every Kaizen event to ensure that its planning activities are properly planned and executed so the event remains on schedule and achieves its objectives. As a result, project leaders should be experienced in leading Kaizen events. If an organization is just beginning a Lean Six Sigma deployment, it should use consultants as project leaders and facilitators. However, over time, an organization should be able to train internal project leaders to lead its Kaizen events. Also, the roles of project leader and process owner should not be filled by the same person. This separation of roles will help to ensure that team discussions are objective and based on fact and all perspectives are considered. This is especially important in the identification and execution of improvement opportunities that impact a process owner and their local work team. As an example, a root cause analysis may show portions of a process workflow should be done elsewhere, or the people currently associated with a workflow may be redundant or perhaps should be assigned elsewhere to increase overall organizational productivity. In these situations, very few process owners would want to lose their resources. They may also have other reasons for not supporting the necessary process changes recommended by a Kaizen team. Another reason for a separation of the team leader and process owner is that a process owner must run the day-to-day operations of the process, whereas the team leader must move his or her team through many focused activities to keep an event on schedule.

Role separation is also important regarding the team leader and the event facilitator. The event facilitator is a person who does not take an active role in a Kaizen event, but instead observes team dynamics during an event. The facilitators also work with the leaders of the event to ensure that the proper facilitation tools and methods are used to involve every team member in the event's activities. An event facilitator also works with an improvement team to evaluate the organizational impact of the team's recommendations on the process owner and local work team, as well as the larger organization. When properly done, facilitation activities will help keep an event on schedule and enhance communication to the rest of the organization.

Team members should be chosen from the process that will be impacted by the improvements of an event. Additional team members may be suppliers or customers of the process depending on the objectives of the project charter. Chapter 3 discussed the fact that teams mature through four stages called forming, norming, storming, and performing. Also, it was mentioned in chapter 3 that team members will always have different perspectives regarding data collection, analysis, and improvement activities. This is especially true if the team is diverse. In summary, a team should be diverse, have the necessary skills to the support their project, and be properly led and facilitated to ensure a Kaizen event's success.

Reserve a Conference Room

A Kaizen team needs a well-equipped conference room that is reserved for a minimum of one week. This room is also called a war room and should be adjacent to the area in which the Kaizen event is being held. A Kaizen team uses this meeting space to build their value stream map (VSM) and display information related to their process analysis activities. A VSM is a graphical display of how materials and information flow through a process as well as the key financial and operational metrics used to evaluate its operational performance. The VSM is built on one of the walls of the conference room using brown paper. In this process, brown paper is attached to a wall and the operations making up a process workflow are represented using sticky notes. These notes are placed on the brown paper to match the flow of materials and information through the process. Each note contains metrics such as cycle time, process yields, and similar metrics for a single operation. The notes enable a Kaizen team to focus their improvement efforts on operations that have the greatest impact on their process. Additional information is also posted on the brown paper. This information includes examples of management reports, data collection forms, and other templates used to move materials and information through the process. Initially, a VSM is built using information provided by the local work team. However, this initial VSM is validated by walking the process to verify its accuracy. Recall that in Chapter 3 we discussed many of the important Lean tools and methods used to analyze a value stream map (VSM).

Obtain Supplies and Equipment

The war room should also have all the necessary supplies and equipment needed by a team because an event is fast paced and a team does not have time to look for materials and supplies when it is necessary to collect and analyze process information. The obvious items required include pencils, paper, tape, staplers, rulers, sticky notes, brown paper, flip charts, and markers. There should also be reference materials and books to help the team when they have technical questions that their leader or facilitator cannot answer. The larger conference room should also have phone lines, video and audio conferencing capability, a camera to photograph the work operations, as well as projectors, fax machines, printers, and similar equipment as required to execute team activities.

Ensure Facilities Are Available, Including Breakout Rooms

In addition to conference rooms, additional breakout rooms may be necessary depending on the size of a team and its activities. This is especially true if a team is large and consists of several smaller work groups which are working groups of activities in parallel to each other. Also, it is important that the work area from which data is collected is directly accessible by a team. In manufacturing environments, conference rooms are reserved close to the process workflow being analyzed. In service systems, the same concept applies except there may be several components comprising a process workflow that span different geographical locations. If a management presentation will be made in the room after an event, then it should be air-conditioned and comfortable and able to accommodate people around a conference table. It was mentioned in the previous section that access to communication should also be available in the form of conference lines and wireless Internet. However, it should be clearly stated up front that the participants must pay attention to the event activities and should not get distracted by wireless Internet during team activities.

Ensure Support Personnel Are Available to Assist the Team

Support personnel are subject matter experts who are required to assist a Kaizen team through its activities. In manufacturing systems, these people could be plumbers and electricians who are available to make minor changes within a process or when equipment is moved within the work area. In service industries these people could be software programmers, finance, and similar subject matter experts. It is important that their support is guaranteed up front, prior to an event, to ensure that scheduled activities are completed on time. This is especially true when team members and support personnel are dispersed geographically or have specialized skills and knowledge that is needed elsewhere within an organization.

Collect Process Information of Floor Layouts, Workflows, and Procedures

Floor layouts are quite detailed and show the location of work stations, meeting rooms, as well as similar details related to the location of people and equipment. In addition, depending on the extent of prior improvement activities, there may also be process maps of workflows as well as work procedures. It is useful to use this information to evaluate the flow of materials and information between work stations using a spaghetti diagram similar to the one depicted in Figure 5.12. As an introduction, these diagrams are constructed by drawing lines between work stations showing how materials and information are exchanged between them. In many situations, the flow of work is inefficient. As an example, it is usually found that the total distance traveled or the cycle time is longer than if the work was routed more efficiently. There may also be rework loops in a process that also increase a process's cycle time. The goal would be to use the floor layouts and workflow information to understand the reasons for the overly complicated workflows and eliminate them. Finally, to the extent that process maps have been quantified relative to time, quality, and cost, they will serve as good sources of information for data collection, analysis, and improvement activities.

Operational and financial reports and similar information are also available to a Kaizen team. This information will be useful to helping a team analyze its process workflows. Ideally, this type of historical information should be collected by an event's sponsor prior to assembling a Kaizen team because data collection and analysis activities will be accelerated as a result.

The exact types of information required for a Kaizen event depend on a team's project charter. In manufacturing systems, information related to floor layouts, electrical wiring, and plumbing systems will be especially important because a team will most likely need to rearrange the location of equipment, electrical, plumbing, and pneumatic lines toward the end of a Kaizen event. In contrast, office projects usually require a different set of activities. However, relative to moving physical objects, a similar approach is taken in regard to the activities that are necessary to identify and eliminate the causes for process breakdowns. As an example, in office environments, most of the data collection and process improvements will require changes to the flow of information rather than the materials that move through the system. In some Kaizen events, partitions and equipment may also need to be physically rearranged and work stations moved. Also, entire process workflows or major components of several workflows may be outsourced to other locations around the world. In this context, most data collection and improvement activities within an office environment will be focused on information technology (IT).

Data collection activities in office environments also require that a Kaizen team work with IT specialists to download data fields for analysis. Also, new data collection systems may be temporarily implemented to obtain information relative to key operational metrics. As an example, time stamps may be temporarily placed on a transaction sequence to record the cycle times between one operation and another. However, in some office systems, time stamps may be manually deployed on a temporary basis. An example would be in a design engineering department in which design changes could be either electronically or manually tracked through the department on an interim basis. As a second example, invoices could be tracked through a procurement process by time-stamping them as they move between operations. In recent years, IT capability has been significantly expanded to include business modeling and analyses (BMA), business intelligence (BI), business activity monitoring (BAM), and workflow management (WM) systems. Several major characteristics of these systems were described in Chapter 3 in the section entitled "10. Continually Update Process Technologies." To summarize that discussion, modern IT systems often provide significant amounts of process information. This information is very useful in focusing a team's attention to areas that need improvement. Also, some of these systems can be modified to provide information to help a Kaizen team with its root cause analysis activities. Process improvements are also relatively easy to make when using some of these IT systems. As an example, some workflow tools enable an analyst to quickly build data collection forms to record the details related to transactions entering a system. In addition, built-in time stamps can be integrated within these systems for future process analysis and improvement. In fact, data fields can be added or deleted in minutes. Finally, these tools can be used to implement one or more process improvements relative to the simplification or elimination of manual work tasks. Typical examples of these work tasks include approval verifications, mistake-proofing data fields, and providing exception reports to flag nonstandard system transactions. There are many other IT tools that can help Kaizen teams improve office environments. This is why having IT experts on a Kaizen team focused on improving office operations is important.

Collect Information on Operational Cycle Times

Conducting a Kaizen event in manufacturing is a straightforward process in which standard operational metrics are collected from the work operations that were identified using a value stream map (VSM). These metrics were discussed in Chapter 3 and include percentages of value-adding (VA), non-value-adding (NVA), and business value-adding (BVA) operations as well as production rates, scrap and rework percentages, equipment downtime percentages, available capacity, setup times, inventory quantities, and the total floor area required by a process. In its data collection activities, a Kaizen team moves into a process to collect information for each operational metric at every operation as described by its VSM. These assessment activities will produce a snapshot of how a process is performing. They also help verify or disprove the original VSM assumptions and show a Kaizen team where it should focus its efforts.

Data collection in service operations is both easier and more difficult than in manufacturing. As an example, transactions between operations are usually electronic rather than physical. If the transactions are also date-stamped operation by operation, then calculating waiting and processing times as well as overall cycle times will be relatively easy. But if this information is not readily available, then IT assistance will be required to obtain the data if it exists. For this reason, it is important that IT professionals be available to support a Kaizen team to enable it to quickly access electronic information. In fact, it would be most helpful if IT information could be extracted and downloaded into spreadsheets prior to a Kaizen event. Also, in addition to completing a physical walkthrough of a process, a Kaizen team, in an office environment, would most likely review the sequence of logic steps used to build the software code that describes a process workflow. This logic sequence includes data input and output as well as the mathematical logic used to run a process.

Another operational assessment issue that is unique to service operations is the behavioral characteristics of service professionals. These are usually difficult to quantify during an event unless specialized data collection methods are used. This is in contrast to manufacturing operations that consist of machines having constant cycle times at well-defined locations. The evaluation of service professionals requires understanding how their activities are performed and integrated with IT systems. Then the time elements of their work tasks must be estimated by an analyst. Recall that these time elements were also shown in Figure 3.9 and included waiting, setup, processing, unloading, inspection, and movement to the next operation. In these systems, data collection takes an inordinate amount of time if the Kaizen team does not have access to date-stamped information. Also, because a Kaizen event is completed in several days, it may be very difficult to quantify cycle times and defect frequencies of highly manual work tasks with sufficient reliability unless data collection activities are carefully planned in advance. In Chapter 5, we will discuss data collection strategies within office operations and provide data collection templates.

Taking Pictures of the Area to Be Improved

In addition to collecting quantitative data, a Kaizen team may also need to take pictures of the work area being improved. Ideally, pictures can be taken of situations where a process has performed and when it has not. A picture conveys a significant amount of information that will enable a team to quickly understand various process issues and more quickly reach a consensus on how to approach a root cause analysis or create solutions for a process problem. Countermeasures to eliminate the root causes of a process problem will also be easier to correlate to process problems. Another advantage of using pictures is that they can be directly attached to a VSM. This information will show a Kaizen team the spatial relationships among equipment, people, and materials, as well as their quantities. Pictures may also be useful to show the process owner and management the "before" versus "after" of a team's improvements activities. This is especially true if the work area was cluttered and other process issues could be seen in the pictures. In manufacturing environments pictures are also useful to show the general state of equipment, the cleanliness of work areas, the presence of excess materials, as well as the relative location of machines and people both before and after process improvements such as 5S.

However, pictures have not been used as extensively in service operations. But they are very useful in showing examples of management reports, data collection forms, examples of defects, computer screen shots, as well as the physical configuration of office work stations. Also, because a major goal of a Kaizen team is cleaning up a work area and applying other 5S methods, pictures may be useful in communicating the before versus after improvements of a Kaizen team's activities.

Obtaining Examples of Process Breakdowns

It is important that as a team engages in its data collection activities it collects work examples showing how a process breaks down during its data collection activities. In manufacturing systems, typical examples of process breakdowns include defective products and components, pictures of work areas clearly showing the process issues, management reports, exception reports, computer screen shots, customer and supplier complaints, and similar information. But this information cannot be a substitute for actually seeing a problem firsthand. A process walkthrough or physical audit of a work area is required to verify the accuracy of the information that a Kaizen team has been provided in advance of their event. In summary, a Kaizen team must see a process problem firsthand and not rely on anecdotal comments from other people.

Obtaining Examples of Best-in-Class Process Conditions

Six Sigma and Lean project examples have shown that most processes perform better under certain operating conditions than under others. If data of "good" operational performance is available to a Kaizen team, it may be possible to analyze the specific process conditions associated with good process performance. These examples may enable a team to more quickly identify the root causes of poor process performance or accelerate process improvements. In Six Sigma, this approach is called an entitlement analysis. An entitlement analysis shows what an organization is "entitled to" if its process operates under the best possible conditions. It also implies that there is an upper limit of process performance based on the design of a process.

Examples of good work should be gathered from a process when it is meeting all required quality and rate-based work standards. Knowing that the work can be performed well under certain conditions will enable a Kaizen team to more quickly identify the root causes for poor process performance. As an example, suppose an analysis shows that ten people answered similar types of incoming calls, but two of the employees completed their calls in one minute versus two other employees, who took three minutes to complete their calls, while the remaining six employees completed their calls in two minutes. The statistic measuring the average length of a call is the average handling time (AHT). Employees are also evaluated using a quality metric that measures the accuracy of the information they provide to customers. An evaluation of the ten employees would require plotting their AHT and quality scores on a two-dimensional graph. Those employees having a low AHT and high quality rating would be considered to be the entitlement group. An assumption is that the AHT and quality scores collected are representative of the process under its normal operating conditions. At this point in an analysis it may make sense to ask why the AHT or quality scores of the poorly performing employees did not match the entitlement group. This approach would begin an investigation in which the performance of some employees having very low AHT and quality scores would be compared to that of employees having high AHT and quality scores. As another example, suppose that the types and frequencies of errors have been collected for three work shifts over several weeks, and that one work shift had a significantly lower error rate than the other shifts. It would make sense to investigate why one shift performs at a higher quality level than others. In summary, comparing best to worse performance is often a useful method to investigate process problems.

Developing a Schedule for the Kaizen Event

The focus of this book is to provide a predefined set of activities that will provide office Kaizen teams with a simple checklist of the activities required for the planning and execution of their Kaizen event. A Kaizen team only has to place predefined dates on the activities listed in Figure 4.1 to create a specific activity schedule for their Kaizen event. However, it should be noted that scheduled dates for the planning portion of a Kaizen event may vary significantly by organization. This variation is due to the available resources as well as project prioritization goals and objectives. In summary, Figure 4.1 provides a standardized checklist for event sponsors, leaders, and facilitators.

Communicating the Event

Communication improves organizational support for Kaizen events. As an example, Kaizen team members, support personnel, the process owner, and local work team must be aware of a planned Kaizen event in order to support its various work activities. Event communication is a set of activities that occur in several forms. These include e-mails, organizational announcements, newsletters, management presentations, and face-to-face meetings, as well as others. It should be noted that communication formats will vary depending on the emotional content of the intended messages and their complexity. Highly complicated messages, which may have a significant impact on others, may need to be carefully communicated. In fact, it is usually best to communicate this information in person. On the other hand, conference calls may be useful when discussing routine planning activities and associated meeting and team logistics. E-mails, newsletters, and the Internet may be useful in communicating simpler messages to the larger organization. Regardless of the communication format, it is important that its message be simple and consistent.

Marking Areas for the Event

In manufacturing, the area in which an event will be held is marked off, using tape, rope, or other methods, to help a Kaizen team identify what is or is not in a work area. As an example, when a work area has been marked off, support people can easily understand the relationships among equipment, people, tools, and other resources, as well as the layout of utilities. This is important because 5S methods, and sorting in particular, will be used to separate materials and equipment that should remain in the work area from those that should not. However, in service or office environments, work areas are seldom formally marked off, because the process workflows reside within information systems (IT). However, there will be situations in which Kaizen events in office environments will require that work areas be isolated and marked off. As an example, partitions may have to be moved, and old reports and similar materials or equipment must be removed from a work area. In these situations work areas must be marked off for safety reasons.

Setting Up Flip Charts and Organizing Other Materials

It was mentioned earlier, in this chapter, that each of the breakout rooms will require materials for the subteams to complete their activities. Flip charts and other supporting materials should be set up in each work area. This will enable the breakout teams to easily communicate with each other by drawing pictures on flip charts and making visible notes as their group works through its discussion activities. Other materials and equipment may also be required by a team. These include sticky notes, copiers, printers, and similar tools, as well as other communications aids.

Date

From: Event Leader

Subject: Upcoming Kaizen Event in Area TBD

To: Distribution of Impacted People

Hello Everyone,

As you know, we have identified several areas within our facility that would benefit from application of the Lean Six Sigma tools and methods. Recall, we were recently trained to identify and eliminate root causes for poor operational performance. Area TBD is the first area we have targeted for improvement, since it has high levels of scrap and rework that are costing our facility $TBD annually. We will need your combined support to make this five-day event a success. I will be meeting with each of you over the next several days to discuss how we should prepare for this event.

Regards,

Event Leader

Figure 4.2   Kaizen event communication letter.

Kaizen Event Communication Letter

Kaizen event communication letters appear in several formats because different organizations have their own standardized approach to communicating process changes. However, Figure 4.2 provides a simple and standardized announcement letter that can be modified to suit your team's needs. Key elements of a communication letter should include the reason for the event, where it will be held, its expected business benefits, who will take part in the event, and the specific support, if any, required from the recipients of the communication letter. Communication letters are particularly important in multicultural and geographically dispersed teams. This is because the logistical process of bringing the resources together for a Kaizen event is enormous given the great distances between team members as well as differences in time zones, which may make meetings difficult.

However, communication between highly diverse teams does not have to be difficult. As an example, a few years ago I consulted with an Asian team of a major international organization to deploy Lean Six Sigma across several countries. The team members were from Japan, Korea, China, India, and Singapore. Throughout the early stages of the deployment, we had a weekly conference call at a mutually agreed-upon time. To facilitate communication between the country teams, the reporting updates from each country were more quantitative than qualitative and the country teams had a leader who could speak and interpret English.

After the operational assessments were completed, black belt training was taught in Japanese, Korean, and English using simultaneous translation. The countries completed their projects on schedule and delivered significant business benefits to their participants. Good team communication greatly enhanced this multicultural team's productivity.

Kaizen Event Kickoff Agenda

At the start of a Kaizen event, the team reviews the event agenda (similar to the one shown in Table 4.2) as a group. It is important that this review take place prior to starting process improvement work. This review begins what is called a kickoff meeting. The purpose of a kickoff meeting is to discuss the upcoming schedule of planned activities that will take place over the next several days. During this meeting, team members may also be provided with training in the tools and methods of Lean, Six Sigma, and other tools and methods that will help a team collect and analyze data from their process workflows. A team kickoff meeting ensures that a Kaizen event is conducted in a standardized manner, that everyone has a basic understanding of the tools and methods integral to an event, and provides an opportunity for team members and local management to ask questions regarding their various roles and responsibilities. A kickoff meeting is also a good forum in which to discuss any operational and financial data that has been collected

Table 4.2   Kaizen Event Kickoff Agenda

1. Kickoff meeting.
2. Learn how to build value stream maps.
3. Building value stream maps.
3.a. Assign people to specific work streams.
3.b. People go out into the process to collect information on key metrics and the management reports and daily forms that are used in the process.
3.c. People return with data collection forms completed, and key metric information is put onto the value stream map.
4. Analyzing value steam maps.
4.a. Lean basics.
4.b. Calculating takt time.
4.c. Lead time reduction.
4.d. 5S opportunities.
4.e. Mistake-proofing opportunities.
5. Changing the process.

in advance by the team's leader and facilitators. This advance information often includes process maps, floor layouts, work and inspection procedures, operational and financial reports, as well as examples of good and poor process performance. Having this type of information prior to conducting a Kaizen event puts a team on a fast learning curve, which is essential to executing the scheduled activities over several days. Advance information is particularly important when process workflows are complex. Also, it may take a long time to obtain information from highly automated systems. This is especially true if several databases must be accessed to create process models.

Once preliminary information has been transferred to a team, the team begins to build either a value stream map (VSM) or a simple floor layout to show spatial relationships between equipment and people. A floor layout is created if a team is focused on a work area having only a few interrelated operations. However, if a team is focused on a major process workflow, then it will construct a VSM or a functional process map to show the flow of materials and information through the process. Once a map has been created, team members are assigned to collect data from specific operations within a process. This information varies by organization and process workflow, but at a minimum it should include the nine key operational metrics listed in Table 4.3 and discussed in Section 2.f of this chapter. In addition, key management reports, data collection forms, and similar information-tracking tools used in the process should be gathered to place on the VSM. Important tools used in these activities were discussed in Chapter 3. Some of them include a takt time calculation, 5S methods, and mistake proofing.

Conducting the Event

Bring Team Together to Discuss Roles and Responsibilities

Table 1.3 listed and defined the key roles and responsibilities of a Kaizen event's team members, and their important roles and responsibilities were discussed in Chapter 1. Roles and responsibilities should be determined in advance of a kickoff meeting. However, during the meeting, some people may prefer to take a different role than the one that was originally assigned to them. This is acceptable if they have the prerequisite skills. Also, if there are subteams involved in an event, then roles and responsibilities may be duplicated across the subteams. As an example, if an event is taking place through videoconferencing, then team members at remote locations may have duplicate roles, such as subteam leader, facilitator, and local subject matter expert. There may also be translators if a videoconference requires that different languages be spoken. Roles and responsibilities may also be rotated during an event, depending on a team's needs. In summary, a team should establish clearly defined roles and responsibilities, but also be flexible in their assignment.

Table 4.3   2. Conduct the Kaizen Event

a. Bring team together to discuss roles and responsibilities.
b. Discuss financial and operational objectives of Kaizen event.
c. Conduct training as required.
d. Create detailed value stream maps and layouts of the process workflow.
e. Facilitate to ensure full participation of the team.
f. Collect data at every operation relevant to:
1. VA/NVA/BVA.
2. Production rate (units/minute) or cycle time.
3. Scrap %.
4. Rework%.
5. Downtime %.
6. Capacity (units/minute).
7. Setup time (minutes).
8. Inventory (units in queue).
9. Floor area.
g. Analyze all data and develop prioritized improvement ideas.
h. Change the process according to a prioritization listing.
i. Apply 5S and mistake-proofing methods.

Discuss Operational and Financial Objectives of the Kaizen Event

The goals and objectives of Kaizen events may differ, although they have similar activities and use common tools and methods. As an example, simple office improvements may not require an in-depth discussion of financial goals and objectives. However, this will not be true for those Kaizen events that significantly impact major process workflows or touch key customers and suppliers. If a Kaizen event is expected to have a major impact on an organization relative to its resource requirements or benefits, or has risks, then a team should know this information. This type of information is usually provided in management presentations. Also, a discussion of operational and financial objectives will be audience-specific because the information may be sensitive.

Conduct Team Training as Required

Team training may also be important if participants of the Kaizen event have had no formal training in Lean and Six Sigma methods. This is not uncommon. As a result, a few hours is usually set aside on the first day of an event to train people in some of the more basic Lean and Six Sigma tools and methods. This training is designed to provide a bare minimum level of competence to enable team members to collect and analyze data from their process workflows. In this context, Chapter 3 provides a good review of the required tools, methods, and other important Lean concepts. Chapters 5 and 6 present additional Lean and some basic Six Sigma tools and methods that can be incorporated into team training activities. The amount of facilitation that will be required to support team training will depend on the team's initial experience with Lean and Six Sigma concepts. As an example, if no team members have been trained in Lean or Six Sigma methods, then extra facilitators will be required to support the team during its Kaizen event.

Create Detailed Value Stream Maps and Layouts of the Process Workflow

In Chapter 3 we discussed the fact that VSMs are an important tool because they show the arrangement of machines, people, and equipment as well as the operational metrics that quantify the flow of materials and information through a process workflow. Chapter 3 also discussed the fact that operational reports, data collection forms, and similar data collection and analysis tools used to manage process transactions should be placed on a VSM. A Kaizen team begins to understand the advantages of using the VSM approach when it goes out into a process and collects operational data for analysis and its VSM is updated with quantitative data. Building a VSM is an organized process in which people are assigned to specific work flows or operations to collect data. The collected data includes the system throughput rate, operational cycle times, and similar metrics, including those listed in Table 4.3. Once a VSM has been constructed and analyzed, a Kaizen team will have a good idea of where operational improvements need to be made within their process workflow. It should be noted that if a team is analyzing just a few integrated operations within a single operation or a few linked operations, then a floor layout may be more useful than a VSM. It is also important to use the voice of the customer (VOC) to identify value-adding (VA) versus non-value-adding (NVA) operations.

Facilitate to Ensure Full Participation of Team

A Kaizen team must be properly facilitated to ensure the full participation of all its members. In addition, a team must be properly balanced in that its members should represent both the process that is the focus of the Kaizen event and processes immediately upstream (suppliers) and downstream (customers) of the process. To ensure full participation of team members, there are several well-established facilitation methods that have been shown to be useful. These include ensuring that an agenda is developed

Table 4.4   Important Event Facilitation Methods

1. A project charter should reflect a business opportunity and be scoped for execution over several days.
2. The Kaizen team should be selected to reflect the project charter's scope and process boundaries.
3. The team should be balanced relative to its experience and work styles.
4. The team should be facilitated be people familiar with team activities and dynamics.
5. The Kaizen event should have a prepublished agenda with roles, responsibilities, and activities.
6. Team members should fully participate in team activities.
7. Team members should be trained as necessary in the proper use of tools and methods for problem identification, data collection, analysis, and changing their process.
8. Facilitators should obtain team feedback every day and make improvements to the Kaizen event as necessary.
9. Keep the event's schedule and make adjustments based on changing circumstances.
10. Celebrate success!

for the Kaizen event and everyone adheres to an event's schedule. In addition, it is important that everyone be encouraged to speak and contribute their ideas.

Table 4.4 lists several important facilitation methods that are useful in managing Kaizen events. First, some of the more important enablers of event facilitation occur up front in an event's planning phase. As an example, it is important that a team's project charter reflect a real business opportunity, is properly scoped for execution over the several days comprising an event, and is quantified to enable a team to measure the success of an event. Second, it is important that team members be selected to reflect the project charter's scope and process boundaries. This means the team should consist, at a minimum, of the people who do the work within a process as well as suppliers and customers to the process. In addition, a team should be balanced with respect to its member's experience and work styles. Once a team meets, it should be facilitated by people experienced with the coordination of group activities and their dynamics. Experienced facilitators may be internal or external to the organization. The fifth important facilitation method is to use a prepublished agenda with roles, responsibilities, and scheduled activities. An agenda communicates to an event's participants the scope and expectations for the event.

An integral part of a Kaizen event's facilitation is ensuring that its team members fully participate in team activities. As a result, team members should also be trained as necessary in the proper use of tools and methods of problem identification, data collection, analysis, and changing their process operations. Also, to keep an event focused and on schedule, its experienced facilitators should obtain team feedback every day. This will enable adjustments to be made to an event's objectives or schedule based on changing circumstances. Finally, it is important to recognize and reward a Kaizen team at the end of a successful event that provides quantifiable business benefits.

Collect Data at Every Operation

Table 4.5 lists the key operational metrics that are the focus of data collection; they were also listed in Table 4.3. One of the most important data collection and analysis activities a team undertakes is construction of a value stream map of a process workflow or a floor layout of a single work area. In Chapter 5, we will provide examples or how data should be collected to build a VSM and analyzed by a Kaizen team. In this section we will discuss data collection and analysis relative to these metrics at a high level.

As a Kaizen team begins to collect process data in an office environment it will face challenges because the flow of information occurs across one or more information technology (IT) systems rather than physically between machines and people. This requires developing data collection strategies that can capture fast-flowing information, which is also heavily dependent on the working habits of employees. This is especially true in client-facing operations as opposed to back-office operations. These processes are characterized by low levels of standardization. Low standardization makes work sampling and similar data collection activities more difficult in office systems. As an example, estimating production rates of a machine is easier than measuring the work habits and performance of professional people, because the relationships between material and labor inputs and their associated transformed outputs are clearly established by the design of a machine. In other words, machines are designed to execute standard work tasks in repetitive cycles. However, useful information related to production rates and cycle times can also be collected in office systems with modifications. As a first approximation, a system production rate can be estimated by counting the transactions exiting the process and dividing by the hours of production. In this calculation, a production rate can be estimated by operation, time of day, job type, shift, employee, customer, and other demographical factors that will enable a Kaizen team to do an analysis of their process. This stratification strategy can also be used to collect data for each of the nine metrics shown in Table 4.5. At a second level of detail, information technology (IT) systems can be used to time-stamp and collect other relevant information on the transactions flowing within a process. This information can then be downloaded for analysis. However, accessing this system information may take several days or weeks. For this reason, it is usually a good idea to collect information from IT systems in advance of a Kaizen event.

Table 4.5 Data Collection Strategies in Service Operations

Metric	Data Collection Strategy	How to Do It
1. VA/NVA/BVA.	Create a value stream map of a process workflow or a floor layout of a single work area.	Bring the team together and create the VSM using sticky notes on a wall. Then "walk-the-process" to verify the VSM.
2. Production rate (units/minute) or operation cycle time.	Count the transactions exiting the process and divide by the hours or operation. This can be done by operation, time of day, job type, shift, employee, customer and other demographic factors which will enable a complete analysis (This type of factor stratification strategy can be used in the analysis of all 9 metrics.)	Ideally, the system will time-stamp all transactions within a process workflow. Alternatively, an audit could be done on completed transactions in e-mail by operation (sent mail). Also, checking personal calendars will show meeting times that in many situations are non-value-adding. People can also be "shadowed" for several days and their activity times recorded at 15-minute time increments. With respect to equipment, materials processed by equipment could be measured or counters designed into equipment can be checked to calculate production rates.
3. Scrap %.	Count the number of transactions that could not be used in production, i.e., reports that were not required, marketing prototypes not sold, etc.	Check financial and operational reports for material or direct labor waste. Audit operations through interviews, e-mail audits, and shadowing to identify scrap.
4. Rework%.	Count the number of transactions that passed through process operations more than once, i.e., any work task with a prefix of *re* such as re-analyze, re-inspect, redo, etc.	Check financial and operational reports for material or direct labor rework. Audit operations through interviews, e-mail audits, and shadowing to identify rework.

5. Downtime %.	Count the time people wait for work, the system is idle, or equipment is not available.	Check financial and operational reports for material, direct labor, and other expenses related to downtime. Audit operations through interviews, e-mails, and shadowing to identify downtime.
6. Capacity (units/minute).	Count the number of units per time produced at the system's bottleneck operation.	Use a VSM with operational reports to identify the bottleneck capacity under typical production conditions. If operational reports are not available, conduct audits to obtain data.
7. Setup time (minutes).	Measure the time to set up a job at every operation and especially at the bottleneck.	Check operational reports for job setup times. Audit operations through interviews, e-mails, and shadowing to identify job setup.
8. Inventory (units in queue).	Measure the work waiting to be done at every operation.	Check operational reports for inventory levels (jobs waiting to be completed and estimate how long it will take to complete these jobs). Audit operations through interviews, e-mail audits, and shadowing to identify inventory levels.
9. Floor area.	Measure the floor area used by a process, including equipment and people.	Review floor layouts and calculate area.

134 ■ *Lean Six Sigma for the Office*

At a more detailed level of analysis, information can be controlled by auditing and taking samples of transactions at an employee level. These completed transactions could include analyzing the types of e-mails that are routinely handled by employees and classifying them based on various stratification criteria. As an example, e-mails could be classified as value-adding or non-value-adding, and according to their reason for being sent, the departments involved in the e-mail transaction, the estimated time spent on each e-mail, and similar demographical information. In addition to these types of audits, an analysis of personal calendars will show the number of employee meetings and time duration. This information can be further broken down by classifying meetings based on their value-adding content, reasons, and demographical factors. Also, it is not unusual to find that employees spend between 25 and 75 percent of their time in meetings. Based on my experience, most meetings are poorly organized, facilitated, and managed, resulting in a significant loss of employee productive time.

Another useful method that can be used to collect operational data from office workflows is the shadowing of people for one or more days. In shadowing activities, people are audited for several hours or days and their activities are recorded at sequential time intervals. Shadowing has been successfully used in manufacturing for many years to observe and improve work tasks of production workers as well as manufacturing professionals. In an office environment, it requires that an analyst sit within an employee's work area and record, at 15-minute intervals, the employee's work activities. This information is related to how and why the work activities are performed. This information is analyzed to determine the percentage of value-adding versus non-value-adding work content as well as the cumulative time duration of major work activities. Shadowing also brings an analyst into close proximity to the employee's work tasks and their interrelationships. As part of shadowing activities, layouts of work areas can also be created, and samples of reports, data entry screens, and other informational tools can be collected and used as examples of how the work is actually done.

Depending on the particular industry, office equipment may either be a major or incidental part of a process workflow. In this context, if a certain type of equipment has a major impact on an office process, then its production rates, availability, ease of use, and similar information can be collected and analyzed to improve operations. A photocopier is an example of a piece of equipment that may periodically become a bottleneck with respect to the flow of materials and information. Equipment audits can be done using sensing devices such as counters to calculate transaction or production rates through the equipment or using a physical audit.

Scrap and rework from office processes can also be measured and analyzed for improvement opportunities by a Kaizen team. Whereas scrap must be thrown away and replaced, rework is work that must be done more than once due to an error. Percentage rework is estimated by counting the number of transactions that passed through the operations of a process more than once. Rework is usually associated by words having a prefix of *re-*, such as reanalyze, reinspect, redo, etc. Another way to estimate scrap and rework amounts and percentages is by analyzing financial and operational reports for variances in material and direct labor that have been classified as scrap or rework. These metrics can be measured in absolute amounts such as pounds, dollars, labor hours, and similar financial and operational units or volume adjusted by converting them into percentages. Office examples include paper that is thrown out, obsolete promotional literature, and similar materials. Operations containing scrap and rework can also be identified using interviews, e-mails, audits, and shadowing people.

Downtime or unavailability percentages can be estimated in a manner similar to scrap and rework percentages. They are also directly related to a system's capacity. Maintenance logs can be analyzed in situations in which equipment downtime is suspected to be a problem. In a different context, records related to tardiness and absences can be analyzed to estimate the availability of people. Operational audits are usually required to break these larger components of downtime or unavailability into lower-level root causes. Capacity is also an important Lean metric that measures the degree of process simplification, standardization, and mistake proofing. Operational capacity increases when materials and labor are effectively utilized. Recall, from Chapter 3, that a system's throughput rate or capacity was constrained by its bottleneck resource. For this reason, improvement efforts should begin at a system's bottleneck. In summary, a system's capacity is estimated by analyzing the throughput rate at its bottleneck operation.

A bottleneck operation should be analyzed using a VSM and the nine metrics listed in Table 4.5. In addition, a Kaizen team should directly observe a bottleneck and estimate its capacity under typical production conditions. It should be noted that an indication that an operation may be a bottleneck is the presence of large amounts of work (inventory in manufacturing) in front of an operation waiting to be processed. Typical bottlenecks found in office processes include managers who fail to sign off on reports in a timely manner, people who work below standard production rates and hold up everyone's work, and equipment or IT systems that are not available or online to do critical work.

Recall that in Figure 3.9 work tasks within operations were broken down into several time components, including setup time. Although any time component other than processing is normally non-value-adding, setup time is usually tracked separately because it increases the scheduling flexibility and capacity of an operation. This enables a process to move toward a mixed-model scheduling system. A mixed-model scheduling system was discussed in Chapter 3 and shown in Table 3.9. In manufacturing, the overall job setup time is easy to measure because the start and end points of a job are recorded by manual or automated systems. However, a careful study is required to quantify the various activities required to set up a job and calculate its time duration. In office processes, information related to job setups will not be available unless transactions are time-stamped by information technology (IT) systems. Common methods used in office environments to estimate setup time include analyzing operational reports, job shadowing, time and motion studies, and conducting periodic employee interviews.

"Inventory" is the eighth metric listed in Table 4.5. Inventory correlates to several of the other metrics listed in the table. As an example, if there are two days of inventory, in front of an operation, then lead time can be estimated as the processing time of the inventory. A system's total lead time can be estimated in a similar manner operation by operation along the system's critical path. Inventory levels for each operation are estimated by counting the number of units in front of an operation during a Kaizen team's VSM activities. This is done by dispersing the team across a process to collect the metric information listed in Table 4.5. The last important metric listed in the table is the total floor area required by a process. Floor area is an important measure of operational efficiency because it is usually proportional to the number of people and equipment required to produce a product or service. In office environments, the relationship is still applicable, depending on the industry, but service systems tend to require proportionally less floor area than, say, heavy manufacturing, with its larger production equipment, raw materials, and finished goods inventories. However, in either system, it has been shown that the proximity and relative spatial relationships between operations have a direct impact on a system's lead time, quality, and cost. These concepts were discussed in Chapter 3 and shown in Figure 3.8. Floor area itself is very easy to estimate by measuring the area required by a process workflow. The goal is to develop very efficient process configurations in which equipment, people, and information are in close proximity either physically or virtually.

Analyze Data and Develop Prioritized Improvements

The goal of a Kaizen event is to collect and analyze data from a process workflow and then make immediate operational improvements. It has been found that a sequential approach to process improvement is often the most effective long-term improvement strategy. Whereas Lean has a process analysis focus, Six Sigma has a data analysis focus. However, both initiatives use subsets of tools and methods from each to fully analyze a process workflow. In other words, their tools and methods are complementary. From a Lean perspective, if an operation adds value from an external customer perspective, then Lean tools and methods can be applied to simplify and standardize its work operations to further increase its value content. On the other hand, whenever data analysis or experiments are required to improve yields or reduce cycle time, Six Sigma tools and methods can be used with Lean tools and methods. In Chapter 6, we will discuss the analysis of common office processes. In summary, it is important to link the root causes of a process problem with solutions using Lean and Six Sigma tools and methods.

Change the Process

A major problem with many Kaizen events is that they are never fully integrated within an organization, after an event. Another common problem is that they are poorly communicated within an organization. This inhibits leveraging their solutions across an organization. For this reason, Chapters 6 to 9 will discuss issues related to the effective communication of Kaizen events and their business benefits throughout the larger organization. This discussion includes developing a list of lessons learned (what did and did not work) and ideas to leverage improvements or solutions across other parts of a Kaizen team's organization. Integral to developing solutions or recommendations are the activities necessary to complete the various root cause analyses and developing countermeasures to eliminate their root causes. Countermeasures will be shown to be combinations of process simplifications, mistake proofing, standardized work, training, and similar methods that depend on a specific root cause. Chapter 6 will discuss six common office processes. Chapter 7 will use this information to discuss several useful methods that enable a Kaizen team to create a business case to influence their process owners and executives to support process changes. This management presentation, which is based on this business case, will show the costs and benefits of the proposed process controls. These controls are in turn based on the Kaizen team's countermeasures to the root causes of the original problem. Project charters will be created by a Kaizen team to implement any longer-term improvements that have been identified, but cannot be completed during their Kaizen event. Chapter 8 discusses the methods necessary to actually implement the solutions developed by a Kaizen team. Implementation occurs toward the end of a Kaizen event, after a management review of the costs and benefits of each improvement. The information contained in Chapter 8 includes developing a control plan, a modified process, new procedures, training materials, a failure mode and effects analysis (FMEA), and a plan to transition the improvements to the process owner and local work team. An additional consideration is the integration of improvements with other organizational initiatives. In this context, Chapter 9 discusses reinforcing behaviors to sustain the process changes.

Apply 5S and Mistake-Proofing Methods

5S methods, standardized work, and mistake proofing were discussed in Chapter 3. At this point in our discussion it is important to note that a Kaizen team should be experienced in the use of Lean methods such as 5S and mistake proofing, or they should receive Lean training. In this context, team member skills should be known prior to a Kaizen event, and if there is ambiguity regarding a team's Lean knowledge, then discussions during the kickoff event should determine what topics need to be presented to ensure everyone has a basic understanding of the required data collection, analysis, and improvement methods. To provide Lean training, workshop facilitators must be experienced in the theory and use of Lean improvement methods. We will continue our discussion of 5S, standardized work, and mistake proofing in Chapters 5 and 6 with examples.

Evaluate the Kaizen Event

A major premise principle of Lean Six Sigma deployments is continuous improvement of all team activities. Figure 4.1 provides a good listing of the required activities that comprise a Kaizen event. Evaluations can be made at several points during an event, but it is important that the first evaluation be made shortly after the kickoff meeting and a final one at the end of an event. Figure 4.3 lists several common evaluation questions, but these can be modified based on a Kaizen team's requirements. These questions relate to event preparation, the effectiveness of team facilitation, whether the event proceeded according to a logical road map, the quality of the training materials, the degree of team member participation, and the overall effectiveness of the event relative to its stated objectives. The final question

Kaizen Event Evaluation Form																	

| Name (Optional):
Work Area:
Date:
How would you improve this training? | Please rate each training segment on a scale of 1 to 5.
1 Do not agree
2 Somewhat agree
3 Neutral
4 Agree
5 Strongly Agree |

	Person 1	Person 2	Person 3	Person 4	Person 5	Person 6	Person 7	Person 8	Person 9	Person 10	Person 11	Person 12	Person 13	Person 14	Person 15	Total	Average
1. Event preparation was well done.																	
2. Facilitation was well done.																	
3. The event proceeded according to a logical road map.																	
4. The training materials were interesting with relevant examples.																	
5. All team members participated in the event.																	
6. The event achieved its stated objectives.																	
7. I would recommend this improvement methodology to others.																	
Total:																	
Average:																	

Figure 4.3   Evaluation of a Lean Kaizen event.

asks whether the team members would recommend this improvement methodology to others in the future.

Summary

The focus of this book is to provide a sequenced set of activities that will enable a Kaizen team to plan all the activities necessary to ensure its Kaizen event is successful. The goal of a Kaizen event is to collect and analyze data from a process workflow to make immediate operational improvements. To accomplish this goal, Kaizen activities were divided into four major sections in this chapter: preparing for the event, conducting the event, presenting the findings, and follow-up activities. The preparation for a Kaizen event begins up front by ensuring that a Kaizen team has an important business project to serve as the focus for their event. Business projects should be integrated within a Lean Six Sigma deployment. In fact, it is best to identify several projects using an operational assessment to increase an organization's productivity and shareholder economic value added (EVA). Project charters provide the essential information necessary to create a Kaizen event. A charter identifies a project's business benefits and required resources. Resources include a team's project leader, facilitators, and team members, as well as facilities, tools, equipment, and other team requirements. A project leader or coordinator is also assigned to a Kaizen event to ensure that all event planning is properly completed and remains on schedule. Project leaders should be experienced in leading these events. In addition, a Kaizen team needs a well-equipped conference room that is reserved for a minimum of several days, because this is a typical time duration for an event. The conference room should also have the necessary supplies and equipment. As an example, flip charts and other supporting materials should be set up in the work area as well as the conference and breakout rooms. Support personnel and subject matter experts may also be required to assist a team through its various team activities.

An organization will usually have a great deal of information related to floor layouts, process maps of its workflows, procedures, operational and financial reports, and so on that will be useful to a team in analyzing the workflow it has been assigned to improve. This information should be gathered for the team prior to its kickoff meeting. Data collection in service operations is both easier and more difficult than in manufacturing. Several data collection methods that are useful in office environments were discussed in this chapter. These concepts will be expanded in subsequent chapters of this book. Once a Kaizen event begins, a team should collect quantified data from their process workflow and create a value stream map (VSM). The VSM is the major integrating tool that ties together all the information gathered by a Kaizen team to describe the workflow. VSMs are important tools because they provide a snapshot of process performance using several useful operational metrics.

Suggested Reading

William Lareau. 2003. *Office Kaizen: Transforming office operations into a strategic competitive advantage*. Milwaukee, WI: American Society for Quality.

Jeffrey K. Liker and David Meier. 2006. *The Toyota way fieldbook*. New York: McGraw-Hill.

James W. Martin. 2008. *Operational excellence—Using Lean Six Sigma to translate customer value through global supply chains*. New York: Auerbach.

James M. Morgan and Jeffrey K. Liker. 2006. *The Toyota Product Development System: Integrating people, process and technology*. New York: Productivity Press.

Chapter 5

Data Collection and Analysis

Overview

In this chapter we will discuss the gathering of process data, including management reports containing financial and operational data, process maps, floor layouts, and similar sources of information, to conduct an analysis of the root causes of process breakdowns. Once identified, root causes can be eliminated when a Kaizen team develops countermeasures. Countermeasures or improvement ideas are the common Lean tools and methods, which were discussed in Chapter 3. In this context, this chapter will show how Lean methods are used in office systems. It should also be mentioned that the tools and templates used in this chapter as well as in other parts of this book can be modified based on a Kaizen team's requirements. In this way, they should be considered as examples and guides. As we discuss process analysis and the improvement of office operations, we will keep our discussion at a level of complexity that any Kaizen team can easily master. Our discussion will begin with value stream mapping (VSM). A VSM should describe how materials and information move through the operations of each major process workflow. However, the exact level of detail required by an initial analysis depends on the team and its project charter. As an example, if a Kaizen team is localized to a manufacturing facility, then its version of a VSM will most likely not include the entire supply chain, although its map should be easy to integrate into a higher-level VSM. Further, if a team has been focused on a single process workflow, then its VSM will most likely resemble a functional process map, although it will be highly quantified relative to key metrics and customer value-adding work. In summary, a Kaizen team should use the correct level of detail to construct its VSM or process map based on its project charter's scope. The construction of a VSM in an office environment may be more complex than in manufacturing. This is because office processes are usually integrated across several organizations and information technology (IT) systems. As a result, several levels of process mapping will often be required to show all operational relationships. As an example, an accounting process may have operational elements within several countries. In these situations, customer-facing operations in the host country are subject to local accounting laws and regulations, but the standardized work tasks may be done in a back office elsewhere in the world. Many banks have this type of system design, in which cancelled checks are sent to centralized clearing facilities for low-cost processing of the checks. Alternatively, an organization may have several accounting systems that vary across countries, but still needs to aggregate their information into one number for the host country.

Although the emphasis in this chapter will be on Lean tools and methods, there will also be a brief discussion of several common data analysis tools and methods. These will be discussed using examples and Minitab® statistical software. These analytical tools will be used to identify statistical relationships among the variables of interest. These relationships will be shown to describe performance characteristics of key operational metrics. In these discussions, the analysis will be restricted to a simple graphical or statistical format, using basic analytical tools and methods. The more complex Six Sigma tools and methods will not be required in a majority of Kaizen events. However, depending on the expected type of root cause analysis, more advanced statistical methods may be necessary to identify the root causes of poor operational performance. Advanced statistical methods should be used in situations in which several variables must be set at levels to optimize a system's performance. As an example, in an office environment we may need to determine the staffing levels to answer customer's inquiries. In this type of analysis, an agent's experience and training level, the time of day, incoming call volume, and several other factors may be relevant to the analysis. This would require building a quantified model to show relationships between the variables. In other words, we would want to meet a service target with a minimum staffing level. In many organizations, the analytical tools and methods presented in this chapter would be categorized as a green-belt skill level. In contrast, a black-belt skill level would include the more advanced statistical tools and methods, such as the advanced methods just mentioned.

In this chapter, our goal is to present tools and methods that will enable a Kaizen team to quickly and simply analyze the data they collect from their process workflows. Also, we will focus on service applications such as those found in office environments. As an example, in manufacturing applications of Lean Six Sigma, a Kaizen team works with local process owners and their teams to create value steam maps (VSMs). In Chapter 3 we stated that this approach is a snapshot of a process workflow's key financial and operational metrics. Several of these common financial and operational metrics were shown in Figure 4.1, Table 4.1, and Table 4.5. After a Kaizen team completes their VSM, it can see where improvements will be necessary. It has also been mentioned that in a manufacturing environment, machines and workers are stationary and the work they do is repetitive. This means their work tasks can be studied over and over under relatively controlled conditions using well-established industrial engineering methods. Also, many manufacturing work tasks are visible, if a trained observer is conducting an analysis. This makes data collection activities relatively straightforward. However, this statement may not always be true, because what should appear to be obvious to some people may not be easy for others to see without a sustained operational analysis. In fact, this is why a Lean deployment is difficult in any system. Although an operational analysis of service workflows uses tools and methods similar to those found in manufacturing, its data collection and analysis is usually more difficult. We discussed these topics in Chapter 4, but will present several useful new tools and methods to facilitate data collection and analysis activities in service systems.

Service processes are usually characterized as having a very high manual content. Also, their work tasks are usually highly integrated within IT systems. These conditions result in a higher variation in work task completion, which can be seen as longer cycle times, lower yields, and higher transactional cost than if these processes were highly standardized and mistake proofed. Complicating Lean Six Sigma deployments in service systems is the fact that operational work tasks may be deployed across the world. Several common examples include computer transactions that are part of a larger and globally integrated process, reoccurring conference calls among teams from several countries, live team meetings using intranet or Internet systems, face-to-face meetings, on-site and off-site team meetings, and similar types of work activities. These types of work activities can be studied and analyzed in a manner similar to those in manufacturing. However, the data collection and associated analytical methods require modification. In this chapter, we will focus on the unique strategies and methods that will enable a Kaizen team to collect and analyze information from their office processes using Lean and Six Sigma tools and methods.

Value Stream Mapping

In this chapter we will discuss the concept of value stream mapping (VSM) in more detail. First, VSM has been around a long time. In its original format, a supply chain was process mapped to include its customers, suppliers, and the materials and information that flowed through its organizational, functional, and operational components. However, a VSM at this level, while very useful, must be broken down into its major workflows and finally analyzed at an operational work task level within each major workflow. In other words, if a Lean Six Sigma deployment has been properly aligned and deployed, then this high-level VSM can be used

Table 5.1   Why Create a Value Stream Map?

1. The value stream map is a visual model of the process including all key operational metrics.
2. Identify areas for operational improvements.
3. Identify rework and non-value-adding (NVA) operations.
4. Provide process documentation.
5. Identify process simplification opportunities.
6. Understand key process input variables (KPIVs) and their effect on key process output variables (KPOVs).

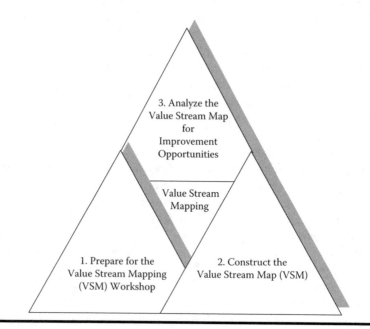

Figure 5.1   Three major steps to creating a value stream map.

to create more detailed maps at lower levels of a supply chain that can be used to create project charters to eliminate process breakdowns. In these situations project charters will be well defined and strategically linked across an organization's supply chain. In other words, our assumption is that a higher-level VSM and project charters have been created to focus a Kaizen team on a specific process workflow as described by a project charter's problem statement and objective. In this chapter, our discussion will be at a project charter level of detail. As a result, when we discuss VSM, it will in the context of a major workflow. Table 5.1 shows several advantages of a VSM.

In Figure 5.1 three sequential steps are shown to be important in creating VSMs. The first step is to prepare for the VSM workshop. This was the major focus of

Chapter 4. Recall that Figure 4.1 listed the activities necessary to fully prepare for a VSM workshop to support a Kaizen event. In this section, we will discuss these major steps in the context of the ten key requirements of an effective VSM. These are listed in Table 5.2. This discussion will be facilitated using standardized templates, tools, and methods with examples. In Chapter 6, six office examples will be discussed to show how these concepts are applied to various services or office workflows, such as finance, accounting, and procurement, as well as several others.

A VSM creates a visual model of a major process workflow describing its key financial and operational metrics, such as those discussed in earlier chapters in relationship to operations within a process. There are also other types of metrics that organizations can measure depending on their specific needs, such as those shown in Figure 5.7. An analysis of metric performance over time against their target levels provides information that can be used to identify projects to close performance gaps. Obvious examples of poor operational performance will be evident as non-value-adding (NVA) operations and process breakdowns such as rework, low process yields, high transaction costs, and long cycle times. In addition, a VSM is useful in providing process documentation to facilitate standardization. As an example, once a VSM has been verified by "walking" its process, it may become a useful source of information for future operational audits or direct process improvements. Another major benefit of a VSM is that it helps identify process simplification, standardization, and mistake-proofing opportunities. As a general rule, simpler process workflows will always have higher quality and lower cost and cycle times than more complicated ones. However, an often overlooked advantage of building a VSM is that once is has been quantified, a dynamic simulation model can be built to analyze its performance, offline, under various process conditions. This information is useful in understanding how a process can be modified to improve its performance. Although a process simulation is not required in a VSM analysis, it may help identify a system's bottleneck and capacity-constrained operations under various simulated process conditions. But one disadvantage of using a simulation model is that its creation and analysis may require expertise from outside the Kaizen team. However, bringing in a simulation expert may be useful in these situations because a model of a single process workflow can be constructed in hours if process data is available. A major advantage of a simulation model is that, in complicated processes, it can show a Kaizen team where increases in the flow of materials and information may be possible.

Although in earlier chapters we have discussed VSMs from several perspectives, Table 5.2 lists the basic requirements of a good VSM. The first requirement is to ensure that a project charter exists to focus a team on a single process workflow, or perhaps just a portion of a workflow. This requires that a project's problem statement and objective be well defined to enable a team to know clearly where they will work, and the available resources, as well as the names of the process owner and local work team. A well-written project charter will enable a team to select its members based on the project's process boundaries. This up-front work,

Table 5.2   10 Requirements Necessary for an Effective Value Stream Map

1. Ensure the project's problem statement and objectives are well defined.
2. Select team members based on the project's process boundaries using a Supplier-Input-Process-Output-Customer (SIPOC) or similar method.
3. Ensure that the level of mapping detail provides information sufficient to analyze and eliminate the problem.
4. Analyze the value stream map for non-value-adding (NVA) operations and rework loops.
4. Analyze the value stream map for process waste such as overproduction, waiting, excess travel, inefficient production, excess inventory, excess movement, or defects.
5. Analyze the value stream map for long cycle times and capacity constraints including the system's bottleneck resource.
6. Identify and prioritize improvements using 5S, mistake proofing, and other Lean methods.
7. Create a modified value stream map of the improved process and use it a guide to the process workflow's "future state."
8. Develop a simple project plan, including a responsibility matrix to migrate to the improved process.
9. Develop controls to ensure the improved process remains in a stable state and in control.
10. Use a visual control system to monitor and continuously improve the process over time.

by deployment leaders and process owners, will ensure sufficient resources will be available to a Kaizen team to complete its data collection and analysis activities. This is important because a Kaizen team is on a very tight schedule. Any activities that can be completed prior to an event will improve its overall execution. A project charter will also help focus a team at a level of a process detail where its work activities correspond to a project's anticipated business benefits.

A method commonly used to construct a VSM map is a brown-paper exercise. Important characteristics of a brown-paper exercise are shown in Table 5.3 and Figures 5.2 and 5.3. A major advantage of a brown-paper exercise is that it is a highly interactive and hands-on workshop within a Kaizen event. Also, the VSM and various supporting documentation are attached to it. And the brown paper can be quickly rolled up and moved to another location or stored as necessary. In this activity, team members work with a local work team to build a VSM and quantify it relative to key operational metrics. In addition, examples of reports, data collection forms, and similar informational and control documents are also gathered by a team. Once a VSM has been constructed on the brown paper, an analysis of

Table 5.3   5 Key Characteristics of a Brown Paper Exercise

1. Hands-on exercise involving people associated with major work stream.
2. Everyone can see the operational relationships and metrics.
3. Captures material and information flow both visually and quantitatively.
4. Shows metric linkages across the process.
5. Major work streams can be broken out for further analysis.

<u>Map the Material Flow</u>

Attach data collected from the process including operations characterized as value-adding (VA), business value-adding (BVA) and non-value-adding (NVA), the production rate (units/minute), scrap %, rework %, downtime %, capacity (units/minute), setup time (minutes), inventory (units), and floor area.

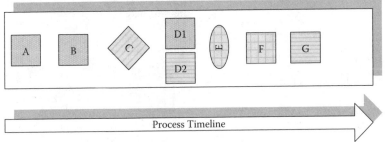

Process Timeline

<u>Map the Information Flow</u>

Attach data collection forms, management reports, inspection forms, procedures, and similar information below the material and information flow.

Figure 5.2   Brown-paper mapping.

non-value-adding (NVA) operations, rework loops, and other areas of process waste can be made. Process waste is evident as overproduction, waiting, excess travel, inefficient production, excess inventory, excess movement, and defects. In addition, a VSM can be analyzed to identify long cycle times as well as capacity constraints within a process, including its bottleneck resource. Countermeasures can then be used to eliminate the root causes of the process breakdowns. A countermeasure is a single solution that helps eliminate one or more root causes. It should also be noted that several integrated countermeasures may be necessary to completely eliminate one or more root causes. Typical countermeasures include a combination of 5S, mistake proofing, and other Lean methods.

The various countermeasures or improvements that were identified by a Kaizen team are incorporated into a future-state process map. Comparing a current- to future-state process map enables a project's business benefits to be estimated. However, more often than not, a team cannot improve its process to its future state, but rather to some intermediate point. The goal then becomes one of continuous

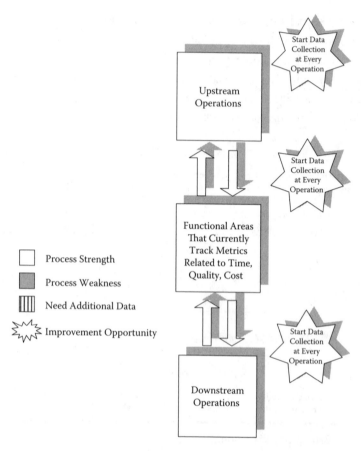

Attach information to the value stream map that shows how the
process is managed, such as management reports, inspection and
data collection forms, quality reports, including scrap and rework,
maintenance reports showing machine breakdowns, and any other
information useful in analyzing the process.

Figure 5.3   Brown-paper mapping at a major work stream level.

improvement to systematically squeeze out the remaining process waste over time
and move a process toward its future state. In summary, every process improvement
is the result of countermeasures applied to the root causes of an identified process
breakdown. In this context, it is important that a Kaizen team develop its countermeasures or process controls in a manner to ensure their sustainability. Ideally,
a team's countermeasures or process controls will contain a high percentage of
visual controls to easily monitor and continuously improve their process. Finally,
any countermeasures that cannot be immediately implemented should be prioritized based on their anticipated business benefits versus resource requirements for
future implementation.

Brown-Paper Exercise

A brown-paper exercise is a hands-on VSM exercise involving a Kaizen team and the local work team of the process. Table 5.3 lists five key characteristics of a typical brown-paper exercise. First, the people who are selected to be included in this exercise should have been identified by the team's project charter as suppliers, customers, the local work team, and various subject matter experts. Second, a VSM should be prominently displayed on a conference room wall so everyone can easily see how the process workflow is organized and the relationships among its operations. This process is facilitated as the Kaizen and local work teams physically add operational information from their process area to the VSM using sticky notes. In this context, a VSM helps to capture the flow of materials and information, both visually and quantitatively, using operational metrics. A fourth characteristic is that a VSM show metric linkages across the process workflow operation by operation. Eventually, a process workflow can be broken down into subprocesses and then into operational work task levels for subsequent analysis. The VSM created by a Kaizen team should remain in the conference room where it was created. But this may not always be possible. However, as mentioned above, an advantage of using brown paper as a background for a VSM is that it can be easily rolled up and moved anywhere. In manufacturing this practice is very common. In fact, a VSM may serve as a source of continuous-improvement ideas for several Kaizen teams. In contrast, the posting of a VSM in office environments is seldom done. This results in a disruption of continuous-improvement activities. As a result, there is a preponderance of process maps in isolated locations throughout office operations. These isolated process maps usually exist within an organization's data repositories, such as sharepoints. In these situations, process maps are used in isolation by single users or small work teams. However, these maps are not usually quantified or completely accurate. In contrast, a major advantage of a visible and easily accessible VSM is that it becomes a highly interactive communication vehicle that helps everyone to identify operational issues.

Figure 5.2 shows how a VSM is created to accurately depict the sequential and spatial relationships of a process. In addition to showing how materials and information flow through a process, data collection forms, management reports, inspection forms, and other information-capturing and reporting documents are attached at the bottom of a VSM. At this point in a Kaizen event, the team has most likely "walked" their process to validate the information used to build their VSM. In service processes, VSMs consist of a combination of manual and computerized work tasks. An interesting characteristic of an office Kaizen event is that operational relationships are easier to see after building a VSM. This is because their complex interrelationships become clear when forms, reports, and similar information are gathered together on a VSM, rather than being scattered across several computer screens or operations. As mentioned earlier, once a VSM has been constructed, a Kaizen team uses it to identify process breakdowns related to poor

Process Step	A	B	C	D	Total Operations	Operation Cost	Total Cost	Setup Time	Delay Time	Processing Time	Inspection Time	Transport Time	Storage Time	Total Time	Yield (RTY)	Value Adding?	Comments
1	1		1	1	3	1.5	$4.50	1.8	3.0	3.0	0.8	1.5	5.3	15.3	99%	Yes	
2	1	1		1	3	1.4	$4.05	1.8	3.6	3.6	0.9	1.8	6.3	18.0	97%	No	Target to Eliminate
3	1	1	1		3	1.6	$4.77	1.8	3.6	3.6	0.9	1.8	6.3	18.0	95%	No	
4	1	1			2	2.4	$4.70	1.8	6.4	6.4	1.6	3.2	11.2	30.6	99%	Yes	
5	1	1	1	1	4	2.1	$8.40	1.8	5.4	5.4	1.4	2.7	9.5	26.1	97%	No	
6	1	1	1	1	4	3.3	$13.08	1.8	0.6	0.6	0.2	0.3	1.1	4.5	99%	No	Target to Eliminate
7	1		1		3	0.1	$0.15	1.8	2.4	2.4	0.6	1.2	4.2	12.6	98%	No	
8	1	1			3	0.2	$0.66	1.8	2.6	2.6	0.7	1.3	4.6	13.5	95%	No	
9	1	1	1		3	0.8	$2.25	1.8	7.8	7.8	2.0	3.9	13.7	36.9	93%	No	
10	1	1	1	1	4	0.9	$3.40	1.8	5.8	5.8	1.5	2.9	10.2	27.9	98%	No	
11	1		1		2	5.2	$10.48	1.8	4.0	4.0	1.0	2.0	7.0	19.8	99%	Yes	
12	1	1			3	0.5	$1.35	1.8	2.0	2.0	0.5	1.0	3.5	10.8	96%	No	Target to Eliminate
13		1			2	0.9	$1.74	1.8	7.0	7.0	1.8	3.5	12.3	33.3	97%	Yes	Target to Eliminate
14	1		1	1	3	1.9	$5.70	1.8	3.4	3.4	0.9	1.7	6.0	17.1	99%	Yes	
15	1	1		1	3	1.5	$4.50	1.8	2.8	2.8	0.7	1.4	4.9	14.4	94%	No	Target to Eliminate
16		1	1	1	3	1.8	$5.25	1.8	2.6	2.6	0.7	1.3	4.6	13.5	99%	No	
17	1	1	1	1	3	1.9	$5.55	1.8	0.4	0.4	0.1	0.2	0.7	3.6	93%	No	
18	1	1	1	1	4	1.9	$7.60	1.8	4.4	4.4	1.1	2.2	7.7	21.6	98%	Yes	
19		1	1	1	2	0.7	$1.30	1.8	3.2	3.2	0.8	1.6	5.6	16.2	92%	No	
20	1	1	1	1	4	0.4	$1.60	1.8	4.2	4.2	1.1	2.1	7.4	20.7	94%	Yes	

	A	B	C	D													
Total	17	15	14	15	61	1.5	$ 91.03	36	75.2	75.2	18.8	37.6	131.6	374.4	$27.27	15	
Sales Price	$32.72	$23.00	$30.94	$24.95													
Total Cost	$27.27	$20.00	$23.80	$19.96			% Total	20%	20%	5%	10%	35%	100%				
Gross Margin %	20%	15%	30%	25%													

Comments

Figure 5.4 Product complexity analysis.

metric performance, non-value-adding operations, and rework loops. Figure 5.3 highlights these breakdowns using starbursts. Recall that two key objectives for building a VSM are that it is interactive among stakeholders and provides a comprehensive visualization of a process workflow. Interactive implies that key stakeholders helped to construct and interpret the VSM. Easy visualization also helps a team understand current versus future operational performance. In addition to placing starbursts on a VSM, other notes are attached by the Kaizen team, the local work team, and other key stakeholders. These comments help clarify the map's information and show where process improvements should be made.

A team may be required to analyze the performance of several process workflows with intent to focus on just one. In fact, even if a team is deployed within a single process workflow, it will usually focus on a few operations that have the greatest business impact or those that are on the critical path impacting the bottleneck. Figure 5.4 shows how a team quantifies several process workflows to identify shared operational and financial metrics. In this example, several product groups have been analyzed to identify the operations they share in common. Operational performance is also analyzed across the product groups relative to their common metrics to identify common process problems. These types of problems are usually related to excessively long cycle times or process yields. Financial metrics are analyzed in a similar manner. This comprehensive information enables a Kaizen team to clearly focus on the analysis of the root causes for process problems. The ultimate goal is process simplification and standardization.

An advantage of using standardized data collection and analysis tools and templates, such as that shown in Figure 5.4, is that they help to quickly focus a team's improvement efforts on the most significant process issues. Also, after a Kaizen event, subsequent analysis of the process information will enable the creation of additional project charters for future teams. However, it must be admitted that the creation of project charters is more of a management role than the responsibility of a Kaizen team that has be tasked with the rapid improvement of a single process workflow. But during its investigative work, many ways to improve a process will usually be identified. In this context, several project charters can be created using the information shown in Figure 5.4. As an example, project charters could be created based on a different metric such as process yield. Measuring process performance in this manner will usually identify numerous ways in which to improve organizational productivity and ensure aligned and prioritized projects.

Process Characterization

A major goal of this chapter is to provide a simple and easy-to-use reference that describes useful data collection and analysis tools and methods for Kaizen events. Figure 5.5 begins this discussion with an overview of data collection strategies in offices. This discussion is divided into three major sections. These include data gathering strategies, analytical tools and methods, and process sampling methods. This chapter also presents several tools and templates that facilitate an efficient collection of these process metrics.

The goal of data collection and analysis is to provide the information necessary to identify the root causes for process breakdowns. Data collection helps to verify that process improvements have been successful and identifies additional project charters for assignment to future Kaizen teams. In this context, Figure 5.5 lists several relevant data collection tools and templates. These include tools and templates related to financial and operational analysis, work sampling, and job shadowing, along with examples. A legitimate question associated with data collection activities is: At which level of analysis should they be applied? The answer will be shown to depend on a Kaizen team's questions, goals, and objectives. As an example, if the team's goal is to develop project charters, then an analysis at an organizational or major workflow level would be appropriate. However, if a team has been assigned to work within a specific workflow, then an analysis of operational work tasks would be appropriate.

Finally, a team must decide on the method that will be used to collect data from their process. Methods range from a 100 percent audit to various types of statistical sampling of a population. Relative to statistical sampling, there are at least four major types of sampling methods. These include random, stratified, systematic, and cluster sampling. Random sampling consists of taking items from a process and measuring one or more characteristics. An example would be selecting

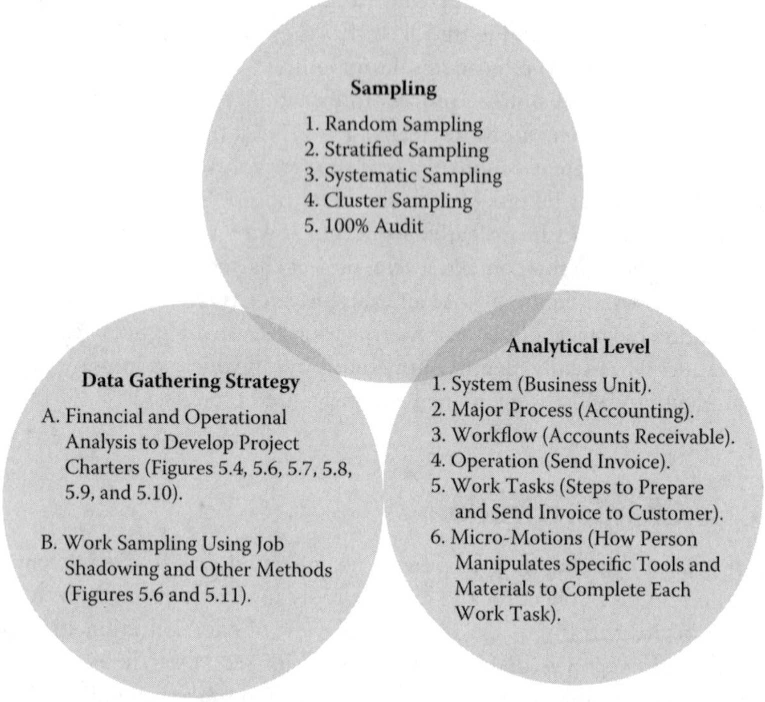

Sampling

1. Random Sampling
2. Stratified Sampling
3. Systematic Sampling
4. Cluster Sampling
5. 100% Audit

Data Gathering Strategy

A. Financial and Operational
Analysis to Develop Project
Charters (Figures 5.4, 5.6, 5.7, 5.8,
5.9, and 5.10).

B. Work Sampling Using Job
Shadowing and Other Methods
(Figures 5.6 and 5.11).

Analytical Level

1. System (Business Unit).
2. Major Process (Accounting).
3. Workflow (Accounts Receivable).
4. Operation (Send Invoice).
5. Work Tasks (Steps to Prepare
and Send Invoice to Customer).
6. Micro-Motions (How Person
Manipulates Specific Tools and
Materials to Complete Each
Work Task).

Figure 5.5   Process analysis.

20 or 30 items from an inventory population to see if they are damaged. Stratified sampling divides a population into groups based on a stratification variable and random samples within each group or stratum. An example would be to divide an inventory population into groups and then draw accounts at random, within each stratum, to estimate the total inventory valuation. But stratification methods are more complicated than other statistical sampling methods and require the help of analysts. Systematic sampling requires that a sample be taken from a process at equal intervals of time or every nth unit. A common example is a control chart that provides a visualization of the variation of a measured characteristic over time. We will discuss control charts in later chapters of this book because they are an important tool to help sustain process improvements. In cluster sampling, a population is divided into naturally occurring groups from which random samples are then drawn. An example would be dividing customers into market segments, then sampling from each segment to measure a particular characteristic such as customer satisfaction. Our goal will be to review the various data collection and analysis tools, as well as sampling methods, to show how they can be used to gather data for process analysis and improvement. In our discussion of specific tools and templates, it should be remembered that some are used to quantify a value stream

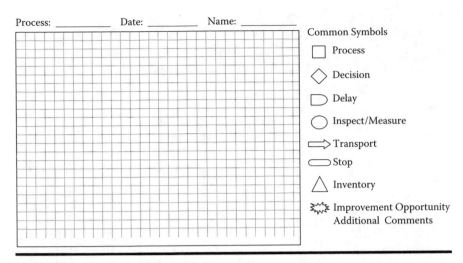

Process: _____ Date: _____ Name: _____

Common Symbols

☐ Process

◇ Decision

◻ Delay

○ Inspect/Measure

⇨ Transport

⊂⊃ Stop

△ Inventory

⚡ Improvement Opportunity
Additional Comments

Figure 5.6   Process analysis worksheet.

map (VSM), while others are used at a more detailed level to investigate operations that have been shown to exhibit poor operational performance.

Figure 5.6 shows a very simple but useful data collection tool called a process analysis worksheet. This tool enables a team to quickly sketch their process workflow, or, if there are just a few operations, sketch a process layout. These simple sketches show the spatial relationships among people, materials, and equipment. Ideally, the relationships will be scaled to enable a quantitative analysis of travel distance. Process analysis worksheets can also be used to describe lower levels of operational detail, such as work tasks and their micro motions. These types of data collection methods help to differentiate value-adding (VA) from non-value-adding (NVA) activities. A Kaizen team should also quantify a process workflow to the greatest extent possible using operational and financial metrics such as those shown in Figure 5.7. This Figure describes an accounting example. Once information has been gathered to complete the data collection templates, a Kaizen team can continue its operational analysis. As additional data collection and analysis activities are required within specific operations, more detailed or modified templates can be used to collect data.

An advantage of measuring and evaluating the variation patterns of operational and financial metrics is that they may show opportuntities for process improvement. As an example, negative metric trends would necessitate that project charters be created to reverse them. Also, if a metric is constant but its performance, especially relative to external customers, is not acceptable, then project charters will be required to make process improvements. Figure 5.7 shows the type of information that should be gathered in an accounts payable process over time. As an example, the initial percentage of value-adding (VA) time is 15 percent of the total process time. Figure 5.7 also shows that a 15 percent process improvement was made that

Operational Performance Measurements

Work Area: Accounting		Average Job Cost:	$22.75		Date: July
Operation: Accounts Payable		Units Per Shift:	50		Auditor: Joe
Process Owner: Mary		Shift Cost:	$1,137.50		Takt Time: 8.4 Minutes/ Unit (50 units in 420 Minutes)
Operation Number: 4TD		Available Time (Minutes):	420		

Operation "Accounts Payable"

Key Metrics	Baseline	Week 1	Week 2	Week 3	Week 4	Week 5	Week 6	Week 7	Week 8	Week 9	Week 10	Week 11	Week 12	Week 13	Week 14	Week 15	Week 16	Average	Improvement %
1. Value Adding %	15.0	15.0	15.0	16.0	16.0	16.0	16.0	17.0	17.0	18.0	18.0	18.0	19.0	20.0	21.0	22.0	13.0	17.3	15%
2. Production Rate (Units/Time) or Operation Cycle Time	50.0	52.0	55.0	55.0	60.0	63.0	55.0	63.0	62.0	63.0	64.0	66.0	65.0	69.0	70.0	73.0	74.0	63.1	26%
3. Scrap%	2.0	2.0	2.0	2.0	1.9	1.8	1.7	1.5	1.4	1.3	1.2	1.1	1.2	1.1	1.1	1.0	1.0	1.5	-27%
4. Rework%	30.0	30.0	30.0	28.0	25.0	31.0	33.0	27.0	25.0	28.0	24.0	22.0	21.0	19.0	17.0	19.0	20.0	24.9	-17%
5. Downtime%	20.0	21.0	23.0	19.0	18.0	20.0	17.0	16.0	18.0	19.0	15.0	16.0	16.0	16.0	14.0	15.0		17.1	-14%
6. Capacity (Units/Time)	54.9	56.4	58.1	62.9	72.4	68.3	60.1	76.1	75.2	72.5	81.7	85.5	87.3	92.8	100.0	100.7	99.6	78.1	42%
7. Setup Time (Minutes)	30.0	29.0	29.0	28.0	27.0	26.0	25.0	26.0	24.0	27.0	25.0	24.0	24.0	21.0	23.0	21.0	20.0	24.9	-17%
8. Inventory (Units in Queue)	20.0	19.0	16.0	18.0	15.0	16.0	14.0	17.0	13.0	18.0	14.0	13.0	12.0	11.0	12.0	9.0	8.0	14.1	-30%
9. Floor Area	10,000	10,000	10,000	10,000	10,000	10,000	10,000	5,000	5,000	5,000	5,000	5,000	5,000	3,800	3,800	3,800	3,800	6575	-34%
Additional Metrics (Depending on Industry or Function)																			
a. Total Process Workflow Cycle Time																			
b. Number of Problem-Solving Teams																			
c. Number of Customer Complaints																			
d. Number Employee Suggestions																			
e. Warranty Expense/ Incidents																			
f. Returned Goods Expense/ Incidents																			
g. Annualized Savings																			
h. Percentage Scheduled Jobs Missed																			
i. First Pass Yield (Rolled Throughput Yield-RTY)																			
j. Profit/ Loss																			
k. Inventory Efficiency (Turns)																			
l. On-Time Supplier Delivery																			
m. Forecast Accuracy																			
n. Lead Time																			
o. Unplanned Orders																			
p. Schedule Changes																			
q. Overdue Backlogs																			
r. Data Accuracy																			
s. Material Availability																			
t. Excess & Inventory																			

Figure 5.7 4. Performance measurements (similar to Figure 3.4).

increased the VA percentage from 15 to 17.3 percent of the total process time. This information implies that additional increases in value-adding time may be possible using Lean methods such as process simplification, standardization, and mistake proofing. Figure 5.7 lists several other metrics whose performance can be improved either immediately using a Kaizen event or through follow-up projects. As an example, rework and scrap percentages could be reduced through a combination of operational improvements. An advantage of using a measurement approach similar to that shown in Figure 5.7 is that a Kaizen team can prioritize their data collection and analysis efforts. Figure 5.7 also lists two additional metric classifications that depend on a specific industry or function. Later in this chapter, we will use the information contained in Figure 5.7 to demonstrate the application of several other important analytical tools within office environments.

There are several other data collection methods that have been shown to be useful in office environments. As an example, Figure 5.8 shows a process audit template of the same accounts payable process, but at a more advanced level of analysis. The initial baseline of non-value-adding (NVA) time in Figure 5.8 is 85 percent because the initial value-adding (VA) time was shown in Figure 5.7 to be 15 percent. This template shows how a detailed audit can be done to identify several process issues, including those commonly called red-flag conditions. The list of issues shown in Figure 5.8 will provide a good source of projects for any Kaizen team. As an example, one of the categories, "frequent changes to a job," is a classic red-flag condition in which increases in the number of changes to a job order negatively impact it from both a quality and a schedule perspective. This is because as the

Process Audit Worksheet				
Work Area: Accounting	Average Job Cost:	$22.75	Date: July	
Operation: Accounts Payable	Units Per Shift:	50	Auditor: Joe	
Process Owner: Mary	Shift Cost:	$1,137.50	Takt Time: 8.4 Minutes/ Unit (50 units in 420 Minutes)	
Operation Number: 4TD	Available Time (Minutes):	420		

Process Breakdowns	Occurrences (Per Shift)	Time (Minutes)	Incremental Expense	Comments
Frequent Changes to a Job	5	17.5	$26.25	Job was interrupted.
Lack of Standards	3	10.5	$15.75	
Lack of Measurement Systems	2	7	$10.50	Lack of clarity regarding start of invoice.
Lack of Training	4	14	$21.00	New employee not familiar with tasks.
Long Cycle Times	4	20	$30.00	Jobs have been pending for weeks.
Infrequent Jobs	2	10	$15.00	Jobs for these suppliers are run once per year.
High Output (Exceeding Capacity)	1	5	$7.50	Job was rushed due to poor planning.
Environmental Conditions	0	0	$0.00	
Attitude (Motivation)	0	0	$0.00	
Waiting	10	50	$75.00	Jobs could not be completed due to incomplete information.
Transport	2	7	$10.50	Jobs had to be walked to another department.
Non-Value-Added Activities	15	53	$79.50	Work tasks that can be eliminated form the process.
Serial Versus Parallel Processes	0	0	$0.00	
Batch Work	10	50	$75.00	Jobs were released at the end of the shift.
Excessive Controls	10	35	$52.50	Jobs required three signatures.
Unnecessary Transfer of Materials	0	0	$0.00	
Scrap	0	0	$0.00	
Rework	10	35	$52.50	Had to call supplier several times.
Ambiguous Goals	2	6	$9.00	Employees confused as to work task.
Poorly Designed Procedures	3	9	$13.50	Work procedures can be made more efficient.
Outdated Technology	0	0	$0.00	
Lack of Information	4	13	$19.50	Employees did not have information to perform job.
Poor Communication	0	0	$0.00	
Limited Coordination	5	15	$22.50	Jobs required several sequential operations.
Total:	92	357	$535.50	
Non-Value-Adding (NVA) Percentage of Total	85%	47%		
Comments:				

Figure 5.8 Process audit worksheet.

number of changes increase, due to a myriad factors, the lead time of a process will increase and a greater probability of error will also occur due to expediting activities and miscommunication. In these situations, a Kaizen team should investigate the root causes of the schedule changes and then eliminate or reduce their occurrence. In this context, the root causes may be due to customer requests, a lack of materials, machine breakdowns, or other reasons. The issues and red-flag conditions shown in Figure 5.8 commonly occur within manufacturing and office processes. These will also serve as excellent sources of projects for improvement teams. The elimination of the process issues shown in Figure 5.8 will increase the percentage of value-adding (VA) time within a process workflow and reduce its lead time as well as its cost.

As a Kaizen team continues to drill down into the root causes of the accounts payable issues, the "standard waste analysis" template shown in Figure 5.9 may be useful. This template can be used to analyze operations at either a process workflow or operational level for the wasted time within operations. The template can also be modified to analyze other important metrics. In the example shown in Figure 5.9, the time spent at every operation is broken down into its lower-level

	Standard Waste Analysis		
Work Area: Accounting	Average Job Cost:	$22.75	Date: July
Operation: Accounts Payable	Units Per Shift:	50	Auditor: Joe
Process Owner: Mary	Shift Cost:	$1,137.50	Takt Time: 8.4 Minutes/Unit (50 units in 420 Minutes)
Operation Number: 4TD	Available Time (Minutes):	420	

Operation Name (Number)	Production Inefficiency	Waiting	Excess Production	Excess Travel	Excess Inventory	Excess Movement	Time Due to Defects	Total Time	Distance	Comments
1	5	10	3	0	0	4	2	24	20	Eliminate Waiting Time
2	0	12	1	0	0	0	0	13	15	Eliminate Waiting Time
3	0	15	0	0	0	1	0	16	5	Eliminate Waiting Time
4	2	8	0	0	0	0	0	10	2	
5	0	3	0	0	0	0	0	3	5	
6	4	2	5	0	0	3	6	20	18	Defect Reduction
7	0	1	7	0	0	0	0	8	0	
8	0	6	0	0	0	0	0	6	2	
9	1	6	0	0	1	2	0	10	2	
10	0	8	0	1	1	0	0	12	3	
11	2	4	9	0	1	0	3	19	50	
12	0	2	0	0	2	0	0	4	0	
13	0	4	0	1	4	0	0	9	3	
14	0	2	0	0	1	0	0	3	25	
15	5	3	4	1	2	4	0	19	2	Improve Work Task Efficiency
16	0	4	0	0	0	0	0	4	5	
17	0	7	0	0	0	5	6	18	2	Reduce Excess Movement
18	0	8	3	1	0	0	0	12	3	
19	6	2	0	0	0	0	0	8	100	Improve Work Task Efficiency
20	0	1	0	0	1	6	0	8	0	Reduce Excess Movement
21	0	4	0	0	0	0	0	4	50	
22	8	6	0	1	0	0	9	24	2	Improve Work Task Efficiency/Reduce Defects
23	0	7	0	0	0	6	0	13	2	Reduce Excess Movement
24	0	8	1	0	1	0	9	19	4	
25	7	8	0	0	0	6	0	21	5	Improve Work Task Efficiency
26	0	8	3	0	0	0	0	11	6	Eliminate Waiting Time
27	0	1	0	0	1	0	0	2	3	
28	5	1	0	0	0	0	0	6	25	Improve Work Task Efficiency
29	0	5	0	0	1	0	0	6	0	
30	5	3	4	0	0	2	0	14	3	Improve Work Task Efficiency
31	0	2	0	0	0	0	2	4	0	
32	1	3	0	0	0	0	3	7	500	
Total:	51	164	40	5	16	44	37	357	862	
Percent of Total:	14.3%	45.9%	11.2%	1.4%	4.5%	12.3%	10.4%			

Figure 5.9 Waste analysis by operation.

time components. Recall that in Figure 5.8 the total non-value-adding time was 357 minutes, which equated to a baseline estimate of 85 percent non-value-adding time. Figure 5.9 shows how these 357 minutes can be broken down at a lower level to identify one or more of the major reasons for the long cycle time within the process workflow. As an example, waiting time represents 45.9 percent of the total non-value-adding time of the accounts payable process. This may be a good place from which to either focus a Kaizen event or, if the analysis is already part of a Kaizen event, focus a team on this process issue as a first priority. Perhaps the focus should also be within operations 1, 2, and 3. These operations are approximately 25 percent of the total waiting time. In the "summary of waste analysis" template shown in Figure 5.10, the data in Figure 5.9 represents just one job. It would also be very useful to gather similar performance information for several jobs to ensure the estimated relative percentages of wasted time across the categories are reflective of longer-term process performance. To summarize our discussion, in the accounts

Summary of Waste Analysis												
Work Area: Accounting		Average Job Cost:			$22.75			Date: July				
Operation: Accounts Payable		Units Per Shift:			50			Auditor: Joe				
Process Owner: Mary		Shift Cost:			$1,137.50			Takt Time: 8.4 Minutes/Unit (50 units)				
Operation Number: 4TD		Available Time (Minutes):			420							

					Time In Minutes							
Job Sequence	Job 1	Job 2	Job 3	Job 4	Job 5	Job 6	Job 7	Job 8	Job 9	Job 10	Average	Percent
Production Inefficiency	51										51	14.3%
Waiting	164										164	45.9%
Excess Travel	40										40	11.2%
Excess Production	5										5	1.4%
Excess Inventory	16										16	4.5%
Excess Movement	44										44	12.3%
Time Due to Defects	37										37	10.4%
Total:	357	0	0	0	0	0	0	0	0	0	357	100.0%

Figure 5.10   Summary of waste analysis for several jobs.

payable process example just discussed, data collection activities are linked at several levels using standardized data collection and analysis templates. Quantitative information facilitates an effective root cause analysis.

Job shadowing is another useful data collection method. It is similar to the templates shown in Figures 5.8 and 5.9 except that it is more easily adapted to complex work tasks such as those involving the flow of information within an office process. The "job shadowing" template shown in Figure 5.11 is useful when work tasks are not standardized and the flow of work is complicated. Typical examples include office workers, managers, and other professionals within both manufacturing and service industries who do not have structured work tasks. In this context, job shadowing is a useful method for processes that are characterized by a large number of meetings, heavy computer use by professionals, and systems in which major components of work time occur repetitively, but not in repeatable sequences. In other words, job shadowing is commonly used to track the time components of complex work tasks or jobs. Using this methodology, an observer records the actions associated with a job over several hours or days and at 15-minute increments. Then the percentages of time, by major work activity, are calculated to show where time is spent by an employee. Most often, the greater percentages are associated with non-value-adding (NVA) work tasks. As an example, it may be found that an employee spends an inordinate amount of time attending meetings, working on NVA analyses and reports, or performing work tasks not directly related to his or her job description. This information is useful because only simple procedural changes may be required to make a process improvement. However, job shadowing may require more time than is available during a Kaizen event. Typically, the method is used in an operational assessment that extends over 20 or more working days. It should also be noted that it may be possible to electronically capture and analyze the time spent on diverse work tasks. In these situations, a Kaizen team will have extensive information at the beginning of their event from which to analyze and improve their process. As a final comment, job shadowing is very useful because it places an operational analyst directly with an employee. As a result of this proximity, in

Job Shadowing Analysis			

Work Area: Accounting	Average Job Cost:	$22.75	Date: July
Operation: Accounts Payable	Units Per Shift:	50	Auditor: Joe
Process Owner: Mary	Shift Cost:	$1,137.50	Takt Time: 8.4 Minutes/Unit (50 units in 420 Minutes)
Operation Number: 4TD	Available Time (Minutes)	420	

Time Period	Observations
15	
30	
45	
60	
75	
90	
105	
120	
135	
150	
165	
180	
195	
210	
225	
240	
255	
270	
285	
300	
315	
330	
345	
360	
375	
390	
405	
420	
435	
450	
465	
480	

Calculations:

Figure 5.11 Job shadowing worksheet.

addition to collecting quantitative data, an analyst could also collect examples of various reports, data collection templates, computer screen shots, and other tools and templates used by employees during the course of their daily work.

A spaghetti diagram is a common data collection method used in manufacturing. But this method can also be adapted easily to an analysis of office operations. A spaghetti diagram template is shown in Figure 5.12. It shows the movement of materials or information in an office environment. In this example, it is apparent that work tasks move back and forth between cubicles or work stations. Using the information provided by a spaghetti diagram, it should be possible to efficiently sequence office work tasks or rearrange their spatial relationships. The concept of minimizing movement between operations is well known, and as a result, it is a common practice to co-locate work teams that interact to a high degree to the greatest extent possible. However, information and material flows may change over

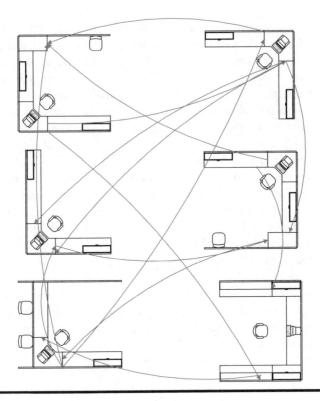

Figure 5.12 Spaghetti diagram.

time, which degrades an optimum co-location solution. This is why a spaghetti diagram may be useful to a Kaizen team trying to understand the unnecessary movements of materials and information within their process.

Data collection, using a spaghetti diagram, can take several forms. As an example, in manufacturing, the movement of people and materials is recorded on a process diagram and every movement is represented by a single line. Distances can be calculated by measuring the length and number of lines between various operations. However, in office environments this type of data collection methodology becomes more complicated because the transaction movements occur between dispersed systems consisting of people and information technology (IT). But it may be possible to have transactions time-stamped as they move from one operation to another. Also, summary reports can be created by IT systems to automate an analysis. In office systems, it may be relatively easy to track time-stamped transactions to calculate cycle times and yields between operations.

A spaghetti diagram analysis will often show that some operations are touched more frequently than others. This may indicate a need to centrally locate the more popular (most frequently touched) operations for easy access by other groups. A common example would be to locate restrooms, break rooms, and office equipment in a central location to minimize walking distance for employees. An analogous situation occurs when people need to share information. Prior to computerization, the information in an organization resided within file folders across diverse locations within a business. A major solution to this problem was the creation of sharepoints. A sharepoint is a place where information is shared remotely by depositing or retrieving it from a central location according to structured rules of use. However, sharepoints must be designed properly, in the sense that they should be simple, standardized, and mistake proofed to ensure that their original design intent is continually met in practice. As an example, imagine that one or more folders in a sharepoint have not been properly labeled or identified; this would require that a person move through several electronic folders before finding the required information. An application of a spaghetti diagram to a sharepoint analysis would trace a person's searching (movement) through file folders looking for information. This data collection and analysis could be done automatically using software.

Another important tool that has been embedded in many of the templates of this chapter is the simple checklist shown in Table 5.4. Checklists can be used separately at any time within a project to show the frequency of occurrence by major category. In the example shown in Table 5.4 we can see that non-value-adding (NVA) activities, batching of work, excessive controls, and rework are categories having a higher frequency of occurrence than others. This information can be analyzed further using some of the tools and methods discussed in the next section.

Simple Analysis of Process Data

It has already been mentioned in earlier chapters that every initiative has its own toolkit for solving certain types of problems. Because there are several operational initiatives and each has its own tools and methods, it becomes confusing to know when to use specific tools and methods to identify and eliminate the root causes of a problem from a process workflow. To help put the two major operational initiatives, Lean and Six Sigma, into perspective, Table 5.5 compares Lean tools and methods relative to the Six Sigma five-phase problem-solving methodology defined as define, measure, analyze, improve, and control. In my experience, Lean methods are preferable for most process analysis and improvement in office processes. This is especially true in situations in which a problem can be identified and eliminated in a matter of days rather than months. Rapid improvement using Kaizen events falls into this latter category. On the other hand, Six Sigma methods are very useful in situations that require intensive data analysis and creation of statistical models to explain relationships between an output (dependent) variables and one or more process input (independent) variables. Notice that the tools listed in Table 5.5 range from the simple to complex, and that both initiatives share several important tools and methods. Common tools and methods are easily seen at the beginning and end of a project. In contrast, Six Sigma tools and methods are heavily represented in

Table 5.4   Checklist

Category	"Checks"	Count
Frequent Changes to a Job	IIIII	5
Lack of Standards	III	3
Lack of Measurement Systems	II	2
Lack of Training	IIII	4
Long Cycle Times	IIII	4
Infrequent Jobs	II	2
High Output (Exceeding Capacity)	I	1
Environmental Conditions		0
Attitude		0
Waiting	IIIIIIIIII	10
Transport	II	2
Non-Value-Adding Activities	IIIIIIIIIIIIIII	15
Serial Versus Parallel Processes		0
Batch Work	IIIIIIIIII	10
Excessive Controls	IIIIIIIIII	10
Unnecessary Transfer of Materials		0
Scrap		0
Rework	IIIIIIIIII	10
Ambiguous Goals	II	2
Poorly Designed Procedures	III	3
Outdated Technology		0
Lack of Information	IIII	4
Poor Communication		0
Limited Coordination	IIIII	5

the analyze and improve phases of Table 5.5. Because they are not the focus of this book, we will not be discussing the more complex tools and methods. However, several books that do explain the more advanced statistical tools are listed in the suggested reading section of this chapter.

Although Lean tools and methods are initially easier to understand because they are process-focused, it should also be stated that they are not necessarily easy to implement without the assistance of experienced facilitators and training. Also, precursor systems must also be implemented to deploy the more advanced Lean methodologies. This concept was discussed in Chapter 3, in which it was stated that to implement a pull system, external demand had to be made relatively stable to implement a stable takt time. Also, the operational systems of a process must be

Table 5.5 How Lean and Six Sigma Tools Compare

Define Phase	Problem Statement	Yes
	Process Map	Yes
	Metric Analysis	Yes
	Benefit Analysis	Yes
Measure Phase	Problem Statement	Yes
	Cause & Effect (C&E) Diagram	Yes
	FMEA	Sometimes
	Measurement System Analysis	Sometimes
	Basic Statistics	Yes
	Process Capability	Sometimes
	Benefits Analysis	Yes
Analysis Phase	Graphic Analysis	Yes
	Hypothesis Testing	No
	Contingency Tables	No
	One-Way ANOVA	No
	Multi-Variant Analysis	No
	Correlation	No
	Regression	No
	Detailed Process Map	Yes
Improve Phase	General Full Factorials	No
	2k Factorials	No
	Fractional Factorials	No
	Response Surface Designs	No
	Mixture Experiments	No
Control Phase	Statistical Process Control (SPC)	Yes
	Mistake Proofing	Yes
	Measurement Control	Yes
	Training	Yes
	Validate Capability	No
	Control Plans	Yes
	Final Benefits Review	Yes

simplified, standardized, and mistake proofed. This requires experience. In addition, many supporting systems must also be deployed. Some examples include quality systems, employee training, and preventive maintenance. In summary, Lean improvements build on each other over time. This is a major reason for the emphasis on continuous improvement and the immediate elimination of process problems using Kaizen events. Deployment of Lean tools also requires the help of specialists who have studied practical applications over many years. This is why organizations retain internal and external consultants in the initial stages of their Lean deployment. In the remaining sections of this chapter, we will discuss several common analytical tools that are useful for Kaizen teams.

Process Mapping—SIPOC

Process maps are used at many levels within a project. What this means is that some process maps will need to describe different levels of process detail than others. We will discuss several types of process maps. As an example, we have already discussed value stream maps (VSMs). Now we will discuss a high-level process map used to identify the boundaries of a process to better define a project and its charter. This type of map is called a SIPOC. SIPOC is an acronym for supplier-input-process-output-customer. A SIPOC is shown in Figure 5.13. This type of process map is useful in defining process boundaries or communicating areas where Kaizen teams should focus their improvement activities. A SIPOC is constructed by working backward into a process from the voice of the customer (VOC) and translating customer needs and requirements into internal specifications. These internal specifications are the outputs of the SIPOC. The major process steps that transform inputs into outputs are also described as the process portion of the SIPOC. Within any of the major process steps there are many internal operational work tasks. This is a very high-level view of a process workflow. At this point

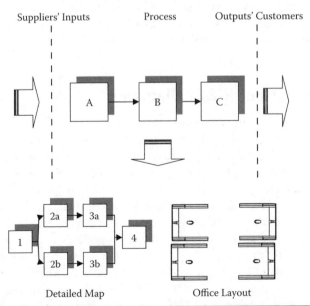

Figure 5.13 Process mapping—SIPOC.

in an analysis the SIPOC is used to identify a major area of a process that will serve as a source of improvement projects. As part of this analysis, input and process variables that transform materials or information into outputs are identified as possible sources of variation for subsequent analysis. In other words, process variables are process settings that transform inputs into outputs. In this context, more detailed process maps may also be created using one or more of these combinations of input and output variables at a particular process step. Suppliers and the specifications that control their performance are associated with the materials and information entering a process at the supplier input boundary. In this context, an input refers to people, materials, information, and other resources that enter a process. As an example in an accounts payable process, internal suppliers may provide information through information technology (IT) systems or contractors to do work. Within a process are the employees who pay the supplier invoices. The process outputs are payments to suppliers that are evaluated based on their accuracy and timeliness. Each of the many operations within this type of process is controlled by specifications related to time, quality, and cost.

At a next lower level of analysis, a Kaizen team could construct more detailed views of their process depending on where the root cause analysis must be focused. As an example, Figure 5.13 shows two different lower-level maps. One is an office layout that depicts materials, people, and information across a few operations. The other lower-level process map shows a portion of the SIPOC's workflow, but at a more detailed level and from a process workflow perspective. In these types of analyses teams work in a top-down and aligned manner from the higher-level SIPOC down into a process to identify and eliminate the root causes for poor performance. In summary, process maps are used to visually describe a process. In this regard they are a very useful communication tool.

Cause-and-Effect (C&E) Diagrams

C&E diagrams are useful in helping a team brainstorm and organize qualitative relationships between a process output variable and several potential input variables. In a C&E diagram the input variables are organized into major categories that are also called themes. These categories are developed using VOC studies related to timelines, quality, and cost that are broken down into subcategories. Figure 5.14 shows a C&E diagram. In this example, the major categories are shown as environment, machines, methods, measurements, materials, and people. But these categories can be modified depending on a project's anticipated root cause analysis. In the current example, high inventory investment is shown as a problem that must be analyzed and improved by a Kaizen team. The effect or problem is that inventory investment increased 25 percent over the previous year without an increase in sales. In other words, 25 percent more inventory is required to meet customer service levels. Note that a C&E diagram contains several branches and

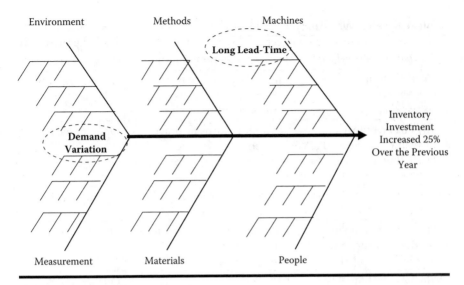

Figure 5.14 C&E diagram.

subbranches. A team would place the inputs or variables they consider to be the major causes of higher inventory investment and then work down to lower-level root causes of the inventory investment problem. As an example, two major causes for higher inventory investment are known to be excessive demand variation and long lead times. At a next lower level, we may find that lead time has increased due to missed supplier deliveries. Then, if we drilled down to still a next lower level of detail, the missed deliveries may be found to be associated with a few suppliers. In this way, a team identifies what may be the important variables or root causes of their process problem. It should be noted that a C&E diagram is based on opinion and is not a substitute for data collection and analysis or factual information. However, it is a first step that enables a Kaizen team to create a data collection plan to either validate or disprove the team's opinion of what may be causing the process problem as represented by the variables placed on the C&E diagram.

Five-Why Analysis

Like a C&E diagram, a five-why analysis is simple analytical tool that may be very useful in identifying the possible root causes of a process problem. Table 5.6 shows how a five-why analysis is applied to the same inventory investment problem shown in Figure 5.15, but with different root causes by way of further example. In this type of analysis, a team will ask why at least five times to drill down to lower levels of detail to uncover the roots causes of a process problem. When using this methodology, it is important that supporting information be gathered to aid in the five-why discussion. There are commonalities between a C&E diagram and a five-why

Table 5.6   Five-Why Analysis

Level of Question	Answer (Opinion)	Supporting Information
Effect (Output)	Inventory Investment increased 25% faster than sales last year.	Accounting report
Why has inventory investment increased 25% faster than sales last year?	Inventory turns (average inventory investment necessary to support sales) decreased by 25%.	Operational report
Why did inventory turns decrease by 25%?	Lead time of production line "XYZ" increased by 5%.	Operational report
Why did lead time of production line "XYZ" increase by 5%?	Machine A has not been running at 95% of the required target rate.	Operational report
Why has machine A not been running at 95% of the required target rate?	There has been a scrap problem with raw material component B.	Quality report
Why has there been a scrap problem with raw material component B?	The component's outer diameter periodically exceeds specification.	Quality report
Why has the component's outer diameter periodically exceeded specification?	Team must investigate the root causes for the diameter variation problem.	Project Charter

analysis, but they also have some important differences. A C&E diagram is useful to organize brainstorming ideas into major themes. In contrast, a five-why analysis is useful to focus down from one major theme into increasing levels of detail. However, they can be used in sequence. As an example, the "effect" in the example shown in Table 5.6 is that "inventory investment increased 25 percent faster than sales last year." Table 5.6 shows an example of how a five-why analysis would be applied to the inventory example. Using the five-why method, a first question a Kaizen team would ask is: Why has inventory investment increased 25 percent faster than sales last year? This increase in inventory investment should be seen in financial or operational reports. Reviewing an operational report, the team may find that inventory turns decreased by 25 percent. Inventory turns is a ratio of the cost of goods sold (COGS) divided by the average inventory investment necessary to produce the COGS. COGS are the labor and material invested in the production of a product or service. This increase in inventory relative to sales could be due to several factors. In answer to the question "Why did inventory turns decrease by 25 percent?" the team may find that lead time of production line XYZ increased by 5 percent, which required that a higher work-in-process (WIP) inventory level be maintained to keep materials flowing through the process. The lead-time information would also be obtained from an operational report. Continuing through the five-why analysis, a Kaizen team might eventually find that the cause of the high inventory investment is that machine A has not been running at 95 percent of the required target rate due to a scrap problem with raw material component B. Finally, the scrap problem may be found to be caused by a quality problem related to a "component's outer diameter that periodically exceeds its specification." Of course, this information must be verified by walking the process to directly observe the problem. But the information gained from this methodology, when based on fact, enables a Kaizen team to quickly investigate the root causes of process problems. In summary, a five-why analysis can be a very useful analytical tool to the extent it is supported by actual financial and operational data.

Histogram

The histogram is another useful analytical tool. It shows the central location and dispersion of a continuous variable. A continuous variable is one that can be measured along a scale that can be divided in smaller intervals as necessary. As an example, a meter can be broken into centimeters, which can be broken into millimeters, and so on. Figure 5.15 shows that the continuous variable "time in minutes" has a central location of approximately 11 minutes and a range of approximately between 2 and 26 minutes. This information would be useful to a team that needs to baseline their current lead time prior to making process improvements. In this scenario average lead-time would be reduced from its current level of 11 minutes to a lower level.

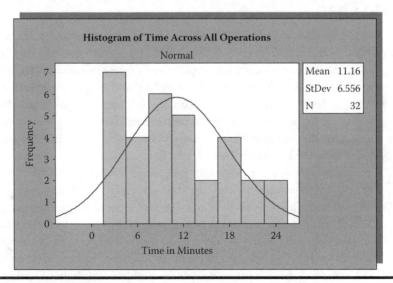

Figure 5.15   Histogram (data from Figure 5.4).

Histograms are also useful in comparing several distributions that share a common scale. In the example just discussed, two histograms could be used to compare lead time before versus after process improvement activities.

In Figure 5.15, the empirical data is shown as rectangular bars. The original data was allocated to classes that correspond to the width of the rectangular bars. The smooth symmetrical curve is a normal distribution approximation to the empirical data. An advantage of graphically displaying continuous data using a histogram is that the data pattern can be analyzed for clues as to how the underlying process is operating. As an example, if the empirical data, as represented by the rectangular bars, is symmetrical, then areas to the right or left of the center of the histogram will be approximately equal. In contrast, a histogram may extend in one direction or another. This is called skew. Highly skewed distributions will usually contain outliers. An outlier is a data value that is far away from the center of a data set. The reasons for outliers may be that the data points are not really representative of the population being sampled, they were measured incorrectly, or perhaps this is just how the process actually operates. A Kaizen team would analyze histograms of the various process metrics with their Six Sigma "belt" for clues as to the root causes of their process problems. A Kaizen team could also use the five-why methodology to verify their countermeasures toward the end of their project. A next step up in analytical complexity would be using summary statistics. Summary statistics describe the central tendency of a dataset as well as its dispersion or variation.

Pareto Chart

A Pareto chart enables a comparison between several discrete variables or categories and their occurrence frequency or total count. Figure 5.16 uses the data from Figure 5.8 to show the occurrence frequency of several process breakdowns. In the display of this data, the Pareto chart shows the number of process breakdowns in decreasing order by category. As an example, the category "non-value-adding activities" has the highest total number of process breakdowns, and "batch work" is shown to have the second highest frequency. Because occurrence frequency is clearly shown from the highest to lowest levels, Pareto charts are useful in focusing a Kaizen team as well as its management on process issues that should have the highest priority for improvement. They are also very useful in working through an analysis of root causes level by level. As an example, Pareto charts could be created as first, second, third, and lower levels. In this context, Figure 5.16 can be broken down into lowers level by analyzing the reasons for the categories associated with non-value-adding (NVA) or batching of work. In summary, Pareto charts are very useful in investigating the root causes of a process problem and communicating the analysis to other people.

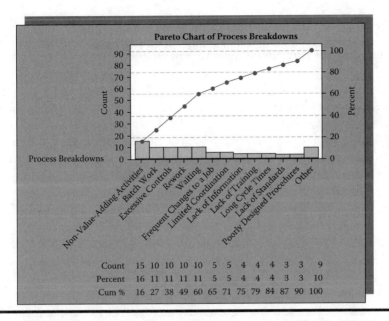

Figure 5.16   Pareto chart (data from Figure 5.9).

Box Plot

The box plot shown in Figure 5.17 is another very useful analytical tool. A box plot provides a graph of a continuous variable that shows both the central location and dispersion of the data set. The dispersion as represented in this example by a range is calculated as the maximum minus the minimum value of the data set. But a box plot provides additional information. These include the 25th percentile, the 50th percentile or median, and the 75th percentile, as well as the minimum and maximum values of the data set. A 25th percentile is a point in a sample at which 25 percent of the values are below. A median is the 50th percentile point in a sample, at which 50 percent of the values are below and 50 percent are above. Finally, a 75th percentile is a point in a sample at which 75 percent of the values are below. Several box plots can also be displayed in a comparative manner. In this type of analysis several discrete variables, having a common and continuous scale relative to each other, are displayed on the same graph. In the sample shown in Figure 5.17 we can see that "lost time" is broken down into various categories, which were shown in Figure 5.9. We also can see that the "waiting" category has a higher median lost time than, say, "excess inventory." Also, the "waiting" category has a higher variation of time relative to any of the other categories. In the example shown in Figure 5.17, an asterisk represents data points that are marked as outliers. An outlier is a data point that may be different from the rest of the sample data, and it is calculated using a formula. Box plots are also an analytical tool from which more advanced statistical methods can be applied to the analysis of process data.

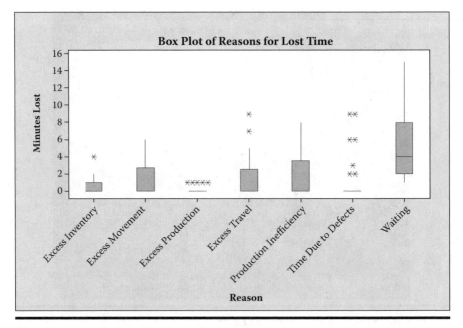

Figure 5.17   Box plot (data from Figure 5.9).

Scatter Plot

A scatter plot is a simple analytical tool that plots two continuous variables relative to each other. In the example shown in Figure 5.18 we can see that the production rate and capacity decrease as the rework percentage increases. It should be noted that the production rate is less than the available capacity. Minitab plots several variables on the same graph and color codes them to provide an easy-to-understand graph showing their qualitative relationships. The data used to construct the scatter plot shown in Figure 5.18 was taken from the example shown in Figure 5.7. A next level up from a scatter plot is developing a quantitative relationship between two continuous variables using a simple linear regression model. A regression model provides statistics that measure the strength of the relationship between the two or more continuous variables and shows their statistical significance.

Time Series Graph

A time series graph compares a continuous variable against its time-ordered sequence. In the example shown in Figure 5.19, we see that "production rate" and "capacity," when plotted against time, appear to be increasing. The data used to construct the graph shown in Figure 5.19 was taken from Figure 5.7. A review of Figure 5.7 shows that they did in fact increase, but rework percentage decreased as

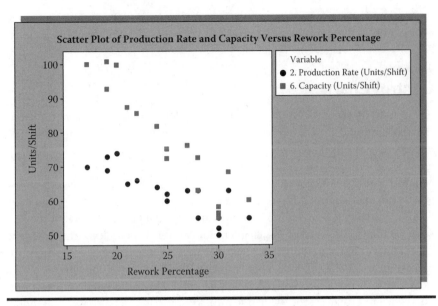

Figure 5.18   Scatter plot (data from Figure 5.7).

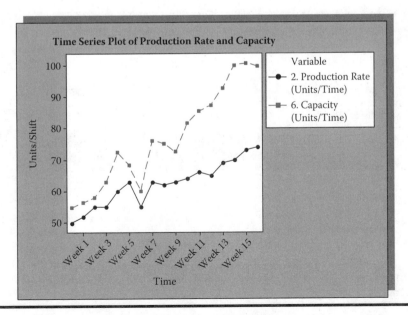

Figure 5.19   Time series graph (data from Figure 5.7).

process improvements were made over time. A time series plot is complementary to a histogram in that it enables data visualization from a different perspective.

Control Charts

Control charts are special types of time series charts in which control limits are calculated around the central location, or mean, of the variable being plotted. A sample mean is calculated by summing all the sample values and dividing by their total. As an example, if a sample consisted of the three data points 1, 2, and 3, then its mean would be calculated as 1 + 2 + 3 = 6 divided by 3 or 2. A description of how to calculate control limits is more complicated, but it will be discussed in more detail in Chapter 8, and additional information is contained in several of the suggested readings at the end of this chapter. But at an elementary level, the upper and lower control limits are statistically calculated at ±3 standard deviations from the process mean. Using this rule, approximately 99.73 percent of the samples drawn from a process would be expected to be within the upper and lower control limits. The concept is that a process in statistical control should not have nonrandom patterns or any outliers beyond the upper and lower control limits.

A first step in constructing a control chart is determining the distribution of the variable being plotted, the sampling plan that will be used to collect data from a process, and the number of time-ordered samples. As an example, the variable shown in Figure 5.20 is continuous and symmetrical (normal distribution

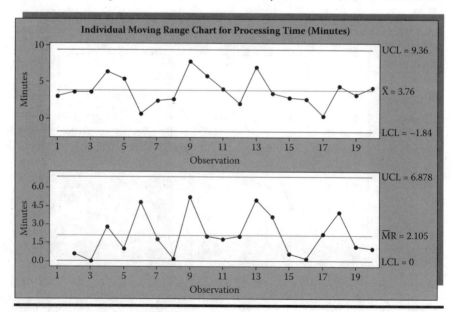

Figure 5.20 Control charts (data from Figure 5.7).

assumption), and sampling is assumed to occur as individual values as opposed to subgroups of various sizes. The initial control limits are calculated at ±3 standard deviations from the mean of the combined sample. The combined sample usually consists of a minimum of 20 to 25 time-ordered samples. This initial control chart will be used as a reference or baseline to compare subsequent samples over time. Then as future samples are taken from the same process, that is, reference distribution, then approximately 99.73 percent of them should remain within the control limits. However, this assumes that the process variable being charted remains symmetrically distributed around its mean and that its mean does not shift over time.

The control chart shown in Figure 5.20 is called an individual control chart. In other words, no subgrouping was used to collect the sample. Two additional control charts that are used to analyze continuous variables and collected as a subgrouped sample are an X-bar chart and range chart. Constructing these charts requires that subgroups of size n be taken from samples as a subgroup from a process at equal time intervals. The subgroup averages are plotted on the X-bar chart and the ranges of each subgroup are plotted on the range or r-chart. Analysis of these control chart patterns requires looking for nonrandom patterns and outliers. In this analysis, an outlier is a subgroup mean or range that is greater than ±3 standard deviations from the mean of the control chart. In an X-bar chart, the mean is the average of all values divided by their number. In a range chart, the mean is the average of the subgroup ranges across all subgroups. Recall that the probability that a subgroup mean or range is beyond either the upper or lower control limits is less that 0.27 percent, that is, 100% − 99.73%. In addition, software such as Minitab also identifies nonrandom patterns that, if they occur, must be investigated by a Kaizen team. In summary, control charts differentiate common cause variation (no pattern) from assignable or special cause variation (outliers or a set of observations forming a nonrandom pattern). It should also be mentioned that there are many other types of control charts that have been developed for various applications. As an example, if a variable is described as a pass or fail, p-charts and np-charts can be used to construct a control chart based on a binomial distribution assumption. Also, if a variable is described as counted data, then c-charts or u-charts can be used to analyze this data based on a Poisson distribution assumption. We will expand our discussion of control charts in Chapter 8.

Once a Kaizen team identifies the root causes for their process problem, using control charts and other tools and methods discussed in this and previous chapters, their project charter should be updated to reflect the most recent analysis. These improvement ideas are formally recorded in an improvement opportunity worksheet, which is shown in Figure 5.21. Many of the improvements will be completed by a Kaizen team during their workshop. However, some improvement activities will require a longer time period to complete, and they may exceed the time available during a Kaizen event's normal schedule. In other words, some improvement activities may have to be completed at a later date.

Kaizen Opportunity Worksheet:		
Date:		Project Number:
Process Workflow:		
Process Owner:		
Team Leader:		
Team Members:		
Kaizen Opportunity:		
Problem Statement:	**Root Causes:**	**Required Actions:**
Current Performance:	**Future Performance:**	**Anticipated Benefits:**

Figure 5.21   Improvement opportunity worksheet.

If the number of identified process improvements is large, then they will need to be prioritized. Figure 5.22 shows how a prioritization can be done using a cause-and-effect (C&E) matrix. The one shown in Figure 5.22 has been modified to prioritize projects relative to their business benefits. Normally, a C&E matrix is used to prioritize process input variables, or Xs, relative to process outputs, or Ys, for data collection activities. In the current example, the prioritization matrix rates several projects or improvements relative to their correlation to key financial or operational metrics using a scale between 1 and 10. A 1 implies no correlation or relationship between a project and benefit, whereas a 10 implies that a high degree

	Rating of Importance to Customer	10	10	8	8	8	7	6	7	5	
		1	2	3	4	5	6	7	8	9	
Sequence	Project	VA%	Production Rate	Scrap%	Rework%	Downtime%	Capacity	Setup Time	Inventory	Floor Area	Total
2	Project B	7	8	8	7	10	10	10	0	8	520
6	Project F	6	8	10	6	7	8	5	7	10	509
10	Project J	10	2	8	9	7	8	10	5	9	508
8	Project H	8	6	5	8	5	5	7	10	8	471
3	Project C	8	6	3	8	9	6	10	0	9	447
9	Project I	9	7	3	8	4	6	9	4	7	439
5	Project E	5	9	0	5	6	9	10	5	10	436
1	Project A	6	3	7	6	5	8	9	7	6	423
4	Project D	4	3	5	9	8	7		2	6	339
7	Project G	7	4	2	7	1	4	8	1	9	318
	Total	700	560	408	584	496	497	468	287	410	

Figure 5.22   C&E matrix—prioritizing projects.

of correlation exists. A second rating is also made relative to business benefits that are important to internal and external customers as represented by metrics such as VA percent, production rate, and others. This rating scale is also between 1 and 10. A 1 implies low importance and a 10 implies very high importance. In the example shown in Figure 5.22, we see that project B has the highest overall rating. The rating of Project B is calculated as a weighted total of $(7 \times 10) + (8 \times 10) + (8 \times 8) + \ldots + (8 \times 5) = 520$. In summary, Project B would be the first project or improvement executed by a Kaizen team if it could be completed within an event's schedule.

Example: Analyzing Job Shadowing Data

In this chapter we have discussed several data collection strategies and presented several tools and methods that are useful in analyzing the collected data. Because data collection is a critical component of process analysis in office environments, we need to use tools and methods that enable the correct information to be collected in an efficient manner. Job shadowing was shown to be an important data collection method in office environments because of the complexity of the work tasks. Job shadowing has been used in manufacturing for many years to analyze complicated operations consisting of people and machines as well as professionals associated with manufacturing activities. In the example that begins in Table 5.7, we see the results

Table 5.7   Example—Analyzing Data Collected from Job Shadowing

Activity	Time	Value
E-mail	5	NVA
E-mail	4	VA
E-mail	3	NVA
E-mail	8	NVA
E-mail	6	NVA
Meeting	30	NVA
Report	60	NVA
E-mail	5	VA
Report	60	VA
Meeting	60	NVA
Phone	20	VA
Phone	10	NVA
Meeting	45	NVA
Meeting	30	NVA
Phone	24	NVA
Meeting	45	NVA
Phone	27	VA
Phone	12	NVA
Meeting	30	VA
Phone	5	NVA
Meeting	20	VA
Phone	16	VA
Phone	34	VA
Total	559	
Total (Hours)	9.32	

from one day's shadowing of an accounts receivable work process. In this simple example, the time durations of several work tasks have been recorded and labeled as value-adding (VA) or non-value-adding (NVA). The total working time is shown to be 9.32 hours, or 559 minutes. This data takes on new meaning when simple analytical tools such as a box plot, shown in Figure 5.23, are used to show relationships between the data elements. Also, it is useful to summarize the shadowing data using simple statistics such as percentages. As an example, in Figure 5.23 it can be seen that 39 percent of the total time is classified as VA. Also, it can be seen that 47 percent of the employee's work time is spent in meetings, some of which add value

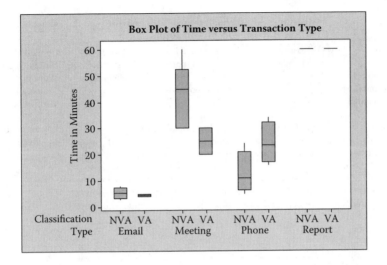

Sum of Time	Classification			
Type	NVA	VA	Grand Total	Percentage
E-mail	22	9	31	6%
Meeting	210	50	260	47%
Phone	51	97	148	26%
Report	60	60	120	21%
Grand Total	343	216	559	
Percentage	61%	39%		

Figure 5.23 Analysis of job shadowing data.

and others that do not. Perhaps some of the NVA meetings could be eliminated or organized to make them more efficient. Overall, 61 percent of the employee's work time contains NVA components. Reducing the percentage of NVA time would provide the employee with the extra time needed to do more useful work. In summary, an advantage of using shadowing and simple analytical tools such as a box plot is that information can be displayed in a format that aids communication and decision making by a Kaizen team.

Example: Inventory Analysis and Reduction

Figure 5.24 shows an example of how Six Sigma tools and methods can be applied to improve inventory management for the specific problem shown in Figure 5.24. It should be noted that Lean methods are a more useful approach to inventory management and reduction. However, in situations in which inventory investment is abnormally high and its root causes lend themselves to statistical analysis, Six Sigma methods in conjunction with standard Lean improvement methods may be the most useful approach. The information contained in Figure 5.24 has

Define	Measure	Analyze	Improve	Control
-Problem statement -Project objective -Process baseline -High level map	-Measurement -Capability -Benefit verification	-Selection of key process input variables (KPIVs) using root cause analysis.	-Final solution -Pilot studies -Benefit analysis	-Control plan -Mistake proofing -Work instructions -Training plan -Verified benefits
Inventory investment increased from 5% to 10% of cost-of-goods-sold (COGS) and inventory turns have decreased from 20 to 10 in the past 12 months.	Verify inventory investment and turns ratios using cycle counting reports and conduct audits of product group "XYZ."	Use basic quality tools and methods to determine the root causes for high investment and low inventory turns.	Develop countermeasures to eliminate the root causes found to contribute to high investment and low inventory turns.	Ensure solutions are effective over time.
The project will focus on product group "XYZ," which has a turns ratio of just 10 and an inventory percentage of 10% of COGS.	Develop a baseline metric charts of inventory investment, turns ratio, service level and project goals by month.			

Figure 5.24 Example: Inventory analysis and reduction.

been organized according to the five Six Sigma phases: define, measure, analyze, improve, and control (DMAIC). The major deliverables listed in Table 5.5 are shown by their DMAIC phase. As an example, the define phase is shown having four major deliverables. These are a problem statement, project objective, process baseline, and a high-level process map. Below the deliverables of each phase are comments of how this inventory management project is structured relative to its project's problem statement and objective. The remaining four Six Sigma phases have other deliverables. The sequential approach of the Six Sigma methodology is evident in this example. As an example, it is reflected in, first, well defining a process problem, then measuring its key metrics or output variables to identify its performance baselines. Once performance baselines have been established, a next goal is to analyze the variables that impact the performance of the output variables through data collection and analysis activities. Finally, once a relationship has been established between outputs and their inputs, a team makes improvements and develops control systems to maintain the newly established performance levels. It should be noted that the specific types of analytical tools used in a given project may vary depending on an analysis of root causes of a process problem.

In the first two DMAIC phases, a team collects information related to the major reasons or issues negatively impacting inventory investment. Figure 5.25 shows these issues, in decreasing order of impact, on inventory investment. These

Reason (Issue)	Count	Percentange	Estimated Impact**	Project
Canceled Order	134	64%	$638,100	A
Schedule Change	36	17%	$171,400	B
Late Deliveries	14	7%	$66,700	C
Large Lot Size	9	4%	$42,900	D
Missing Materials	9	4%	$42,900	E
Quality Issue	8	4%	$38,100	F
Total	210	100%	$1,000,000	

Cost-of-Goods-Sold (COGS)	$10,000,000
Inventory Investment Due to Issues	$1,000,000
Total Inventory Investment	$2,000,000
Inventory Turns Ratio	5

** Subject to verification

Figure 5.25   High inventory investment—first level.

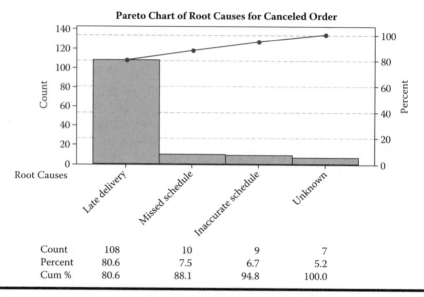

Pareto Chart of Root Causes for Canceled Order

	Late delivery	Missed schedule	Inaccurate schedule	Unknown
Count	108	10	9	7
Percent	80.6	7.5	6.7	5.2
Cum %	80.6	88.1	94.8	100.0

Figure 5.26 Major reasons for canceled orders.

are canceled orders, schedule changes, late deliveries, large lot sizes, missing materials, and quality issues. A Kaizen team could investigate and improve any or all of these issues depending on their magnitude and ease of elimination. But if an issue or problem is too complicated or requires several days or weeks of investigation, then it should be identified as a separate project for future solution. Figure 5.26 shows the same data, but graphically, using a Pareto chart. In the Pareto analysis the issue "canceled orders" represents 64 percent of the $1,000,000 inventory investment associated with all issues. This is also approximately 50 percent of the overall inventory investment of $2,000,000. Based on this analysis, there appear to be six separate projects that can be applied to reduce inventory investment. If the $1,000,000 associated with these problems could be completely eliminated, then inventory turns would increase from 5 to 10 and investment would decrease from $2,000,000 to $1,000,000.

Figure 5.27 shows a next-level root cause analysis in which the "canceled orders" issue is broken down into several lower-level reasons that orders are canceled. These include an inaccurate schedule, late deliveries, missed schedules, and unknown reasons. At this level of an analysis, late deliveries are shown to represent 81 percent of the cost of inventory investment associated with canceled orders. It also represents 51.8 percent of the entire inventory investment problem. This is calculated as 64% × 81% × $1,000,100 = 51.8%. What this implies is that if the Kaizen team eliminated late deliveries as an issue, then the reduction in inventory investment would be $518,000. Figure 5.28 shows an alternative root cause analysis of canceled orders relative to demand variation. Figure 5.29 continues the root cause analysis of late deliveries down to a third Pareto level. The issue "customer not notified"

Root Cause (Canceled Orders)	Count	Percentange	Estimated Impact**	Project
Inaccurate schedule	9	7%	$42,862	A1
Late delivery	108	81%	$514,341	A2
Missed Schedule	10	7%	$47,624	A3
Unknown	7	5%	$33,337	A4
Total	134	100%	$638,164	
Inventory Investment Due to Canceled Orders	$638,164			

** Subject to verification

Figure 5.27 High inventory investment—second level.

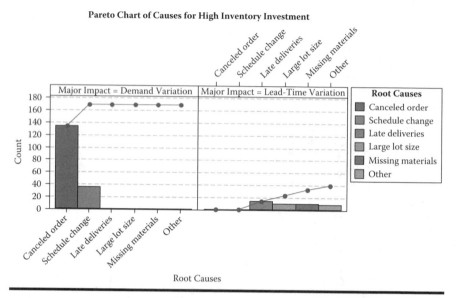

Figure 5.28 Major reasons for high inventory investment.

is shown to be the major contributor to late deliveries. If we could eliminate the "customer not notified" issue, then the inventory investment reduction would be 64% × 81% × 54% × $1,000,000 = 28%, or $280,000. Figure 5.30 is an alternative view of Figure 5.29 using a Pareto chart. The difference in percentages between Figures 5.29 and 5.30 relates to the fact that in Figure 5.29 the percentages are calculated by using inventory investment, whereas in Figure 5.30 counts are used in the percentage calculation. A Kaizen team could use this type of root cause analysis to communicate the business benefits of their project's improvements.

Summary

In this chapter we discussed several useful methods for gathering process information to analyze the root causes related to poor process performance. In this discussion classical manufacturing tools and methods were discussed in the context of office workflows and applications. It was shown that an operational analysis of service workflows is in many ways more difficult than in manufacturing because of the high degree of automated work tasks that are often dispersed globally. The concept of value stream mapping (VSM) was expanded, but from several new perspectives, using the information presented in earlier chapters. In this discussion the advantages of using a brown-paper exercise were also shown to be a hands-on exercise involving all stakeholders in the data collection and analysis activities of a Kaizen event. This chapter also provided several simple and easy-to-use data collection and analysis templates, tools, and methods. These included a SIPOC, metric

Root Cause (Late Delivery)	Count	Percentange	Impact**	Project
Incorrect Invoice		16	12%	$76,199	A21
Carrier Issue		13	10%	$61,911	A22
Customer Not Notified		73	54%	$347,656	A23
Unknown		6	4%	$28,574	A24
Total		108	81%	$514,341	
Cost-of-Goods-Sold (COGS)	$10,000,000				
Inventory Investment Due to Late Deliveries	$514,341				

** Subject to verifcation

Figure 5.29 High inventory investment—third level.

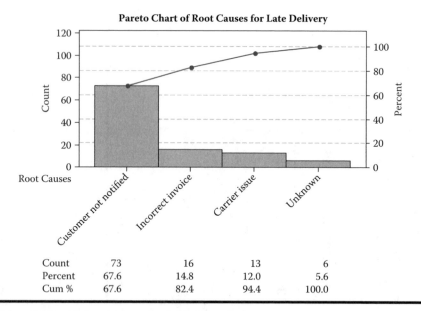

	Customer not notified	Incorrect invoice	Carrier issue	Unknown
Count	73	16	13	6
Percent	67.6	14.8	12.0	5.6
Cum %	67.6	82.4	94.4	100.0

Figure 5.30   Major reasons for late deliveries.

summarization templates, shadowing templates, spaghetti diagrams, checklists, C&E diagrams, five-why analysis, histograms, Pareto charts, box plots, scatter plots, time series graphs, and control charts. Examples using some of the tools were presented at the end of the chapter. We will continue our discussion of process analysis in Chapter 6 using six common office processes as examples to show how Lean and Six Sigma methods can be applied by Kaizen teams.

Suggested Reading

Davis R. Bothe. 1997. *Measuring process capability*. New York: McGraw-Hill.

Charles R. Hicks and Kenneth V. Turner, Jr. 1999. *Fundamental concepts in the design of experiments*. 5th ed. New York: Oxford University Press.

J. M. Juran and Frank M. Gryna. 1993. *Quality planning and analysis*. New York: McGraw-Hill.

James W. Martin. 2008. *Operational excellence—Using Lean Six Sigma to translate customer value through global supply chains*. New York: Auerbach.

Douglas C. Montgomery. 1997. *Introduction to statistical quality control*. 3rd ed. New York: John Wiley & Sons.

Chapter 6

Process Improvement

Overview

The purpose of this chapter is to discuss process improvements using several office examples. This discussion includes asking general questions related to the why, where, how, and who of making process improvements, as well as reviewing the general and specific methods necessary to implement improvements. Our goal will be to demonstrate the linkage between process improvements, which we have also called countermeasures, to a Kaizen team's analysis of root causes. These concepts will be demonstrated using six common office workflows: finance, accounting, sales and marketing, product design, human resources, and procurement. These office examples have been provided to demonstrate data collection and analysis tools and methods. The chapter ends with a discussion of several ways in which a Kaizen team can present its recommendations to obtain a consensus from management and the process owner for process changes.

Common Process Changes

Table 6.1 presents a listing of several common process changes that are routinely implemented to improve process performance. This list is not exhaustive because there can be several variations of these common tools and methods. Table 6.1 is divided into three sections. The first section encourages a Kaizen team to "think outside the box" prior to jumping into their solution discussion. The second section focuses on general methods of process improvement using higher-level tools and

Table 6.1 Common Process Changes

General Questions	General Methods	Specific Process Change
■ Should the work be performed?	■ Eliminate operations and work tasks.	■ Modify organizational reporting structures.
■ Where should an operation be performed?	■ Manage bottlenecks to maximize the flow of materials and information.	■ Eliminate portions of a process.
■ When should an operation be performed?	■ Apply mixed model scheduling to reduce lead-time.	■ Create new or modified process designs and layouts.
■ How should an operation be best performed?	■ Deploy transfer rather than production batches.	■ Mistake proof portions of a process.
■ Who should do the work?	■ Deploy Lean, just in time, and quick response methods.	■ Purchase or design new types of equipment.
	■ Deploy Six Sigma and related initiatives.	■ Implement 5S, mistake proofing, and similar Lean methods.
		■ Create new operational and financial metrics.
		■ Create new information reporting systems.
		■ Modify work, testing, inspection, maintenance, and other procedures.
		■ Process audits and monitoring such as statistical process control.
		■ Training programs.
		■ Group meetings (huddles), written procedures, and verbal instructions.

methods, which were discussed in Chapter 3. It should be noted that specialized training is required to use these tools and methods in any but the simplest applications. This is why a Kaizen team normally requires ancillary team members and experts to help in their analysis and improvement work. The last section of Table 6.1 describes specific changes Kaizen teams can make to improve their processes.

Prior to any process improvement activities, a Kaizen team should first ask the questions listed in the section entitled "General Questions" in Table 6.1. In this context, relevant questions are: Should the work be done by this facility or our organization? Should the work be outsourced? Should the work be modified or augmented to increase its value content? Where should this work be performed and by whom? Who should be doing the work? Should the work tasks be automated? These types of questions as well as others may enable a team to achieve rapid productivity gains without major resource expenditures. The logic behind this type of rationalization is that a Kaizen team should first understand the value content of their current process prior to implementing process improvements. After this discussion, a team should estimate potential increases in the value content of their process using the information that has been collected during their event. It is assumed that a team has the appropriate leadership to facilitate these discussions. In summary, work should migrate to where it will have the highest value content, and a Kaizen team should be empowered to make these types of recommendations based on its project's scope.

Our focus on value content is an extension of the concepts that were discussed in Chapter 1 and shown in Table 1.4. In these discussions the emphasis was on a rationalization of products and services to simplify an organization's process workflows based on the voice of the customer (VOC). In that context, we wanted to understand the concept of customer value and how it related to our current process design. The stated goal was to ensure that products and services, as well as the processes producing them, have high value content, be profitable, and be efficiently produced. This implied that they were well designed, having a low level of complexity but a high degree of standardization. In other words, prior to improving a process, a team should reduce its complexity to create a simpler workflow, if possible. As a result, the first question of Table 6.1 is perhaps the most important. In other words, a team should always ask, given their new knowledge of customer needs and requirements: Is this work necessary? The logic behind this question is that if the work is non-value-adding (NVA), then it should be quickly eliminated from a process. This also implies that expensive countermeasures will not have to be deployed, and that resources can be allocated elsewhere within an organization. The balance of the questions listed in the first column of Table 6.1 follow from this first question.

The second question related to process improvement is: Where should an operation be performed? In this context, an organization should determine if the work should be located to another area within a facility or to another facility within the organization or outsourced elsewhere based on various considerations. For example, outsourcing of work may be required if it is very dangerous, is difficult to control because it may require specialized training and equipment, or is expensive on a per unit cost basis. In these situations, suppliers may have the necessary resources due to economies of scale, across several customers, to more efficiently do the work. As an example, perhaps one part of an organization has a tax expert or experts in intellectual property management or compensation management expertise. These resources can be shared across an organization. In other situations, work can be moved to areas of expertise within an organization or outsourced where it can be done more efficiently. Work can also be broken up into operational work tasks with portions done at different locations. Relative to the question, When should an operation be performed? it should be noted that some types of work should be done more or less frequently. Also, it may be better to do work at certain times of the day or during the week. As an example, perhaps the setup time for a certain type of job is very long. In an absence of analyzing and reducing job setup times, perhaps it would make sense to batch the work based on an economic analysis. Or perhaps if the cycle times of jobs are too long and job setup times are inexpensive, it would make sense to do a job more frequently. This may be the situation in which office workers are very skilled and can easily switch from one task to another, but through personal habit they tend to batch their work. As another example, the refreshing of computer systems, database backups, or other system maintenance may be best done when the workforce is not online or in the office. The question, How should an operation be best performed? is a major topic of this book as well as many other process improvement books. In this book, we discuss ways to increase operational efficiencies using a Kaizen event. The best way to answer this type of question is through a thorough root cause analysis. Answering the first four questions of Column 1 in Table 6.1 will make it easier to answer the question: Who should do the work?

The second section of Table 6.1 discusses several internal improvement methods. These have been shown to be very useful in process improvement and control activities, and they have been discussed in earlier chapters. As a result, we will not discuss them in further detail except to make a few additional comments. The elimination of operations and work tasks is a very effective way to eliminate root causes from a process workflow. Also, reductions in cycle time and cost are directly proportional to the number of work tasks eliminated from a process. Quality is also improved, in a simplified process, because defects that were created by former operations are no longer impacting the modified process. In Chapter 3 we also discussed the fact that balancing work within a system, relative to its bottleneck's production rate, will tend to minimize the probability of abrupt changes occurring within a system. In an environment in which the workflow has been balanced, errors will also be easier to identify and eliminate. This is in contrast to situations in which errors are not immediately discovered, which then requires a more complicated analysis of their root causes. However, it should be noted that it may take a significant amount of time and resources for an organization to be able to achieve the full operational benefits from balancing materials and information flows through a system. As a result, this type of process improvement is generally outside the scope of most rapid improvement teams because it depends on many subordinate activities and process improvements. These usually require an extended period of time to fully implement. The third general improvement method is the implementation of mixed-model scheduling systems to reduce lead time. This method was discussed in Chapters 3 to 5. However, mixed-model scheduling requires an extensive redesign of products and services and their associated processes because the number of job setups is increased due to their lower cost. However, to the extent these design changes can be made, mixed-model scheduling is an effective solution to reduce cycle time and cost. It has already been mentioned that the deployment of transfer rather than production batches will also directly reduce a system's lead time because product units are moved to downstream operations rather than batched based on their economic lot size. The other general methods to improve operational performance, which are listed in Table 6.1, include Lean, Six Sigma, just-in-time, and quick-response methods. However, the application of these methods requires significant changes to an organization's infrastructure as well as resource commitments for an extended period of time. These were also discussed in Chapters 3 to 5. Later in this chapter, we will discuss how to integrate these general methods of process improvement into office processes using six common office examples.

The third section of Table 6.1 lists several common process changes routinely implemented by Kaizen teams to improve their office operations. But the specific combination of improvements will depend on an analysis of root causes. As an example, sometimes a modification of organizational reporting structures eliminates functional silos and operational handoffs to more effectively align financial and operational metrics across a process workflow. This type of process change reinforces teamwork and creates a single source of accountability for processing issues. It has also been shown to be a very effective way to improve process workflows because many operational issues are due to an organization's bureaucracy and politics. As an example, the absence of operational procedures or the existence of overly complicated procedures increases a system's complexity, cost, and lead time. Typical examples include a requirement for management sign-offs rather than reinforcing employee accountability, the addition of NVA operations such as inspection, and confusion when employees do not understand their work tasks. Finally, competition and a failure to share information between departments or working toward conflicting performance goals and objectives create organizational conflicts. These situations result in an inability to identify and eliminate chronic process problems.

Common process changes also include creating new or modifying current process designs and layouts to improve operational performance. However, a redesign of products and services may require significant resources and an extended schedule that exceeds the time available during a Kaizen event. As an example, some changes may require the purchase of expensive equipment or require a long lead time for their implementation. As a result, Kaizen teams are seldom involved in the direct creation of new products or services because their implementation schedule is only a few days. However, to the extent that process workflows, including those related to design, can be modified to satisfy current customer and business requirements, they will be more effective and efficient if they contain a higher percentage of value-adding work. In this context, design simplification and technology innovation may enable work tasks to be done more efficiently as well.

It is common that older process workflows will tend to have a higher non-value-adding (NVA) context due, in part, to the misalignment caused by customer value migration. In these situations, process breakdowns will occur, resulting in ineffective or nonaligned operational and financial metrics. Metric misalignment drives the wrong organizational behavior because there is conflict between groups working toward different goals and objectives and competing for scarce resources. As an example, poorly aligned sales incentives may encourage salespeople to sell low-margin products or services or the wrong types of products. This practice will tend to lower organizational profits and create production inefficiencies. As a contrasting example, an organization may overly emphasize operational efficiency rather than process throughput rates of saleable products. As a direct result, local production supervisors will tend to utilize their resources near a 100 percent level rather than balancing their utilization rates to their system's bottleneck resource. This practice has been shown to cause the production of incorrect products, higher inventory levels, and the nonavailability of capacity for products that customers need. Another problem is often higher rework due to job start-up when schedules change. These situations also occur within office environments for a variety of reasons. One reason is insisting that people be kept busy on work tasks regardless of their usefulness to an organization. This does not imply that people should be idle, but that their work should be focused on activities that increase organizational productivity. Busy people working on NVA work tasks still require materials and information from their co-workers. This distracts co-workers from value-adding work tasks and reduces organizational productivity. Also, doing work too far in advance may require that it be reworked if customer requirements change. This situation may result in more important work not being completed on time, resulting in higher overtime expense. Revenue may also be adversely impacted. This is why work standards must be carefully designed and managers trained to use of efficient work methods rather than poor work habits that become reinforced with time.

Referring again to the third column in Table 6.1, a team may also create new information reporting systems. These reporting systems provide information in several different formats, but with a goal of providing useful information rather than an enormous amount of process data. Useful information facilitates more effective management of a process. One example would be to provide a graphical display of higher-level performance metrics, but also providing an analytical capability to drill down into the reasons for variations in higher-level performance. As an example, an accounts receivable process, could be measured using three higher-level performance metrics related to quality, cycle time, and cost. If any of these performance metrics should deteriorate, an effective reporting system would enable a manger to analyze successively lower-level metrics for clues to improve process performance. Using the quality metric "percentage invoice accuracy" as an example of this concept, at a next lower analytical level, percentage invoice accuracy can be broken down into customer segment, region of the country, industry, invoice aging, and amount. Also, at a lower level of analysis, perhaps customer segment can be broken down by specific customers and their invoiced amounts. Alternatively, account aging can be broken down by customer and invoice amount. This type of analytical capability will enable any organization to monitor and improve its process performance over time. Along this line of thought, project charters can be created and Kaizen teams deployed to improve operational metrics that have degraded. Exception reports can also be created to highlight process issues. They are a useful reporting method because processes are measured using myriad operational metrics, which are in turn based on an enormous amount of data that has been automatically captured by information technology (IT) systems. Figures 6.1 and 6.2 demonstrate these concepts. Also, process monitoring and reporting will be discussed in more detail in Chapter 8. In summary, new reporting systems will increase an organization's operational efficiency.

The balance of the common improvements listed in Table 6.1 include the purchase or design of new types of equipment, the implementation of 5S, mistake proofing, and similar Lean or Six Sigma methods, as well as the modification of procedures related to work tasks, testing, inspection, and maintenance. It should be noted that decisions to modify or purchase new equipment should be made only after a thorough analysis of a process problem. In other words, all proposed equipment improvements should be countermeasures that have been directly tied to a root cause analysis. An advantage of using fact-based methods such as those found in Lean and Six Sigma are that equipment improvements will have a higher probability of being successful. It was also mentioned that these Lean Six Sigma methods take time to implement. However, an exception occurs when an organization has already deployed a Lean Six Sigma improvement program. In these environments, Kaizen events, 5S, and other Lean methods can be easily implemented because the supporting infrastructure is already in place. In addition to the major improvements just discussed, there are myriad supporting process changes that are necessary to train employees to work within a modified process. These include modifications to work, testing, and inspection and maintenance procedures as well as employee training. Finally, small work group meetings (huddles) and verbal instructions should be reinforced on a daily basis to help ensure that process improvements are sustained over time.

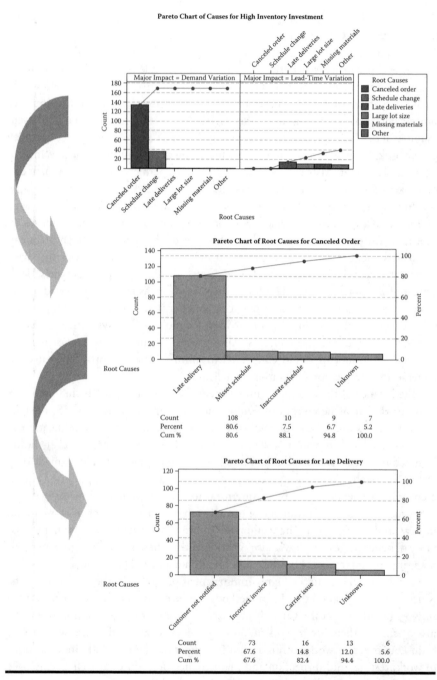

Figure 6.1 Root cause analysis: Levels 1, 2, and 3 (Figures 5.26, 5.28, and 5.30).

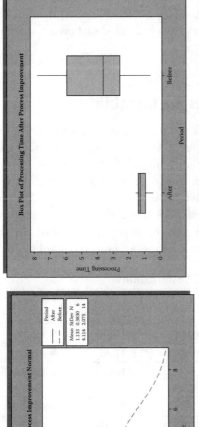

Box Plot of Processing Time After Process Improvement

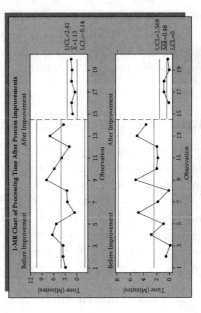

I-MR Chart of Processing Time After Process Improvements

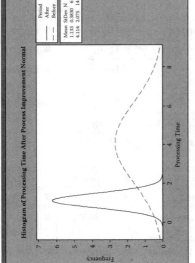

Histogram of Processing Time After Process Improvement Normal

• These graphs show that the average processing time and its variation decreased after a process improvement.

• There may be several ways to communicate process improvements depending on the intended audience.

• Several graphs may be used together if they help communicate process improvements.

Figure 6.2   Use graphics to show process improvements.

In summary, project controls are a combination of specific process changes. These process changes are the countermeasures necessary to eliminate the root causes of process breakdowns. We will continue to discuss the application of process controls to office processes in the next several chapters. In Chapter 7, these discussions will also include the cultural aspects of process change. Chapter 8 will discuss the methods necessary to integrate these control tools into an organization. In Chapter 9, we will discuss transferring control of the modified process back to the process owner and local work team.

Control Tool Effectiveness and Sustainability

Table 6.2 lists several common control tools and then compares their effectiveness and sustainability. Effectiveness means the process change eliminates the root cause or source of the process problem. Sustainability implies that the process change is very difficult to eliminate or avoid by the employees impacted by the change. Control tools vary relative to their effectiveness and ability to sustain process changes over time. For this reason, they are often used in combination to eliminate the root causes of a process problem to achieve a project's original objectives. In this context, it is useful to discuss the pros and cons of various process control tools.

Table 6.2 Control Tool Effectiveness and Sustainability

Specific Process Changes	*Effectiveness*	*Ability to Sustain*
■ Modify organizational reporting structures	■ High	■ High
■ Eliminate portions of a process	■ High	■ High
■ Create new or modified process designs and layouts	■ High	■ High
■ Mistake proof portions of a process	■ High	■ High
■ Purchase or design of new types of equipment	■ Medium	■ High
■ Implement 5S, mistake proofing, and similar Lean methods	■ High	■ Medium
■ Create new operational and financial metrics	■ Medium	■ Medium
■ Create new information reporting systems	■ Medium	■ Medium
■ Modify work, testing, inspection, maintenance, and other procedures	■ Medium	■ Low
■ Process audits and monitoring such as statistical process control	■ Medium	■ Low
■ Training programs	■ Medium	■ Low
■ Group meetings (huddles), written procedures, and verbal instructions	■ Low	■ Low

If a root cause is due to communication breakdowns between several organizational functions or to interpersonal issues, then a modification of organizational reporting structures may significantly increase operational efficiency. This is because changing an organizational reporting structure eliminates redundancies within an organization. This type of process improvement will typically improve communication, lower lead time, and reduce errors. This is because different organizational functions may have divergent goals and objectives as well as performance metrics. Different goals and objectives will usually result in miscommunication and other issues at functional interfaces. However, most Kaizen teams are not structured or authorized to make these types of improvements. For this reason, it is important that a Kaizen team, which is focused on modifying an organization's structure, consist of senior-level executives who have the authority to do this work. In these situations, the goal will be to determine an optimum organizational structure in a very short period of time. The effectiveness of these types of changes is very high and sustainable when properly analyzed and implemented.

Another very effective and sustainable control method is an elimination of portions of a process or a redesign of its operational work tasks. The effectiveness and sustainability of this type of countermeasure are very high because the complexity of the resultant system will decrease. The reasoning behind this statement is that if work operations are eliminated, then cycle time and cost will be directly reduced and the errors associated with the prior work operations will also be eliminated from a process. In a similar manner, but at a lower operational level, if work tasks within operations can be eliminated, then a process will be less complex and can be standardized and mistake proofed to increase its efficiency and availability.

Implementation of 5S, mistake proofing, and similar Lean methods has a high degree of effectiveness, but is somewhat difficult to sustain over time because these methods consist of combinations of manual work tasks and information technology (IT) systems. As a result, employees may deviate from using standard work instructions or not follow prescribed control measures. On the other hand, the purchase of new equipment is classified, in Table 6.2, as having a medium effectiveness level, but a high level of sustainability. This is because purchased equipment does not always eliminate a process problem if a root cause analysis was not properly conducted. However, once effectively deployed, improvements are usually easy to sustain.

Whereas the process changes described above have various levels of high effectiveness and sustainability, the next several changes are classified as having medium effectiveness and sustainability. In other words, they must be frequently audited over time to ensure they remain in place as effective process controls. As an example, in some situations, in lieu of an organizational restructuring, it may be possible to achieve similar results through modifications of operational and financial metrics. But these types of modifications must be carefully analyzed, deployed throughout the impacted areas of an organization, and consistently evaluated to ensure they remain effective. As a result, this type of process change has a medium level of effectiveness and sustainability because there may be problems gathering data for the timely metric reporting, and people may not fully comply with a new reporting system for many reasons. These reasons may include not having been involved in the development of the metrics, a lack of confidence in the measurement system itself, or a lack of understanding of the importance of the process change due to poor communication. The creation of new reporting systems is also classified as having a medium level of effectiveness and sustainability for the same reasons.

The balance of the process changes listed in Table 6.2 are less effective or sustainable. These include process audits; statistical process control; modification of work, testing, inspection, maintenance, and other procedures; training programs, group meetings; and verbal instructions. It should also be mentioned that statistical process control (SPC) is very effective in monitoring and controlling a process, but it is also manually intensive and difficult to sustain unless it has been automated. However, one way to increase the sustainability of SPC is to apply it only to control important or critical process variables. These variables should have been identified as significant through a root cause analysis. Audits are also a very useful process control tool, but manually intensive, and they must be done periodically by employees. As a result, they are costly and time-consuming to sustain over time. Employee training, although useful, must be clearly aligned with the countermeasures identified by a Kaizen team and frequently updated. However, organizations seldom maintain their training programs at their required frequency. In these situations, management is often a key obstacle in delaying training to ensure that employees are available to work on higher-priority issues. As a result, process controls that are heavily dependent on maintaining employee training are difficult to sustain over time. An exacerbating situation occurs when employees leave their jobs. This necessitates having to train new employees. Unfortunately, this situation is very common in service industries, with annualized employee turnover rates routinely exceeding 25 percent in some situations. Employees may also simply forget information. The operational impact when these situations occur is a degradation of service performance. In service industries, perhaps the most impartment component is a well-trained employee providing service in a predictable and standardized manner. If training is to be a major component of one or more process changes, then there may be several ways to keep employees up to date. In office systems, information technology (IT) can be used to prompt an employee for action, offer a menu of possible choices, or provide explanations of job tasks. This type of continuous employee training can be provided at a very low cost. The last few process changes listed in Table 6.2 include meeting and verbal instructions. Although these are important, they should be incidental to other, more robust process changes because they are very difficult to sustain.

Root Cause Analysis and Improvement Strategies

In Chapter 5 we discussed several tools and methods that are useful in the collection and analysis of process data as well as simple analytical tools and methods. In

Table 6.3   Root Cause Analysis and Improvement Strategy

1. Project selection aligned with business goals.
2. Obtain approval from process owner, finance, and key stakeholders.
3. Communicate project results to key stakeholders.
4. Root cause analysis drives all improvements.
5. Prove causal effect Y = f(x) using tools.
6. Process controls must be tied to root cause analysis.
7. Standardize procedures and implement training.
8. Mistake proof the process or change process design.
9. Measurement systems improvement.
10. Detailed control plan and audits.

this section we will discuss a general process improvement methodology, shown in Table 6.3. This sequential methodology is useful in the analysis and elimination of the root causes of process problems, and it can be modified to fit a Kaizen team's project. As an example, Step 5 can be modified if an analysis is not heavily dependent on statistically based tools.

A successful root cause analysis begins with a well-defined problem statement and project objective. It is very easy to get this step of a root cause analysis wrong. This may be particularly true if the project's charter was not created in advance of a team's deployment. Recall that in earlier chapters we discussed the concept that project charters need to be aligned with business goals and objectives. Also, project charters must be fully investigated and quantified prior to team selection and deployment. This requires that a project charter be approved by a process owner, finance, the Lean Six Sigma deployment champion, as well as other relevant stakeholders. Once a team has been assigned a fully vetted project charter, it should be reviewed for its relevance. A diverse and well-facilitated Kaizen team is usually very effective in reviewing their team's project charter from several different perspectives. This is important because a Kaizen team should discuss all aspects of a process problem prior to working on its root cause analysis. A first step in this review process is gathering all the information related to the process problem using the methods discussed in earlier chapters of this book. Ideally, a project champion will have gathered preliminary process data for his or her team in advance of the Kaizen event.

The assumption at this point in our discussion of process improvement is that a project has been selected to ensure its alignment with business goals in a manner discussed in earlier chapters. Recall that in these discussions, it was stated that a root cause analysis must drive all process improvements to ensure a project's success. In other words, a Kaizen team must prove causal relationships between the financial and operational metrics that must be improved and the variables that must be changed through an application of one or more countermeasures. Countermeasures must be sustained after they have been applied to eliminate the root causes for poor process performance. It has already been mentioned in the previous section that some countermeasures are easier to sustain than others. As an example, those that require a high degree of manual intervention will usually require a standardization of procedures, implementation of training programs, and creation of process audit systems. In addition, a process should be mistake proofed to the highest extent possible. The cumulative impact of these activities will be an improved measurement system, and enhanced metric and process status reporting, as well as a detailed process control plan in either physical or electronic format.

Prior to turning to how the concepts examined up to this point can be used to analyze common office workflows, we must have a preliminary discussion showing how the diverse concepts should be put together to complete a root cause analysis of process issues. Figure 6.1 begins this discussion using the inventory investment example discussed toward the end of Chapter 5. Recall that as a Kaizen team collected and analyzed data associated with the reasons for canceled orders, the root cause analysis extended down to successively lower levels. This concept is shown in Figure 6.1, which is an aggregate of Figures 5.26, 5.28, and 5.30. The root cause analysis moved from the inventory investment problem to canceled orders and then to late deliveries as a major problem causing high inventory investment. Finally, it was found that the "customer not notified" issue was the major contributor to the late delivery of materials. At this point in the investigation, a Kaizen team may rescope its original project charter to focus on the problem at hand, that is, to eliminate the root causes for the late delivery of materials; fix several related issues, if the schedule permits; or create new project charters for future Kaizen teams.

In addition to identifying the reasons for the high inventory investment problem, a financial analysis is required to ensure a Kaizen team focuses on eliminating root causes having the most severe impact on the organization. A thorough financial analysis will also be useful when balancing implementation costs against anticipated business benefits. As an example, Table 6.4 uses the information shown in Figure 5.29 to evaluate each of the proposed countermeasures to calculate business benefits net of implementation costs. Also, the process improvements have been divided into three separate project charters for assignment to other Kaizen teams. The net business benefits shown in Table 6.4 will be realized if the countermeasures or improvements are executed according to their project schedule. It should also be noted that all financial numbers should link to the higher-level inventory investment problem. It is easy to see that a complete elimination of the "customer not notified" issue would reduce inventory investment by \$347,656. Recall that the total inventory investment associated with the process issues was \$1,000,000. Thus, the percentage of the investment problem represented by "customer not notified" is 34.8 percent. Also, because the total inventory investment is \$2,000,000, the percentage reduction in overall inventory investment is 17.4 percent. When a Kaizen team can communicate to its management using such clear language describing a project's business benefits, it will be able to easily obtain resources for its project's

Table 6.4   Countermeasures at 4th-Level Root Cause—Late Deliveries

Root Cause	Incorrect Invoice	Carrier Issue	Customer Not Notified
Countermeasure	System match to customer zip code	Assign a specific and load/unload time for each carrier.	Send an automatic e-mail to customer when order is shipped.
Business Impact	$ 76,199		
Implementation Date	January	February	March
Implementation Costs	$ 10,000	$ 6,000	$ 25,000
Net Business Benefits	$ 66,199	$ 55,911	$ 322,656
People Responsible	Team 1	Team 4	Team 3

Data from Figure 5.29

improvements. Also, note the clear linkage between the financial estimates and specific operational improvements that are tied to a rigorous root cause analysis. Finally, it is also clear that the major problem the team should eliminate is "customer not notified" because it is associated with $347,656 of inventory investment.

An important part of process improvement is also showing, through the types of countermeasures, that a problem will be permanently eliminated from a process. This information should be reviewed with a process owner and local work team prior to transferring the modified process back to them. In this context, Figure 6.2 shows one of several ways in which process improvements can be clearly communicated to an organization. The hypothetical example shown in Figure 6.2 describes a reduction of processing time (or cycle time) after a process improvement. Any of the three graphs shown in Figure 6.2 can be used to demonstrate that a performance improvement occurred relative to its baseline level. Also, more advanced statistical methods can be applied to the same example with the assistance of people familiar with such methods. The histogram and box plot were discussed in Chapter 5. The control chart shown in Figure 6.2 was also discussed briefly in Chapter 5, and it will be discussed in more detail and from several perspectives in Chapter 8. The remainder of this chapter will examine how the six common office processes can be analyzed and improved, using the methods discussed in Chapters 3 through 6. Then, in Chapters 7 to 9 we will expand our discussion to include several elements of organizational change in the context of Kaizen events, management presentations, and process control.

Examples Using Common Process Workflows

An organization is a system consisting of numerous process workflows. In turn, these process workflows are aggregates of lower-level operations and work tasks. In this section, we present several very simplified office processes common to both manufacturing and service organizations. The goal of reviewing these six examples is to show that they can be analyzed using the tools and methods discussed in Chapters 3 to 6. As a general statement, mapping and quantifying a process workflow using financial and operational information is always an important analytical strategy for a Kaizen team. Communication aids are also very useful in describing process breakdowns. These include symbols and other information placed directly on a process map. This approach was discussed in Chapter 3 and shown in Figure 3.5 and includes using starbursts and attaching data collection, analysis, and reporting forms and reports to the map. Figures 3.4 and 3.5 demonstrated these concepts by showing how to mark up a process map for analysis by a Kaizen team and key stakeholders. Relative to quantification there are several useful approaches to metric quantification that have been discussed in earlier chapters. As an example, Figures 3.7 and 3.8 show how takt time calculations can be used to measure the throughput rates of materials and information as they flow through a process. In addition, process yields and failure points should be identified to include scrap and rework percentages, maintenance, and similar process issues. This quantitative information will provide a Kaizen team with a long list of prioritized ideas to improve its process. Using this combined analytical approach as well as the information contained in Chapters 4 to 6, we will provide a general discussion of Lean Six Sigma improvement opportunities in the context of these examples.

Example 1: Financial Forecasting

A finance department is made up of several workflows, including the forecasting and control of an organization's budgets. The basis for developing a financial forecast is an organization's revenue goals. These goals or targets are set as a percentage increase over the previous year if there is no macroeconomic, industry, or other reasons for setting it at lower levels. These revenue goals are allocated to every product and location by adjusting the previous year's sales or next year's forecast by the required percentage increase or decrease. In this discussion, products also mean services, and the budgeting process is similar for both manufacturing and service industries. In fact, wherever services are provided and resources are necessary to provide them there will be a planning or budgeting process. Also, financial forecasting is itself an office process that is common in any organization with a financial budget. In a financial budgeting process, several functional groups meet to review an organization's annual revenue forecasts. This is done in the context of how revenue targets will be achieved through product sales. In these discussions, marketing and sales determine sales targets for products. In addition, operational functions such as procurement, production, and logistics provide capacity information broken down by facility and product group showing how production will be made to satisfy sales and, by implication, revenue forecasts.

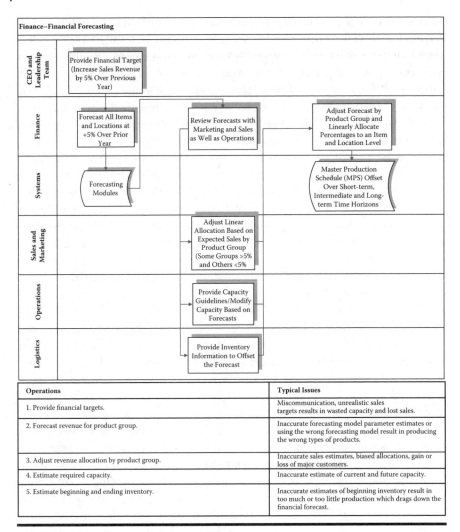

Figure 6.3   Example 1: Financial forecasting.

Figure 6.3 shows a simple example of how this type of process workflow functions using five operations as well as several places where it could break down. In Operation 1, typical process breakdowns include miscommunication between finance and other functions, unrealistic financial targets, and lost sales revenue. Miscommunication issues may be caused by inaccurate or missing information. As an example, sales and marketing may agree they can increase sales and revenue, but they may not know that industry sales are declining because of inaccurate marketing research data. Nonaligned sales incentives cause other breakdowns in a financial forecasting process because they contribute to building products that compete for scarce production capacity or have a low profit margin. This may cause a buildup of inventory for some products but lost sales for others. Other failure modes include misapplication of forecasting models, inaccurate parameters, and a failure to adjust the historical basis of a forecasting model when its time series abruptly changes. The wrong types or quantities of products and services will be produced in these situations. A financial forecast may also be in error due to the gain or loss of major customers. These and other issues can be mitigated by formally communicating them through an organization's sales and operations planning (S&OP) team. From an operational perspective, process breakdowns may also occur if resources are not available to produce products or beginning and ending inventory estimates are inaccurate. As an example, inaccurate estimates of beginning inventory result in too much or too little production, which drags down a financial forecast for the associated products or services. Any of these types of process issues can serve as a basis of one of more Kaizen events, depending on the complexity of their root causes. In other words, if the anticipated root causes of a process breakdown are easy to identify and eliminate, then a Kaizen team may be able to eliminate them quickly within a few days. But more complicated analyses may require deploying formal Lean and Six Sigma projects.

These types of process breakdowns show that even a very simple office process has multiple places where failure could occur. The best way to identify these types of process issues is through a formal financial and operational analysis of an organization's major process workflows. This is best done using a Kaizen team and working with key stakeholders, such as the process owner and local work team, to build a value stream map (VSM). In parallel, a Kaizen team should gather financial and operational reports, forms, templates, and other tools that are used to manage, control, and improve the various process workflows. Another important reason to analyze financial workflows is to ensure an organization's financial controls are compliant with governmental laws and regulations. In the United States this would mean meeting Sarbanes–Oxley and Financial Services Accounting Board (FASB) standards. As financial and accounting processes become increasingly geographically dispersed, they have a higher probability of breakdown given the differences in language, culture, and other similar issues that adversely impact operations.

Example 2: Accounts Receivable

An accounts receivable process is one of several accounting functions. Additional functions include auditing, accounts payable, and similar activities. In the simple example shown in Figure 6.4 we see that the process workflow consists of several major operations beginning when a customer places an order to the payment of an invoice. The eight operations shown in Figure 6.4 contain many work tasks that can fail to meet requirements. These requirements include specifications related to cycle time, accuracy, and per unit transaction cost. Process breakdowns within each of

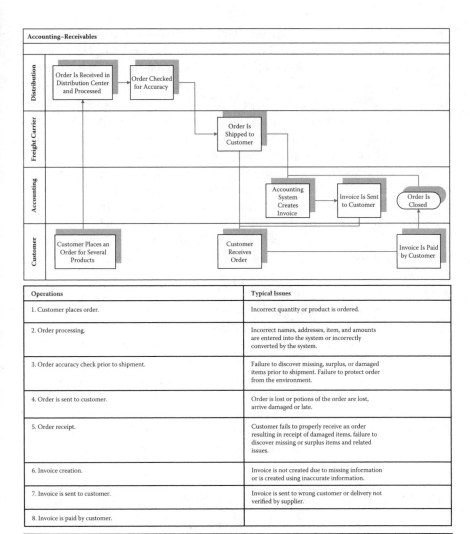

Figure 6.4   Example 2: Accounts receivable.

the eight operations of the accounts receivable process are shown in Figure 6.4. Any one of these process issues could serve as a basis for a Kaizen team's project charter or become part of a team's analysis of root causes. In the first operation, a customer places an order for a product or service. At this step in the process, a common error is incorrectly ordering a product. This may include an inaccurate type of product or its quantity. In the second operation, even if a customer correctly orders a product, an employee taking the order may have misinterpreted the customer's request. This misinterpretation may be related to entering an incorrect name, address, product type, or similar customer information. However, in automated systems this may

not be a major issue because a system simply records a customer's order information. A second part of Operation 2 is filling an order that has been placed into the
system. In service systems, this may include employees providing a service to a customer. In manufacturing or logistic systems, orders may be processed though manufacturing and warehousing operations and finally staged for shipment. Once an
order has been completed and prepared for shipment, it may have missing, surplus,
or damaged items. These conditions occur for various reasons and may be shipped
to customers even if dock audits are performed on outgoing orders. As an order is
transported to a customer, it may be lost or damaged through poor handling by a
carrier or if exposed to adverse environmental conditions. The result is that when
an order is received by a customer, it may arrive damaged or be late. At the sixth
operation, customers receive their orders. Invoice payment depends on customers
receiving their order without defects and on time; otherwise, payment of the invoice
will be delayed by the customer. Once the order has been successfully received by a
customer, an invoice is created by the supplier. An error may also occur at this part
of a process due to missing information and other issues that result in an invoice
having incorrect information or being sent to a wrong customer.

Accounts receivable processes are common to almost every organization. As a
result, Kaizen teams can be deployed to identify and eliminate problems within
these processes. This is very important because the negative cost impact associated
with accounts receivable breakdowns can be significant. In fact, in some organizations, accounts receivable that are more than 90 days old cannot be collected
at all, resulting in a complete loss of materials and labor for sold products. Also,
accounting processes are subject to governmental laws and regulations such as
Sarbanes–Oxley and the Financial Accounting Standards Board (FASB).

Example 3: New Product Market Research

A major process workflow within the sales and marketing function is new product
marketing research. Product in this context refers to manufactured goods or services
provided to customers. Marketing research is an important set of activities for an
organization because inaccurate demand estimates will result in a sales forecast that is
significantly higher or lower than actual sales. The result will be either excess inventory
or product shortages. In the first situation, if products are not sold, then inventory
levels build up. This increases the expenses related to the invested materials and labor
as well as the warehousing expense necessary to store the inventory. In a worst-case
scenario, inventory may never be sold. This type of situation would necessitate its
disposal at a financial loss. This situation is analogous in a service organization, but
inventory investment appears in the form of excess operational capacity, that is, hiring
of employees in anticipation of future sales. In either situation, poor forecasts of new
products will result in significant operational issues for an organization.

Although marketing research is a complicated process, a simplified version is shown in Figure 6.5. In the first operation, customer needs and requirements are estimated by marketing analysts. Even under the best of circumstances this is a very complicated and error-prone process that requires a significant amount of education and experience. Six Sigma tools and methods are very useful in these data-intensive environments. But Lean methods and their process analysis focus are also very important in understanding the relationships among operational work tasks. Common issues or process breakdowns in the new product marketing research process include a lack of relevant and quantifiable information. This is often caused by a failure to use efficient survey methods to obtain and analyze the voice of the customer (VOC). VOC activities consist of identifying market segments and using survey methods to identify customer needs and values expectations by market segment. Survey methods include determining the right mixture of e-mails, interviews, focus groups, on-site visits, as well as other data collection methods that are necessary to adequately capture customer information. These activities are also very complex, which increases the probability of process breakdowns. A new product marketing research team will work with its product designer's team to translate the VOC into design concepts, prototypes, and specifications. A breakdown within this translation process could also occur if VOC information is not translated accurately. The result will be a new product or service that does not meet customer requirements. This may result in lost sales and high inventory expense for an organization. A different problem may occur if requirements that customers do not need or value are added to a product's specifications. This will increase the cost of a product or service. Finally, a review of alternative product designs with external customers is important. In other words, it is important to go back to customers with working prototypes to show how a new product will look, feel, and function. A failure to properly review new concepts with customers to obtain their feedback may result in a suboptimal product design that is more costly and less reliable than alternatives. Kaizen teams can be formed around any of these issues, or alternatively, they may discover one or more of these issues as they analyze the new product marketing process.

Example 4: New Product Development

Almost every organization has a new product development group that coordinates the creation of new products and services. This group works at the functional interfaces with sales, marketing, procurement, production, logistics, and external customers. Figure 6.6 shows a simple view of a new product development process with several key functions displayed. The goal of a new product development process is to accurately and efficiently translate customer needs and requirements into design specifications. These specifications are related to functional, performance, and aesthetic features. In this work, myriad specialized tools and methods are used

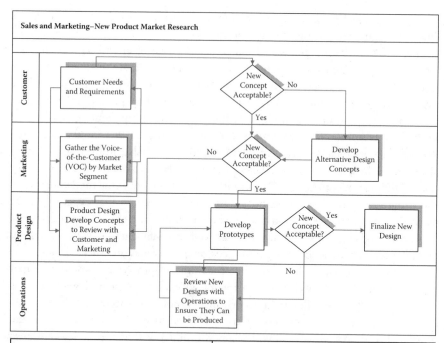

Operations	Typical Issues
1. Estimate customer needs and requirements.	Lack of quantification or methodical survey methods used to obtain the voice of the customer (VOC).
2. Gather the VOC.	Ineffective or inefficient survey choice of methods (emails, interviews, focus groups, site visits, and similar data collection methods).
3. Work with product design to translate VOC into design specifications and prototypes.	All VOC information is not transmitted to product design or additional requirements are added that customers do not value or need.
4. Review concepts with customers.	Failure to review new concepts with customers to obtain their feedback in a methodical manner.
5. Develop alternative designs.	Failure to develop alternative designs that meet customer and business requirements and their characteristics be evaluated using structured methods.

Figure 6.5   Example 3: New product marketing research.

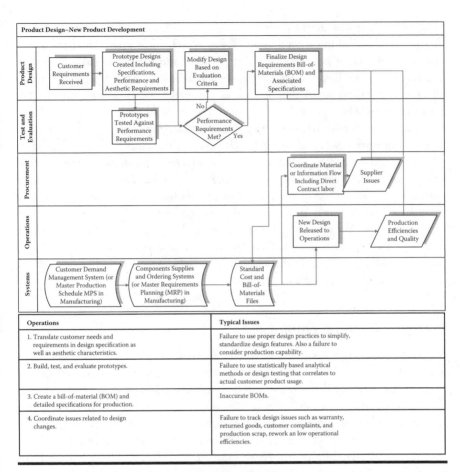

Figure 6.6   Example 4: New product development.

to efficiently design products and services. A failure to use proper design practices to simplify, standardize, and mistake proof design features will result in a longer product development cycle time and higher error rates and cost.

Because this is a very complicated process consisting of several major work-flows, there will be many ways in which it can break down. But Kaizen teams can be deployed to eliminate many of these process issues. Alternatively, Kaizen teams that have been deployed to one or more new product operations may identify several process issues that are caused by design activities as part of their assessment activities. As an example, a failure to obtain the VOC information or to consult with production or other key stakeholders will cause the probability of miscommunication and design errors during the development process of new products. Also, mistakes may be made during the building, testing, or evaluation of alternative designs and prototypes. This is especially true when these activities are not based on statistically valid analytical methods or modern project management methods such as concurrent engineering (CE). CE is a set of tools and methods that promote communication among all key stakeholders when deploying a new product or service. When deploying new products and services it is also important that laboratory and field testing correlate to actual customer use of a product under all expected conditions. A product bill of material (BOM) or a service's scripts are other areas where there may be issues. Process issues may also occur after a new product or service has been released for production. These issues are seen as increases in warranty and returned goods expense, customer complaints, production scrap and rework, as well as other conditions contributing to low operational efficiencies. In summary, a well-functioning new product development process is critical in the prevention of these types of process issues. In this context, because these issues occur across several organizational functions, Kaizen teams are an excellent way to identify and implement process improvements. In fact, a quick review of the typical issues listed in Figure 6.6 shows that several are related to communication problems. In this regard, Kaizen teams are an excellent resource to improve organizational communication.

Example 5: Hiring Employees

Recall that our original purpose in discussing these six common office workflows was to show that any process consists of a complicated set of work tasks. As a result, there will usually be many ways to improve a process relative to reducing its cycle time and cost while improving its quality. Along this line of thought, we will continue our discussion into the human resources (HR) process related to hiring new employees. Hiring qualified employees is difficult because it includes several organizational functions. As an example, it includes a hiring manager, the human resources organization, perhaps a third-party employment agency, advertising agencies, as well as the local employment market relative to the availability and skills of potential employees. The expenses related to hiring and retaining employees can be very high if this process is broken. In earlier chapters, it was mentioned that some industries and organizations have turnover rates exceeding 25 percent or more. This is because when employees leave an organization, others must be recruited and trained to take their place. It is also interesting to note that whereas retaining employees is difficult, the yields associated with employee hiring are also very low. As an example, I worked with several organizations that were located in rural areas. Over several years the available pool of potential employees had become effectively exhausted. But instead of trying to attract the limited, but available, pool of applicants for interviewing and hiring, the employment policies of these organizations were very complicated and actually turned away available candidates. To provide a more specific example of the impact of a broken process, in one organization, the potential workforce consisted principally of working mothers with small children. This organization had a corporate policy that mandated that

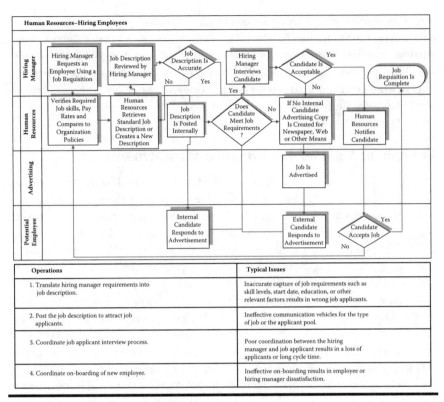

Figure 6.7   Example 5: Hiring employees.

employees be terminated if they missed a certain number of days per year. The policy resulted in an annual employee turnover rate of more than 100 percent as well as $1,000,000 in hiring and termination expenses for this one division. A solution was found using a Kaizen team in which employee policies were changed to accommodate employees having special work-hour requirements. It has been my experience that once a process becomes broken, people often do not see where it needs to be improved without making a concerted effort to analyze its performance. Kaizen teams are an excellent way to measure, analyze, and improve the HR processes related to hiring and retaining new employees.

Figure 6.7 shows a simple example of a process workflow for new-employee hiring. Important operations in this type of process include the translation of hiring manager requirements into a formal job description, posting the job description, coordinating interviews between job applicants and the hiring manager, as well as new-employee on-boarding activities. Each of these operations consists of lower-level work tasks. In a manner similar to that in the previous examples, there are typical issues with each operation. Issues associated with the translation of job requirements include a failure to accurately capture requirements related to skills, experience, education, or other relevant factors from a hiring manager. Inaccurate requirements may result in interviewing unacceptable applicants, resulting in a longer cycle time to hire and on-board new employees. Issues may also occur when posting a new job description in a timely manner because some jobs are time sensitive. Finally, there may be poor coordination of the activities associated with the interviewing process. Kaizen events can be deployed within any of these operations to identify and eliminate the root causes of process breakdowns.

Example 6: Supplier Performance Management

The supplier performance management (SPM) process workflow is critical in providing suppliers with the information they need to improve their performance over time. An additional organizational benefit is higher competition between suppliers. This situation will contribute to lower material, labor, and other procurement costs. SPM processes exist with varying degrees of professionalism across industries and organizations. Larger organizations tend to create professional SPM processes, whereas smaller ones most likely use informal systems. The specific types of performance information collected in these systems also varies, but it tends to focus on timeliness of providing products and services, year-over-year cost reductions, the quality or accuracy of service, and other factors that may be important to an organization. SPM systems can also range from very simple ones, which are best characterized as simple Excel-based spreadsheets, to more complicated Web-based systems in which there are many handoffs as different functions add information to build a final supplier report. The complexity of the larger systems also varies. As an example, procurement evaluates suppliers based on their pricing, design engineering evaluates suppliers based on their level of innovation, and production evaluates suppliers based on their quality and on-time delivery performance.

The SPM process shown in Figure 6.8 is a relatively simple one consisting of only a few operations. The process begins with developing an approved supplier listing in which supplier performance has been fully evaluated by a cross-functional team. Typical issues at this point in the evaluation relate to the relevancy of the supplier rating system or improperly conducting supplier audits. In the second operation of an SPM process, orders are sourced with suppliers who have been added to an approved supplier listing. In these sourcing activities, there may be miscommunications of the order requirements relative to delivery time, quality, or cost. These conditions may result in process breakdowns between suppliers and their customers. Miscommunication issues also increase the probability of errors. In turn, these conditions increase procurement cost. The coordination activities are very complex and often span several organizations within a supply chain. At this point in the SPM process, several problems may impact the coordination of supplier evaluations among internal organizational functions. This may result in a failure to properly evaluate a supplier's performance from several organizational

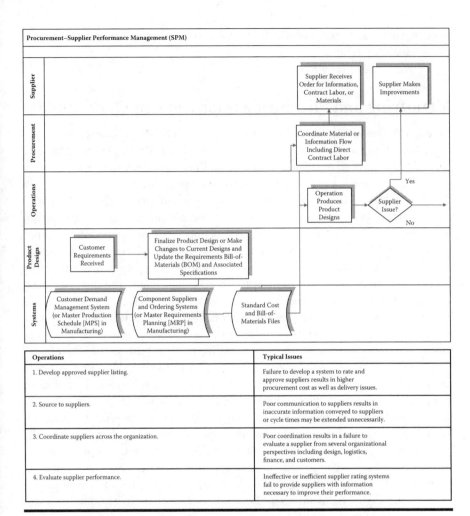

Figure 6.8   Example 6: Supplier performance management (SPM).

perspectives, including design, logistics, finance, and external customers. An ineffective or inefficient supplier rating system will not provide suppliers with the information necessary to improve their performance over time.

Although the emphasis of this book is on highly interactive and manual creation of process workflows using a value stream map (VSM), in some systems, especially those having complicated rework loops and parallel operations, it may be useful to create simulation models of a process workflow. As a result, we will discuss Crystal Ball® software in Appendix 1 as an approach to simulate quantified versions of office processes. An advantage of this approach is that once a simulation model has been built, it will be possible to evaluate changes in operational outputs such as time, process yield, and cost to relative to various process inputs.

In these analyses, a system's critical path and bottleneck are an important focus of the simulation activities.

Identifying and Prioritizing Improvement Opportunities

An organization should always have a listing of projects that will improve its productivity. Our discussion in earlier chapters emphasized that projects should be aligned with business goals and objectives and prioritized relative to their anticipated business benefits as well as resource requirements. This identification process was done using a variety of quantitative analyses. Recall from earlier chapters that these analyses included a review of financial and operational reports, the gathering of information related to customer complaints, warranty issues, and returned products, and information showing where customer satisfaction was low. Using this information, Kaizen teams can be deployed to identify and eliminate the causes for poor process performance or to identify improvement projects to increase operational performance and productivity.

The Kaizen project worksheet shown in Figure 6.9 demonstrates how ideas to improve a process are formally recorded during a Kaizen event to build actionable project charters that can be prioritized relative to their business benefits. Recall that in the new product market research example, one potential problem was poor translation of customer requirements into internal design specifications. Kaizen teams can create a list of project ideas using this approach, which can be immediately executed by the team. These ideas may also become future project charters for other Kaizen teams in the future. An advantage of this approach is that formally characterizing productivity opportunities in this manner provides management with a strong incentive to provide additional resources to Lean Six Sigma improvement teams to continue their activities. It should be noted that the Kaizen project worksheet in Figure 6.9 is shown without a root cause analysis. This implies it was created through an operational assessment using a root cause analysis. A Kaizen team will eventually complete the sections entitled "root causes," "required actions," and "future performance." In the next few chapters we will discuss several additional ways in which a Kaizen team can communicate improvement suggestions to their leadership team.

In addition to identifying projects, a Kaizen team should also prioritize projects using a tool similar to the one shown in Figure 6.10. Figure 6.10 is similar to the cause-and-effect (C&E) matrix discussed in detail in Chapter 5. Prioritization of projects should not be difficult if the project worksheet shown in Figure 6.9 has been properly completed. This concept is shown as an example in Figure 6.10 in which several potential improvement projects are prioritized within the new production marketing research process. These projects include issues related to a lack of VOC quantification, problems with reviewing design concepts, inaccurate information being transferred back and forth between the customer and supplier, a failure to

Kaizen Project Worksheet:		
Date:		Project Number:
Process Workflow: New Product Marketing Research		
Process Owner:		
Team Leader:		
Team Members:		
Kaizen Opportunity: Improve the process for translating sales information to design engineering.		

Problem Statement:	Root Causes:	Required Actions:
All VOC information is not transmitted to product design or additional requirements are added that customers do not value or need. This has increased the lead-time of new product releases from 100 to 200 days and increases development costs by 50%, or $2,000,000 annually.	TBD	TBD

Current Performance:	Future Performance:	Anticipated Benefits:
Insert metrics, charts, and graphs to show current performance baselines of operational, financial, and other metrics.	TBD	TBD or, if historical information is known, this can be taken from the projects charter.

Figure 6.9   Kaizen project—new product marketing research.

identify suitable alternative designs, the deployment of incorrect survey methods, and adding superfluous specifications to meeting customer requirements. The prioritization shown in Figure 6.10 enables a weighted total to be calculated, in the manner described in Chapter 5. Projects having a higher weighted total are ranked more important to a customer and business than those having a lower weighting.

Summary

Table 6.1 presented a listing of several common process changes that can be made to eliminate one or more of the root causes for poor process performance. It was

Rating of Importance to Customer	10	9	7	9	9	10	9	9	9	
	1	2	3	4	5	6	7	8	9	
Sequence / Project	Customer Satisfaction	Standard Cost	Cycle Time	Warranty Cost	Returned Goods	Customer Complaints	Scrap Cost	Rework Costs	Design Labor Costs	Total
6 Lack of VOC quantification	6	7	8	7	6	7	8	6	9	573
4 Reviewing concepts with customers	9	7	7	8	8	9	4	5	5	562
1 VOC information not given to design	6	6	7	8	7	6	7	7	8	556
5 Lack of alternatie designs	8	6	5	4	4	7	4	3	6	428
2 Incorrect survey methods	4	3	5	5	6	5	5	3	5	368
3 Nonessential information added	3	7	6	3	4	3	3	2	7	336
Total	360	324	266	315	315	370	279	234	360	

Figure 6.10   Prioritizing new product marketing research projects (similar to Figure 5.22).

mentioned that prior to improving a process, we may want to consider asking questions such as those listed in the section entitled "General Questions" and then apply internal improvements. It was also mentioned that control tools and methods vary in their effectiveness and sustainability. As a result, they should be used in combination to achieve a project's improvement goals. This is particularly important in situations where some process controls may be less effective or sustainable. These types of process controls include process audits, statistical process control (SPC), modification of procedures related to work, testing, inspection, and maintenance, training programs, group meetings, and verbal instructions. These concepts were demonstrated using the inventory investment example shown in Figure 6.1 and Table 6.4. In addition, Figure 6.1 and Table 6.4 as well as Figure 6.2 demonstrated how a root cause analysis should be used to create a business case for process improvements. These are the types of analyses Kaizen teams should use to gain management's support for their project recommendations.

The balance of the chapter discussed six common office processes and the typical process issues that occur within these processes. These issues increase cycle time and cost and lower process yields. As an example, in Figure 6.3 it was shown that financial forecasting consists of several operations related to the establishment and control of organizational budgets. Typical process breakdowns included miscommunication between finance and other functions, poor model specification, and operational issues relative to asset valuation, such as inventory. Figures 6.4 through 6.8 showed five additional office processes with various related process issues. The conclusion from this discussion is that process improvement opportunities are numerous. As a result, an organization should always be identifying improvement projects through a variety of methods, including operational assessments by Kaizen teams.

Suggested Reading

Wil van der Aalst and Kees van Hee. 2002. *Workflow management models, methods, and systems.* Cambridge, MA: MIT Press.

David Bustard, Peter Kawalek, and Mark Norris, eds. 2000. *Systems modeling for business process improvement.* Norwood, MA: Artech House, Inc.

Mikell P. Groover. 2007. *Work systems and the methods, measurement and management of work.* Upper Saddle River, NJ: Pearson-Prentice Hall.

Paul Harmon. 2003. *Business process change—A manager's guide to improving, redesigning, and automating processes.* San Francisco: Morgan Kaufman Publishers.

Michael Havey. 2005. *Essential business modeling.* Sebastopol, CA: O'Reilly Media, Inc.

Peter Hines, Richard Lamming, Dan Jones, Paul Cousins, and Nick Rich. 2000. *Value stream management.* New York: Prentice Hall.

James W. Martin. 2008. *Operational excellence—Using Lean Six Sigma to translate customer value through global supply chains.* New York: Auerbach.

James P. Womack and Daniel T. Jones. 1996. *Lean thinking—Banish waste and create wealth in your organization.* New York: Simon & Schuster.

IMPLEMENTING SOLUTIONS

3

Chapter 7

Building a Business Case for Change

Overview

If a Kaizen team's analysis of root causes was correctly done, then making effective process changes should be a straightforward set of activities. These activities will ensure that the correct things have been changed and improvements are sustained over time. There are many ways to describe the key elements of an effective change initiative. Figure 7.1 shows one such description in which several important elements that have been known to influence an organization's change effectiveness are shown in sequential order. Several of these variables were discussed in earlier chapters of this book. The balance will be discussed in this and subsequent chapters. Figure 7.1 shows that in addition to being used in combination, some elements naturally follow others. As an example, project alignment would naturally be a prerequisite for tool training because different projects require different combinations of tools and methods for the analysis of the root causes associated with the project's problem statement. Also, countermeasures must follow an analysis of root causes. Process improvement activities fail or become diluted when one or more of these basic elements is missing or not done efficiently according to its sequence. There are also simpler versions of this concept in which key elements are multiplied to indicate that they reinforce each other. As an example, one major organization uses the following relationship to express the effectiveness of change: cultural acceptance × business strategy = change effectiveness. But this relationship hides several of the important elements shown in Figure 7.1.

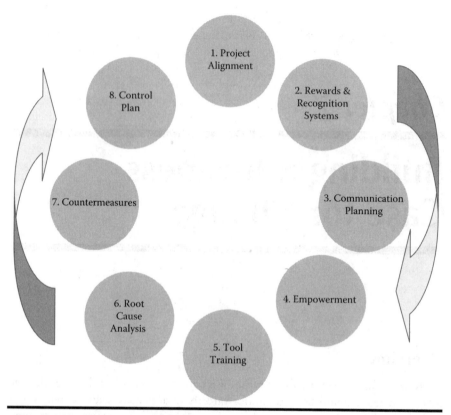

Figure 7.1   Major change elements.

Effective organizational change begins with a project's alignment with higher-level management goals and objectives. This ensures that the project will be important to key organizational stakeholders to obtain the support and resources necessary for its success. We have already discussed the importance of project alignment in Chapters 1 and 2. In this context, an organization has many goals and objectives that must be achieved in any given year. In the execution of these goals and objectives, it is important that resources be prioritized and allocated according to their anticipated business benefits. In these prioritization activities, improvement projects are analyzed and their alignment to higher-level organizational goals and objectives is verified by deployment leaders. A Lean Six Sigma initiative and Kaizen teams, in particular, will face significant challenges in the execution of their Kaizen events if their projects are not aligned with their management's goals and objectives. Unfortunately, this situation occurs quite often in some organizations. The result is isolated Kaizen events that create little synergy or justification for organizational change.

Creation of reward and recognition systems is critical to the execution of any business activity. But they become especially important when a new initiative is being deployed within an organization. This is because employees will only expend their energy on work activities that their managers have told them are important to their performance review or impact their other incentives. In this context, there are many case studies and examples where an initiative began to fail until an organization changed its incentive systems. It should be noted that incentives can be either positive or negative. Positive incentives include promotions, awards, pay increases, bonuses, and similar positive reinforcements. Negative incentives include disciplinary action, termination, a reduction in bonus or pay decreases, and similar actions. What gets rewarded gets done in an organization. As a result, an organization should ensure its reward and recognition systems promote its goals and objectives through teamwork. This is because organizational change and even changes at a project level require both coordination and the cooperation of many individuals.

Communication is important for any business activity. This is especially true when a Kaizen team needs to obtain help from very busy people within their organization. Communication can take very different forms, but the message should always be simple and consistent across all types of communication. As an example, there are many types of communication formats and vehicles. These also change depending on the level of the organization at which their message must be delivered as well as the target audience. For these reasons, it is important that a Kaizen team properly communicate their activities both prior, during, and after their event and at the appropriate levels of the organization. The exact format of the communication and the vehicle used for sending a message also depend on the message content. As an example, complicated and politically sensitive information should be communicated through one-on-one meetings with recipients, whereas simple messages, having a high degree of organizational consensus, perhaps can be communicated using e-mails. Implicit in an organizational environment that promotes change is an assumption that rapid improvement teams should be empowered, within the scope of their project charter, to investigate and eliminate process issues and breakdowns. This assumption is strengthened when teams are aware of the importance of a Kaizen team's project and its importance to their organization.

Empowerment is an interesting concept. In its simplest form, it implies that employees have the permission, training, resources, and other support necessary to accomplish specific goals and objectives under defined conditions of work. Extrapolating this concept to a higher level, employee empowerment varies depending on an organization's culture, an employee's status within an organization, and the type of work. At a minimum, a Kaizen team should be empowered to execute its project charter with regard to all its deliverables, including team formation, Kaizen event planning and execution, and implementation of the process improvements that have been shown to be tied to an analysis of the root causes for the project's problem statement. However, in some organizational cultures, employees have a higher degree of discretion relative to forming and deploying process improvement teams. In these circumstances, there is less management intervention in deploying Kaizen teams. Also, senior management executives and budget holders have a greater degree of discretion in selecting and providing resources to improvement projects and teams. Empowerment is an important characteristic of a team in its ability to execute its assigned goals and objectives.

Teams also require training on the tools, methods, and concepts that they are expected to use to execute their project charter. It should be noted that different projects may require a different combination of analytical tools and methods for their analysis, and elimination of the root causes of their problem statement. As an example, a data-intensive analysis of root causes in which data is downloaded from information technology (IT) systems and analyzed for reoccurring or non-random patterns may require the use of Six Sigma tools and methods or more advanced forms of mathematical analysis. In these situations, a Kaizen team should be trained to use the types of data analysis tools discussed in Chapter 5. However, if more complex analyses are required, then technical experts should assist a team. On the other hand, if a project's objective is to value stream map (VSM), simplify, standardize, and mistake proof a process, then classical Lean tools and methods would be required by a team. Usually, an analysis and elimination of root causes requires a combination of Lean and Six Sigma methods—hence the creation of the phrase "Lean Six Sigma." In summary, team members should be trained in the tools and methods necessary to accomplish their project's goals and objectives. In most situations, this will require a basic level of training in Lean and Six Sigma tools and methods. However, more advanced methods from these initiatives as well as others may also be necessary to execute a project. In these circumstances, a decision must be made regarding conducting more advanced team training or the retention of technical experts and facilitators.

Countermeasures or specific process improvements must be developed to eliminate root causes from a process. We have discussed many of these activities in earlier chapters. However, we will now discuss how to incorporate a Kaizen team's countermeasures into a project's control plan. In this chapter our discussion will focus on the analysis activities related to implementation costs versus benefits, key stakeholders, organizational resistance, infrastructure analysis, and implementing process changes. Additional topics that are prerequisite to building a control plan are communication planning, change readiness, project transitioning, and building a business case for change. This information will help to implement and sustain a Kaizen team's countermeasures.

In summary, process change must occur with organizational support. In this context, we have discussed several important characteristics of a Kaizen event. These included creating aligned projects, organizing a team, collecting and analyzing information from a project's process workflow, and developing one or more countermeasures to eliminate the root causes of process breakdowns. In the balance of this chapter our focus will be on the review and verification of proposed countermeasures to ensure that the proper process changes, communications, and control elements are in place prior to a management presentation and a transition of an improved process back to its process owner and local work team.

Change Readiness

Lean and Six Sigma initiatives have well-structured improvement methodologies. These include using a well-defined project to work sequentially through data collection and root cause analysis activities to eliminate process breakdowns. These activities require that a Kaizen team work closely with a process owner and their local work team. As a result, there is a high likelihood that process improvements will be successfully implemented by a team. But the support of other people outside of the immediate process is also critical to implementing process improvements. As an example, a local process owner and work team may have successfully identified several ways to improve their process, but one or more senior managers may not agree with their improvement suggestions. This will certainly be the situation if the team has not properly done their analysis of root causes or been able to easily describe the business benefits of the corresponding countermeasures. In these situations, it may not be possible to obtain the resources necessary to make process changes. As a result, a Kaizen team must realize that their activities are part of a larger organization having many other competing priorities and gain commitment from key stakeholders. This is critical to their project's success.

Table 7.1 lists several important criteria that will increase the likelihood that a project will be supported by key organizational stakeholders. Recall that we stated that all project work within an organization must align with senior management's goals and objectives. This is because resources are scarce, and there are

Table 7.1   Change Readiness

1. Are goals and objectives at all levels of an organization integrated to support change activities?
2. Are rewards and recognition systems in place? (These include promotions, bonuses, pay increases, employee recognition, and other benefits.)
3. Have organizational barriers to the change activities been identified and countermeasures developed to mitigate their impact?
4. Is a communication infrastructure in place to support change activities?
5. Have project charters been created to support the change objectives?
6. Are resources available to support the improvement projects?
7. Have roles and responsibilities have been defined to support the improvement projects?
8. Has training been created to provide the relevant tools and methods necessary to support the improvement projects?
9. Once countermeasures have been identified, have process workflows been modified and controls implemented to ensure the changes are sustained over time?
10. Have process controls been fully integrated into the performance management and control systems?

many other competing projects at any given time within an organization. This implies that employees should be working on improvement projects that have been properly prioritized and integrated into an overall strategy for process improvement. In many organizations these umbrella programs are called Lean Six Sigma, Operational Excellence, or Process Excellence. Another important consideration is the assignment of people to projects. In this context, employees should be working on projects that are integrated with their personal annual performance plans, so their organization can formally evaluate their performance and provide the proper incentives for continued improvement work. Incentives include promotions, bonuses, pay increases, employee recognition, and similar rewards that will support a project's execution and drive the correct types of behavior. This is another reason that projects must be fully integrated into a deployment rather than deployed as stand-alone events. It may also be the situation that many of these competing projects have expected business benefits that are higher than a project planned by a Kaizen team.

In any organization, there will be various degrees of structural, technological, cultural, economic, and other organizational barriers to making process changes. In an environment in which there are other competing priorities, there will always be individuals who are pursuing their own interests according to their assigned goals and objectives, which may require a different prioritization than those of a Kaizen team. But sometimes individuals pursue activities to the detriment of their organization's goals and objectives. Still other individuals may be required to support an initiative but are busy with day-to-day activities. There will also be individuals who just do not agree with the premise of a given initiative or its recommendations despite their senior management's statements to the contrary. This is especially true if the improvements negatively impact an individual through loss of power or employment. As a result, it is important for process improvement professionals to understand the types of organizational barriers that impede their activities as well as their extent. This requires an analysis of the proposed process changes or countermeasures, their business benefits, the required resources to implement the process improvements, and the key stakeholders that will be impacted by the changes. We will discuss how to do a stakeholder analysis later in this chapter. However, it has already been stated that a proven way to eliminate barriers to process changes is to obtain the formal support of senior management by creating project charters having quantifiable business benefits.

Communication is essential when deploying an initiative or even localized Kaizen projects, especially within larger organizations. Communication provides information describing an initiative's major characteristics as well as its benefits. In this context, it was mentioned earlier in this chapter that communication should be made across several organizational levels, but a simple and consistent message should be its key characteristic. As an example, there may be an initial announcement by senior executives describing the major benefits of an initiative to the larger organization. Follow-up communications may include monthly newsletters and websites. Local-level mangers may also be required to reinforce key talking points every day. Over time, as an initiative is deployed project by project, its benefits should become obvious to the larger organization; otherwise, there may be problems with its execution. In this context, project successes should also be communicated to key stakeholders throughout an organization. It is also very important that the various roles and responsibilities within an initiative be defined in an easy-to-understand manner. Finally, it is important that the new process controls are fully integrated into an organization's management and control systems to increase the interaction between employees and the process changes.

Project Transition

At this point in a project, it is important that a Kaizen team ask questions similar to those listed in Table 7.2. For example: Have the project's improvement recommendations been tied to its root cause analysis? Are the process controls effective, and how do we know this? Have all control systems and reaction plans been documented? Have people been trained to use the new process controls? Can the process controls be sustained day to day? Did the project solution provide the expected business benefits? How will the process improvements be measured going forward? Are there any known risks to the project? These questions are useful in ensuring a Kaizen team has reached a consensus with a process owner regarding what the problem was and how it was eliminated by the team's countermeasures. A project transition back to a process owner and local work team will proceed more smoothly if these questions have been answered during a Kaizen event and its root cause analysis. Eventually, this information will be formally documented using a control plan. This topic will be discussed in Chapter 8 because implementing process changes through a documented control plan is a first step in the transition of a project back to the process owner and local work team.

Table 7.2 Important Project Transition Questions

1. Have the project's improvement recommendations been tied to its root cause analysis?
2. Are the process controls effective? How do we know?
3. Have all control systems and reaction plans been documented?
4. Have people been trained to use the new process controls?
5. Can the process controls be sustained day to day by the local work team?
6. Did the project's countermeasures or solutions provide the expected business benefits?
7. How will the process improvements be measured going forward?
8. Are there any known risks to the project?

Table 7.3 Building a Business Case for Change

1. Identification of countermeasures including their benefits and resource requirements as represented in the form of a cost-benefit analysis.
2. A stakeholder analysis to identify key stakeholders and their positions regarding the countermeasures or process changes as well as the impact of the changes on key stakeholders.
3. A stakeholder impact analysis to evaluate the impact of the changes on key stakeholders.
4. A resistance analysis of the cultural, political, and other organization factors that may impede the deployment of process changes.
5. An analysis of the infrastructure factors and risks that facilitate or inhibit the proposed changes.
6. Scheduling of countermeasures or improvements as well as related activities such as training, creation of procedures, and similar supporting activities.
7. Development of a communication plan of the changes in an easy-to-understand format for the organizational stakeholders.

Building a Business Case for Change

Table 7.3 lists several key characteristics of a business case for change. In this type of analysis it is necessary to identify the specific countermeasures that will eliminate the root causes for poor process performance, including their benefits and resource requirements. A major component of a business case is a cost-benefit analysis. An example of how this is done was discussed in Chapter 6 and shown in Figure 6.1 and Table 6.4. A second important characteristic of a business case is a stakeholder analysis. This analysis describes expected customer and business benefits by their positive and negative impacts on key stakeholders. An important characteristic of a stakeholder analysis is an understanding of stakeholder positions regarding the countermeasures associated with process changes. In addition to conducting a stakeholder analysis, a team must also understand organizational barriers to change that may prevent the implementation of their project's countermeasures. In this type of analysis, the elements comprising an organization's infrastructure are evaluated relative to their ability to inhibit or promote change activities. As an example, infrastructure includes organizational factors related to technology, culture, rewards and incentives, recognition, and other factors that may impact the proposed process changes. These infrastructure elements must be aligned in order. Once a full understanding of the organizational impact of changes has been made, a detailed deployment plan can be developed to include scheduling of the activities directly related to the process improvements. This includes training and the creation of supporting documentation. Integral to the successful deployment of these important change activities is creation of a high-level communication plan for organizational stakeholders.

Cost–Benefit Analysis

In the balance of this chapter we will discuss the key activities that are necessary to ensure projects are properly transitioned to a process owner and local work team. In this transitioning process, a cost-benefit analysis is important to promote project implementation. In fact, a highly favorable cost-benefit analysis relating process improvements to resource requirements and other costs will help increase a project's priority. A cost-benefit analysis calculates the net financial benefits of improvements after their implementation costs have been subtracted from the initial financial benefits. Figure 7.2 shows that a cost-benefit analysis begins up front when a project has been aligned with an organization's strategy. This alignment is made through the project's charter and its description of the process problem, the impact the problem has on an organization both financially and operationally, and the expected benefits from eliminating the process problem. As a team completes its data collection and analysis activities, which are based on a project charter's scope and process boundaries, it will also be building a business case for the process changes it will ultimately recommend to the process owner and local work team. Ideally, the project identification process is done by senior managers or deployment leaders and integrated into an overall strategy to increase organizational productivity. This will reinforce the importance of a project to the larger organization. In this context, project charters are created in a top-down manner to ensure they produce business benefits for an organization. This project deployment process will also help to align Kaizen events and other process improvement activities throughout an organization. Project metrics and the original cost-benefit analysis can be periodically updated as circumstances require.

Projects differ in the types of benefits they produce for an organization as well as their implementation costs. This concept is shown in Figure 7.2, where benefits are broken down into four separate classifications. These classifications include revenue increases, cost of goods (COGS) expense, other expense reductions, and increases in cash flow. There are also other, nonfinancial benefits that may be created by a project. These are related to increases in customer, supplier, and employee satisfaction and cost avoidances related to changes in technology, laws, and regulations. An example of a revenue-enhancing project can be seen through volume or pricing improvements. Volume increases are new sales in units. Pricing improvements are higher sales prices per unit. Ideally, volume increases and per unit pricing increase to dramatically raise sales revenue. However, other projects decrease various types of expenses. These expenses are directly related to materials, labor, sales and administrative expenses, overtime, warranty, returned goods, indirect labor, premium freight, research and development, and similar expenses. A project will usually include financial and nonfinancial benefits. However, it will be much easier to gain management support for a project when it has clear financial benefits. In this context, it is important that the financial analyses that form the basis of a cost-benefit analysis should always be reviewed with financial representatives prior

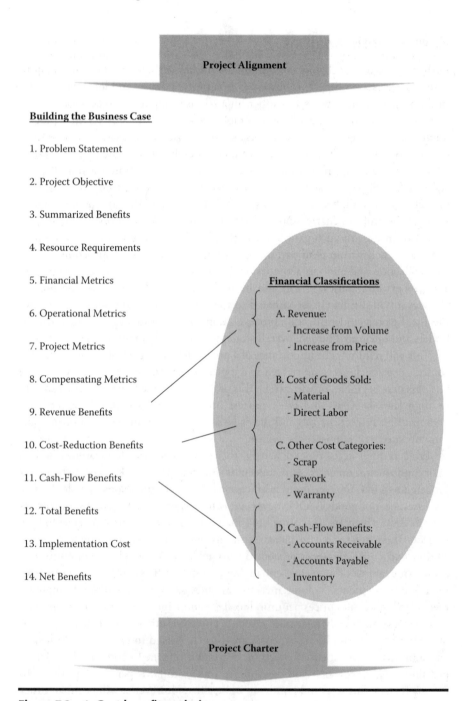

Figure 7.2   1. Cost-benefit analysis.

to communication to management or the larger organization. Financial analysts are trained in this type of analysis, including the various assumptions required to analyze revenues and expenses. An added advantage of including financial analysts in a preliminary review of a cost-benefit analysis is that they may suggest alternative analyses or other ways to increase a project's benefits or reduce its expense.

In addition to financial benefits, there are other types of project benefits. These include cost avoidance projects or projects that increase key stakeholder satisfaction. Cost avoidance projects lower expenses in future time periods. An example would be reducing the expense of material or labor today, but receiving the productivity improvement in the future. Another example would be to create a project to eliminate a hazardous material this year to avoid future governmental fines. Projects designed to improve stakeholder satisfaction would include eliminating the root causes of problems that result in poor quality, long delivery times, or noncompetitive costs to customers. Additional projects can be created to solve supplier issues related to quality, long delivery time, and cost. In summary, there are many types of project benefits. But benefits and costs must be clearly described and supported with documentation. Also, Kaizen projects will usually have several different benefits that must be communicated to the process owner and local work team using a cost-benefit analysis approach.

Key Stakeholder Analysis

Figure 7.3 shows several key elements of a stakeholder analysis. A key stakeholder analysis begins by identifying the organizational groups or stakeholders that are likely to be impacted by a project both during its data collection and analysis activities and after its eventual improvements. Once key stakeholders have been identified, a Kaizen team methodologically identifies its concerns as well as recommendations for the implementation of process improvements. This analysis is designed to ensure that process improvements are modified in a way to ensure key stakeholder support. The process modifications are the countermeasures identified by the analysis of the root causes of the original process problem. From a Kaizen team's perspective, a key stakeholder analysis is useful in identifying where key stakeholders need to support a project's improvements, through either organizational intervention or providing resources for the team. It should be noted that a key stakeholder analysis is useful whenever an improvement team engages its key stakeholders. The information provided by a key stakeholder analysis helps a Kaizen team to identify the actions it must take to ensure its project is executed according to its planned schedule.

A modified version of the key stakeholder analysis that includes a net promoter score (NPS) is shown in Figure 7.3. An NPS is a useful approach to a key stakeholder analysis because it enables a Kaizen team to quickly identify a project's potential promoters and detractors. The team strategy should be to reinforce project

Stakeholder Group	What are their concerns?	How do we need their support?	What actions should we take?

Stakeholder Group	Baseline Promoter	Revised Promoter	Follow-up Actions

Promoter Question: Would you support this project by recommending it to others?

0=Unlikely　1　　2　　3　　4　　5　　6　　7　　8　　9　　10=Highly Likely

- An average NPS of 16% was calculated over 400 companies in 28 industries. A world-class NPS benchmark is in the range of 75% to 80% (*Harvard Business Review*), Frederick F. Reichheld, Article Number 5534, entitled "The One Number You Need to Grow," December 2003.

Figure 7.3　2. Key stakeholder analysis.

attributes that are important to its key stakeholders and also to consider modifications to project attributes that are identified as issues by a project's detractors. The NPS was discussed by Frederick F. Reichheld in December 2003 in a *Harvard Business Review* article (5534) entitled "The One Number You Need to Grow." In the NPS method, customers are asked if they would recommend a product or service to others. It was reported in this article that an NPS question correlated, across more than 400 organizations in various industries, to incremental sales better than other types of customer survey questions. The NPS concept is that people will often summarize their various experiences with a product or service into one final decision, that is, to recommend the product or service or not. The NPS scale ranges from a 0 to a 10. A 0 correlates to the rating "extremely unlikely to recommend" and a 10 correlates to a rating of "extremely likely to recommend." Promoters are usually defined as ratings of 9 and 10 on the 0 to 10 scale. Detractors are defined as ratings between 0 and 6 on the same scale. Ratings of 7 and 8 are considered to be neutral and are not calculated as part of the NPS statistic. The NPS is calculated by subtracting the percentage detractors from the percentage promoters without using responses classified as neutral. It was reported that an average NPS is approximately 16 percent, and a world-class percentage is in a range between 75 and 80 percent. In summary, the goal of a team's NPS analysis is to determine specific ways to gain key stakeholder support for their project by eliminating barriers to project execution.

A key stakeholder analysis is important because key stakeholders will have differing views of a project's risks and benefits. This requires that a team consider

Stakeholder Group	Countermeasure/ Improvements	Positive Impacts	Negative Impacts

Negative Impacts	Mitigation Activities	Potential Issues	Success Probability (Risk)

Figure 7.4   3. Impact analysis of key stakeholders.

these diverse key stakeholder viewpoints. This type of introspective analysis results in a more efficient project execution process because more effective solutions may be developed than those originally considered by a Kaizen team. An important concept of a key stakeholder analysis is development of a mitigation plan to address all stakeholder concerns. These mitigation plans are based on an in-depth analysis of the potential positive and negative impacts of the proposed countermeasures using the information shown in Figure 7.4. In this analysis the risk level of each counter-measure is estimated. Countermeasures having a high risk require additional focus by the Kaizen team. Figures 7.3 and 7.4 have been shown to be very useful tools to evaluate the impact of a Kaizen team's countermeasures on its organization.

Certain organizational characteristics will tend to promote process changes and minimize organizational resistance by key stakeholders. These concepts are sum-marized in Figure 7.5 as promoters and barriers of change. Several of these charac-teristics have been discussed in previous chapters. These include project alignment, ensuring process changes have been effectively communicated, team empower-ment, training people in the tools and methods necessary to collect and analyze data, and establishing reward and recognition systems. On the right-hand side of Figure 7.5 are the barriers to change. The first barrier is conflicting priorities. In this context, it is difficult to obtain the help of busy people whose goals and objectives do not include a Kaizen team's recommended improvements. A solution to this situation is to ensure that a Kaizen project is aligned with an organization's goals and objectives up front, prior to its deployment. Also, fear of the unknown can

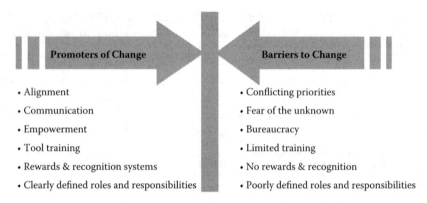

Promoters of Change	Barriers to Change
• Alignment	• Conflicting priorities
• Communication	• Fear of the unknown
• Empowerment	• Bureaucracy
• Tool training	• Limited training
• Rewards & recognition systems	• No rewards & recognition
• Clearly defined roles and responsibilities	• Poorly defined roles and responsibilities

Balance Point
(No Change)

Figure 7.5   4. Resistance analysis of proposed changes.

slow down a project if people do not understand how the project positively impacts their work activities or organization. Well-designed and -coordinated communication will help manage these types of issues. Bureaucracy is a significant barrier to change. In fact, bureaucracy is often the cause of excessively complicated processes. This is due, in part, to managers creating non-value-adding (NVA) policies and procedures. Empowering employees is a proven way to reduce the negative impacts of bureaucracy. In fact, Kaizen teams are empowered improvement teams designed to attack this common barrier to process change. Limited training and a lack of rewards and recognition are the next two barriers to change shown in Figure 7.5. The causes of these barriers may be complicated. As an example, lack of training is a very common organizational issue. One reason for this situation is that if the root causes of a process problem are not known, then countermeasures cannot be developed to eliminate them and the required employee training cannot take place. In summary, employee training should be designed to reinforce the correct process controls, but this is not always obvious. Developing effective rewards and recognition systems is a complicated process that assumes organizations develop their lower-level goals and objectives in an aligned manner, and then reinforce the importance of their execution. Human resource (HR) professionals should be consulted for assistance with reward and recognition issues.

The final barrier to change shown in Figure 7.5 is roles and responsibilities. Clearly defined roles and responsibilities have been shown to be a significant factor in promoting organizational change. Properly defined roles and responsibilities help to ensure that important deployment activities are well organized and managed properly. This avoids misunderstandings and conflicts. These concepts were also discussed in Chapter 1 and shown in Table 1.3. In this discussion, it was mentioned that the deployment leader role is a critical one. Recall that deployment leaders develop deployment plans to ensure that the required resources are aligned with improvement opportunities and business benefits. In this alignment process, deployment leaders work with the process owners and their local team members to identify projects and align resources. Other important roles include a Kaizen event sponsor, who provides resources for the Kaizen event, and the Kaizen event facilitator, who coordinates the planning, execution, and follow-up activities associated with an event. Team members also fulfill an important role because they collect and analyze data to identify ways to improve a process. Additional people associated with these Kaizen activities may include process experts and support people who attend meetings as necessary.

Infrastructure Analysis

An infrastructure analysis is also conducted to identify the basic organizational systems that tend to promote or inhibit the planned process improvements once a Kaizen team develops countermeasures to eliminate the root causes for process breakdowns. An infrastructure analysis is used to analyze the impact of external and internal factors that may positively or negatively impact process improvements. These factors include cultural, technological, scheduling, customer, supplier, economic, and regulatory risks. Figure 7.6 cross-references these factors by key stakeholder because different stakeholders may be differentially impacted by different factors and risk. The goal of using this type of analysis is to identify implementation risks in advance to reinforce positive or minimize negative impacts of improvement activities. As an example, typical cultural risks may include a unionized environment, a workforce that has never been asked to change its behavior, or a consensus-based workforce. These work environments will tend to slow process changes. But this is not necessarily a negative situation if a workforce is proactive. As an example, a consensus-based workforce may contribute significantly to improvement efforts. However, organizational cultures having a strong history of embracing new and diverse ideas will tend to accept change more readily than those that do not. Technological risks occur when project improvements are dependent on new machines, materials, work procedures, and other process elements that have not been fully tested over extended periods of time. Scheduling risks are impacted, both positively and negatively, by the other risk factors shown in Figure 7.6, but may become a separate risk factor if they are set unrealistically by a deployment leader or Kaizen team. Customer risks include the impact of a Kaizen team's countermeasures on major customers. In these situations, the loss or gain of a major customer may also impact the demand for a product or service. This would then affect a project's financial assumptions. Also, countermeasures may positively or negatively impact a product or service's specifications. The result may be changes to a project's original cost, profit, and schedule assumptions. Countermeasures may also impact suppliers. As a result, a Kaizen team should evaluate countermeasures relative to their supplier impact. The risk factors discussed so far may also independently impact a Kaizen team's project. As

	Stakeholder Group	Countermeasure/ Improvements	Positive Impacts	Negative Impacts
Cultural Risks				
Technological Risks				
Scheduling Risks				
Customer Risks				
Supplier Risks				
Economic Risks				
Regulatory Risks				

	Negative Impacts	Mitigation Activities	Potential Issues	Success Probability (Risk)
Cultural Risks				
Technological Risks				
Scheduling Risks				
Customer Risks				
Supplier Risks				
Economic Risks				
Regulatory Risks				

Figure 7.6   5. Infrastructure analysis.

an example, a key technology that is the basis for a team's recommended solutions may change, impacting its original assumptions regarding process sustainability and business benefits. Also, the gain or loss of key customers and suppliers as well as general macroeconomic conditions may also have positive or negative impacts on a team's countermeasures or solutions. Finally, regulatory risks may have a significant impact on a team's solutions. In these situations, a Kaizen team should work with human resources, legal, and other organizational functions as necessary. The goals of an infrastructure analysis are to enable a team to easily review and consider all project risks related to the factors shown in Figure 7.6.

Scheduling Process Change Activities

Effective project scheduling is important to ensure that projects and their solutions are well managed so that they meet quality, time, and cost targets. As an example, our focus has been on rapid improvement using Kaizen events. These events are characterized as having very short time durations of three to five days, with perhaps some follow-up activities. But recall that, depending on the complexity of an event relative to data collection and analysis, up-front work by a deployment champion and his or her team may be required prior to assignment of a project to a Kaizen

Deliverable Complete (Y/N)	Project Name: Team: Major Activity	Person Accountable	Day 1	Day 2	Day 3	Day 4	Day 5	Day 6	Day 7	Day 8	Day 9	Day 10
	1. Customer CTQs											
	2. Define Problem											
	3. Team Charter											
	4. Stakeholder Analysis											
	5. High-Level Map											
	6. Project Plan											
	7. Perform. Standards											
	8. Data Collection											
	9. Detailed Proc. Maps											
	10. COPQ											
	11. Root Cause Analysis											
	12. Vital Few Xs											
	13. Potential Solutions											
	14. "Should-be" Process											
	15. Cost/Benefit Analysis											
	16. Validate Improvements											
	17. Mistake Proof											
	18. Process Performance											
	19. Control Plan											
	20. Response Plan											
	21. New Process Map											
	22. New SOPs											
	23. Standardize operations											
	24. Transfer Control											
	25. Follow-up Activities											
	Activity 1											
	Activity 2											
	Activity 3											
	Activity 4											
	Activity 5											
	Activity 6											

Figure 7.7   6. Scheduling process changes.

team. In this context, Chapter 4 showed how the various work activities associated with planning and conducting a Kaizen event had to be carefully scheduled to achieve the goals and objectives of the event. In this current discussion, the generic schedule or activity checklist shown in Figure 4.1 is a useful guide. A summarized version of key activities occurring during a Kaizen event is shown in Figure 7.7, but with an emphasis on those that normally occur toward the end of an event. Figure 7.7 is presented in the form of a Gantt chart. In this format Kaizen event activities are completed in sequence based on their time duration. Notice that the time duration is very short because Kaizen events, as defined by their project charter, are structured or scoped to be completed in just a few days. Improvement activities that require a longer implementation time are scheduled as follow-up activities. In summary, the goal of effective project management, including work scheduling, is that all activities be identified, sequenced, and scheduled to ensure that a team's improvements are well managed and executed according to schedule.

Communication

The importance of effective communication has been discussed repeatedly throughout this book. In these discussions, communication was shown to be an important

	Stakeholder Group	Countermeasure/ Improvements	Positive Impacts	Negative Impacts	Communication Format				Due Date	Person Responsible
					In-Person	Telephone	E-mail	Other		
Cultural Risks										
Technological Risks										
Scheduling Risks										
Customer Risks										
Supplier Risks										
Economic Risks										
Regulatory Risks										

Figure 7.8   7. Communication planning.

set of activities necessary to both obtain resources for a project and ensure that the correct format is used to announce the team's proposed countermeasures to key stakeholders. In Figure 7.8, each communication activity has been correlated to its countermeasure and key stakeholder group. In addition, the person responsible for the specific communication is also listed. It is apparent that there are several formats that can be used to communicate to organizational stakeholders. These include e-mails, telephone calls, videoconferencing, newsletters, and similar formats. The key concept is that the communication format should be simple and consistent. It should also be selected based on its message content. As a general example, complicated messages that impact key stakeholders should be communicated in person rather than e-mail. On the other hand, simple and routine messages can be communicated using e-mails.

Summary

Changing a process should be a straightforward set of activities, using a structured improvement methodology, which ensures that process improvements are sustained over time. Integral to these activities should be a well-defined business case for every deployed project. Table 7.1 listed several important change elements that will increase the probability that improvement projects will be supported by an organization. These change elements are important because at any given time there are other competing priorities within an organization. These priorities are associated with the numerous programs and initiatives necessary to manage modern organizations across the world. In this competitive environment, there will always be individuals who are pursuing their own interests based on their organization's reward and recognition systems. The first step in changing a process is an implementation of process controls. The next step is a transition of the modified process back to the process owner and local work team with the tools and methods necessary to sustain the process improvements. The tools and methods discussed in this chapter have been designed to facilitate the important elements of change. As an example, a key stakeholder analysis is important to the implementation of countermeasures, because key stakeholders may have differing views of a project's risks and benefits as well as the recommended improvements. Also, certain organizational characteristics will tend to promote or inhibit process change. Once a team has developed the countermeasures necessary to eliminate the root causes for their process breakdown, then an infrastructure analysis should also be conducted to identify the factors that may promote or inhibit the planned process improvements. The importance of scheduling project activities was also discussed in the context that projects should be well managed relative to quality, time, and cost. Finally, communication activities are another important consideration that is necessary to obtain project support of key stakeholders.

Suggested Reading

Sanjiv Augustine. 2005. *Managing Agile projects*. Englewood Cliffs, NJ: Prentice Hall.
Rosabeth Moss Kanter. 1983. *The change masters*. Innovation and Entrepreneurship in the American Corporation. New York: Simon and Schuster.
John P. Kotter. 1996. *Leading change*. Boston: Harvard Business School Press.
John P. Kotter and James L. Heskett. 1992. *Corporate culture and performance*. Free Press, New York, NY.
James W. Martin. 2008. *Operational excellence—Using Lean Six Sigma to translate customer value through global supply chains*. New York: Auerbach.
Tom Peters. 1999. *The circle of innovation*. Vintage Press, New York, NY.

Chapter 8

Implementing Solutions

Overview

Once an improvement team has identified the root causes for process breakdowns and developed countermeasures to eliminate or prevent them from occurring, this information must be documented in a control plan and integrated within an organization's normal quality control system. These quality systems range from internationally recognized systems such as those promoted by the International Standards Institute (ISO), the Automotive Industry Action Group (AIAG), and similar organizations. Although there are many ISO standards, three are of particular importance for process control. The most basic is ISO 9000. This ISO standard describes a basic quality management system that every supplier should have to meet basic customer requirements. It includes procedures and standards related to the control of documents, quality measurement records, internal audits, nonconforming materials, corrective actions, and activities designed to prevent quality problems. ISO 9000 is used to develop a mutual understanding of quality requirements between customers and suppliers. ISO 9001 is a next-higher level of control. It is a formal set of requirements that a quality management system must have to demonstrate that a supplier can consistently meet customer and regulatory requirements. The difference between ISO 9000 and 9001 is that 9000 only demonstrates that a supplier has the basic elements of a quality system, but not that the system will consistently meet customer requirements.

At a more advanced level, the ISO 9004 standard is used to certify that a supplier can also continuously improve its quality systems. AIAG standards specify the design and manufacture of products using detailed road maps, tools, and templates.

239

AIAG methods can also be used in service functions, but with modifications. It should be noted that there are several other major quality management systems, such as the Malcolm Baldrige award. The Malcolm Baldrige award is an auditing process that measures organizational maturity relative to several categories, including leadership, strategic planning, customer and market focus, the measurement, analysis, and management of knowledge, the management of human resources, process management, and performance results. Typically, organizations use these systems in an integrated manner. As an example, the Malcolm Baldrige criteria may be used as an overall measure of organizational performance, then products or services could be designed using AIAG criteria and procedures and systems. Once designed, these would be subject to ISO standardization requirements. In summary, quality control systems must also be differentiated from simple quality improvement initiatives such as Lean and Six Sigma. The reason for this differentiation is that while Lean and Six Sigma methodologies are characterized by many useful tools and methods, they must rely on an integrated system to implement and sustain process improvements.

In our discussion of quality control systems, several themes will emerge. These include ensuring that controls have been based on a thorough analysis of the root causes of a process problem and their countermeasures, and also that controls are placed within a process to control the process variables impacting what exits the process. In other words, we want to control process inputs (Xs) to ensure that process outputs (Ys) remain in control. It is also true that control strategies usually consist of a combination of several different tools or methods. As an example, a control system may consist of a combination of training, procedures, the application of 5S methods, mistake-proofing activities, statistical process controls, the application of preventive maintenance, and quality and process audits. Note that these controls are usually applied after a process has been simplified and standardized through an elimination of operations and work tasks. More detailed control tools may also be deployed to support other methods employed to control a process. As an example, teams will usually use control plans, failure mode and effects analysis (FMEA), metric dashboards, and automatic process monitoring, as well as other supporting tools and methods to reinforce their major process controls.

Key Questions

Process controls are developed when a Kaizen team completes its analysis of root causes and determines the types of countermeasures that are necessary to reduce or eliminate process breakdowns. In this context it is important that a team ask the following basic questions as it develops solutions. But the answers to these questions should be easy to answer based on the knowledge that has been gained from a Kaizen team's activities. An important question is: Which operations or work tasks need to be eliminated, modified, or controlled using one of several control

Table 8.1   Key Process Improvement Questions

1. What process?
2. What countermeasures or improvements?
3. How will countermeasures or improvements be applied?
4. Who is responsible?
5. When will the countermeasures or improvements be made?
6. How will we know when they are successful?

methods? A second question is: Which types of controls or countermeasures will be most useful in controlling the process, and how will they be applied and by whom? Other important questions are related to developing a schedule to execute process improvements and assigning resources to the improvement activities. This chapter will discuss the answers to these questions as well as others.

Control Plan Requirements

The various control strategies and their systems should be incorporated into a quality control plan. A quality control plan is used by an organization to communicate important process characteristics, their target levels, the measurement methods necessary to monitor metric performance levels, and reaction plans that, when executed, will bring a process back into control. In other words, control plans document the controls that are placed on a system's operational work tasks to ensure key metric performance is sustained over time. This control documentation may appear in many formats, including paper and electronic. In this chapter we will discuss the major attributes of a control plan and how to interpret the information it provides to a process owner and the local work team. In this discussion, we will review the basic requirements shown in Table 8.2. These include the inputs (Xs) that were found to be important in the Kaizen team's analysis of root causes. Ideally, controls will be

Table 8.2   Control Plan Requirements

1. Document system characteristics of key process input variables (KPIVs) and key process output variables (KPOVs) including their definition, target performance level, and measurement systems.
2. Specifies tolerances on key process input variables (KPIVs) and key process output variables (KPOVs).
3. Specifies measurements of KPIVs and KPOVs.
4. Specifies controls on KPIVs and KPOVs.
5. Specifies reaction plans to out-of-control conditions.
6. Describes who is responsible for what corrective action.

placed on the inputs, but outputs will also need to be monitored using a control plan. A second requirement of a control plan is describing specifications and their tolerances of key process input variables (KPIVs) and output variables (KPOVs). A tolerance is the range of a specification. A specification is the target value of a metric and should be directly related to customer requirements though the voice of the customer (VOC). Measurement tools and procedures, including sample size and the frequency of data collection, should also be specified for each variable. As an example, an inspection procedure should describe the data collection method as well as the definition of each error type with an example. In this context, if invoices were being sampled, errors could be incorrect customer names and address, incorrect quantities, as well as inaccurate descriptions of products and services. This information will be incorporated into a quality control plan. A control plan also describes specific actions that must be taken if process performance degrades, and who should take these actions as well as how.

Important Control Tools

Process control strategies require the combined application of several control tools. These control tools should be carefully selected as the correct countermeasures to eliminate the root causes that were found to have caused the original process problems. However, control tools vary in their effectiveness as well as their ease of use, and hence sustainability over time. As an example, controls relying on employee training must be continually audited and updated to ensure that employees remember how to correctly do their work tasks. On the other hand, an elimination of several process operations that have been shown to be causing a problem will permanently eliminate the original problem. An advantage of this type of robust solution is that it does not require sustained efforts for its maintenance. As a result, it would be a preferable control method to a less robust one such as employee training as the only control. In other words, employee training should be supported by more robust process controls to ensure process performance is sustained over time.

Table 8.3 lists several important control tools that can be used in combination to ensure process performance is sustained over time. There may also be additional control tools and methods that depend on an industry or organization. In this context, Table 8.3 describes the common tools and methods used for process control. The first critical tool is training. It is required wherever a process change impacts manual operations requiring that employees be educated to work procedures associated with various control tools. However, training must also be designed based on an analysis of root causes to ensure it is effective. In other words, training should not be haphazardly deployed as a solution. It must be clearly documented so employees will understand their work requirements. This training documentation may include

Table 8.3   Important Control Tools

1. Training
2. Updating procedures
3. Audits
4. Statistical process controls
5. Measurement system improvements
6. Failure mode and effects analysis (FMEA)
7. 5S (simplification and standardization)
8. Mistake proofing
9. Eliminating operations and work tasks
10. Process modification and redesign

written procedures, examples of poor and excellent work, as well as periodic testing and similar controls to ensure that the quality of training is sustained over time. Also, the responsibility for the periodic evaluation and delivery of training should be assigned to one department. However, this does not imply that other departments should not assist with training activities. In summary, training information and methodologies should be standardized and incorporated into a control plan. In addition to training documentation, work and inspection procedures will usually need to be created or updated to provide information to a process owner and local work team to help them sustain their process at its expected performance levels. Typical procedures include work, inspection, maintenance, and similar types of instruction documents. Ideally, procedures will be developed using a highly standardized and modularized format to make them easy to understand. Audits are another integral part of a process control strategy. This is especially relevant when a process contains several manual operations. This is because manual operations depend on the judgment and skill of the people comprising them. People forget work instructions or training and become distracted and fatigued from their work activities. As a result, to sustain process improvements, an audit system should be designed to periodically gather information from a process to ensure that process controls are effective in maintaining performance levels. Audits may take many forms, but they are the most effective when process information has been meticulously collected and evaluated according to required standards and procedures. In addition to the control tools mentioned above, there are several others that are very effective in maintaining process performance. Some of these control tools, such as 5S, mistake proofing, and the elimination of operations and work tasks, were discussed in earlier chapters. Others, such as statistical process control (SPC) and failure mode and effects analysis (FMEA), will be discussed in the next several sections of this chapter.

Statistical Process Controls

Statistical process controls are used to monitor the performance of key process variables to identify nonrandom patterns that may indicate a loss of process control. Key process variables are inputs or outputs. In addition, control charts apply statistical tests on the pattern of a process variable to determine if it is different from its baseline performance level. Recall that this is the information used to construct a control chart. As an example, the various statistical tests conducted on control chart patterns will enable its users to detect outliers, trends across several sequential data points, as well as other types of nonrandom patterns. Although there are several control chart patterns that are common across all industries, some industries have unique processes and patterns that require the use of different types of control charts. In this section, we will show how control charts are selected based on the distribution assumptions of the variable being charted.

Table 8.4 lists ten key control chart concepts. The first key concept is that a stable process should only contain random or common cause variation. Also, its variation pattern should be similar to the baseline that was calculated using an initial sample taken from a process. As an example, if the variable being charted is the cycle time to review customer invoices, and its distribution is symmetrical around

Table 8.4 Key Concepts of Control Charts

1. The variation of a stable process contains random or common cause variation.
2. Common cause variation is due to many sources, it is stable, sampling can be applied to a process having common cause variation, and it is difficult to eliminate from a process.
3. Special or assignable cause variation is due to one or a few sources, it is not stable, sampling cannot be used to monitor process performance, and it may be easy to eliminate it from a process.
4. Control charts differentiate special from common cause variation.
5. Statistical evaluations of process performance can be made for a stable process.
6. It enables the identification and elimination of special cause variation.
7. A process will operate with less variability if it is in a state of statistical control.
8. Control charts promote less frequent process adjustments.
9. A process variable must exhibit both statistical control and meet customer requirements (these are not the same analysis).
10. Specialized control charts are used to monitor specific conditions such as metric performance over short periods of time, when small samples are used to collect process data, and when small changes must be detected within a process.

its mean value, then it would make sense to assume that future samples taken from the same process and under similar conditions would exhibit a similar cycle time pattern. The second key concept is that common cause variation is due to many sources of variation, which makes it difficult to eliminate from a process because there are no obvious patterns. However, if special or assignable sources of variation are present in a process, then a control chart will detect a nonrandom pattern. This enables assignable causes of variation to be identified and eliminated. In summary, a control chart differentiates between common and special cause variation. This enables a statistically based evaluation to be made of its control chart pattern. Depending on the specific pattern, process adjustments can be made to eliminate the special cause variation. As a result, process variation will be decreased because fewer manual adjustments will be required to maintain process control.

The ninth key concept of control chart usage is that there is a difference between the control of a process and its capability to meet customer requirements. In other words, a process could be very stable, but its performance may not meet customer requirements or internal specifications. Also, a process could easily meet customer requirements due to a very wide specification range, but not be in statistical control. In the former situation customers will not be satisfied, while in the latter situation internal resources may be wasted because of high variation. In summary, a process should be stable, in a state of statistical control, and fully capable of meeting customer requirements. It should also be noted that there are several specialized control charts that can be used to monitor specific process situations. These situations include monitoring process performance over short periods of time, using small samples to collect process data, and detecting small changes within a process. In this chapter, we will discuss the most common control charts and their interpretation. Specialized control chart applications are discussed in several of the suggested readings at the end of this chapter.

There are many different types of control charts, which differ based on their assumed reference distribution as well as the historical time frame of the variable being charted. Table 8.5 lists the most commonly used control charts. These charts are individual-moving range charts, X-bar and r-charts, p-charts, and c-charts. It should be noted that different data formats and assumed probability distributions require the use of different control charts. As an example, cycle time is a continuous variable that is measured on a scale that can be broken into smaller and smaller intervals. Applicable control charts that could be used to monitor the variation of cycle time are either individual-moving range control charts or X-bar and range control charts. Individual-moving range control charts monitor the patterns of a continuous variable individually for each time period. In contrast, X-bar and range charts monitor averages and ranges of subgrouped values. A subgroup range is calculated as the maximum minus the minimum value of the subgroup. An advantage of using X-bar and range charts is that if the original distribution of individual values is slightly skewed, that is, not symmetrical, then the distribution

Table 8.5 Control Chart Control Overview

Control Chart	Individual Moving Range Charts	X-Bar and Range Charts	P-Chart/NP-Chart	C-Chart/U-Chart
Data Format	Continuous	Continuous	Percentage or Proportion	Counts
Basic Application in Office Environments	Cycle time, hours, incident rates, costs, etc.	Cycle time, hours, incident rates, costs, etc.	Number of units failing a standard, i.e., percentage defective invoices, percentage days late, etc.	Number of defects per sampling unit, i.e., number of errors per invoice, number of accidents per building, etc.
Sample Size	25 to 125 observations in total sample with subgroup size=1.	4–6 observations per subgroup and 20–25 subgroups in the initial baseline sample.	50 or more observations per subgroup. P-charts are constructed using subgroups of equal or unequal size. np-charts are used in situations where subgroup sizes do not vary.	Convenient sampling unit that is constant from one sample to another. U-charts are used in situations where the size of the subgroup size varies.
Assumed Distribution	Normal	Normal	Binomial	Poisson

of subgrouped means (transformed from the original skewed individual values) will often be symmetrical and appear as a normal distribution.

Figure 8.1 was created using Minitab® software. It shows an example of how individual-moving range control charts and X-bar range control charts can be used to monitor the variation of invoicing cycle time. It should be noted that the control limits of an individual control chart are wider than those of the X-Bar chart because the standard deviation is larger than that for a corresponding X-bar chart based on subgrouped values. This is because the standard deviation of the subgroups is calculated as $s/\sqrt{n}$, which is a smaller quantify than s. Note that n is the size of the subgroups. This can be seen in Figure 8.1, where the upper control limit of the individual-moving range chart is 14.62 days versus that of the X-bar chart, which is 12.02 days. We will discuss these control chart calculations later in this chapter.

A variable could also be evaluated using a pass-or-fail criterion. Practical examples of this situation are found in office work environments and include statistics such as percentages of invoices without errors, deliveries on time, and hours lost due to illness. In these situations, the variable being charted is distributed as a binomial distribution because it is being measured as the proportion of successes of an event of interest, that is, pass or fail. The variation of proportions can be monitored using the p-chart shown in Table 8.5. It should be noted that a p-chart can be used with subgroups having either equal or unequal sample sizes. In contrast, an np-chart can only be used in situations in which subgroups have an equal subgroup size. A second invoicing example is shown in Figure 8.2, but now as a p-chart. The evaluation criterion in this example is the proportion of invoicing cycle times that are less than 12 days. The proportion is calculated as the fraction of invoices per subgroup that are less than 12 days. In this example the proportion or percentage of observations having a cycle time of less than the 12-day standard is 91.13 percent, and the upper control limit is calculated as 99.66 percent.

Table 8.5 also shows that a variable can be measured as counts falling into a predetermined category. As an example, we could count the number of errors found in a sample of 100 invoices or the number of employees per shift who are late every week. In these situations, the variable being charted has a Poisson distribution. Data in the form of counts can be collected using either an equal or unequal sample size. A c-chart is used to monitor the counts of a predefined quality characteristic using a constant sample size. As an example, a c-chart would be created using the number of errors found on an invoice when the sample sizes were equal day to day. In other words, we would count the number of errors for 100 invoices each day and plot this statistic on a c-chart. As a modification of this concept, if there were 200 data fields with an error in a sample of 100 invoices, with each invoice having 5 data fields, then the average error count per invoice, or c, would be 2, that is, 200 errors/100 invoices. Another way to look at the situation is that there are 500 data fields in the sample of 100 invoices. The original calculation can be revised using a different statistic calculated as 200 errors per 500 data fields. The error count c per data field,

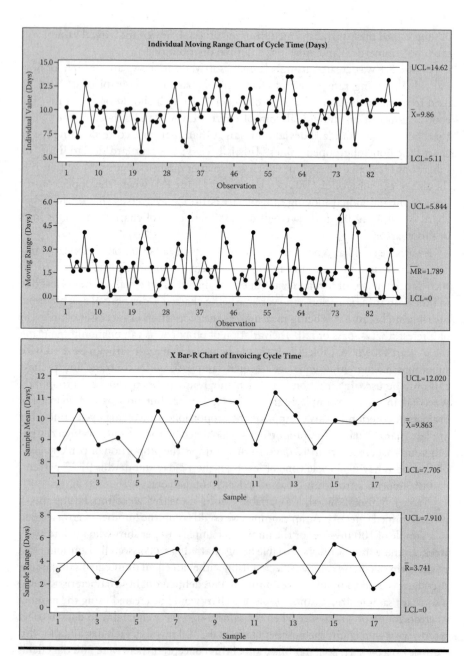

Figure 8.1 Control charts for normally distributed variables (continuous).

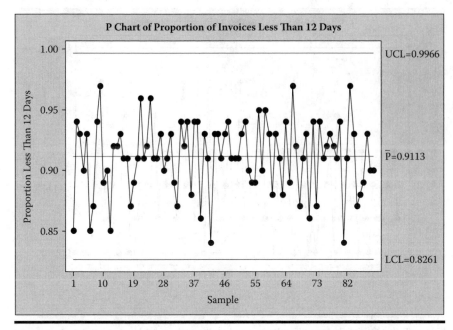

Figure 8.2   Control charts for binomially distributed variables (pass/fail).

in this revised example, would be 0.4, that is, 200 errors/500 data fields. A u-chart is used when a sample's subgroup size varies and its metric is based on counts. In the example just provided, a u-chart could be used if different numbers of invoices were collected every time period. In a u-chart, the proportion of errors is plotted based on the average counts found in each subgroup. A second invoicing example, using a c-chart, is shown in Figure 8.3.

Table 8.6 lists the steps necessary to set up a control chart. It should be noted that the calculation of control chart lower and upper control limits is complicated. However, the suggested readings at the end of this chapter will provide the detailed calculations necessary to manually construct and interpret several common control charts. Also, these calculations can be automatically done with software. In this book, we used Minitab to automatically create control charts and interpret their patterns. A subject matter expert may need to be brought into a Kaizen event to help the team create and interpret control charts.

The first steps in creating a control chart are to select the type of control chart that is consistent with the distribution of the variable being monitored. It should be noted that the default setting for the calculation of a control chart's lower and upper control limits is ±3 standard deviations from its mean. However, control limits can also be set at other distances from their mean value. As an example, limits of ±1 (~68 percent); ±1.96 (~95 percent), and ±3 (~99.73 percent) can be set, with the percentage of the reference distribution contained within the control limits shown in parentheses. As an example, if control limits have been set at ±3 standard

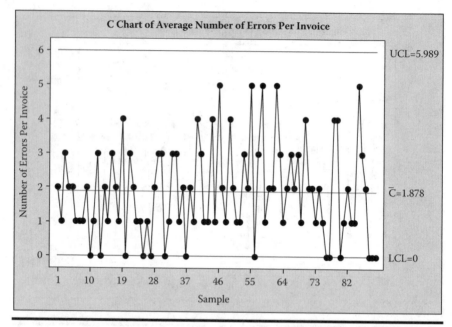

Figure 8.3 Control charts for Poisson distributed variables (counts).

Table 8.6 How to Create a Control Chart

1. Select the metric, i.e., input or output variable.
2. Select the type of control chart based on the distribution of the variable.
3. Calculate the control limits (standard deviations): +/1 (~68%); +/− 1.96 (~95%) and +/− 3 (~99.73%).
4. Determine the rational subgroup size and frequency of sampling.
5. Determine the data collection system, including where the data will be collected, by whom, the measurement criteria, and the evaluation methods.
6. Plot the data and interpret the control chart patterns.

deviations from a mean, then approximately 99.73 percent of the reference distribution is within the lower and upper control limits of the chart. This implies that the probability of being outside of the control limits is low, at 0.27 percent. This implies that if a point is outside of a control limit, we can assume with high statistical confidence that it is different from its original reference distribution due to an assignable cause of variation. In addition to calculating control limits, the rational subgroup size and its frequency of collection must be established. In this context, rational implies that a subgroup contains the smallest level of variation of interest to the analysis. As an example, if cycle times are collected on a daily basis, then the subgroup size may be 5 because there are five days in a typical workweek. In this situation, the control chart would exhibit week-to-week variation. On the other hand, if cycle times are collected on a weekly basis, then a rational subgroup could be a month. Data collection methodologies are another important consideration when constructing control charts. This includes information related to where the data will be collected, by whom, and the specific evaluation or measurement criteria used to classify the data. As a final step, the collected data is plotted on a control chart and its variation patterns interpreted by members of the local work team.

Our next discussion will focus on the interpretation of several common variation patterns. These variation patterns are shown in Figures 8.1 to 8.4. At this point in our discussion we will review the variation pattern of the individual-moving range and X-Bar range charts for the invoicing cycle time example shown in Figure 8.1. The individual control chart shows invoice cycle times arranged in their daily sequence. The mean cycle time is shown to be 9.86 days. This implies that 50 percent of the sample data had a cycle time greater than 9.86 days. Also, the lower control limit is 5.11 days and the upper control limit is 14.62 days. This implies that 99.73 percent of the observed cycle times are expected to be within this interval. It should be noted that an outlier that exceeds these control limits would be expected to occur with a probability of only 0.23 percent, that is, 100% − 99.73% = 0.23%. Another interesting observation is that all the cycle times fluctuate within the control limits. This indicates that only common cause variation exists within the process. In other words, if we need to reduce the daily cycle time to less than 9.86 days, then a significant process modification or redesign may be necessary. Otherwise, the process will remain at its current performance level. It is also important to note that the associated moving range chart is in statistical control. A moving range control chart monitors the variation between successive observations. To assume a stable process, both charts must be in statistical control. As a second example, the X-bar and range charts shown in Figure 8.1 show that the average cycle time of the invoicing process is in statistical control. In this example, the average of each subgroup is calculated as an average of five daily cycle times, which are averaged by week. However, the control limits are closer together than in the previous example, because they are calculated as the variation of subgroup means rather than individual values. Recall that the standard deviation of a distribution of means, that is, X-bar control chart, is less that that of individual values as shown by the formula $s/\sqrt{n}$.

Figure 8.2 shows the same data set, but now reclassified as the proportion of invoices having a cycle time less than 12 days. The subgroup size is 100 invoices per day. In this example, an average of 91.13 percent of the 100 invoices in the sample had a cycle time of 12 days or less. The control limits show that 99.73 percent of the subgroups will have a calculated proportion between 82.61 and 99.66 percent. This implies that a proportion less than 82.615 percent or greater than 99.66 percent would be expected to occur, with less than a 0.23 percent probability. This would most likely be due to an assignable cause of variation. However, it should be noted that this performance level may not be acceptable to an organization. In these situations, improvement projects will need to be created to change the current

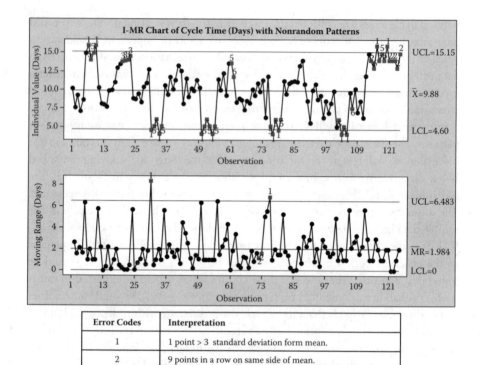

Error Codes	Interpretation
1	1 point > 3 standard deviation form mean.
2	9 points in a row on same side of mean.
3	6 points in a row all decreasing or increasing.
5	2 out of 3 points > 2 standard deviations from mean.
6	4 out of 5 points > 1 standard deviation from mean.

Figure 8.4 Control chart interpretation.

process performance level of a variable that has been shown by its control chart pattern to be stable.

The c-chart shown in Figure 8.3 is a control chart used to monitor counts. The sampling unit, area, or size is constant from one subgroup to another. Recall that the metric being monitored in this example is a count of the number of data fields in error. In this context, examples of data fields could include customer names, addresses, invoice amounts, item descriptions, and similar data elements. In these types of control charts a sampling unit may contain zero, one, or more defects. It should be noted that it is not unusual for a c-chart or even a p-chart to have its lower control limit as 0, and several observations on the lower control limit when the observed error or defects is zero. In Figure 8.3, the average number of data field errors per subgroup is 1.878. The assumptions used to create this control chart were that 100 invoices per subgroup were collected each day and each invoice contained five data fields. Note that the lower control limit was 0 and the upper control limit was 5.989 defective fields. This implies that 99.73 percent of the subgroups are expected to contain between 0 and 5.889 errors. Subgroups containing greater than six errors are outliers and are assumed to be caused by assignable causes of variation.

Recall that a process is not stable if there are outliers beyond the control limits or variation patterns in the control chart. Figure 8.4 shows several nonrandom control chart variation patterns. Minitab software evaluates data patterns and flags eight nonrandom patterns if the data distribution is continuous and normally distributed, and four nonrandom patterns if the data is discrete and distributed either binomially or as a Poisson distribution. We will use Figure 8.4 to discuss the basic variation patterns that may be observed when using individual and moving range control charts, some possible underlying root causes of the nonrandom variation pattern, and potential correction actions that a Kaizen team can be take to bring the process back into a state of statistical control. There are many types of variation patterns that may occur due to the underlying sources of variation within a process. A Kaizen team will use this information to identify the causes of the assignable variation. As an example, an outlier will usually indicate a major change in process conditions due to one or more sources of variation. Some of these variation sources may include materials, work procedures, people, measurement methods, machine settings, environmental factors, machine adjustments, maintenance, and others. In these situations, the underlying root causes may be easy to detect because their occurrence is recorded on a control chart. This makes it easier to correlate process conditions that may have existed at the time of the process problem to the observed variation.

Minitab will label subgroups that are more than three standard deviations from a process mean as outliers using a code of 1. However, Minitab software also allows a user to set control limits at another level, such as ±2 standard deviations from a process mean. As an example, outliers are evident at several places in the I-MR charts shown in Figure 8.4. An advantage of detecting outliers when they occur is that they signal that something unusual occurred within a process to force the level of the variable being charted to such an extreme value. However, from a different perspective, the existence of an outlier may indicate that its operating performance has actually improved. As an example, a long cycle time may be caused by a missed schedule. In contrast, a low cycle time may indicate a high adherence to schedule. In the former situation, immediate action would be necessary to identify the reasons for the long cycle time to return the process to its stable or steady-state condition. However, the latter situation may be an opportunity to improve the process. In this context, it would be useful to understand the process conditions that created the favorable result.

A second nonrandom pattern shown in the I-MR chart is error code 2. This error code is associated with nine sequential points on the same side of a process mean. This indicates a sustained shift in the process mean. A third nonrandom pattern detected in the I-MR charts shown in Figure 8.4 is a trend that is identified by error code 3. A trend is identified when there are six sequential points all decreasing or increasing. Other nonrandom patterns, such as cycles or clustering within or toward the extremes of the control chart, also indicate process issues. Finally, two additional error codes are shown in Figure 8.4: error codes 5 and 6. These error codes indicate that there are two out of three points greater than two standard deviations from the process mean, and four out of five points greater than one standard deviation from the process mean, respectively. These two types of error codes show there is higher process variation in this portion of the control chart. Minitab also identifies several other nonrandom patterns.

Measurement System Improvements

Every office process has one or more measurement systems. These can be seen in the form of management reports, metric dashboards, and other system information that is used to monitor, control, and manage process work activities. A measurement system is impacted by environmental factors, measurement procedures, equipment, people, work procedures, materials, and others. In other words, because a management report is created from information that has been gathered by manual or automated systems, it may be in error. In fact, depending on the variable being measured or the measurement system itself, there may be at least six components of measurement error. A Kaizen team needs to understand the importance of these measurement components to ensure their measurement systems accurately and precisely provide the information necessary to make correct decisions regarding process status.

The six common components of measurement system error are its resolution, accuracy, stability, linearity, reproducibility, and repeatability. These components are integral parts of Six Sigma "belt" classes. But the discussions within these classes are usually manufacturing-centric. Our focus will be to explain how the six components impact the measurement and evaluation of data collection within an office environment. The resolution of a measurement system is related to its ability to detect changes in the variable being measured. It is also dependent on the scale used by the measurement system. As an example, to detect changes in distance of a meter with adequate resolution, a team might measure distance in centimeters or millimeters. Referring again to an invoicing example, if a team must detect changes in cycle time measured in hours, then a time stamp based on days would not have adequate resolution. In this situation, a team would need to increase the measurement resolution by moving it to a time stamp that measures in minutes. Resolution issues, once recognized, are often the easiest measurement system error to reduce or eliminate. The second measurement system component is accuracy. Accuracy is also called bias or offset. If the average measured value of a variable differs from its true value, then the system has an accuracy problem. An example in office environments is when a computer system rounds up or down, or when a "fudge factor" is added to a measured quantity.

Stability errors occur when a variable's measured average value changes over time, but its true values do not change. An example would be a deterioration of employee performance skills acquired through training. This is because these skills must be periodically reinforced through ongoing training activities. Linearity refers to the ability of a measurement system to measure a variable with the same variation around its true value over its full range of measurement. An example of a possible linearity problem is when rating scales are skewed toward one end or another in customer satisfaction surveys. Skew of the survey responses may occur if there are more levels on either side of the scale, or if they are more heavily weighted. As an example, customer feedback surveys may be organized using the following levels: poor, neutral, fair, good, very good, excellent, outstanding. In this type of scale, positive responses will tend to dominate the survey.

The final two measurement error components are reproducibility and repeatability. Reproducibility is a situation in which the average measurements of two or more people or machines differ from each other when measuring the same thing under identical conditions. Identical implies the same measurement device and procedure is used to obtain the measurement. An example of a reproducibility problem is when several people are trained to evaluate work tasks, but they differ on average relative to their evaluations. Examples would include managers who rate their employees higher or lower than an established evaluation standard, or when several call center agents differentially escalate similar complaints based on the same evaluation criteria. The sixth measurement component, repeatability, refers to a small variation between successive measurements when measuring something several times under identical conditions.

It is important that a Kaizen team understand the impact of these six measurement components on their project's data collection and analysis activities and their final controls. In fact, in some projects, the root causes of the original process problem may have been actually caused by its measurement system. As a result, some of a project's countermeasures may be designed to eliminate the measurement issues. As an example, in Figure 8.5, the two graphs appear to show that cycle time has been reduced by a team's process improvements. In the first graph, a control chart is used to show that both the average cycle time and its variation decreased over an initial baseline. In the second graph, a box plot is used to show the same information, but in a different format. However, in this example, it is important that a Kaizen team be able to show the impact of measurement error on the project's key metric, which is cycle time. In fact, management support for process improvements may differ if the extent of measurement error was only ±10 percent versus ±50 percent. In many project presentations, typical questions include "How did you obtain your data?" and "How do you know that your data is accurate?"

Failure Mode and Effects Analysis (FMEA)

The FMEA template shown in Figure 8.6 is used to systematically review every operational work task to look for ways in which it may fail. Up-front in a project, this type of analysis is also useful in identifying potential failure causes that a

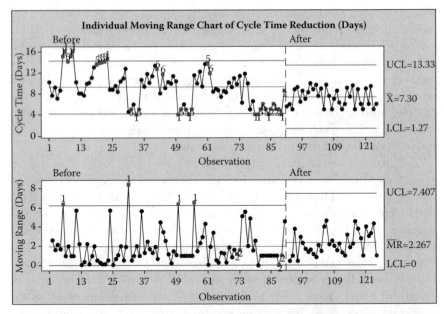

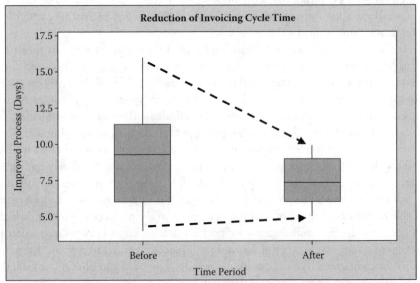

Figure 8.5 Measuring process improvement.

Kaizen team would investigate during its data collection and analysis activities. At the end of a project a Kaizen team could also use an FMEA to evaluate the ability of countermeasures to prevent process failures. In an FMEA, specific process failures are called failure modes. As an example, in Figure 8.6, a potential failure mode is associated with a customer calling to make a reservation and the call not

Process or Product Name: Call Center–Making an Airline Reservation									Prepared by:			Page 1 of 1						
Responsible:									FMEA Date (Orig) _____ (Rev) _____									
Process Step/Part Number	Potential Failure Mode	Potential Failure Effects	S E V	Potential Causes	O C C	Current Controls	D E T	R P N	Actions Recommended	Responsible	Actions Taken	S E V	O C C	D E T	R P N
Customer calls into call center.	Customer call not answered according to standard cycle time.	Customer leaves queue.	8	Staffing level not correct.	2	Analyze staffing levels versus customer average waiting time every week.	7	112	Implement a real-time service analysis system that will dynamically display average customer wait times and customers leaving the queue.	Joe and IT team.	Complete	8	1	1	8
Make airline reservation.	Select incorrect times.	Arrive too early/late.	4	Not confirming departure/ arrival times.	1	Have agent read back itinerary prior to accepting flight reservation.	5	20	Have agent read back itinerary and send the itinerary by e-mail prior to accepting flight reservation.	Joe	Modified software algorithm to automatically send itinerary to customer for review.	4	1	2	8

Figure 8.6   Failure mode and effects analysis (FMEA) example.

being answered within a standard cycle time. In this example, a customer may have been promised that a call would be answered within 60 seconds. If the call is not answered within 60 seconds, then this incident would be a failure relative to service level. The next column of Figure 8.6 is the potential failure effect. In the example shown in Figure 8.6, one effect of having to wait for their calls to be answered is that customers may leave a queue. The severity or seriousness of a failure effect is rated on a 1 to 10 scale in the severity column of the FMEA template. A 10 is very serious and a 1 is a minor impact, depending on the context of the analysis. The next column lists the potential causes of a failure mode (we skip over the potential failure effect column). In the travel example, there are three causes of the failure to answer a customer call in a timely manner: the staffing level was not adequate, agents were not properly trained, and agents are not provided with standard tools and information. These failure causes are variables that a Kaizen team could eliminate from their process to reduce customer waiting time. Each of the three failure causes also has an occurrence probability that is rated on a scale between 1 and 10. A 10 is a high occurrence and a 1 is a very infrequent one. Once a team lists failure causes and their occurrence probabilities, current process controls are evaluated for their effectiveness in detecting and preventing the causes of failure. Some controls are more effective in detecting and preventing failure causes than others. As mentioned earlier, verbal or written instructions tend to be weaker controls than the application of Lean methods such as 5S and mistake proofing. The detection column is an inverse rating scale in which a 1 implies controls are very effective in detecting failure causes, whereas a 10 implies current controls are relatively ineffective. The rating scales are multiplied to calculate the risk priority rating (RPN) column. As a result, the RPN number can range between 1 and 1,000. Each failure cause is prioritized for improvement based on its RPN number. Higher RPN numbers have a higher prioritization for improvement. The balance of the columns in the FMEA template capture information related to the corrective actions that are developed to reduce the impact of a failure cause or to eliminate it from a process workflow. In summary, an FMEA is a useful tool both up-front in a project to help in data collection and analysis activities, and at the end of a project to ensure countermeasures remain effective over time.

Other Control Tools

Other control tools and methods were discussed in Chapter 6 and listed in Tables 6.1 and 6.2. These included:

Modifications to organizational reporting structures
Elimination of portions of a process
Creation of new or modified process designs and layouts
Mistake proofing portions of a process

Purchase or design of new types of equipment
Implementation of 5S
Mistake proofing and similar Lean methods
Creation of new operational and financial metrics
Creation of new information reporting systems
Modifications of work, testing, inspection, maintenance, and other procedures
Development of process audits and monitoring such as statistical process control
Deployment of training programs
Holding group meetings (huddles)
Creation of written and verbal instructions

Quality Control Plan

Figure 8.7 provides an example of the types of information necessary to create a quality control plan. Quality control plans can exist in different formats. As an example, they may exist in paper or electronic form. If electronic, there could be dynamic links to referenced procedures and other templates that are being updated by other organizational functions. A Kaizen team's final recommendations should be incorporated within a quality control plan because it is a communication document that describes the variables found to be important to sustain the process improvements and the levels at which they must be maintained. These could be input (Xs) or output (Ys) variables. Examples of output variables include the cycle time for issuing customer invoices or answering customer calls within an agreed-upon time. Process inputs would impact these output variables. Once control variables have been specified, methods can be created to measure their performance. Corrective actions are also identified that will bring the controlled variables back into control if their performance degrades. However, once a Kaizen team has reached this step in their process improvement project, all the information necessary to complete a quality control plan template should be available.

Communicating the Proposed Changes to Management

Table 8.7 shows a portion of Figure 4.1, but in more detail. We are currently at Step 3 of the Kaizen event schedule as described by Figure 4.1. Table 8.7 lists four key deliverables that a Kaizen team should review, in advance, with their project champion and process owner to verify that the team has the information their management needs to know to move the project and its improvements forward. This is the point at which a Kaizen team's project recommendations and findings are presented to the process owner and other leaders. This step in the Kaizen event is critical for presenting a team's project recommendations to secure resources for improvement activities in both current and future projects. Also, at this point in time, a Kaizen team has the most up-to-date information regarding the root causes

Process Name: Team:		Customer: Office Location:						Date: Revision:	
Process Step/ Work Operation	Key Outputs (Y)	Key Inputs (X)	Requirements			Measurement Method	Testing/ Evaluation Method	Work Procedure Reference	FMEA Reference
			Lower	Target	Upper				
Customer calls into call center	Time to answer call	NA	NA	5 seconds	15 seconds	Automated time- stamp	Daily call summary report	Call Center Procedure 35/ Revision 4	Call Center Incoming Calls Revision 2

Figure 8.7 A generic quality control plan.

Table 8.7   Present Findings to Organization

| a. Develop a presentation of all analyses and implementation activities. |
| b. Develop lessons learned (what did and did not work). |
| c. Develop ideas to leverage improvement ideas. |
| d. Present findings to management in an easy-to-understand presentation format using clear presentation roles and a standardized template. |

Similar to Step 3 of Figure 4.1.

and the countermeasures required to eliminate them. The team's management is naturally interested in learning about this information.

The presentation must be structured to provide the team's information in a coherent and linear manner with relevant and supporting documentation. In other words, it should use a standardized presentation format that is easy to understand. It should also include the lessons learned from the data collection and analysis as well as improvement activities. In addition, team members should determine in advance the people who will be presenting their findings to management. A team should also practice its presentation in advance to ensure its success. Although there are many types of presentation formats, Figure 8.8 shows the basic concept. A team should use the information gathered from its root cause analysis as well as the countermeasures and related process improvements to show management the types of new process changes that need to be implemented and their impact on organizational stakeholders. It is also important in the stakeholder analysis to specify what activities key stakeholders need to take to support the changes. In addition, the management presentation should describe how the changes will be supported by the process owner and local work team, as well as any required future process changes. It is always a good idea to obtain specific questions from a Kaizen team's project champion and process owner in advance of a team's presentation.

Finally, although every organization has its own standardized way to communicate process improvements to management, it is always useful to discuss a project's original problem statement, and then show how the data collection activities and root cause analysis are linked to the problem statement and to the team's countermeasures and improvements. Every countermeasure should also have a corresponding business impact, including its benefits and cost. In addition, the schedule of how process improvements will be implemented should be discussed in the presentation. The tools and templates discussed in this book, with modifications, should help your Kaizen team adequately prepare for its management presentation.

Follow-Up Activities

Although a Kaizen team will normally complete most of their work activities during their event, some activities may be more complicated or require an extended

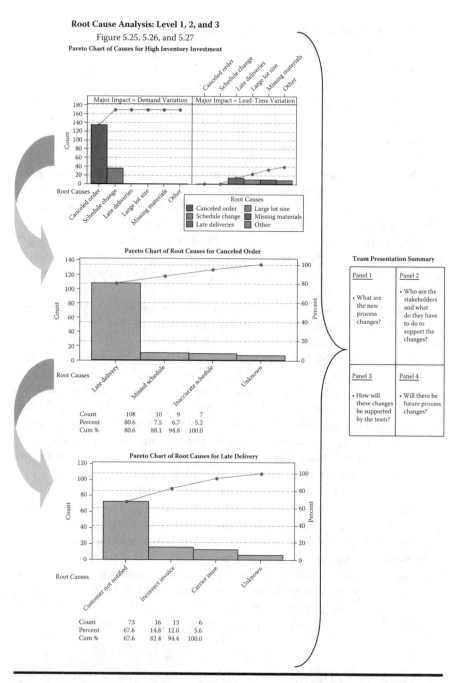

Figure 8.8 Communicating the proposed changes to management.

Table 8.8   Improvement Event Follow-Up Activities

a. Complete all prioritized improvements not completed during Kaizen event.
b. Communicate the Kaizen event results.
c. Celebrate with team.

Similar to Step 4 of Figure 4.1

period of time to complete. As a result, there may be several follow-up activities from a Kaizen event. The basic activities are listed in Table 8.8. Table 8.8 is similar to Step 4 of Figure 4.1. These follow-up activities are divided into three components. The first includes improvement activities not completed as part of the Kaizen event. These activities can be documented using a format such as that shown in Figure 8.9, or a simple listing can be created of the unfinished work tasks, completion dates, and the people responsible for their completion. In addition to the various follow-up activities required to make the final process improvements, there are a few additional actions a team will need to complete to close out their Kaizen event. These include communicating the findings of the Kaizen event to the larger organization and celebrating the team's success.

Creating Metric Dashboards

Metric dashboards will be our final discussion in this chapter. A metric dashboard provides an easy-to-understand reporting format that enables those using it to monitor the status of a newly improved process and take appropriate corrective actions, if its performance begins to degrade. There are many versions of these metric dashboards, but the basic concept is that they should be highly graphical and, ideally, enable a user to drill down to lower levels of a performance metric to identify the root causes for performance degradation. As an example, in Figure 8.10, total cycle time is broken into its time components by major process step. This is a useful feature, because if the higher-level cycle time performance degrades, a process owner can immediately see which operations have caused the cycle time problem. Ideally, this type of metric dashboard would also enable its users to drill down further into a root cause analysis. As an example, it would be very useful to be able to see the information related to cycle time at a work task level within each of the process steps shown in Figure 8.10.

Summary

Once a Kaizen team has identified the root causes for process breakdowns and developed countermeasures to eliminate and prevent them from occurring, this information must be documented in a control plan and integrated within an organization's

Action Item Listing (Follow-up Activities)												
Kaizen Event Number:			Facilitator:									
Department:			Date:									
Process:			Operator:									
Workflow:			Takt Time:									
Operation Number:			Required Production:									
				Improvements								
Identified Process Breakdown	Person Responsible		Completion Date	Production Rate	Scrap %	Rework %	Downtime %	Capacity	Setup Time	Inventory	Floor Area	
Comments:												

Figure 8.9 Follow-up activity list.

normal quality control system. A quality control plan is used by an organization to communicate important process characteristics, their target levels, the measurement methods necessary to monitor their performance, and reaction plans that are activated when process performance degrades. Effective process control strategies will usually require a combination of countermeasures to eliminate the root causes for process breakdowns. Although several types of control tools were discussed in previous chapters, this chapter presented several new control concepts. These included statistical process control (SPC), and failure mode and effects analysis (FMEA), as well as others. Another important topic discussed in this chapter was presentation of a team's project findings to obtain resources for improvement activities in both current and future projects. Metric dashboards were our final discussion. In this

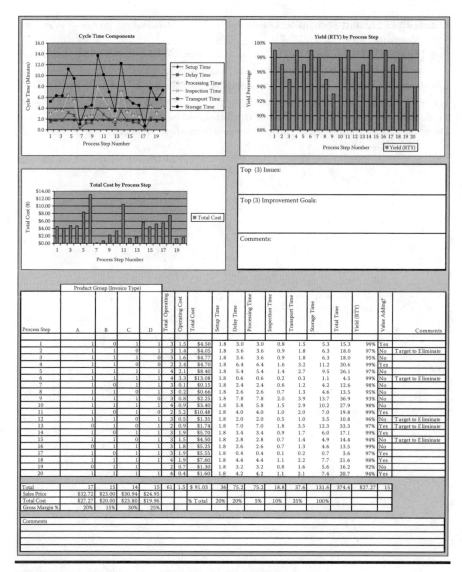

Figure 8.10 Creating metric dashboards (similar to Figure 5.1).

discussion, it was mentioned that metric dashboards should enable a process owner and local work team to monitor the status of higher-level metrics and take appropriate corrective actions to maintain their performance.

Suggested Reading

Davis R. Bothe. 1997. *Measuring process capability.* New York: McGraw-Hill.

Eugene L. Grant and Richard S. Leavenworth. 1988. *Statistical quality control*. 6th ed. New York: McGraw-Hill.

Paul Harmon. 2003. *Business process change—A manager's guide to improving, redesigning, and automating processes*. San Francisco: Morgan Kaufman Publishers.

J. M. Juran and Frank M. Gryna. 1993. *Quality planning and analysis*. New York: McGraw-Hill.

James W. Martin. 2007. *Operational excellence—Using Lean Six Sigma to translate customer value through global supply chains*. New York: Auerbach.

Douglas C. Montgomery. 1997. *Introduction to statistical quality control*. 3rd ed. New York: John Wiley & Sons.

Chapter 9

Reinforcing New Behaviors and Organizational Change

Overview

An organization will only support change when the argument for it is logical and compelling and its employees are actively engaged in aligned process improvement activities. However, most isolated Kaizen projects are implemented without much resistance because the process owner and local work team are involved with the process analysis and subsequent changes. However, a disadvantage of this bottom-up approach is that if the deployment's activities are isolated, then its process improvements will be difficult to sustain or propagate through an organization. As a result, a major theme of this book has been that Lean and Kaizen events should be an integral part of an organization's operational strategy with other reinforcing initiatives, such as Six Sigma. When properly deployed, Lean and Kaizen events have the potential to dramatically increase tremendous productivity for an organization.

The subject of reinforcing new behaviors and organizational change can be discussed at two levels. The first is at an organizational level within an environment where there are many integrated projects being simultaneously deployed through an organization. At this level, several specific change elements must be simultaneously developed to help create new organizational behaviors. At a second and lower level, the focus should be on the effective deployment of teams and execution of improvement projects where process changes are specific to a local work team. Effective organizational change depends on this tactical project alignment and execution.

In earlier chapters, we discussed the strategic alignment and efficient allocation of organizational resources to execute an initiative's projects. Effective project execution increases an organization's core competency in the areas improved by a project's solutions. In other words, an organization learns as new process knowledge is created through the collection and analysis of data, as well as the development of solutions to chronic process problems. Because initiatives are important in increasing organizational productivity, their effectiveness should be continuously measured relative to their financial and operational benefits. One measure of an initiative's effectiveness is the percentage of people within an organization who are using its tools and methods to make process improvements to increase productivity. In this context, effectiveness can be measured by project benefits that are correlated with employee surveys and training activities. It is also important, in the early stages of an initiative, that its invested resources be significantly higher than its benefits. Common statistics or metrics that can be used to measure the effectiveness of an initiative include the total projects deployed, the average cost savings per project, the total people deployed, the total investment cost, the average cost savings per person, the total cycle time to initiate and close a project, and the net promoter scores (NPSs) for the key stakeholders who are impacted by an initiative. An organization can also use other measurements to calculate its initiative's success. Recall that the NPS statistic discussed in Chapter 7 and shown in Figure 7.3 was a measure of key stakeholder satisfaction. Key stakeholder satisfaction is important in obtaining organizational resources and cooperation for an initiative's project activities. These measurements of effectiveness are important to sustain and expand an initiative. Communication is also an integral success factor. These combined measurements are also important to evaluate the effectiveness of Kaizen events and, as a justification, to secure resources for future Kaizen events.

In earlier chapters, we also discussed the fact that organizational change is enhanced when the correct tools and methods are used to deploy an initiative. In other words, tools should be matched to business opportunities. In this context, some projects should be deployed as Lean, Six Sigma, Kaizen, capital expenditure, or other types. This concept was shown in Figure 2.4. An organizational infrastructure should also be created to support different types of reinforcing initiatives. As an example, to the extent that an organization's senior management is engaged in an initiative's deployment through an executive steering committee, its success probability will be higher than if it were deployed in a bottom-up or isolated manner. This is because members of an executive steering committee can help select and align projects and also help implement the necessary organizational changes. Change is also facilitated by organizational training, in advance of an initiative's deployment, based on employees' anticipated roles and responsibilities. Also, at a project execution level, the people who will be impacted by a project's improvements should be integrated into Kaizen or other process improvement teams. Finally, change is enhanced when project metrics and business benefits are tracked and measured against key performance targets to show success.

Process Change across Global Supply Chains

Organizational change is particularly difficult within a global supply chain because of the large distances and cultural differences across its various locations. In my recent book entitled *Operational Excellence—Using Lean Six Sigma to Translate Customer Value through Global Supply Chains*, I discussed several success factors that facilitated organizational change within a global supply chain environment. One enabling characteristic was collaboration through interorganizational projects, joint ventures, and partnerships. These collaborative activities tend to improve supply chain communication and build interpersonal relationships among its participants. Another enabling characteristic is the development of high-performance teams that reflect the demographics of supplier and customer organizations. Diversity facilitates organizational change by improving group dynamics in a multicultural environment. Multicultural work environments also improve the ability of an organization to consider and adopt new ideas.

The design of a supply chain's products and services can also accelerate or inhibit change. In these leading-edge systems, operational simplification and standardization are enhanced through deployment of simple product and service designs and global operational standards that meet customer requirements, but are also flexible and easy to change over time. People are more apt to improve and change a process if the time and effort to make changes is low. This is possible through design simplification and standardization. As another example, enhanced technology, elimination of intermediaries within a process, and similar improvements reduce operational cycle times and improve quality. These increase the flow of materials and information through a system and enable a global supply chain to more easily match capacity to demand.

In his book entitled *Leading Change*, John P. Kotter discussed several successful characteristics that will tend to reinforce new organizational behaviors. Two critical success characteristics discussed by Kotter were empowerment of teams and the execution of short-term projects that provide business benefits. Kaizen events have these characteristics. But from an organizational change perspective, more is required to sustain improvement activities over time. These concepts have been the central focus of this book and are summarized in Figure 9.1 using a sequence of activities that build on each other and are continually improved as lessons are learned and deployment activities mature from one generation to another. As an example, an organization's steering committee and deployment leaders translate an organization's strategic goals and objectives into an initiative's projects by identifying financial and operational performance gaps. In turn, the closure of

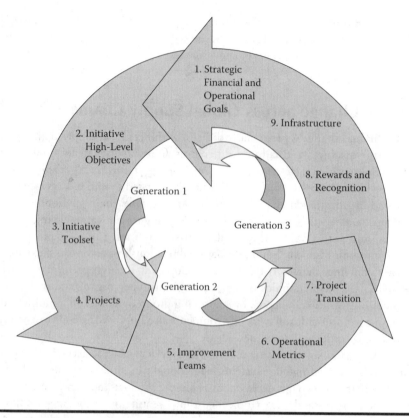

Figure 9.1 Reinforcing new behaviors.

performance gaps requires the use of unique tools and methods that are associated with an initiative. It is at this point when people may become confused if an initiative is being poorly executed by an organization. A complicating problem may also arise if an organization thinks it is easier to select just one initiative and then apply it to several problem areas where its tools and methods fit poorly. As an example, if a root cause analysis is not expected to be data intensive, then Lean methods, and Kaizen events in particular, may be the most efficient use of an organization's resources to eliminate the process problem. On the other hand, if a problem's root cause analysis is very data intensive, then perhaps Six Sigma tools and methods would be more useful. It should be noted that even within a Lean initiative there are numerous subspecialties, such as setup methods, preventive maintenance programs, ergonomic applications, and several other stand-alone initiatives. These may have a higher priority at various times depending on business requirements. Once a performance gap analysis has been completed, then actionable project charters are created and improvement teams can be deployed to execute them. Then as projects are executed over time, an organization's operational competency and the value-adding content of its processes will increase. Competency enhancement

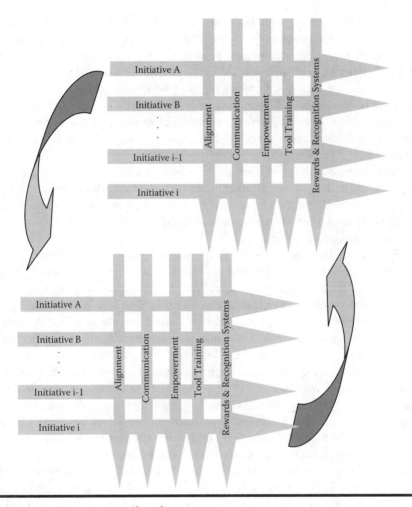

Figure 9.2 Competency migration.

occurs when an organization matches its product and service designs and its operational performance to its customer needs and requirements. At this point, process change becomes a reinforcing attribute that can change an organization's culture. This is particularly true when an organization's reward and recognition systems as well as its infrastructure are modified to support process change.

Figure 9.2 suggests that initiative competency migrates through an effective alignment of projects, the correct types of communication, team empowerment, training in relevant tools and methods, and the creation of reward and recognition systems that promote organizational change activities. Project alignment was discussed in Chapters 1 and 2. As a result, we will focus our discussion on several important communication elements and then on the creation of rewards and recognition systems.

Communication to key stakeholders is particularly important to accelerate organizational change across the larger organization. It was previously mentioned that communication is a complex process in which different communication channels must be used to match the message with its intended audience. These channels include messages from an organization's senior management, e-mails, newsletters, brochures, and advertising, as well as the day-to-day reinforcement by key stakeholders. In this context, all communicated messages should describe the necessity and advantages of process changes as they positively impact customers, employees, and suppliers. However, communication messages must be simple, clear, and consistent; otherwise, stakeholders may become confused. It is also important to match the correct communication format to the information being conveyed to the larger organization. As an example, routine and simple messages can be communicated informally and impersonally using e-mail, but complicated messages are best communicated in person.

Rewards and recognition systems are another important area that is used to support an organization's goals and objectives. As an example, rewarding people who oppose improvement projects or not rewarding participants of successful improvement projects will guarantee that an initiative will fade away. These situations occur when improvement activities are isolated and not aligned with an organization's goals and objectives. Another mistake is delegating the deployment of an important initiative to lower-level employees rather than senior managers. This will tend to send a message that these improvement activities are not important. This situation will also eventually result in a nonalignment of projects with degeneration of business benefits and will place an organization in a position in which the original opponents of an initiative's deployment will be able to point to its failures as proof that the original deployment concept was wrong. Organizational cultures having these behaviors will invariably exhibit poor project execution and numerous process breakdowns. The correct way to modify a rewards and recognition system is through a human relations (HR) department with the guidance of senior management. It is a complicated process that requires a strong commitment from an organization's leadership.

An organization must also simultaneously prioritize and allocate its scarce resources across several initiatives. This requires that each initiative be evaluated against its productivity opportunities. Some initiatives will be more important at any given time to an organization than others. Also, prioritization will change over time. As an example, Lean and Six Sigma initiatives receive a large amount of organizational support when they are first deployed within an organization. As they mature, organizational support levels off as their investment is matched to benefits or productivity opportunities. People often make a mistake in thinking that prior initiatives should not be supported after their tools, methods, and concepts have been integrated into an organization's processes. In summary, an initiative should be properly supported and communicated by its management to the extent that it is important to an organization.

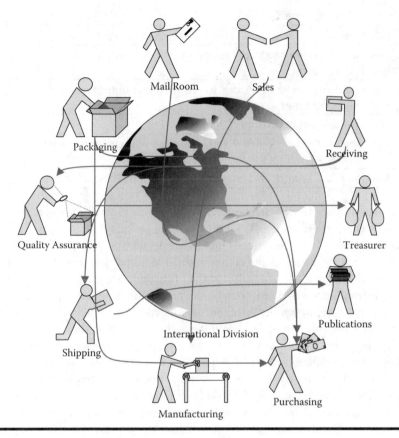

Figure 9.3 **Sharing knowledge across the world.**

An organization should also fully validate a model prior to deploying it to international locations. In other words, an organization should pilot or test its deployment with internal and easily accessible process workflows prior to internationally expanding an initiative across its other locations. This concept is captured in Figure 9.3. This is because an initiative requires that modifications be made after its introduction. Modifications are difficult when made in one language and at few locations, and having to make them across several countries makes the process even more difficult. It is also important to recognize that deployments across a global supply chain encounter significant cultural and language differences from one country to another. As a result, communication must be carefully designed to meet its intended objectives. Also, organizational hierarchies may be more or less structured depending on the country and its local culture. Organizational goals and objectives may also differ from one country to another. This includes its rewards and recognition systems. Communications describing Kaizen events must also be carefully crafted, if the audience is not local, to ensure their full meaning

Table 9.1 Transferring Control

1. What are the business benefits of the team's improvements?
2. Has the team demonstrated a strong root cause analysis with countermeasures?
3. Has a control plan been created to ensure the countermeasures will be sustained over time?
4. What work is left to be done?
5. Have the local process owner and local work team been trained to use the new process?
6. Have all process work and inspection instructions been updated?

is translated intact for the diverse locations in which the workflows reside. As an example, the various work tasks of an invoicing process may be scattered across several countries. In these systems, improvements within these process workflows must be carefully managed and communicated to all participants of the workflow wherever they may reside, regardless of their function.

Transferring control of a Kaizen team's process improvements is an important first step to changing an organization. In this context, John P. Kotter considers short-term wins, through project execution, to be one of the eight important factors reinforcing cultural change. As a result, we will complete our discussion of organizational change with a review of the questions listed in Table 9.1. The first critical question is "What are the business benefits of the team's improvements?" At this stage of the Kaizen event a team should have detailed data collection, analysis, and presentation material to support the business improvements it has created for the organization. In this context a team should have demonstrated a strong root cause analysis with countermeasures and incorporated their improvements into a quality control plan to ensure the countermeasures will be sustained over time. Additional considerations for the transference of process control are identifying how the follow-up activities, which could not be completed by the Kaizen team, will be completed in the near future. Finally, the Kaizen team should also have trained the process owner and local work team to use the new improved tools and methods to control their process. These include an effective alignment of projects, the use of the correct types of communication formats, team empowerment, training in relevant tools and methods, and the creation of reward and recognition systems. Another success characteristic that was previously discussed is communication to key stakeholders throughout a deployment.

Summary

Change will be supported by an organization only under circumstances in which the argument for it is logical and compelling and employees are actively engaged in the process improvement activities. My experience has been that most Kaizen or rapid improvement projects are implemented without much resistance because their impact is small and isolated. In contrast, there can be tremendous productivity increases for an organization when its Kaizen events and Lean Six Sigma activities are integrated with its other initiatives as part of a long-term strategy to improve operations. It was also mentioned that organizational change across global supply chains is particularly difficult given the large distances and cultural differences between its various participants. However, I have found through both research and practical experience that there are several key success factors that promote organizational change. These factors have been discussed several times in preceding chapters as well as this one.

Suggested Reading

Rosabeth Moss Kanter. 1983. *The change masters—Innovation and entrepreneurship in the American corporation*. New York: Simon and Schuster.

John P. Kotter. 1996. *Leading change*. Boston: Harvard Business School Press.

John P. Kotter and James L. Heskett. 1992. *Corporate culture and performance*. New York: Free Press.

James W. Martin. 2007. *Operational excellence—Using Lean Six Sigma to translate customer value through global supply chains*. New York: Auerbach.

Thomas E. Volkmann. 1996. *The transformation imperative*. Boston: Harvard Business School Press.

Conclusion

The book was written to provide information that is useful to plan and conduct a Kaizen event. In addition, data collection and analysis templates have been used throughout the book to enable a Kaizen team to immediately begin their process improvement activities. It is my opinion that effective and sustainable organizational change can be accomplished by applying the proven principles found in this book. This book has also been written in a modular format so that people who are familiar with Lean tools and methods can skip several chapters. In this way, the book should enable a Kaizen team to immediately begin planning and then conducting a Kaizen event, and in a systematic manner that is also clearly aligned with organizational goals and objectives. In this context, Kaizen events and their projects must be planned and executed and their solutions implemented with the support of process owners and local work teams.

Strategic alignment of Kaizen projects included a discussion of several key topics related to ensuring that an organization's goals and objectives were met in practice. This is an important concept because a major problem of many Lean Six Sigma activities, and Kaizen events in particular, is that their strategic alignment is often missing and process improvements become disconnected from organizational goals and objectives. As a result, an organization's management may have a feeling that a Kaizen event was not worth its resource expenditure or that the resultant process improvements are not sustainable. As a result of these personal observations, the discussions in earlier chapters of this book focused on the activities necessary to reduce system complexity in the context of the strategic alignment of Kaizen projects. This is done using an operational assessment prior to their deployment. Lean, Six Sigma, or Kaizen methods can then be applied to projects requiring a specific set of tools and methods for their effective execution. In summary, the strategic integration of Kaizen events in the context of project selection, team building, and the management of organizational change is important.

Service systems, and office processes in particular, have unique operational characteristics. In contrast to manufacturing processes, in service systems, the production process transforms information as it moves through integrated workflows in which manual work tasks are highly integrated with information technology

(IT) systems. Modern service system environments are characterized by a global integration of people, reports, data collection and analysis templates, and similar types of components across different countries, cultures, and with language differences. As a result, data collection tools and methods are different in service systems that are highly automated and globally dispersed. However, a problem in these types of work systems is a high degree of system complexity that is directly related to the fact that work teams are geographically dispersed and culturally disparate across organizational functions. Also, information gathering and sharing activities are heavily dependent on the efficient use of IT. As an example, process workflows in office environments include several hierarchal IT systems, such as business process management (BPM), business modeling and analysis (BMA), business intelligence (BI), business activity monitoring (BAM), enterprise application integration (EAI), and workflow management (WM). The hierarchal nature of these systems was discussed in Chapter 3 in the section entitled "10. Continually Update Process Technologies."

In earlier chapters of this book, I mentioned that a common but unsatisfactory approach to process improvement in office environments is to apply, without modifications, Lean manufacturing tools and methods. This overly simplistic approach tends to create overly complicated and disconnected activities. This is because manufacturing people are not expert in office processes such as financial forecasting, accounts receivable, new product marketing research, new product development, hiring employees, and supplier performance management (SPM), to name just a few examples. Consultants have not helped this situation. As a result, although useful, the application of Lean methods has not reached their full potential within office environments in the past 40 years.

It was also mentioned in earlier chapters that office cultures are different than those found in manufacturing because their workflows heavily rely on information technology and are highly dispersed functionally as well as globally. In this context, several major elements of a successful change model were discussed relative to transitional improvements to a process owner and local work team. In other words, this book has been written from the perspective that people and the cultural aspects of process improvement activities are as important as the analytical tools and methods used to identify and implement them.

The road map shown in Figure 4.1 is the basis of the book. This road map is a representation of the sequential activities that are necessary to plan, conduct, and follow up on all process improvements that comprise a Kaizen event. A Kaizen event is normally completed in three to five days depending on the application or project. But if up-front work is required to collect data and organize an event, then the schedule related to planning an event could easily exceed several weeks. This is a major differentiating characteristic between Kaizen events in service and those in manufacturing systems. As an example, once a Kaizen team has been brought together, it must have sufficient data, information, and resources to accomplish its work activities within the prescribed event schedule of between three and five days.

But it should be noted that an event schedule can be modified based on an organization's specific requirements.

Another major goal of this book was to develop modified versions of Lean and Six Sigma tools and methods that are currently used in manufacturing. The goal was to better characterize service systems, including their process workflows and operational work tasks. As an example, over the past 20 years, I found that data collection and analysis activities were more difficult in service applications, and especially those that touch office operations. To a large extent this situation is caused by the fact that process characterization and improvements in service systems rely to a great degree on implementation of IT to identify and eliminate the root causes related to high cycle time, low yields, and high transaction costs. A major recommendation of this book is to gather information prior to Kaizen events in service systems to provide a quantified description of the performance of key operational metrics related to cycle time, uptime, yield, inventory, setup time, and similar metrics. This is in contrast to a manufacturing operational assessment in which a Kaizen team is deployed across a manufacturing facility to physically count materials and collect operational information related to various workflows comprised of machines, materials, and people. Preliminary data collection in these situations is usually not difficult in manufacturing environments because machine operations are repeatable hour to hour. However, this does not imply that a detailed process analysis will not be eventually required to identify the causes for process issues. In contrast, service systems are heavily dependent on a combination of computerized systems and manual work tasks. This is because information rather than materials is created by a service system. In this context, a lack of standardized work tasks may complicate operational assessment activities in service systems. As a result, the efficient collecting of process information is usually more difficult. However, several useful methods were presented in earlier chapters of this book to collect and analyze data from service systems and their process workflows.

A value stream map (VSM) was shown to be an integral part of the data collection and analysis discussion and subsequent process assessment activities. Recall that a VSM is constructed as part of a hands-on operational assessment in which a Kaizen team is brought together to create its VSM using sticky notes that are placed on a wall. These notes represent the operations making up a process workflow. It was also shown that there were several data collection approaches to the quantification of a VSM. These included enabling IT systems to automatically time-stamp the transactions moving among operations, shadowing of office workers, and analyzing management reports and similar supporting materials. To obtain this type of information from service systems, and office processes in particular, audits are typically done on completed transactions or software code is written to automatically time-stamp and collect the transaction data within IT systems. Other relevant data collection activities include analyzing e-mails, personal calendars, and meetings, as well as job shadowing of employees over hours or days. The purpose of these data collection activities is to determine the percentage of time an employee spends on various non-value-adding (NVA) work tasks. Additional audits can also be done to assess transactions related to various types of work processed using office equipment. Finally, financial operational reports that describe issues related to cycle time, quality as they relate to expenses, customer complaints, health, safety, and environmental issues, and supplier performance can also be analyzed by a Kaizen team.

After data was collected, its analysis was discussed. These topics focused on only the several simple, but effective, analysis tools that have been shown to be very useful in Kaizen events. However, if more advanced analytical methods are required by a Kaizen team, then experts can be brought into a team's analytical activities. In other words, advanced statistical analysis was not the major focus of this book because Kaizen events require process characterization and simple data analysis. In this context, VSMs are critical to an effective process analysis. These topics were the focus of this book. It was also shown that Lean, Six Sigma, and Kaizen events were complementary and shared many of the same characteristics. In fact, Kaizen events consist of process improvement activities that use a combination of Lean and Six Sigma tools and methods. But the goal of a Kaizen event is to very quickly identify and eliminate process problems within days rather than weeks, months, or years. However, a common requirement of any process improvement method is that it should be aligned with the voice of the customer (VOC) and voice of the business (VOB).

In addition to a discussion of Lean and Six Sigma initiatives, as well as project selection, it was shown that organizations have several options when deploying an initiative, with some being more effective than others. These deployment options include a top-down, bottom-up, or isolated deployment. This discussion also compared and contrasted deployment strategies relative to organizational structure, roles and responsibilities, benefit identification, resource prioritization and allocation, communication, execution, organizational integration, and continuous improvement. The conclusion from these discussions was that top-down deployments are the most successful because they are aligned with an organization's goals and objectives. Strategy alignment implies Kaizen events will be linked to higher-level organizational goals and objectives. This prevents the deployment of projects to improve low-priority work areas. Also, it forces an evaluation of the correct tools and methods to identify and eliminate the underlying root causes of a process problem as it is originally identified in a Kaizen team's project charter.

However, prior to the deployment of process improvement activities, it was recommended that system complexity be reduced to the greatest extent possible. In this context, project identification and deployment activities were discussed from the perspective that they may be selected and impact several process workflows and locations. As a result, the discussion focused on ensuring that the specific projects assigned to a Kaizen team be properly described using a project charter that was integrated with an operational assessment across an organization's applicable processes to ensure a strategic linkage with its Kaizen events. In this context, an operational analysis could be focused at several organizational levels if the improvement work could be completed in a short period of time.

Another major focus of this book was a discussion of basic Lean tools and methods. The purpose of presenting this information was to provide background information for team members not familiar with these concepts. Of course, this basic information may need to be augmented for specific situations. This discussion began with the VOC and showed why reducing system complexity at all levels throughout an organization is important. Additional topics included:

Deploying Lean Six Sigma teams
Creating performance measurements
Creating VSMs of major process workflows
Eliminating unnecessary operations within workflows
Implementating just-in-time (JIT) systems to eliminate process waste
Reorganizing physical workflow configurations
Implementing 5S and standardized work
Operational linkage and spatial relationships
Balancing material flows
Bottleneck management
Using transfer batches
Mistake proofing
Improving quality
Reducing setup time
Deploying total preventive maintenance (TPM)
Leveling demand
Reducing lot sizes
Deploying mixed-model scheduling systems
Creating supplier networks
Implementing visual controls and pull systems using Kanban
Importance of continually updating process technologies

These Lean concepts were described from a service or front-office perspective.

After a complete discussion of Lean tools and methods, projects were assigned to a specific initiative based on their anticipated root cause analysis. As an example, projects whose major root cause analysis and improvement focus should most likely be process simplification, standardization, and mistake proofing would be assigned to Lean teams. On the other hand, projects requiring extensive data analysis and mathematical model building should be assigned to Six Sigma teams. Kaizen projects should be created when root causes need to be investigated and eliminated in a matter of days. Once a Kaizen event becomes necessary, the activities related to preparing, conducting, and presenting its findings to management were discussed. These include the logistics of selecting projects, roles and responsibilities, teams, meeting logistics, and communication to all key stakeholders.

Activities associated with conducting a Kaizen event include data collection and analysis using Lean and simple Six Sigma tools and methods. The focus of this discussion was on the use of simple data collection and analysis templates using six office processes. Some of these key analysis tools and methods included VSM, spaghetti diagrams, developing time standards, auditing of operational work tasks, and job shadowing activities. Six Sigma tools included cause-and-effect (C&E) diagrams, X to Y matrices, five-why analysis, data collection checklists, histograms, Pareto charts, box plots, scatter plots, time series graphs, and control charts.

The final activities of a Kaizen event included a discussion of how to summarize a Kaizen team's root cause analysis and findings and present them to their management team. Management presentations of the Kaizen team's findings are designed to show how improvement recommendations were developed and their business impact. Key elements of a management presentation include an analysis of operational data, a root cause analysis, and the countermeasures, which include mistake proofing, standardized work, training, and so on, found to be necessary to eliminate each root cause. Related information includes the lessons learned (what did and did not work) and a discussion of how a Kaizen event's lessons learned can be translated to similar processes.

Throughout this book, the discussions highlighted the difficulties often encountered when a Kaizen team attempts to change an organization's work activities. Important topics related to changing a process by implanting improvements included:

Integrating project improvements to a team's root cause analysis
Developing effective process controls and systems
Training people in the new process controls
Estimating a project's business benefits
Conducting a risk analysis of the recommended process improvements
Transitioning a project back to a process owner and local work team
Reinforcing the newly learned behaviors over time

In these discussions, the emphasis was on developing sustainable process improvements that were aligned with an organization's strategic goals and objectives.

Changing a process can be a very straightforward set of activities that ensure that process improvements are sustained over time. In this context, carefully planning the activities necessary to effectively change a process is important because there may be conflicting priorities within an organization because of the competing initiatives being deployed and managed at any given time within the organization. It was shown that effective communication is essential to gain support for process improvements.

Another important aspect of deploying Kaizen events is ensuring that change management tools and methods are fully integrated with process improvements and incorporated into an organization's quality control systems. It was shown that process control strategies require the combined application of several control tools that have been carefully selected as countermeasures to eliminate the root causes of process breakdowns. In this context, the controls or countermeasures implemented by a team must be tied to the root cause analysis of the original problem stated in the team's project charter. It was also shown that a metric dashboard can enhance process control by providing process status information in an easy-to-understand format that enables those using a metric dashboard to monitor metric status and take appropriate corrective actions to maintain process performance at its target level.

My reason for writing this book is that organizational change across global supply chains is particularly difficult given the large distances and cultural differences between its various locations. But it has been my experience that process change will be supported when its argument is logical and compelling and employees are actively engaged in identifying and working on process improvement activities in an empowered way. This is the strength of the Kaizen event approach to process improvement. It is a proven fact that many process problems can be quickly analyzed and solved using Kaizen events. In this context, bringing together a cross-functional team to completely focus on a process problem has been shown to work very well. Indeed, many operational issues associated with office processes can be best investigated and eliminated using a Kaizen event approach rather than more complicated methods. As a result, I have attempted to create a book that would provide a simple and easy-to-understand guide to plan and conduct Kaizen events in office environments for rapid improvement.

Appendix 1: Crystal Ball® Software

Most process analyses and improvements can be completed using either manual or simple computerized methods. These methods consist of drawing process maps and using graphical and simple statistical analyses as well as Lean methods such as value stream maps (VSMs), 5S, and mistake proofing. In this context, simulation methods can also be very useful when analyzing complicated process workflows that consist of numerous rework loops as well as changing levels of key process variables.

As an example, a simulation model relating how long a customer waits for his or her call to be answered by an agent may depend on employee staffing levels, the volume of incoming calls, time of the day, days of the week, type of customer request, and similar factors. A clear understanding of how important system variables drive customer waiting time would enable a Kaizen team to more realistically estimate its organization's required staffing levels and other factors to provide the expected customer service level, that is, minimum waiting time at a minimum system cost. As another example, if a process contains several rework loops that tend to increase a system's cycle time or lower its process yield, a Kaizen team could use a simulation model to analyze how eliminating each rework loop would reduce cycle time and improve quality of the process workflow.

You may ask, "Why do we need a simulation model to do these analyses?" The answer is that a simulation is useful in quickly evaluating how a system's outputs change when the levels of its input variables change in a complicated manner. In other words, if a process contains only a few operations, then a simulation model may not provide new information. But if the process contains parallel operations and rework loops, then a simulation model will usually be necessary to understand the dynamic relationships among its many process variables.

Real-world process workflows are difficult to characterize. This is because they consist of complicated and unknown interrelationships among their process components. Think of these systems as black boxes in which an analyst knows what

285

enters and exits the system, but not exactly how the system's inputs are transformed into outputs. The reason for this lack of knowledge is that real work systems are a dynamic combination of operational variables that may have significant time delays between when an event occurs and when it is finally measured by an observer. The existence of time delays results in ambiguity as well as poor resolution of actual system performance. Of course, many Lean methods, such as building and analyzing a value stream map (VSM), help a Kaizen team to create a process model and understand its dynamic performance. But a simulation model could also be used at a next lower level of quantification to understand the dynamic relationships between a system's input and output variables. This methodology is particularly useful in estimating system yields, availability, and cycle time. As mentioned above, simulations can also be used to clarify the relationships of input and output variables in response to changing levels of a system's parameters. In effect, the creation of a simulation model requires a mapping of real-world process performance into a virtual world using known process parameters and decision rules that characterize the interrelationships between known system components. Simulation models enable a Kaizen team to compress time between events to rapidly evaluate multiple process scenarios to understand the complex interrelationships among work operations.

However, it must be admitted that simulation methods are not easy to understand or learn in a few days. For this reason, it is important that a Kaizen team consult with local experts who are familiar with simulation methods. But on the other hand, it may be very easy to develop simulation models given that a Kaizen team has already quantified its VSM and operational relationships are known. Analysts can immediately use this information to create a basic simulation model that can be used to develop improvement scenarios for a Kaizen team's cost-benefit analysis. But how would an organization develop its capability to create simulation models to improve its process workflows?

A first step would be to hire analysts or industrial engineers who have received educational training in simulation and statistical methods. All industrial engineers should have received this type of training. However, the training is also readily available in industry at training seminars. In this context, an organization would need to organize a group of people who have been trained to build simulation models. This training can be attained through several ways, including educational institutions, corporate seminars, and from suppliers such as those providing Crystal Ball® software, a global business unit of Oracle® Corporation. A good way to gain this type of analytical capability is to develop, in advance, a list of work applications that would benefit from simulation methodology.

Simulation methodology has been applied to most organizational functions. As a result, a quick review of the numerous available case studies will enable an organization to quickly develop a justification for the training of a few individuals in simulation methodologies. A next step in the process to develop this type of analytical capability is to research and select off-the-shelf modeling software to match expected process applications such as manufacturing, service systems, warehousing, and logistics, as well as other operational and business functions. Also, some software packages have been highly customized for certain functions, such as logistics or manufacturing. Others enable development of three-dimensional models of process workflows. Prices, of course, vary significantly. However, an advantage of using Crystal Ball software is that it is very versatile and can be applied to any process workflow, in both office and manufacturing applications. It is also relatively inexpensive. A next step in building this type of analytical capability is to create a library of relevant applications that are typical for your organization. This will save time and expense when simulation models are needed by a Kaizen team, because off-the-shelf models can be easily adapted to similar workflows but may have different parameters levels. Developing a library of applications will also facilitate the training of new employees.

Once an initial analytical capability has been created by an organization, an analyst can more easily work with a Kaizen team to model a process workflow. Building a simulation model requires that all the operational work tasks be quantified by an analyst. This includes estimating the probability distributions of the operational metrics at every operation of the VSM. As an example, if a Kaizen team needs to build a simulation model of a system's cycle times, then an analyst can estimate the cycle time distribution at every operation. This is not difficult for an experienced analyst, because there are both exact and approximate methods that can be used to estimate these distributions. As an example, a goodness-of-fit test can be used to estimate the most likely standard probability distribution that fits a particular data pattern. Also, approximate methods can be used if the minimum, maximum, and average operational cycle times are known for every operation. An approximation of a cycle time distribution could be estimated using a triangular distribution to estimate an operation's mean cycle time and variance.

Once the probability distribution has been developed for every operational metric, an analyst develops decision rules of a model that reflect how the process functions. These rules include a specification of the initial and final states of a simulation model. As an example, one decision rule may be to estimate the overall cycle time by adding the average operational cycle times on a system's critical path. A critical path consists of a series of sequential operations having the maximum total cycle time relative to any other path through a system or network. In this context, a comparison of two parallel operations in which one has a time duration of one day while the other has a ten-day time duration would indicate that the one-day operation could be started as late as nine days from the initial starting date of the operation that requires ten days for its completion and still not impact the system's total cycle time. The operation with a time duration of only one day has nine days' slack time in its completion schedule. Decision rules show how system components interact to create process functionality.

As a second example, another decision rule may require that there be a rework cycle after an operation. A rework cycle would have the effect of lowering the preceding operation's throughput rate because work must be made up or reworked. Once an analyst builds and executes a simulation model that reflects a Kaizen team's VSM, its accuracy must be compared against actual system performance. After all analytical activities have been completed, a Kaizen team documents its simulation analyses and develops plans to implement its improvement solutions.

Accounts Receivable Example

In Chapter 6, six common office processes were presented and discussed in the context of Lean methods. We will use the accounts receivable process described in Figure 6.4 to show how a Kaizen team could use simulation methods to improve its analysis and final recommendations. In Figure A1.1, the eight operations shown in Figure 6.4 have been quantified to create a simulation model using Crystal Ball software. This type of quantification would be obtained using a Kaizen team's VSM. Also, recall that a VSM quantifies a process workflow relative to key operational metrics. As part of this quantification, a team could also calculate several simple summarized statistics, such as an operational metric's minimum, maximum, mean, and standard deviation, or collect the data reflecting the metric's performance history. Although estimation of probability distributions is beyond the scope of this book, analysts can use Crystal Ball to perform distribution fitting of empirical or historical data to known probability distributions, or use an approximate distribution such as the triangular one discussed above to create probability distributions.

However, a few of the more common distributions, which are shown in Figure A1.1, can be described at a basic level. A normal distribution is symmetrical around its mean and exhibits a bell-shaped curve. An exponential distribution is highly skewed. It should be noted that a distribution of cycle times is commonly described using an exponential distribution when there are outliers in the data set that skew it. A uniform distribution is described as having minimum and maximum values as well as a rectangular shape. A common example of a uniform distribution occurs when a vending machine fills a coffee cup for every customer within a relatively constant time interval once the customer pushes the vending machine's start button. As a final point, Crystal Ball can also be used to run larger numbers of simulations, for example, 10,000, to accurately estimate the areas at the ends of the simulated distributions. This may help better identify outliers within a distribution.

The example shown in Figure A1.1 is an analysis of the cycle time from when a customer places an order to when he or she pays it. This cycle time interval is the total cycle of the nine operations shown in Figure A1.1 and is also called the accounts receivable cash flow cycle. Figure A1.1 also shows typical process issues or

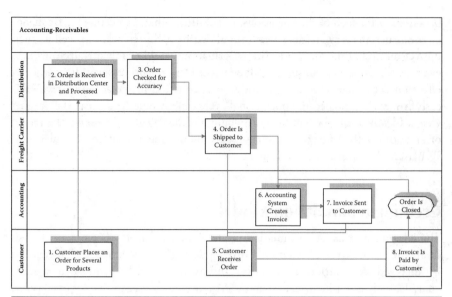

Operations	Distribution	Mean	Std. Dev.	Typical Issues
1. Customer places order.	Normal	.5 Hours	.1 Hours	Incorrect quantity or product is ordered.
2. Order processing.	Normal	8 Hours	4 Hours	Incorrect names, addresses item and amounts are entered into the system or incorrectly converted by the system.
3. Order accuracy check prior to shipment.	Exponential	.5 Hours		Failure to discover missing, surplus or damaged items prior to shipment. Failure to protect order from the environment.
4. Order sent to customer.	Lognormal	48 Hours	3 Hours	Order is lost or potions of the order are lost, arrive damaged or late.
5. Order receipt.	Uniform	Minimum = 8 Hours	Maximum = 16 Hours	Customer fails to properly receive an order resulting in receipt of damaged items, failure to discover missing or surplus items and related issues.
6. Invoice creation.	Uniform	Minimum = .25 Hours	Maximum = .5 Hours	Invoice is not created due to missing information or is created using inaccurate information.
7. Invoice sent to customer.	Normal	24 Hours	12 Hours	Invoice sent to wrong customer or delivery not verified by supplier.
8. Invoice paid by customer.	Normal	4 Hours	2 Hours	

Figure A1.1   Accounts receivable simulation: distribution assumptions (similar to Figure 6.4).

breakdowns for each of the operations. It is assumed that the occurrence frequency of the issues at every step has been calculated by a Kaizen team as well as their impact on cycle time and cost. This information would enable a Kaizen team to evaluate the impact of eliminating these issues from the process workflow. The net effect on cycle time would be an additional reduction in the accounts receivable cash flow cycle time because operational cycle times would be decreased by higher yields. Ideally, a cost-benefit analysis would also be calculated to show the return on investment (ROI) of the various process improvement scenarios. Simulation is very useful in modeling complicated systems.

Creating a Simulation Model

The advantage of using a simulation model is that it enables a complete analysis of a process workflow's operational distribution relative to important metrics to be analyzed from various perspectives and assumptions. In contrast, in a static analysis, such as a value stream map (VSM), only the average values of operational metrics are analyzed by a Kaizen team. Also, a simulation is useful when changing a process workflow to quickly evaluate the likely impact on a process. As an example, the quantitative information shown in Figure A1.1 has been transformed into probability distributions for every operation on the critical path of the accounts receivable process. This was done using Crystal Ball software. These distributions are shown in Figure A1.2. Notice that the summarized cycle time statistics from the process map shown in Figure A1.1 were used to create each distribution. Also note the different shapes or patterns of each distribution. As an example, the exponential distributions are highly skewed right. This implies that some events have a very high cycle time compared to other events. In contrast, the normal distributions are symmetrical around their mean value. Crystal Ball also provides other standardized distributions for a simulation analysis.

A summarized analysis is also shown in Figure A1.3. In addition to a total cycle time analysis, simulated cycle times can be compared to a specification, which in this example has been set between 40 and 120 hours. Notice that the mean cycle time is ~98 hours and that the simulated range of cycle times, as measured by their minimum and maximum values, respectfully, was ~58 to ~140 hours. Also notice that some orders fell outside this cycle time specification. An advantage of using this approach is that a Kaizen team can look for ways to reduce the overall cycle time for a process. As an example, in Figure A1.4 we can see that the subprocess associated with sending invoices to customers represents ~80 percent of the total cycle time of the accounts receivable process. This statistic shows that a Kaizen team should be working on the subprocess for sending invoices to customers.

This analysis is aided by Crystal Ball's sensitivity analysis graph. It can be seen that the subprocess for sending invoices to customers represents ~80 percent of the total cycle time of the accounts receivable process. Notice that in the statistical analysis

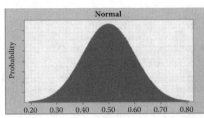

Normal distribution with parameters:
Mean   0.50
Std. Dev.   0.10

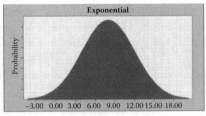

Normal distribution with parameters:
Mean   8.00
Std. Dev.   4.00

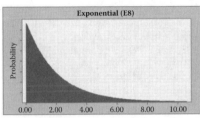

Exponential distribution with parameters:
Rate   0.50

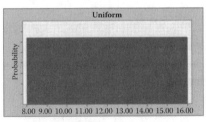

Lognormal distribution with parameters:
Mean   48.00
Std. Dev.   3.00

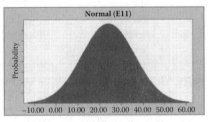

Uniform distribution with parameters:

Minimum   8.00
Maximum   16.00

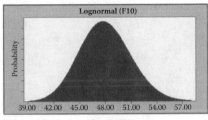

Normal distribution with parameters:
Mean   24.00
Std. Dev.   12.00

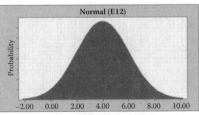

Normal distribution with parameters:
Mean   4.00
Std. Dev.   2.00

Crystal Ball® software is a global
business unit of Oracle® Corporation.

www.crystalball.com

Figure A1.2   Some Crystal Ball® software statistical distributions.

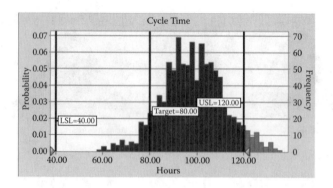

Trials	1,000.00
Mean	98.56
Median	98.31
Mode	---
Standard Deviation	13.49
Variance	182.04
Skewness	0.07
Kurtosis	3.15
Coeff. of Variability	0.14
Minimum	58.91
Maximum	139.45
Range Width	80.53
Mean Std. Error	0.43

Crystal Ball® software is a global business unit of Oracle® Corporation.

www.crystalball.com

Figure A1.3   Crystal Ball® software cycle time analysis.

shown in Figure A1.1, this subprocess has an average cycle time of ~24 hours and a standard deviation of ~12 hours. This cycle time is less than that for the subprocess associated with shipping orders to customers, which has an average cycle time of 48 hours. A Kaizen team would have missed the fact that the process of sending invoices to customers was the largest contributor to overall cycle time. Recall that simulation is useful in identifying and understanding dynamic metric patterns within a process workflow. The advantage of augmenting value stream analysis using simulation methods is that various improvement scenarios can be studied without actually changing a process workflow. As an example, a team could analyze reductions in the cycle times associated with sending invoices to customers, building a business case for process improvement. Once management approves the recommended process improvements, then actual versus predicted reductions in cycle time can be compared by a Kaizen team.

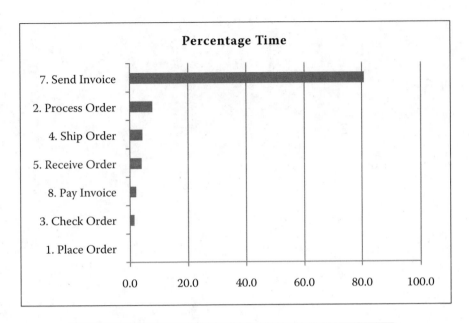

Operation	Distribution	Percentage
7. Send Invoice	Normal	80.8
2. Process Order	Normal	7.8
4. Ship Order	Lognormal	4.1
5. Receive Order	Uniform	4.0
8. Pay Invoice	Normal	2.1
3. Check Order	Exponential	1.2
1. Place Order	Normal	0.0

Crystal Ball® software is a global business unit of Oracle® Corporation.

www.crystalball.com

Figure A1.4   Crystal Ball® software sensitivity analysis.

Appendix 2: Minitab® Statistical Software and Quality Companion by Minitab

There are many software packages that a Kaizen team can use to collect, analyze, and report their project information. Examples that come to mind include Excel, and PowerPoint, as well as the numerous specialized software packages that provide Pareto charts, cause-and-effect (C&E) diagrams, project scheduling templates, and similar information. However, an advantage of using the new Quality Companion by Minitab™ from Minitab® is that all the common data collection and analysis activities associated with Kaizen events can be captured and reported using this one software package. The software also encourages a sequential problem-solving methodology such as Six Sigma's define, measure, analyze, improve, and control (DMAIC), but it does not force a particular solution methodology on its users. In other words, a project could be structured as a Lean or Six Sigma project or to the sequential phases of any other initiative. It is very flexible in this way. Specific capabilities of the software include creating, managing, and reporting project activities. These activities include most of the tools and methods discussed in this book. As an example, they include building process maps, brainstorming tools such as a C&E diagram, and related Lean and Six Sigma tools. Other capabilities include creating data collection and analysis forms, exporting and importing data and graphs from Minitab Statistical Software, and creating PowerPoint presentations using the accumulated information. The various software tools and templates also include help information in the form of a "coach."

Figure A2.1 shows how a project schedule can be created using the Quality Companion 2. The project activities shown in Figure A2.1 are similar to those

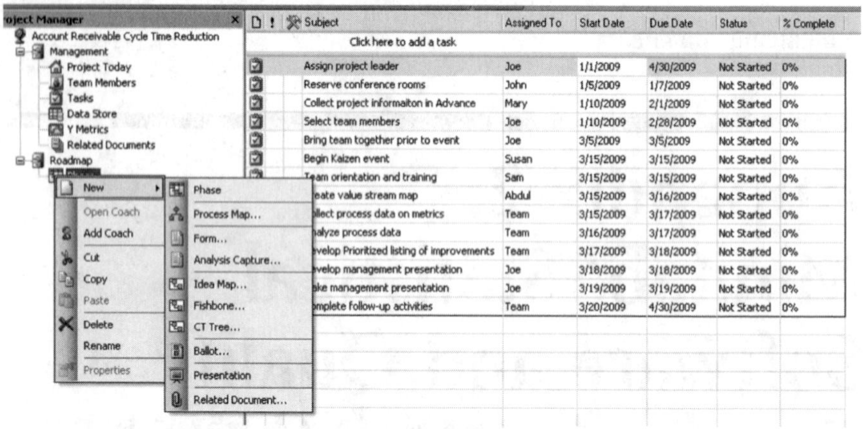

Figure A2.1   Creating a project schedule using Quality Companion by Minitab®.

shown in Figure 4.1. These activities are the major ones required to plan and conduct a Kaizen event and report its results to management. Also included are follow-up activities. In addition to this list of activities, this section of Quality Companion 2 enables a user to create phases within the project's road map by selecting "new," as shown in Figure A2.1. From "new," another pull-down menu appears. This second pull-down menu enables a user to create and label a new phase, create some basic quality tools such as process maps and C&E diagrams, and insert data collection and analysis templates or import analyses from Minitab Statistical Software. This information can also be incorporated into a PowerPoint presentation file. A project's Roadmap® can be easily built using these integrated options.

The specific tools and templates available in Quality Companion 2 are shown in Figure A2.2. The list is extensive, so three screen shots are shown in the Figure. The list includes basic quality templates such as audit plans, control plans, data collection planner, Gantt charts, financial analysis, project risk assessment, stakeholder analysis, value stream maps (VSMs), and project charters, as well as many other tools and templates which are used in Lean, Six Sigma, and other process improvement initiatives. These tools and templates can be incorporated into the various phases of a project's road map and can be used over and over from one phase to another. Another extensive list of statistical tools and methods has been imported from Minitab Statistical Software. These are shown in Figure A2.3. In this listing, the tools and methods range from the very basic to more advanced. If a Kaizen team needs these types of tools and analyses, then Six Sigma or similar statistical experts should be brought into the team. A discussion of these tools and methods is beyond the scope of this book because they are required infrequently by most Kaizen teams. Once a Kaizen team completes its data collection and analysis activities and develops a list of prioritized improvements, a management

Figure A2.2   Incorporating Quality Companion's Lean forms and templates.

presentation is developed to present the team's fact-based recommendations to the process owner and local work team. Quality Companion 2 has this function completely integrated within its software. Presentation slides can be easily created and edited to develop a management presentation in minutes. The slides are taken from Quality Companion 2's phased Roadmap. In this context, Quality Companion 2 is very useful because a presentation can be created at various levels of detail depending on the expected audience.

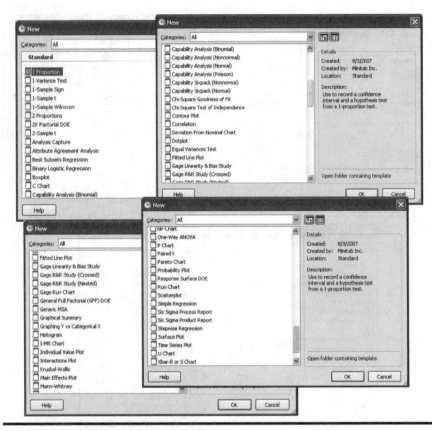

Figure A2.3   Incorporating Six Sigma tools from Minitab® into Quality Companion.

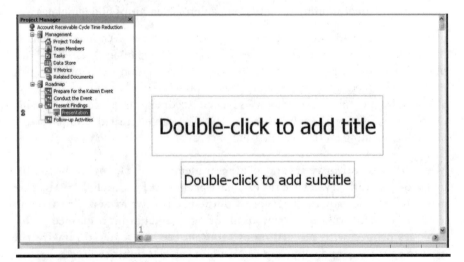

Figure A2.4   Creating PowerPoint presentations using Quality Companion.

Appendix 3:
Figures and Tables

Chapter 1

Figure 1.1   What is Kaizen?
Figure 1.2   Strategic alignment.
Figure 1.3   Ten important elements of a Lean system.

Table 1.1   How Do Lean, Six Sigma, and Kaizen Compare?
Table 1.2   Comparing Deployment Strategies
Table 1.3   Deployment Roles and Responsibilities
Table 1.4   Reducing System Complexity
Table 1.5   How to Deploy Kaizen Events in Three Steps
Table 1.6   Building a Business Case for Improvement
Table 1.7   Translating the Voice of the Customer (VOC)

Chapter 2

Figure 2.1   Project identification—breaking down high-level goals.
Figure 2.2   Project identification—process analysis.
Figure 2.3   Project charter example.
Figure 2.4   Prioritizing projects.
Figure 2.5   Generic financial statements—profit-and-loss statement.
Figure 2.6   Generic financial statements—balance sheet.

Table 2.1   Analytical Levels of Process Analysis
Table 2.2   Typical Project Examples
Table 2.3   Key Metric Definitions

Chapter 3

Figure 3.1	JIT philosophy—the seven major types of process waste.	
Figure 3.2	1. Voice of the customer (VOC).	
Figure 3.3	3. Deploy Lean Six Sigma teams.	
Figure 3.4	4. Create performance measurements.	
Figure 3.5	5. Create value stream maps (VSMs) of major workflows.	
Figure 3.6	Takt time calculation.	
Figure 3.7	Takt time calculation—original process.	
Figure 3.8	Takt time calculation—future state.	
Figure 3.9	6. Eliminate unnecessary operations within workflows.	
Figure 3.10	7. Implement just-in-time (JIT) systems—eliminate waste.	
Figure 3.11	7.a. Reorganize physical configurations.	
Figure 3.12	7.c. Link operations.	
Figure 3.13	7.d. Balance material flow.	
Figure 3.14	7.d.1 Bottleneck management.	
Figure 3.15	7.d.2 Transfer batches.	
Figure 3.16	7.e. Mistake proofing.	
Figure 3.17	7.i. Level Demand.	
Figure 3.18	7.j. Reduce lot sizes.	
Figure 3.19	7.j.1. Mixed-model scheduling.	
Figure 3.20	8. Supplier networks and support.	
Figure 3.21	9. Implement pull systems in offices using visual controls and Kanban.	
Figure 3.22	10. Continually update process technologies.	

Table 3.1	Ten Key Steps to Implementing a Lean System
Table 3.2	2. Create Robust Product and Process Designs to Reduce Complexity
Table 3.3	7.b. 5S and Standardized Work
Table 3.4	7.f. High Quality "Zero Defects"
Table 3.5	7.g. Reduce Setup Time (SMED) "Single Minute Exchange of Die"
Table 3.6	7.h. Total Preventive Maintenance (TPM) "Preventive...Autonomous...Predictive"

Chapter 4

Figure 4.1	Kaizen event checklist.
Figure 4.2	Kaizen event communication letter.
Figure 4.3	Evaluation of a Lean Kaizen event.

Table 4.1	1. Prepare for the Kaizen Event
Table 4.2	Kaizen Event Kickoff Agenda

Table 4.3   2. Conduct the Kaizen Event
Table 4.4   Important Event Facilitation Methods
Table 4.5   Data Collection Strategies in Service Operations

Chapter 5

Figure 5.1   Three major steps to creating a value stream map.
Figure 5.2   Brown-paper mapping.
Figure 5.3   Brown-paper mapping at a major work stream level.
Figure 5.4   Product complexity analysis.
Figure 5.5   Process analysis.
Figure 5.6   Process analysis worksheet.
Figure 5.7   4. Performance measurements (similar to Figure 3.4).
Figure 5.8   Process audit worksheet.
Figure 5.9   Waste analysis by operation.
Figure 5.10   Summary of waste analysis for several jobs.
Figure 5.11   Job shadowing worksheet.
Figure 5.12   Spaghetti diagram.
Figure 5.13   Process mapping—SIPOC.
Figure 5.14   C&E diagram.
Figure 5.15   Histogram (data from Figure 5.4).
Figure 5.16   Pareto chart (data from Figure 5.9).
Figure 5.17   Box plot (data from Figure 5.9).
Figure 5.18   Scatter plot (data from Figure 5.7).
Figure 5.19   Time series graph (data from Figure 5.7).
Figure 5.20   Control charts (data from Figure 5.7).
Figure 5.21   Improvement opportunity worksheet.
Figure 5.22   C&E matrix—prioritizing projects.
Figure 5.23   Analysis of job shadowing data.
Figure 5.24   Example: Inventory analysis and reduction.
Figure 5.25   High inventory investment—first level.
Figure 5.26   Major reasons for canceled orders.
Figure 5.27   High inventory investment—second level.
Figure 5.28   Major reasons for high inventory investment.
Figure 5.29   High inventory investment—third level.
Figure 5.30   Major reasons for late deliveries.

Table 5.1   Why Create a Value Stream Map?
Table 5.2   10 Requirements Necessary for an Effective Value Stream Map
Table 5.3   5 Key Characteristics of a Brown-Paper Exercise
Table 5.4   Checklist
Table 5.5   How Lean and Six Sigma Tools Compare

Table 5.6   Five-Why Analysis
Table 5.7   Example: Analyzing Data Collected from Job Shadowing

Chapter 6

Figure 6.1   Root cause analysis: Levels 1, 2, and 3 (Figures 5.26, 5.28, and 5.30).
Figure 6.2   Use graphics to show process improvements.
Figure 6.3   Example 1: Financial forecasting.
Figure 6.4   Example 2: Accounts receivable.
Figure 6.5   Example 3: New product marketing research.
Figure 6.6   Example 4: New product development.
Figure 6.7   Example 5: Hiring employees.
Figure 6.8   Example 6: Supplier performance management (SPM).
Figure 6.9   Kaizen project—new product marketing research.
Figure 6.10   Prioritizing new product marketing research projects (similar to Figure 5.22).

Table 6.1   Common Process Changes
Table 6.2   Control Tool Effectiveness and Sustainability
Table 6.3   Root Cause Analysis and Improvement Strategy
Table 6.4   Countermeasures at 4th-Level Root Cause—Late Deliveries

Chapter 7

Figure 7.1   Major change elements.
Figure 7.2   1. Cost-benefit analysis.
Figure 7.3   2. Key stakeholder analysis.
Figure 7.4   3. Impact analysis of key stakeholders.
Figure 7.5   4. Resistance analysis of proposed changes.
Figure 7.6   5. Infrastructure analysis.
Figure 7.7   6. Scheduling process changes.
Figure 7.8   7. Communication planning.

Table 7.1   Change Readiness
Table 7.2   Important Project Transition Questions
Table 7.3   Building a Business Case for Change

Chapter 8

Figure 8.1   Control charts for normally distributed variables (continuous).
Figure 8.2   Control charts for binomially distributed variables (pass/fail).

Figure 8.3   Control charts for Poisson distributed variables (counts).
Figure 8.4   Control chart interpretation.
Figure 8.5   Measuring process improvement.
Figure 8.6   Failure mode and effects analysis (FMEA) example.
Figure 8.7   A generic quality control plan.
Figure 8.8   Communicating the proposed changes to management.
Figure 8.9   Follow-up activity list.
Figure 8.10   Creating metric dashboards (similar to Figure 5.1).

Table 8.1   Key Process Improvement Questions
Table 8.2   Control Plan Requirements
Table 8.3   Important Control Tools
Table 8.4   Key Concepts of Control Charts
Table 8.5   Control Chart Control Overview
Table 8.6   How to Create a Control Chart
Table 8.7   Present Findings to Organization
Table 8.8   Improvement Event Follow-Up Activities

Chapter 9

Figure 9.1   Reinforcing new behaviors.
Figure 9.2   Competency migration.
Figure 9.3   Sharing knowledge across the world.

Table 9.1   Transferring Control

Appendix 1

Figure A1.1   Accounts receivable simulation: distribution assumptions (similar to Figure 6.4).
Figure A1.2   Some Crystal Ball® software statistical distributions.
Figure A1.3   Crystal Ball® software cycle time analysis.
Figure A1.4   Crystal Ball® software sensitivity analysis.

Appendix 2

Figure A2.1   Creating a project schedule using Quality Companion by Minitab®.
Figure A2.2   Incorporating Quality Companion's Lean forms and templates.
Figure A2.3   Incorporating Six Sigma tools from Minitab® into Quality Companion.
Figure A2.4   Creating PowerPoint presentations using Quality Companion.

Glossary

5S techniques: Lean techniques that encourage local work teams to sort, set in order, shine, standardize, and sustain.

Activation: Using a resource only when it is needed.

Actual capacity: A capacity less than that which should be available due to unexpected process breakdowns.

Affinity diagram: Used to organize large amounts of data into natural groups based on a common theme.

Agile project management (APM): A project management system based on Lean concepts and used to develop software products.

Analysis of collected data: The process of applying analytical tools to understand relationships in data to obtain information.

Analyze phase: The third phase of the Six Sigma DMAIC methodology.

Application programming interfaces (APIs): The software used to transfer data between different manufacturing systems.

Arrow diagram: Used to show the spatial relationships between many factors to qualitatively identify causal factors.

As-is map: A graphical depiction of a process that is usually quantified and created by "walking the process."

Assessment: A methodology for evaluation process performance.

Attribute control chart: A control chart that monitors a variable that is discrete, i.e., pass/fail or counts.

Available capacity: Capacity less than the design capacity with normal inefficiencies factored into its calculation.

Balance sheet: A financial statement that records assets and liabilities.

Basic need: One of the three types of Kano needs. Customers expect basic need to be met by all suppliers.

Batch-and-queue system: A transformation system in which production is moved using discrete lots.

Benchmarking: A system of tools, methods, and techniques that compare the performance attributes of one system to another.

Bottleneck management: The process of ensuring system bottlenecks are utilized to meet the takt time without disruption.

Box plot: A graphical analysis tool showing the first, second, third, and fourth quartiles and median of the sample data.

Breakthrough improvement: Changing process performance by a discontinuous amount, i.e., a step change improvement.

Budget variance: A difference between a budgeted actual and amount.

Business activity monitoring (BAM): A software system that monitors changes in process workflow status.

Business intelligence (BI): A software system that analyzes data and provides information useful for process workflow control.

Business metrics: A measure of operational performance used to provide information or control a process.

Business process management (BPM): A software system that integrates several other software systems to manage process workflows.

Business process management suite (BPMS): A software system that integrates data and storage among many IT platforms.

Business modeling and analyses (BMA): A software system that allows a process workflow to be simulated and optimizes offline.

Business value-added operations: Operations valued by the external customer and required to meet their requirements.

Capability analysis: A set of tools, methods, and concepts that compare the voice of the process (VOP) to the voice of the customer (VOC).

Capability ratio: The ratio of the range of customer specification limits and the process variation measured in standard deviations.

Capacity: The amount of material or information that can be put through a system in a unit amount of time.

Capacity-constrained resource: A resource that can become a bottleneck if process conditions change.

Capacity requirements: The amount of capacity required to produce a unit of material or information.

Capacity requirements planning (CRP): Planning material, labor, equipment, and facilities necessary to produce products and services.

Capacity utilization: The process of using capacity whether it is necessary or not.

Cash flow statement: A financial statement that estimates the amount of free or available cash by time period.

Cash-to-cash cycle: The cycle time between paying for material, labor, and other expenses and receipt of payment from the customer.

Cause-and-effect (C&E) diagrams: A graphical tool that shows qualitative relationships between causes (Xs) and their effect (Y).

Cause-and-effect matrix: A matrix used to prioritize several inputs Xs for data collection across several outputs, or Ys.

c-Chart: A control chart that monitors a count data based on a Poisson distribution with equal subgroup sample size.

Champion: A person who removes project barriers.

Cluster sampling: Drawing a sample based on natural grouping of the population, i.e., by geography.

Common sampling methods: The four basic ways in which a random sample can be drawn from a population.

Compensating metric: A metric used to ensure other project metrics do not adversely impact a project.

Continuous-flow environment: A process workflow where there are no discrete units, such as oil refining.

Continuous improvement: Process improvement activities that are deployed over an extended time.

Control: The fifth DMAIC phase, in which process improvements are transitioned back to the process owner.

Control chart: A time series chart used to distinguish between common and special cause variation.

Control phase: The fifth Six Sigma phase, in which key process input variables (KPIVs) are controlled.

Control strategies: Combining various control tools to ensure process improvements are sustained over time.

Corrective maintenance: A set of tools and methods that attempt to prevent unexpected equipment failures.

Cost avoidance: A potential cost to an organization that will occur if not prevented.

Cp: The process capability when the process is on target and estimated using short-term variation.

Cpk: The process capability when the process is off-target and estimated using short-term variation.

Critical to quality (CTQ): A product or service feature that is important to an external customer.

Cultural change: A situation in which an organization begins to practice one or more new behaviors.

Cultural survey: A method that asks employees their opinion of its strengths, weaknesses, external threats, and opportunities.

Current map: A graphical representation of the process as it currently exists.

Customer value: Cost, time, function, utility, and importance of a product or service as perceived by a customer.

Data accuracy: The requirement that data not be biased from its true average level.

Data analysis: Various tools and methods designed to create information to answer questions from data.

Data collection: The process of bringing people and systems together to obtain information from a process.

Decision tree: A mathematical method to assign probabilities and expected payoffs to several alternative decisions.

Defect: A nonconformance relative to a specific customer requirement.

Defect per million opportunities (DPMO): A normalized quality metric calculated by multiplying DPU by 1,000,000 and dividing by the opportunity count.

Defects per unit (DPU): The ratio of total defects in a sample to total units sampled.

Define phase: The first DMAIC phase, in which a project is defined relative to business benefits and customer requirements.

Demand aggregation: The process of combining unit demand for several items and locations by time period (usually one month).

Demand forecast: The process of estimating demand in the future by time period (usually one month).

Demand management: The process of estimating future demand based on a combination of mathematical models and real-time demand information.

Demand pull: The scheduling process in which actual customer demand is used to schedule upstream operations.

Demand push: The scheduling process in which forecasted demand is used to schedule operations.

Dependent demand: Demand that is related to independent demand through a bill of materials (BOM).

Dependent variable: The variable that is explained by one or more other variables (independent).

Descriptive statistics: Summarized information relative to the central location and dispersion of a sample.

Design capacity: The maximum capacity a system can attain at 100 percent efficiency.

Design failure mode and effects analysis (DFMEA): A tool and related methods used to identify how a design can fail to meet requirements and the causes of this failure.

Design for Manufacturing (DFM): A design methodology using several rules and techniques that attempts to simplify and modularize designs.

Design for Six Sigma (DFSS): A set of tools, methods, and concepts used to ensure designs meet customer requirements at a Six Sigma performance level.

Design standards: Information used to ensure designs meet minimum accepted standards related to fit, form, and function.

DFSS scorecard: A summarization of a design's capability relative to all its components and related services.

Direct labor: An expense component on the profit-and-loss statement representing the cost of non-salary labor.

Disaggregating: The process of breaking a larger workflow system into components for insourcing or outsourcing.

Display board: A board placed in areas to show key metrics and other information useful to improve and control processes.

Diverse team: A group of people brought together to work a project and having diverse viewpoints, skills, or demographics.

DMAIC: The Six Sigma five-phase problem-solving methodology, i.e., define, measure, analyze, improve, and control.

DPMO: Defects per million opportunities.

Economic order quantity (EOQ): An optimally calculated quantity that balances inventory ordering cost versus inventory holding cost.

Economic value added (EVA): The income shareholders receive for their investment in an organization.

Economy of scale: A situation in which the variable cost of a product decreases as its sales volume increases.

Effectiveness: A situation in which the right things are being done.

Electronic data interchange (EDI): An electronic system that allows IT systems between organizations to exchange information.

Enabler initiative: An initiative used to execute improvement projects.

Engineer to order: A system in which unique products and services are designed and built for a customer.

Enterprise application integration (EAI): A software system that manages and controls information between several legacy systems.

Enterprise Information Systems (EIS): Separate software systems that manage specific protons of a supply chain.

Entitlement analysis: An analysis showing the best process performance, i.e., an on-target process having short-term variation.

E-supply: Electronic supply chain processes between supplier and customers.

Excess inventory: Inventory quantities exceeding expected demand during the order cycle.

Excitement need: One of the three types of Kano needs in which customers are delighted by a design characteristic.

Failure mode and effects analysis (FMEA): An analytical tool that shows the relationship of failure modes to causes and evaluates their risk levels.

FIFO inventory valuation: First-in-first-out inventory management.

Financial justification: The process of developing financial estimates of improvement project benefits.

Financial metric: A project metric that shows its cost savings, revenue increases, or cash flow increases if successful.

Finished good inventory: Inventory that has been completely built and packaged and is ready to ship to the external customer.

Finite loading: Scheduling a product with consideration for demand on the work center (available capacity).

First come first serve (FCFS): A prioritization system used in queuing models.

First in first out (FIFO): A prioritization system used in inventory valuation systems that values materials as they are received.

First-pass yield: The number of units meeting requirements at a single operation, excluding rework.

First quartile: The point at which 25 percent of the observations from a sample are below.

Force field analysis: A method used to analyze barriers to countermeasures necessary to eliminate root causes of process breakdowns.

Forecast: A set of quantitative and qualitative methods used to predict future events.

Forecasting new products: The process of estimating demand for new products by time period (one month).

Forecasting products: The process of estimating demand for current products by time period (one month).

Forecasting reconciliation: The process of smoothing out the forecast based on factors external to the forecasting model to ensure one number.

Forecasting system: A system of people, software, and other tools used to estimate future demand based on historical demand patterns.

Forecasting time horizon: The time period into the future.

Forming stage: The first stage in a team maturation process.

Forward scheduling: A scheduling method that uses a forecast to schedule manufacture of a product.

Functional interface: The handoff between organization functions.

Functional process map: A detailed process map showing all process workflow operations by function and time sequence.

Functional silos: Different departments or work areas within an organization having different responsibilities and work tasks.

Functionality: How a product or service functions.

Gantt chart: A chart that shows the start and finish times of work tasks in a project.

Globalization: An economic evolutionary process in which organizations compete across the world.

Green belt: A process improvement specialist within the Six Sigma program who works within a function.

Gross margin: The profit before taxes calculated by subtracting cost of goods sold from revenue minus adjustments.

Groupthink: A situation in which team members consistently agree with each other even if their decision is incorrect.

High-performance work team: A diverse team that has been through all four maturation stages and consistently achieves its objectives.

Histogram: A statistical method that graphically summarizes continuous data to show its central location and dispersion.

Historical demand: Actual customer demand over time.

House of quality (HOQ): A graphical method used to show quality function deployment information.

Hybrid decentralization: A system that locates work where it is performed best at lower cost and cycle time and higher quality.

Improve phase: The fourth Six Sigma phase, in which key process input variables (KPIVs) or X levels are changed to optimize Y.

Income statement: A financial statement that records income and expenses by time period.

Independent demand: Customer demand for products or services.

Indirect labor: Labor actually making a product or providing a service to a customer.

Individual control chart: A time series chart that separates common cause from special cause variation for nonsubgrouped continuous data.

Infinite loading: Scheduling a product without consideration for demand on the work center (available capacity).

Information disaggregating: Taking information associated with producing a product or service and sending it to different locations for processing.

Input/output matrices: Matrices that correlate input variables relative to output variables.

Insourcing: A practice of bringing work into an organization to improve its productivity.

Integrated supply chain: A supply chain that is linked by information technology to provide system status in real-time.

Interrelationship diagram: Used to show the spatial relationships between many factors to qualitatively identify causal factors.

Inventory age: 365 days divided by inventory turnover.

Inventory investment: The amount of money required to maintain inventory in anticipation of demand to meet target service levels.

Inventory make-to-stock model: A model that calculates required finished goods inventory quantities by item and location.

Inventory turnover: Cost of goods sold divided by average inventory investment.

Inventory turns: A ratio calculated by dividing cost of goods sold (COGS) by the average on-hand inventory investment.

ISO 9000: International Standards Organization standard describing basic quality system requirements.

ISO 9001: International Standards Organization standard describing system elements needed to meet customer requirements.

ISO 9004: International Standards Organization standard describing system improvement potential.

JIT system: Just-in-time supply of materials or information dependent on several underlying systems for success.

Job shop: A type of production process characterized by low volumes and high product diversity.

Just in time (JIT): A Lean system in which material or information arrives when needed and in the required quantity.

Kanban: A Kanban is a sign attached to inventory to show order status. There are transport, production, and signal Kanbans.

Kanban calculation: Sets the WIP inventory based on lead time, demand, and service level.

Kano: A system that classifies customer needs into basic, performance, and excitement needs.

Key process input variable (KPIV): Independent variables that have a significant impact on key process output variables (KPOVs).

Key process output variable (KPOV): Dependent variables that are directly correlated to voice of the customer (VOC).

Kitting: The process of bringing together components for use in service kits, replacement parts, and other applications.

L-shaped work cell: A work cell layout arranged as an L.

Lead time: The time to complete all work tasks.

Lead-time analysis: The process of decomposing lead time into its time elements.

Lead-time components: Lead time can be broken into transportation, setup, waiting, processing, inspection, and idle time.

Lead-time reduction: The process of reducing non-value-adding time within a process.

Lead-time variation: The dispersion of task completion times within a process.

Lean: A system designed to create simple, standardized, and mistake-proofed processes based on customer value.

Lean enterprise: A organization that exhibits Lean principles.

Lean performance measurements: A series of operational and financial metrics that can be used to evaluate the effectiveness of a Lean deployment.

Lean supply chain: A supply chain that uses a minimum amount of resources to satisfy customer demand.

LIFO inventory valuation: Last-in-first-out inventory valuation.

Long-term variation: The variation that impacts a process over a long period of time.

Lower specification limit (LSL): Lower level of a customer specification.

Make to order: A production system that produces products or services based on firm customer orders.

Make to stock: A manufacturing system that makes products for inventory storage.

Malcolm Baldrige Award: An award presented to organizations having best-in-class quality systems.

Mass customization: A system of production recommending lower-level design and process commonality, but higher-level product diversity.

Master production schedule (MPS): System that aggregates demand for the MRPII system.

Master requirements planning (MRPII): System that uses demand from the MPS and explodes it to the MRPII system.

Mean: A central location statistic calculated by summing all observations and dividing by their number.

Mean absolute percentage error (MAPE): A forecasting error statistic useful in comparing the forecasting error of different time series.

Measure phase: The second Six Sigma phase, in which the ability to measure a metric and its capability is established.

Measurement accuracy: The ability to measure a characteristic and be correct on average over many samples.

Measurement linearity: The ability to measure a characteristic over its entire range with equal variation (error).

Measurement repeatability: Variation between measurements when made by the same person (or machine) on the same thing when measured several times.

Measurement reproducibility: The ability of two or more people (or machines) to measure a characteristic with low variation between each person (machine).

Measurement resolution: The ability of the measurement system to discriminate changes in the characteristic being measured (1/10 rule).

Measurement stability: The ability of the measurement system to obtain the same measured value over time.

Measurement systems analysis (MSA): A series of methods used to verify accuracy and identify sources of measurement variation.

Median: A central location statistic calculated by taking the number separating 50 percent of observations on each side.

Metric: A characteristic that can be measured as either a discrete or continuous variable.

Metric dashboard: A tool used to collect information on several related metrics to provide information on process status.

Metric scorecard: A matrix that is used to record and track process metrics by metric type.

Micromotion studies: Analysis using cameras that break down work into its smallest motions to set work time standards.

Milk run: A delivery system in which suppliers are co-located near customers and supply them based on Kanban quantities.

Min/max inventory system: An inventory system that reorders based on an item's reorder point.

Mistake proofing: A system of tools and methods that prevent or detect errors and their defects.

Mixed-model scheduling: A scheduling system that allows more frequent scheduling of products or services through low-cost setups.

Monte Carlo simulation: A mathematical technique in which randomly generated numbers are transformed into a reference distribution.

Multivari chart: A graphical method used to analyze the impact of changing levels of independent variables on a dependent variable.

Nominal logistic regression: A logistic regression model in which a dependent variable has several discrete labels.

Nonlinear regression: A method that does not use linear coefficients to explain the variation of a dependent variable.

Non-value-adding (NVA) operations: Operations within a process workflow that customers do not want.

Normality test: A goodness-of-fit test that compares a sample to an assumed normal distribution.

Norming stage: The third stage of team maturation, in which team members begin to agree on team objectives.

np-Chart: A control chart for binomially distributed data in which the subgroups must be constant.

Obsolete inventory: Inventory that cannot be used to produce products or provide services.

On-time delivery: When a supplier's shipment quantity is received at the agreed-upon lead time without process defects.

Open system: A system in which the consequences of its actions are not necessarily relevant to its decisions.

Operational balancing: Every operation in a system contributes the material or information flow necessary to maintain the takt time.

Operational efficiency: How well a system functions relative to a target of 100 percent.

Operational excellence: An umbrella initiative including Lean, Six Sigma, and total productive maintenance (TPM).

Operational linkage: Ensuring operational metrics are consistent across functional boundaries.

Operational metrics: Metrics other than financial that indicate process status relative to time, performance, or quality.

Operational planning overview: A group of cross-functional people who meet to determine the best mix of supply necessary to meet demand.

Operational strategy: The high-level operational goals and objectives that must be achieved to meet financial goals and objectives.

Operations management: A field of study that includes tools and methods used to transform process inputs into outputs.

Opportunity: A product or service characteristic that can be either a pass or fail state.

Optimum map: A process map containing only value-adding operational work tasks.

Order book: Firm demand that is based on customer orders.

Order cycle (T): The time-to-time interval between sequential incoming order quantities from suppliers.

Outsourcing: A process of sending work to other organizations to increase productivity.

Overdue backlog: Quantity of product that could not be manufactured according to customer demand due to capacity constraints.

p-Chart: A control chart for binomially distributed data in which the subgroups are either equal or not equal.

Pareto chart: A graphical analysis tool in which discrete categories are arranged in descending order by their counts.

Parts per million (PPM): A metric that adjusts a fraction in terms of 1 million, i.e., $10\% \times 1,000,000 = 100,000$ PPM.

Payback: The number of years required to recover an initial investment.

Percent error: The number of defects found in the sample divided by the total sample and multiplied by 100.

Performance gap: The difference between a target versus actual performance level.

Performance measurements: Metrics used to measure process changes.

Performance need: A Kano need that helps differentiate one supplier from another.

Performing stage: The fourth stage in a team maturation process, in which a team works toward common goals and objectives.

Periodic review inventory system: An inventory model checking inventory at specific times and ordering quantities to bring inventory up to a target.

Perpetual inventory model (PIM): An inventory model in which inventory is continually monitored and orders are released at a reorder point.

PERT: Program evaluation and review technique.

Pilot of solution: A test of proposed process change within the actual process, but under controlled conditions.

Plan-do-check-act: Deming cycle used for problem solving.

Point of sale (POS): A system that collects sales data as it occurs and provides it to suppliers to plan production.

Pp: The process capability when the process is on-target and estimated using long-term variation.

Ppk: The process capability when the process is off-target and estimated using long-term variation.

PPM: Parts per million.

Preventive maintenance: A system of tools, methods, and concepts designed to ensure systems are available for use.

Primary metric: A metric, including financial, business, or project, that must be improved for a project to be successful.

Prioritization matrices: Used to prioritize decisions based on various weighting schemes.

Proactive data: Data that is actively collected by an organization.

Problem statement: A verbal description of the operational problem that must be solved by the project.

Process batch: A system that transfers materials or information to subsequent operations when all units have been processed.

Process capability: A method used to compare process performance against customer specifications.

Process failure mode and effects : A method that analyzes how a process can fail to correctly build a product or provide a service.

Process improvement projects: Projects used to close performance gaps.

Process mapping: A method used to show the movement of materials and information through the system.

Product group: A collection of products having similar characteristics.

Product life cycle: The demand phases a product goes through over time, including its introduction, growth, maturity, and decline.

Product proliferation: Many organizations allow products having little demand or margin contribution to remain active in their systems.

Production activity control (PAC): A manufacturing function on the shop floor used to schedule work through work centers.

Production Kanban: A quantity of material or information used in operations to signal an operation to process another Kanban quantity.

Productivity: A year-over-year measure of outputs divided by inputs; usually expressed in financial terms.

Profit and loss (P/L): A key financial statement that shows income and costs to show if a profit has been made by the organization.

Profitability index: The ratio of present value of cash inflows to present value of cash outflows.

Project activity: A major set of project work tasks that have been assigned a time duration and starting and ending dates.

Project charter: A document in either electronic or paper format that provides justification for the project.

Project evaluation and review technique: A project probabilistic scheduling methodology used to find a network's critical path.

Project identification: A process of identifying projects to increase organizational productivity or stakeholder satisfaction.

Project management: A set of tools and techniques used to manage project deployment.

Project metric: An operational metric used to measure project success; correlates to financial and business metrics.

Project milestone: A major set of project activities used to monitor project schedule completion.

Project objective: A section of the project charter that states the specific business benefit of the project.

Project plan: A combination of work tasks, budgets, schedules, and resources brought together to complete a project.

Project planning: The process of scheduling the various work tasks and elements necessary to complete the project.

Project resources: Materials, labor, money, and information necessary to complete the project.

Project selection: The process of identifying work to benefit the business and customer according to strategic goals and objectives.

Prototype phase: A phase in product development in which samples or prototypes are created for test and evaluation.

Pugh matrix: A tool that enables several alternatives to be compared against a baseline scenario.

Pull scheduling: A visual scheduling system in which the manufacturing system produces according to external customer demand.

Push scheduling system: A manufacturing scheduling system that uses a forecast through the master production schedule to schedule orders.

Quality control plan: A combination of documentation indicating important product features that must be controlled.

Quality function deployment (QFD): A system of tools and methods used to translate the VOC into internal specifications.

Quantitative forecasts: Forecasts that rely on mathematical models to predict future demand.

Quick response manufacturing (QRM): A system that provides local control of resource scheduling in an MRPII environment.

Random sampling: A sample drawn from a population without bias.

Range chart: A control chart of ranges in which a range equals the maximum minus the minimum values of each subgroup.

Rational subgroup sampling: A sampling method that collects data from a process at time intervals smaller than that which must be analyzed.

Raw material inventory: Inventory that has been received from an external supplier and has had no work done on it.

Reactive data: Information that customers volunteer in the form of complaints, warranty charges, and returned goods.

Reorder point (ROP): A quantity of inventory based on the lead time to receive an order times the expected daily usage over the lead time.

Residual: The difference between a model's fitted versus actual value.

Return on investment (ROI): Net income divided by available total assets.

Reverse logistics: Operations associated with receipt of customer returns.

Rework: A situation occurring when something must be done more than once due to defects.

Rolled throughput yield (RTY): Calculated as the multiplicand of the first-pass yields at every operation.

Root mean square deviation (RMSD): A forecasting error statistic calculated as the square root of the mean summed differences of forecast to actual.

Rough-cut capacity planning: An estimate of capacity needed at a future time period for a process workflow.

Run chart: A time series chart used to analyze time dependent data in which observations are arranged by time order.

S-shaped work cell: A work cell layout arranged as an S.

Safety stock: An inventory quantity that is kept due to demand or lead-time variation.

Safety-stock calculation: Inventory quantity calculated as service factor times standard deviation of demand and lead times square root.

Sales and operational planning: The process of coordinating demand and supply based on system constraints.

Sample mean: Calculated as the sum of the observations divided by their number.

Sample standard deviation: The square root of the variation around the mean; expressed in units. Useful to estimate safety-stock levels.

Sample variance: The variation around the mean; expressed in units.

Sampling: The process of obtaining samples from a larger population.

Sarbane–Oxley Act: A series of governmentally mandated requirements for disclosure and accuracy of financial data.

Scatter plot: A graphical analysis tool that plots two continuous variables against each other to identify patterns.

Scheduling algorithms: Mathematical models that help schedule resources.

Seasonal component: A time series component that models periodic patterns.

Seasonal index: A constant used to increase or decrease the level of a time series based on the seasonal variation.

Second quartile: The point at which 50 percent of the observations from a sample are below.

Secondary metric: A project metric used to prevent negative consequences of changes in the project's primary metric.

Service level: A percentage of time, units, or orders the customer will receive his or her orders.

Short-term variation: Variation acting on a process for a limited amount of time.

Should-be map: A graphical depiction of a process with non-value-adding operations removed.

Sigma level: The short-term capability of a metric.

Single minute exchange of dies (SMED): A set of techniques to reduce job changeovers.

SIPOC: Acronym for supplier-input-process-output-customer.

Six Sigma: A process improvement program characterized by five phases: define, measure, analyze, improve, and control.

SMED: Acronym for single minute exchange of die.

Standard operating procedures (SOPs): Procedures that determine the best way to do a job.

Statistical sampling: A set of methods that specify how observations are to be drawn from a population.

Stocking location: A specific place where an item is stored.

Storming stage: The second stage of the team maturation process, in which a team disagrees on a project's goals and objectives.

Strategic flow down: A method used to ensure alignment of strategic goals and objectives throughout an organization.

Strategic project selection: The processes of ensuring projects are selected to align with senior management's goals and objectives.

Stratified sampling: A type of sampling technique in which the population is broken into subgroups having minimal variation within each subgroup.

SWOT analysis: Strengths, weaknesses, opportunities, and threats to an organization.

System model map: A quantified map of a process showing input and output metrics.

Systematic sampling: A sampling method in which every nth observation is taken from the subgroup.

Takt time: The time in which one unit must be produced to meet customer schedules.

Takt time calculation: A calculation that determines how many time units it takes to manufacture one unit.

Target costing: Determining the price at which a product or service will sell and subtracting out the desired profit margin.

Theory of inventive problem solving (TRIZ): A structured brainstorming technique used to apply analogous and previously discovered solutions to new problems.

Third-party logistics: Outsourcing one or more functions to external organizations.

Third quartile: The point at which 55 percent of the observations from a sample are below.

Throughput: The cycle time between paying for material, labor, and other expenses and receipt of payment from the customer.

Time fence: The cumulative lead time to build a product.

Time series: A data series sequentially arranged by time order.

Time series graph: A graphical analysis tool that shows how a variable changes over time.

Total productive maintenance (TPM): A set of methods that ensure machines are maintained and available at a predetermined percentage of time.

Transfer batch: A system that moves units of production immediately to downstream operations.

Tree diagram: Used to map higher- to lower-level relationships.

Trend component: A time series component showing the average change of a time series over time.

u-Chart: A control chart for a Poisson distributed variable in which sample size can vary.

U-shaped work cell: A work cell layout arranged as a U.

Unidentified task: Goals and objectives that do not currently have projects assigned to ensure their solution.

Unplanned orders: Orders put into the schedule without regard for the product's lead time or time fence.

Upper specification limit (USL): The customer's upper level for the product characteristic.

Utility: A customer value element describing the usefulness of a product feature to a customer.

Validate phase: A fourth Design for Six Sigma (DFSS) phase used to evaluate design specifications' capability levels.

Value-adding operations (VA): Operations that a customer desires in a product or service.

Value elements: These consist of time, price, utility, function, and relative importance to a customer.

Value stream mapping (VSM): A process of mapping material and information flows through a process.

Variable control chart: A group of control charts used to evaluate continuously distributed variables.

Variance inflation factor (VIF): A statistic that calculates the degree of collinearity between independent variables.

Virtual capacity: Having available capacity when needed, but not owning or having to pay for its existence.

Visual controls: A system in which process status can be easily seen at a glance.

Visual displays: Graphics used to convey system status in the workplace.

Visual workplace: A workplace in which system status can be determined immediately by looking at visual metric displays.

Voice of the business (VOB): Financial and operational goals and objectives that must be considered in process improvements.

Voice of the customer (VOC): Customer requirements that are translated into specifications.

Voice of the process (VOP): Characteristic-by-characteristic central location and dispersion (variation) measured within a process.

Working capital: Current assets minus current liabilities.

Work-in-process inventory: Inventory that is within the process and acts as a buffer against disruptions in material flow.

Xs: Independent variables that have a significant impact on key process output variables (KPOVs).

Ys: Dependent variables that are directly correlated to the voice of the customer (VOC).

Index

A

Accountability, 189
Accounting, 115
Accounting processes, 21
Accounts payable, 153, 156
   process workflows, 43
Accounts receivable, 57, 191, 202–203, *203*, 278
   process breakdowns, 202, 204
   process workflows, 202
   simulation: distribution assumptions, *289*
   simulation model example, 288
Activity checklist, 123, 235
Actual capacity, 94
Airport check-in, service workflows, 67
Alignment, 23
   organizational goals and objectives and, 29,
      227, 233, 274, 277
   strategic, 8–9
Apathy, organizational, 4
Assessment activities, 39
Asset utilization, 46, 52, 100
Audits, 280, 296
Automation, work tasks and, 105
Automotive Industry Action Group (AIAG), 239
   criteria, 240
   methods, 240
   standards, 239
Available capacity, 57
   waiting and, 58
Average handling time (AHT), 123

B

Back-office operations, 38

Balance material flow, 84–86
   bottleneck management, 85–86
   transfer batches, 87
Balance sheet, 52
Basic needs, 62, 63
Behaviors, changing, 22
Bell-shaped curve, 288
Benchmarking, 53
   targets, 52
Best Buy, 28
Best-in-class process conditions, obtaining, 122
   Kaizen event and, 122
Bill of material (BOM), 208
Black belt skill level, 14, 15, 16, 126, 142
Bottleneck management, 59, 85–86, 103, 135, 147
   analyzing, 135
   photocopiers and, 134
   process improvement, 188, 212
Box plot, 169, *170*, 184, 282
Brand awareness, improving, 46
Brown-paper exercise, 146, 149–150, 182
   five key characteristics of, **147**
   Kaizen team and, 149
   mapping and, *147*, *148*
Bureaucracies, 104, 232
Burger King, 102
Business activity monitoring (BAM) systems,
     105, 120, 278
Business benefits, 23, 269
Business intelligence (BI), 120, 278
Business metrics, 46, 48
Business modeling and analysis (BMA), 105,
     120, 278
Business process management (BPM), 278
Business process management suite (BPMS), 105

Business value-adding (BVA) operations
  Lean Six Sigma and, 106
  Lean system and, 30
  process improvement and, 121
  reduce setup time (SMED), 91
  strategy alignment and, 7
  unnecessary operations, eliminating, 74, 75
  value stream map (VSM) and, 71

C

Call centers, 28, 37, 96
  international, 38
  process flow, 61
Canceled orders, reasons for, *180*, 198
Capital expenditure, 268
Case studies, 41
Cash flow projects, 48
Cash management systems, 45
Cashflow, increased, 36
Cause-and-effect (C & E) diagrams, *165*
  control charts, 174
  Crystal Ball® software and, 282
  data collection and analysis, 184
  identifying and prioritizing improvement
    opportunities, 212
  information technology (IT) and, 164
  Kaizen team and, 164
  Minitab® statistical softwear and, 295, 296
  prioritizing projects, *175*
C-charts, 247, *252*
Change
  corporate cultures and, 26
  cultural factors, 20
  organizational resistance to, 222, 231
  organizational support for, 274
  readiness for, **223**, 223–224
Change, building a business case for, 22, **23**,
    215, 219–238, **226**
  change readiness and, 223–224
  communication, 235
  cost-benefit analysis, 227–228
  information technology (IT) and, 222
  infrastructure analysis, 233
  Kaizen teams and, 219, 222
  key stakeholder analysis, 229–232
  overview, 219–222
  project transition, 225
  scheduling process change activities, 234

Change, organizational barriers to, 226, 236, 282
  bureaucracy, 232
  conflicting priorities, 231
  lack of rewards and recognition, 232
Change initiative, effective, 219
Change model, 278
Channel gross margin, improving, 46
Checklists, 160, **161**
China, 125
  process workflow, 114
Cluster sampling, 152
Common process workflows, supplier
    performance management, 210–211
Communication, 235, 268, 281
  key stakeholders and, 272
Communication activities, 236, 237
Communication planning, *236*
  format and, 236
Comparison of Lean, Six Sigma, and Kaizen,
    6, **162**
Compensating metrics, 48–49
Competency migration, *271*
Competitors, Lean system and, 38
Complexity, 32
  avoiding in tools or procedures, 67
  reducing in product and process, 28
  reducing in products and services, 64–66,
    65–66
  seven key concepts of reducing, 64
Concurrent engineering (CE), 208
Consensus-based workforce, 233
Consultants, 11, 20, 278
Continuous improvement, 67, 69
  activities, 77
  processes, 67
  work, 33
Control charts, *172*, 172–174, 184, 255, 282
  for binominally distributed variables
    (pass/fail), **249**
  calculations, 247
  c-charts, 245
  control overview, **246**
  creating, **250**
  individual-moving range charts, 245
  interpretation, *252*
  Kaizen events and, 249
  Kaizen team and, 173
  key concepts of, **244**, 244–245
  for normally distributed variables
    (continuous), **248**
  p-charts, 245

for Poisson distributed variables, *250*
r-charts, 245
specialized, 245
steps for setting up, 249
types of, 245
variation patterns, 251
X-bar chart, 245
Control limits, calculating, 250
Control plan, 263, 296
building, 222
requirements, 241, **241**
Control systems, visual, 37
Control tools, 242–243, 258
effectiveness and sustainability, **194**, 194–196
elimination of portions of a process, 258
group meetings (huddles), 259
implementation of 5S, 259
mistake proofing, 258, 259
modification of organizational reporting structures, 258
modification of work, testing, inspection, maintenance, and other procedures, 259
new information reporting systems, 259
new operational and financial metrics, 259
new or modified process designs and layouts, 258
process audits, 259
purchase or design of new types of equipment, 259
training programs, 259
written and verbal instructions, 259
Core products, 64
Core services, 64
Cost avoidance, 229
Cost of goods sold (COGS), 48, 166
Cost-benefit analysis, 226, 227–228, **228**, 286, 289
Countermeasures, 274, 282
at 4th level root cause—late deliveries, **199**
business impact of, 226, 261
changing the process and, 137
control tools and, 242
failure mode and effects analysis (FMEA) and, 255
implementing solutions, 148, 236–237, 239, 263–264
key questions and, 240
key stakeholder analysis and, 231, 232
root cause analysis and, 197, 219, 222
supplier impact and, 233

value stream map (VSM) and, 147
Critical-to-quality (CTQ) characteristics, 27
Critical-to-quality (CTQ) flow down, 41, 43, 55
Crystal Ball® software, 211, 285–294
cycle time analysis, *292*
cycle times, 288
Kaizen events and, 288
Kaizen team and, 282, 288, 289, 290
Lean methods and, 285, 286
Lean tools and methods, 281
sensitivity analysis, *293*
sensitivity analysis graph, 290
statistical distributions of, *291*
value stream map (VSM) and, 285, 286, 287, 288
Customer demand, 38
Customer satisfaction, improving, 46
Customer value migration, 190
Customer-facing operations, 38
Customers, 87
complaints, 31
interviewing, 62
requirements of, 245
satisfaction levels of, 38
Cycle times, 36, 71, 82, 92, 214, 245, 250–251, 255
analysis of, 290–292
control tools, 258
errors and, 77
high, 40
implementing solutions, 263
long, 11, 147
process improvement and, 253
reducing, 46, 73, 188
transfer batches and, 87

D

Data collection and analysis, 22, 136, 141–184, 200, 223, 278
box plot, 169
brown-paper exercise, 149–150
cause-and-effect (C & E) diagrams, 164
control charts, 172–174
five-why analysis, 165–166
histogram, 167
information technology (IT), 120, 279
inventory analysis and reduction, 177–181
job shadowing data, 175–176

methods, 151, 154
operations and, 131–135
Pareto chart, 168
prioritizing, 154
process characterization, 151–159
process data, 160–162
process mapping—SIPOC, 163
scatter plot, 170
in service operations, 121, **132–133**
spaghetti diagram, *158*
standardized, 151
time series graph, 170–171
tools, 222
value stream map (VSM), 143
Data collection planner, 296
Defects, in product or services, 61
Define, measure, analyze, improve, and
    control (DMAIC) project execution
    methodology, 5, 178, 295
Dell, 66
Demand
level, 94–95, *95*
level loading of, 31
patterns of, 94
variation in, 31
Deployment, types of
aligned, 12
bottom-up, 12, 16, 67
hierarchical, 12
top-down, 12, 15, 40, 67, 280
Deployment champion, 234
Deployment leaders, 12, 40
Deployment options, 280
Deployment roles and responsibilities, **14**
Deployment strategies, 10–16, **13**
Design errors, reducing, 46
Design failure mode and effects analysis
    (FMEA), 66
Design for Manufacturing (DFM), 89, 90
    methods, 66
Design for Six Sigma (DFSS), 89, 90
    methods, 66
Design for Six Sigma (DFSS) tools and methods,
    67
Design simplification and standardization, 269
Distributions, 290
common, 288
exponential, 288
normal, 288
uniform, 288
Diversity, organizational change and, 269

Downtime percentages (equipment and people),
    135
Drumbeat time, process and, 37

E

Economic value added (EVA), 98, 106, 116, 139
    targets, 9
E-mail, impact of development of, 104
Employee training, continuous, 196
Employee turnover rate, 209
Empowerment, 221, 222
English language, 19
Enterprise application integration (EAI), 105, 278
Entitlement analysis, 123
Equipment
classifying, 93
purchasing, 195
Error conditions, prevention of, 66, 87, 89
Error rates, high, 11
Event facilitation methods, **130**
Event facilitator, 15
Everyday low pricing, minimizing demand
    variation and, 31
Excel, 295
spreadsheets, 104, 210
templates, 25, 36
Exception reports, 191
Expense reduction, 36

F

Facilitators, 19, 117, 222
    Kaizen events and, 130
Fact-based methods, 191
Failure causes, 258
    risk priority rating (RPN), 258
Failure mode and effects analysis (FMEA), 137,
    240, 255–257, 264
example, *257*
template, 255, 258
Failure modes, 256
Failure points, 200
Finance, 14, 115
Finance department, 200
Finance reports, 119
Financial analysis, 11, 52, 55, 198, 229, 296

Financial and operational metrics, improvement through Kaizen events, 36
Financial assessments, 24
Financial forecasting, 57, 200–201, *201*, 202, 278
    process breakdowns in, 214
Financial metrics, 29, 38–39, 48, 55, 113, 143, 145, 150
    project examples, 48
Financial operational reports, 280
Financial projects, 46
Financial statements, improvement teams and, 53
Financial workflows, analyzing, 202
Five-S (5S) methods (sorting, setting in order, shining, standardizing, and sustaining), 8, 122, 127, 137, 195, 258, 285
    implementation of, 191
    self-discipline, 82
    sorting process, 80
    standardization, 80–81, **81**, 82
Five-why analysis, 165–166, **166**, 167–168, 184, 282
    Kaizen team and, 165
Follow-up activities, 261, *264*
    (for implementing solutions), 261–262
"Functional silos", elimination of, 39

G

Gantt charts, 235, 296
Generic financial statements—balance sheet, *54*
Generic financial statements—profit-and-loss statements, *53*
Global service system, 32
Global supply chains, 31, 32, 275
Global teams, 19
Goals and objectives, breaking down high-level, 41–42
Goodness-of-fit test, 287
Graphics, using to show process improvement, *193*
Green belt expert, 14

H

Harvard Business Review, 230
High level road map, 22

High quality, 89, **90**
    process improvement activities and, 89
Hindi language, 19
Hiring process, 208–209, *209*, 278
    steps in, 209
Histogram, *167*, 167–168, 172, 184, 282
    Kaizen team and, 167
    skew and, 168
Human resources (HR), 43, 46, 115
    process breakdowns, 209
    process workflows, 208, 209
    processes, outsourcing, 209
    reward and recognition systems, 232, 272

I

Immediate defect detection, 66
Implementation risks, 233
    cultural factors, 233
    customer risks, 233
    economic risks, 234
    identifying, 233
    regulatory risks, 234
    scheduling risks, 233
    supplier impact, 233
    technological risks, 233
Implementing solutions, 219–276
    building a business case for change, 219–238
    changing behaviors and, 25
    reinforcing new behaviors and organizational change, 267–276
Improvement event follow-up activities, 235, **263**
Improvement methodologies, 32
Improvement opportunities, 23
    alignment of, 3–110, 22, 23
    identifying and prioritizing, 212
    worksheet, 173, *174*
Improvement projects, 236
    identifying, 53
Improvement recommendations, 225, 282
Incentives, positive and negative, 224
    change and, 221
India, 125
    process workflow, 114
Individual-moving range charts (I-MR charts), 247, 253
Information flow, 32
Information reporting systems, 190

Information technology (IT), 14, 124, 159,
  277–279
  balanced material flow and, 84
  control tools, 195
  data collection and analysis, 131, 135, 142
  efficiency of service operations, 32
  information on operational cycle times and,
    120, 121
  process changes, 191
  process designs and platforms, 38
  root cause analysis and improvement
    strategies, 196
  service workflows and, 26
  supplier networks and, 31
  systems, 103, 105
Infrastructure analysis, 222, 233, **234**, 237, 268
Initiatives, 53
  prioritizing, 272
Internal improvement methods, 188
Internal specifications (Ys), 27
Internal vs. external work tasks, 92
International Standards Institute (ISO), 239
  ISO 9000, 239
  ISO 9001, 239
  ISO 9004, 239
  standardization requirements, 240
Internet, 66
Interorganizational projects, 269
Inventory, 59, 135, 136
  analysis and reduction, 177–181, **178**
  asset utilization and, 37
  excess, 60, 204
  obsolete, 60
  waste, 60
Inventory investment, 198
  canceled orders and, 180
  problem, 165, 198
  reduction of, 182
Inventory investment, high
  first level, *179*
  major reasons for, *182*
  second level, *181*
  third level, *183*
Inventory management, improving, 177
Inventory turns ration, 37
Invoice payment, 203
Invoicing cycle times, 247, 251

J

Japan, 125
Japanese language, 19
Job candidates, prescreening, Internet and, 92
Job shadowing, 134, 175
  analysis of data, *177*
  as data collection method, 157
  worksheet, *158*
Job shadowing data, analyzing, 175–176, **176**
Just in time (JIT) systems, implementing, 30,
    76–98
  5S and standardized work, 80–81
  balance material flow, 84–86
  high quality, 89
  level demand, 94–95
  link operations, 82–83
  mistake proofing, 87–88
  reduce lot sizes, 96–98
  reduce setup time (SMED), 90–91
  reorganize physical configurations, 78–79
  total preventive maintenance, 92–93
Just-in-time (JIT) systems, 77, 94, 97, 189
  continuous improvement of operational
    work time, 77
  implementing to eliminate waste, *76*
  operational stability and, 77
  philosophy of seven major types of process
    waste, 59
  stable demand and, 76

K

Kaizen, 4, 105
  defining, *4–5, 4–7*
  deployment of, 7
Kaizen event, 15, 19–20, 40, 80, 105, 139–140,
    275, 278–281
  activities in, 24, 235
  analyze data and develop prioritized
    improvements, 136
  apply 5S methods, 137
  apply mistake-proofing methods, 137
  building a business case for change and, 227
  change the process, 137
  checklist, *112*, 116
  communication and, 124, 273
  communication letter, 125, *125*
  conducting, 22, 24, 111–218, **128**

data collection and analysis of workflows
and operations, 119–120, **131**,
131–135, 139, 282
deployment in three steps, **22**
evaluating, 138
facilitating, 117, 129–130, 233
facilities for, 117, 118, 124
follow-up activities, 263
implementing solutions, 222
improvement activities, 115
infrastructure analysis and, 233
international process workflows and, 114
Kaizen team and, 130
kickoff agenda, 126, *126*, 126
obtaining examples of best-in-class process
conditions, 122
obtaining examples of process breakdowns,
121, 122
operational and financial objectives, 36, 128
organize and train team, 116, 127, 128
planning, 8, 22, 111–112, 277
preparation for, 113–124, **114**
process change across global supply chains,
269–270
process workflow layouts, 129
project charters, 116
project identification and, 55
project transition and, 225
rapid process improvement, 22, 26, 32, 160,
234
schedule for, 123, 235, 259
sponsors and, 15
strategic alignment with organizational
goals and objectives, 23, 220, 277
supplies and equipment for, 118, 124
support personnel, 115, 118
value stream maps, 129
video and audio conferencing, 114
voice of the customer (VOC) and, 63
Kaizen methodologies, 5
Kaizen projects, 26, 36, 42, 229, 267–268
alignment with organizational goals and
objectives, 231
communication and, 224
new product marketing research, *213*
project charters, 50
resistance and, 275
strategic alignment and, 277
worksheet for, 212
Kaizen team, *54*, 277
activities, 240

alignment with organizational goals and
objectives, 220
analysis of data and development of
prioritized improvements, 136
analysis of root causes, 185
change readiness and, 223, 224
communication and, 12, 221
consultation with local experts, 286
control tools, 195
data collection and analysis, 25, 134–135,
141, 182, 184
decision-making and, 177, 180
empowerment and, 221, 232
evaluation of Kaizen event, 138
facilitation of, 129
failure causes, 258
failure mode and effects analysis (FMEA)
and, 256
general questions and, 187
identifying and prioritizing improvement
opportunities, 212
implementation risks and, 234
implementing solutions, 191
improvement activities, 163
Kaizen events and, 115–116, 117, 119–123,
139
key stakeholder analysis, 229, 231
Lean Six Sigma teams and, 29, 30
Lean system and, 26
Lean training, 137
measurement components and, 254
net promoter score (NPS), 229
process change across global supply chains,
269
process characterization and, 151, 153, 155
process improvement, 189, 190, 215
process workflows and, 200, 202–203, 205,
207–209
project charters, 280
project leader and team members, 116
rapid deployment of, 112
recommendations of, 259
roles and responsibilities, 127
roles and responsibilities of, 127
root cause analysis and improvement
strategies, 196–198
scheduling risks and, 233
six measurement components, 255
support personnel and, 118
training of, 128, 222
transferring control, 274

Kaizen team, Lean system and, 28
Kanban, 100, 102
  cards, 31, 32, 101
Kano, Dr., 62
Kano needs, 63, 64
  basic needs, 62
  excitement needs, 62
  performance needs, 62
Key metric definitions, 46–49, **49**
Key process input variables (KPIVs), 242
Key process output variables (KPOVs), 242
Key stakeholders, 237, 268, 274, 281
  analysis of, 229–232, **230**, 233, 236
  communication and, 236
  diverse viewpoints of, 231
  impact analysis, **231**
  satisfaction of, 268
Kobayashi, metrics of (listed), 78
Korea, 125
Korean language, 19
Kotter, John P., 26, 269, 274

L

Language and cultural differences, impact of, 19
Late deliveries, 180, 198
  major reasons for, *184*
Lead time, 136
  inventory and, 135
Leading Change by John P. Kotter, 269
Lean, 98, 137, 240
  concepts of, 96, 112
  culture of, 4
  integrated approach, 24
  methodologies, 240
  process analysis focus, 136
  process improvement initiatives, 61, 296
  rapid improvement and, 55
  six common process workflows, 57
  tools and methods of, 41
Lean, deployment of, 7, 22–25, 44, 143
  Step 1: align improvement opportunities, 23
  Step 2: plan and conduct the Kaizen event, 24
  Step 3: Implement solutions and change behaviors, 25
Lean 5S philosophy, 90
Lean and Design for Six Sigma (DFSS) concepts, 18

Lean and Six Sigma, 160, 222
  initiatives, 223, 280
  performance metrics, 67
  projects, 202
  tools and methods, 90, 282
Lean assessment, conducting, 39–40
Lean events, 267, 280
Lean expert, 14
Lean improvement projects, 8, 24, 42, 268, 295
  examples, 45, 122
  financial, 46
  human resources (HR), 46
  marketing, 46
  operational, 46
  procurement operations, 46
  product design, 46
  sales, 46
Lean initiatives, 4
  deployment characteristics of, 11
Lean Kaizen event, evaluating, *138*
Lean masters, 14
Lean methods, 5, 30, 177
  changing processes and, 137
  common workflow processes, 205
  control tools and, 195, 258
  data collection and analysis, 184
  deployment strategies and, 10
  operational and financial objectives of the
      Kaizen event, discussing, 128, 129
  operational metrics and, 36
  process change across global supply chains,
      270
  process changes and, 189, 191
  reduce setup time (SMED), 90
  reducing complexity and, 66
  supplier networks and, 31
  voice of the customer (VOC) and, 61
Lean metrics, 44, 45
Lean production, 105
Lean Six Sigma, 5
Lean Six Sigma, 32, 69, 77, 125, 222, 224
  activities, 19, 68, 82, 275
  concepts of, 31
  implementing, 57
  improvements, 71, 191, 200
  initiatives, 70, 220
  metrics, 29
  organizational level, 23
  prioritizing, 55
  process, 32
  process workflow level, 23

projects, 24, 39, 41, 111
reducing system complexity, 16
simplification of process work flow, 29
strategic alignment and, 277
team selection, 69
teams, 212
tools and methods of, 16, 94
Lean Six Sigma Basics, 22, 57–110, 105, 106–110
continually update process technologies, 102–104
create robust product and process designs to reduce complexity, 64–66
create Value Stream Maps (VSMs), 70–73
deploy Lean Six Sigma Teams, 67–68
eliminate unnecessary operations, 74–75
implement Just in Time (JIT) systems, 76–98
implement visual control and pull systems - Kanban, 100–101
performance measurements, 69
supplier networks and support, 98–99
understand the VOC (Voice of the Customer), 61–63
Lean Six Sigma deployment, 12, 14, 16
business metrics, 46
communication and, 15
compensating metrics, 46
evaluating the Kaizen event and, 138
executive training (leadership workshops and), 41
financial metrics, 46
four high-level metrics in, 46
Kaizen event planning and, 112, 117
Lean assessment and, 39
Lean system elements and, 26
in an office environment, 23
plan and schedule, 29
planning and conducting the Kaizen event, 24
problem-solving teams and, 33
project champion training (middle management workshops), 41
project charters and, 50
project identification and, 55
project metrics, 46
root cause analysis and improvement strategies, 197
value stream map (VSM) and, 143
Lean Six Sigma initiative, 33
continuous improvement and, 29
Lean Six Sigma methods, 22
global process workflows, 21

Lean Six Sigma teams, 14, 64
deployment of, 29, 67–68, *68*
Lean Six Sigma tools and methods, 24, 32
manufacturing systems, 279
service systems, 279
Lean supply chain, 36–38
Lean system, 37, 55, 78, 100
alignment of operational capacity, 39
benefits of, 38
continuously update process technologies, 32
develop supplier networks, 31
elements of, 26–32
eliminate unnecessary operations, 30
flow of information and materials, 32
high process yields, 38
high value-adding (VA) content and, 36
implement Just in TIme (JIT), 30
implementation of, 30, 97
Lean Six Sigma Teams, 29
low cycle time, 38
low operational cost, 38
low variation of internal demand, 38
performance measurements, 29
problem-solving teams and, 29
reduce product and process complexity, 28
supply chains and, 31
technology, 102
ten key elements of, 26, *27*
ten key steps to implementing, **58**
visual controls and pull systems, 32
voice of the customer (VOC) and, 26–27
Lean tasks, 100
Lean teams, 281
Lean tools and methods, 3–4, 21, 32, 53, 61, 63, 85, 142, 277–278
analysis of process data, 161
building a business case for change, 222
rapid improvement and, 35
Leanness of system, 37
Link operations, 82–83, *83*
Local work team, 274
Lot sizes, reducing, 96–98, *97*
mixed-model scheduling, 98

M

Maintenance, 14
Maintenance logs, 135
Major change elements, *220*

Major toolsets, 53
Malcolm Baldridge award, 240
Malcolm Baldridge criteria, 240
Management, 185
Mandarin language, 19
Market penetration, increasing, 46
Market research, 66, 204
Marketing analysts, 205
    voice of the customer (VOC), 205
Materials, flow of, 32
    balancing, 84, *85*
Mathematical modeling, Six Sigma teams and,
        281
McDonald's, 20, 21
    buffer inventories, 102
    pull scheduling system, 102
Measurement system error, components of, 254
    accuracy, 254
    linearity, 254, 255
    repeatability, 254, 255
    reproducibility, 254, 255
    resolution, 254
    stability, 254
Measurement system improvements, 254
Metric dashboards, 29, 264, 265, 283
    creating, 263, *265*
    Kaizen team and, 263
Metrics
    define, 46
    financial, 36
    operational, 36
Metrics, higher level, 29
Minitab, Inc., *297*
Minitab® Quality Companion 2, 295
    creating a project schedule using, *296*
Minitab® statistical softwear, 142, 173, 247,
        253, 295–297, *297*
    control charts and, 249
    error codes and, 254
    Kaizen event and, 296
    Kaizen team and, 295, 296
    Pareto chart and, 295
    process mapping and, 296
    value stream map (VSM) and, 296
Minitab® statistical softwear and Quality
        Companion, 295
Minitab® Statistical Software and Quality
        Companion by Minitab (Appendix 2),
        295–298
Misalignment, 190
Miscommunication issues, *201*

Mistake proofing, *89*, 92, 127, 162, 191, 195,
        198, 285
    common strategies of, 87
    control tools, 258
    design features, *207*
    Kaizen and, 7
    Lean Six Sigma and, 66, 87–88
    Lean supply chain and, 37
    methods of, 137
    processes, 222
Mistake-proofing methods, 66
    functional testing, 66
    simplification, 66
    standardization, 66
Mistakes, 61
Mitigation plans, 231
Mixed-model scheduling, 98, *99*, 135, 189

N

Net promoter score (NPS), 230, 268
    key stakeholder analysis and, 229
    method, 230
New behaviors, reinforcing, *270*
New products
    development of, 57, 205–207, *207*, 278
    market research, 57, 204–205, *206*, 278
    prioritizing research products, *214*
New reporting systems, 191, 196
Nonrandom control chart variation patterns, 253
Non-value-adding (NVA) operations, 23, 280
    analyzing job shadowing data example,
        176–177
    balance material flow, 84–85
    eliminating, 37, 38, 44, 64, 74–75, 91
    inventory analysis and reduction example, 177
    Lean Six Sigma, 106
    Lean system and, 29–30
    operational cycle times and, 120
    Pareto chart and, 168
    policies and procedures, 232
    process changes, 189–190
    process characterization, 153–154, 156–157
    process data analysis, 160
    process improvement, 187
    process workflows and, 129
    project examples and, 45
    reduce product and process complexity, 28
    strategy alignment and, 7, 11

transportation activities, 60
value stream map (VSM), 71, 145, 147
voice of the customer (VOC) and, 61
Np-charts, 247

O

Obsolescence, 60
Office environments, 32
Office environments, defects in
    mathematical mistakes, 61
    repetition of work task, 61
    sending incorrect information, 61
Office processes, 184, 277
    measurement systems and, 254
    rapid improvement of, 26
Operating expenses, 41
Operational analysis, 11, 53, 55
Operational and financial objectives of the
        Kaizen event, discussing, 128
Operational assessments, 24, 39, 40
Operational cycle times, collecting information
        about, 120
Operational data from office workflows, 134
Operational Excellence, 224
*Operational Excellence—Translating Customer
        Value through Global Supply Chains*,
        James W. Martin, 19, 269
Operational metrics
    brown-paper exercise, 149–150
    Kaizen event and, 113
    Lean supply chain, 38–39
    Lean system and, 29
    prioritizing projects, 55
    value stream map (VSM), 143, 145
Operational performance, 44
Operational reports, 119
Operational stability, 37
Operations
    mistake proofing, 31, 71
    simplifying, 31
    standardizing, 31
Operations research (OR) methods, 84
Oracle® Corporaton, 286
Organizational barriers to change
    limited training, 232
    roles and responsibilities, 232
Organizational behaviors, new, 267
    reinforcing, 269

Organizational change, 25, 268, 269, 274, 277
    cultural differences, 269
    effective, 268
    global supply chains, 269, 283
Organizational cultures, 233, 272
Organizational environment, change and, 221
Organizational goals, 55
Organizational productivity, 9
Organizations, 43
    dysfunctional, 39
    reporting structures, 195
Outliers, 253, 288
Outsourcing, 18, 19, 188
Outsourcing products or services, 64
Overproduction, 57, 58

P

Packaging lines, 82
Pareto chart, 168, *169*, 180, 182, 184, 282
    Kaizen team and, 168
    process breakdowns, 168
P-charts, 247
Performance gaps, 11, 40
    analysis of, 270
    identifying, 55
Performance measurements, 69
    creating, *70*
    implementing, 29
Performance measurements, common, **154**
    allocated floor space required for production,
        70
    downtime percentages (equipment and
        people), 69
    inventory investment by operation, 70
    percentage of value-adding (VA) content or
        time, 69
    production or throughput rate (units per
        minute), 69
    rework percentages, 69
    scrap percentages, 69
    setup time and cost of jobs within workflow,
        69
Performance metrics, 63
    critical to safety (CTS) themes, 63
    critical-to-cost (CTC) themes, 63
    critical-to-delivery (CTD) themes, 63
    critical-to-quality (CTQ) themes, 63

Physical configurations, 82
impact on workflow, 78
reorganizing, 78–79, *79*
Pilot study, 36
Poisson distribution, 247, 253
Potential failure effect, 258
PowerPoint, 295
Present findings to organization, **261**
Pricing levels, optimizing, 46
Priorities, conflicting, 38
Prioritized improvements, developing, 136
Probability distribution, 287, 288, 290
Process
changing, 137
floor area required for, 135
Process analysis, *152*, 191, 279
analytic levels of, **44**
Process analysis tools, 7
Process analysis worksheet, *153*, 153
Process audit worksheet, *155*
Process audits, 82
Process breakdowns, 60, 149, 168, 190, 202,
233, 239, 263
lack of procedures, 57
lack of process standardization, 57
obtaining examples of, 121, 122
poor process design, 57
poor training methods, 57
reducing, 240
root cause analysis, 141, 147, 151, 264
variable demand, 57
Process change activities, scheduling, 234, 237
Process changes, 194, 196, 226, 271
across global supply lines, 269–273
common, 185–193, **186**, 189, 213
implementing, 222
organizational barriers to, 224
organizational barriers to change, 237
organizational characteristics and, 231
organizational support, 222
scheduling, *235*
Process characterization, 151–159
Process complexity, reducing, 28
Process control strategies, 242, 264
Process control tools, 242, **243**
5S methods, 243
audit systems, 243
elimination of operations and work tasks, 243
employee training and, 242
failure mode and effects analysis (FMEA), 243
mistake proofing, 243

statistical process control (SPC), 243
training, 242
work and inspection procedures, 243
Process controls, 148, 240
implementation of, 236
training and, 196
Process data, 141
simple analysis of, 160–162
Process documentation, 22
Process Excellence, 224
Process improvement, 22, 185, 188–189,
195–218, 222
common process changes, 185–193
control tool effectiveness and sustainability,
194–196
cost-benefit analysis, 227
examples using common process workflows,
199–211
identifying and prioritizing improvement
opportunities, 212
implementing, 223
Kaizen event approach, 283
key questions, 240, **241**
measuring, *256*
methodologies, 197
office processes and, 189
root cause analysis and improvement
strategies, 196–198
Process improvement experts
full-time, 10
part-time, 10
Process information (floor layouts, workflows,
and procedures), 119
collecting, 119
Process inputs, 240, 241
Process layouts, 30
Process mapping, 7, 44, 53, 163, 200
Process mapping—SIPOC, 163
Process operations, eliminating, 242
Process outputs, 240
Process owner, 185, 223, 225, 236, 274
Process simplifications, 30, 137
Lean teams and, 281
Process standardization, Lean teams and, 281
Process technologies, 32
continual updating of, 32, 102, *104*
Process variation, 245
Process walkthrough, 122
Process waste
excess inventory, 60
overproduction, 57

product or service defects, 61
  seven classics forms of, 57
  unnecessary processing by people and or
    machines, 60
  unnecessary transport of materials or
    information, 59
  waiting, 58
  waste of motion, 60
Process workflows, 8, 11, 15, 279, 289
  analysis of by Kaizen team, 27
  analyzing, 119
  balance material flow, 84
  brown-paper exercise, 149
  collect data at every operation, 135
  common process changes, 188, 190
  financial metrics, 142
  improving, 24
  Kaizen events and, 117
  layouts of the process workflow, 129
  Lean assessment and, 40
  Lean supply chain and, 37, 38
  mistake proofing, 21
  operational metrics, 142
  operations and, 43
  outsourced, 19, 20
  prioritizing projects and, 53
  process characterization, 153
  process technologies, 32
  project identification, 55
  project identification and process analysis, 43
  pull systems, 32
  quantification of, 288
  reduce setup time (SMED), 90
  simplifying, 30
  simulation model and, 290
  standardization and, 30
  three-dimensional models of, 287
  transfer of, 21
  value stream map (VSM), 72, 144
Process workflows, common, 199–211
  accounts receivable, 57, 202–203
  financial forecasting, 57, 200–201
  financial forecasting and, 200, 201
  hiring employees, 208–209
  new product development, 57, 205–207
  new product market research, 204–205
  new product marketing research, 57
  supplier performance management, 57
Process yields, 36, 200
Processes
  auditing, 154

outsourcing, 18–21
Processes, mistake proofing
  Lean teams and, 281
Processing waste, available capacity, 60
Procurement operations, 115
Product complexity analysis, *150*
Product design, 115
Product rationalization, 18
Product redesign, 190
Production work, mistake proofing, 77
Productivity
  metrics, 9
  waiting and, 59
Profit-and-loss (P/L) statement, 24, 52
Project alignment, 55, 219, 220, 268
Project champions, 14, 41, 197, 261
Project charters
  accounts receivable example, 50, **51**, 203
  changing processes, 137
  communication and, 50, 235
  control charts and, 173
  control tools and, 191
  cost-benefit analysis, 227
  example, 50
  example of, 50
  Excel-based, 50
  financial information, 52
  formal, 36
  goals and objectives and, 42
  implementing solutions, 222
  Lean assessment and, 40
  Lean deployment and, 24
  Lean supply chain and, 36
  manufacturing systems, 119
  Minitab® statistical softwear and, 296
  office environments, 119
  performance measurements and, 69
  preparation for Kaizen events and, 113
  prioritizing, 55
  process characterization, 151, 153
  project identification and process analysis, 43
  quantifiable business benefits, 224
  selecting, 116
  value stream map (VSM) and, 145
Project control plan, 222
Project controls, 194
Project examples, 45, **47**
Project identification, 35–56, 227, 233
  breaking down high-level goals, *42*
  breaking down high-level goals and
    objectives, 41–42

conducting a Lean assessment, 39–40
key metric definitions, 46–49
Lean supply chain, 36–38
overview, 35–56
prioritizing projects, 51–54
project charter example, 50
project identification—process analysis,
43–44
suggested reading, 56
summary, 55
typical project examples, 45
Project identification activities, *52*
Project identification—process analysis, 43–44,
45
Project improvement, 219
Project leaders, 117
assigning, 116
Project metrics, 48
Project plan, 35
Project prioritization, 12
Project risk assessment, 296
Project teams, 40
Project transition, 225
important questions, **225**
Project worksheets, 212
Projects
prioritizing, 51, *52*, 55, 212, 213
short-term, 269
Projects, financial benefits of
cost of goods sold (COGS), 227
expense reduction, 227
increased cashflow, 227
revenue increases, 227
Projects, nonfinancial benefits of
cost avoidance, 227
increased customer satisfaction, 227
increased employer satisfaction, 227
increased supplier satisfaction, 227
Proposed changes, communicating to
management, 259–260, *262*
Pull production, daily customer demand and, 39
Pull scheduling system, 37, 100, 102
Toyota manufacturing, 100
Pull systems, 31–32, 60, 100–101
implement in using visual controls and
Kanban, *103*
implementing solutions, 100
information technology (IT) systems and, 32
Kanban cards and, 32
minimize work-in-process (WIP) inventory,
31

stable external demand and, 161
Push scheduling system, 100, 102

Q

Quality Companion 2, Roadmap, *297*
Quality Companion, PowerPoint presentations
and, *298*
Quality Companion's Lean forms and
templates, *297*
Quality control plan, 239, 259, 264, 274, 282
generic, *260*
Quality control systems, 240
Quantification methodology, 40
Quick-response methods, 189

R

Random sampling, 151
Range charts, 251
Rapid improvement, 4, 105, 160, 234
resistance to projects, 275
Rebates, processing, 28
codes, 28
Recommendations of product or service to
others, 230
Red-flag conditions, 89, 154
eliminating, 66, 87
Red-tagging process, 80
Reduce setup time (SMED), 90–91
single minute exchange of dies (SMED), **91**
SMED and, 90
Redundancies, eliminating, 195
Regulatory constraints, 7
Reichheld, Frederick F., 230
Reinforcing new behaviors and organizational
change, 22, 267–276
Kaizen events and, 267–268
Kaizen team and, 274
overview, 267–268
process change across global supply chains,
269–273
Relocation teams, 20
Resistance analysis of proposed changes, **232**
Resources, 15
allocation of, 12
Return on investment (ROI), 14, 15, 39, 50, 289

Revenue increases, 36
Reward and recognition systems, 236, 272
  change and, 231
Rework, 135
  loops, 11, 119, 190, 285
  percentages, 200
Risk priority rating (RPN), 258
Road map, 278
Roadmap, Quality Companion 2, *297*
Role separation, 117
Root cause analysis
  accounts receivable process workflow
    example, 202
  building a business case for change, 219,
    222, 237
  cause-and-effect (C & E) diagrams, 164
  change readiness and, 223
  changing processes and, 137
  common process changes, 188
  communication breakdowns, 195
  data collection and, 141, 142, 182
  example: inventory analysis and reduction,
    180
  failure mode and effects analysis (FMEA),
    255
  follow-up activities, 261
  histograms and, 167
  identifying and prioritizing improvement
    opportunities, 212
  implementing solutions, 25, 240
  improvement strategies and, 196–198, **197**
  infrastructure analysis and, 233
  Kaizen events and, 113
  Kaizen team and, 116
  key stakeholder analysis, 232
  level 1, *192*
  level 2, *192*
  level 3, *192*
  metric dashboards, 263
  process breakdowns, 194
  process change across global supply chains,
    270
  process characterization and, 157
  process improvement, 214
  project transition and, 225
  reduce setup time (SMED) and, 90
  reinforcing new behaviors and
    organizational change, 274, 281, 282

S

Sales and marketing, 115
  operational capacity and, 39
  process workflows, 204
Sales and operations planning (S&OP) team, 202
Sales promotional activities, minimizing, 31
Sarbanes–Oxley and Financial Services
    Accounting Board (FASB), 204
  standards, 202
Scatter plot, 170, *171*, 184, 282
Scrap and rework, office environments and, 134
Scrap percentages, 200
Senior management
  aligning improvement opportunities, 23
  conducting a Lean assessment, 40
  control tools and, 195
  cost-benefit analysis, 227
  Kaizen events and, 115, 221
  process change across global supply chains,
    272
  process improvement and, 223
  reward and recognition systems, 272
Service industries, 196
Service processes, 143
  workflows, 64, 67
Service professionals, 121
Service systems, 277
  collect and analyze process data, 279
  waiting and, 96
Setup time, estimating, 135
Sharepoints, 160
  disorganized, 80
Sharing knowledge across the world, *273*
Shining, 80
Simplification, 92, 150, 162, 222, 269
Simplification projects, 53
Simulation methods, 285, 286, 287
Simulation model, 286, 287, 288
  accounts receivable example and, 288
  cost-benefit analysis, 286
  creating, 286, 290
  Kaizen team and, 287, 292
Singapore, 19, 125
Single minute exchange of dies (SMED), 8, 77,
    90, 91
Six Sigma
  activities, 30
  concepts of, 26
  data analysis focus, 136
  deployment of, 7

events, 280
implementing solutions, 240
methodologies, 111, 240, 295
Minitab® statistical softwear and, 296
mistake proofing, 137
outsourcing processes, 21
process breakdowns, 122
process improvement initiatives, 61, 296
reinforcing new behaviors and
    organizational change, 267
supplier networks and support, 98
tools and methods, 41, 205
voice of the customer (VOC) and, 61
Six Sigma "belt", 168
components of measurement system error,
    254
Six Sigma five-phase problem-solving
    methodology
    (define, measure, analyze, improve, control),
    160
Six Sigma improvement methodologies, 10
data collection and analysis, 184
inventory analysis and reduction example,
    177, 178
Kaizen and, 5
Kaizen events and, 128, 129
Lean system and, 30
process improvement and, 189, 191
Six Sigma initiatives, 5
deployment characteristics of, 11
Six Sigma phases
analyze, 61
control, 61
define, 61
define, measure, analyze, improve, and
    control (DMAIC) project execution
    methodology, **178**
improve, 61
measure, 61
Six Sigma projects, 8, 42, 268, 295
examples, 122
projects requiring extensive data analysis and,
    24
Six Sigma teams, 281
data analysis and, 281
deploying, 67
Six Sigma tools and methods, 25, 32, 63, 142,
    177
building a business case for change, 222
data collection and analysis, 35
reinforcing new behaviors and
    organizational change, 270

Six Sigma tools from Minitab® statistical
    softwear, incorporating into Quality
    Companion, *297*
Small work group meetings (huddles), 191
SMED activity, 92
SMED principles, 96
Solutions, implementing, 22, 239–266
communicating proposed changes to
    management, 259–260
control plan requirements, 241
creating metric dashboards, 263
failure mode and effects analysis (FMEA),
    255–257
follow-up activities, 261–262
important control tools, 242–243
key questions, 240
measurement system improvements, 254
other control tools, 258
overview, 239
quality control plan, 259
statistical process controls, 244–253
Southeast Asia, 19
Spaghetti diagram, *159*, 184
Kaizen team and, 159
Stakeholder analysis, 224, 226, 261, 296
Stakeholders, 16, 222, 224
commitment and, 223
improving satisfaction of, 229
Standard waste analysis, template, 155
Standardization, 30, 89, 92, 137, 150, 162
building a business case for change, 222
process change across global supply chains,
    269
projects and, 53
work methods and, 60
Statistical methods, 142
Statistical process control (SPC), 196, 214,
    244–253, 264
Kaizen team and, 253
key process input variables (KPIVs), 244
key process output variables (KPOVs), 244
key process variables, 244
Statistical sampling, 151, 152
Strategic performance gaps, identifying, 51
Strategy alignment, 3–34, *9*, 280
general deployment strategies, 10–16
how to deploy lean in three steps, 22–25
important elements of a Lean System, 26–32
outsourcing processes, 18–21
overview, 3–34
reducing system complexity, 17
suggested reading, 33

summary, 32
what is Kaizen?, 4–7
Stratified sampling, 152
Summary of waste analysis for several jobs, *157*
Supplier networks and support, 98–99, *101*
developing, 31
Supplier performance management (SPM), 57,
210, *211*, 278
process breakdowns, 210
process workflows, 210
Supplier-input-process-output-customer
(SIPOC), 163, 164, 182
constructing, 163
Supplies and equipment, obtaining, 118
Supply chains, 95
dysfunctional, 38
global, 31, 105
"Lean", 77
System
dysfunctional, 38
value-added content of, 37
System availability, 93
System complexity, reducing, **16**, 17, 33

T

Takt time, 8, 58, 85, 103
calculation, *72*, 127
calculation—future state, *74*
calculation—original process, *73*
predetermined production rate, 37
process and, 37
Team members, 15, 117
assigning, 117
Team training, conducting, 128
Teams, forming, 117
Testing new products or services, 67
"The One Number You Need to Grow"
(Frederick Reichheld, *Harvard
Business Review* article), 230
Time and motion studies, 82
Time series graph, 170–171, *171*, 184, 282
Top-down initiatives, 12
Total cost of good sold (COGS), 37
Total preventive maintenance (TPM), 8, 10,
92–93
information technology (IT), 92, 93
key strategies, 92

"Preventive...Autonomous...Predictive", **93**
Total productive maintenance (TPM), 77, 92.
see also total preductive maintenance
(TPM)
Toyota, just-in-time (JIT) systems and, 77
Toyota manufacturing, pull scheduling system,
100
Toyota Production System (TPS), 76, 77
just-in-time (JIT) systems and, 76
Training, 137
Transfer batches, 87, *88*, 96, 189
production batches and, 87
Transferring control, **274**
Transition of modified process, 236
Travel expenses, reducing, 28
Trends, identifying, 253
Trial run, 69

U

U-charts, 249
Unionized environment, 233
Unit flow concept, 97
United Parcel Service, standardized work
procedures, 38
United States, 202
process workflow, 114
supply chain in, 100
Unnecessary movement, 61
of materials and information, 59, 61
Unnecessary operations, eliminating, 28, 30,
60, 74–75
within workflows, *75*
U-shaped work cells, 30

V

Value expectations, 63
functionality, 63
price and, 63
relative importance, 63
time and, 63
utility, 63
Value stream map (VSM), 149–150
analyze data and develop prioritized
improvements, 136
benefits of, 145

brown-paper exercise, 146
building, 7
building a business case for change, 222
creating, 70–73
data collection and analysis, 131, 135,
    141–148, 150, 182
eliminating unnecessary operations and, 74
just-in-time (JIT) systems and, 76, 87
Kaizen event planning and, 115, 117, 118,
    120, 121
Kaizen events and, 127, 129, 139
Kaizen team and, 279
Lean Six Sigma basics and, 72, 106
objectives of, 150
pictures and, 122
prioritizing projects and, 53
process characterization, 153
process mapping–SIPOC, 163
process workflows accounts receivable
    example, 202
process workflows and, 30, 39, 70, *71*
process workflows supplier performance
    example, 211
project identification and process analysis, 43
quantification of, 37, 279
reasons to create, **144**
reinforcing new behaviors and
    organizational change, 280
strategy alignment and, 11
ten requirements for, **146**
three major steps to create, 144
visual model of process workflow, 145
voice of the customer (VOC) and, 27
workshop, 145
Value-adding (VA) operations, 7
    balance material flow, 84
    calculating time duration of, 37
    eliminating unnecessary operations and, 30,
        74
    example analyzing job shadowing data, 176
    Kaizen and, 10
    Lean Six Sigma basics and, 106
    mistake proofing, 38
    process characterization, 153, 154, 156
    process workflows and, 120, 129
    reduce setup time (SMED), 91
    standardization of, 38
    value stream map (VSM) and, 71, 73
    voice of the customer (VOC) and, 61

Variation patterns, 253
    common cause, 251
Visio® software, 79
Visual control systems, implementing, 100
Visual controls and pull systems, implementing,
    32
Voice of the business (VOB), 63, 280
Voice of the customer (VOC), *62*, 164, 280, 281
    activities, 205
    alignment with, 67
    collecting information about, 63
    common process changes, 187
    critical to safety (CTS) themes, 63
    critical-to-cost (CTC) themes, 63
    critical-to-delivery (CTD) themes, 63
    critical-to-quality (CTQ) themes, 63
    implementing solutions, 242
    just-in-time (JIT) systems, 89
    Kaizen and, 7, 10
    Lean Six Sigma and, 29, 61, 105
    Lean system and, 26
    outsourcing processes and, 21
    process workflows and, 129
    process workflows new product development
        example, 207
    quantification of, 212
    reduce setup time (SMED), 90
    reducing system complexity and, 17
    strategy alignment and, 3
    translating, **27**
    understanding, 26–27, 61–63

W

Waiting, 58
"Walk the process", 11, 40
Wal-Mart, 31, 95
War rooms, in office environments, 115
Waste analysis by operation, *156*
Waste of motion, 60
Work
    elements of, 44
    outsourcing, 21
    standardization of, 7, 37
Work activities, 35
Work cells, U-shaped, 79, 83
Work environments, multicultural, 269
Work operations, eliminating, 195
Work space, analysis of, 84

Work stations, 119
  overloaded, 84
Workflow management (WM) systems, 104,
     105, 120, 278
  Internet-based, 104
Workflows, 277, 285
  internal, 43
Work-in-process (WIP) inventory, 31, 60, 166
  reducing, 76

X

X-bar chart, 173, 247, 251

Z

Zip codes, 66